WALKING IN THE HAUTE SAVOIE

Looking down on the Lac de Lessy. (Walk 48)

WALKING IN THE
HAUTE SAVOIE

by

JANETTE NORTON

CICERONE PRESS
MILNTHORPE, CUMBRIA

ISBN 1 85284 196 6
A catalogue record for this book is available from the British Library.

ACKNOWLEDGEMENTS

I would like to thank the many wonderful friends who accompanied me on the walks, especially: Rosemary and Roger Beattie, Janet Locke, Lynn Mermagen and Cheryl Roberts.

A special thanks to Roger Ratner of Village Camps who gave me the time to accomplish the book and Jennifer De Gandt for telling me I could do it!

Last but not least my long suffering husband Alan whose analytical hand took out all the unnecessary waffle!

I am also extremely grateful for the information provided by the various Tourist Bureaux and Syndicats d'Initiative of the Haute Savoie region.

All the photographs were taken by Janette Norton unless otherwise indicated.

Front Cover: Climbing up to the summit La Dent d'Oche. (Walk 17)

CONTENTS

ADVICE TO READERS

As walking has become increasingly popular in recent years and more and more visitors are flocking to this part of France, the various communes of the Haute Savoie region are reorganising their walking areas by resignposting and in some cases re-routing their mountain paths.

It could be that since some of these descriptions were written up there have been various changes. It is advisable to check locally on transport, accommodation, shops etc. Please note that the author is not responsible. She would, however, be grateful to hear from readers c/o the publishers as regards major changes, so that any future edition could be updated.

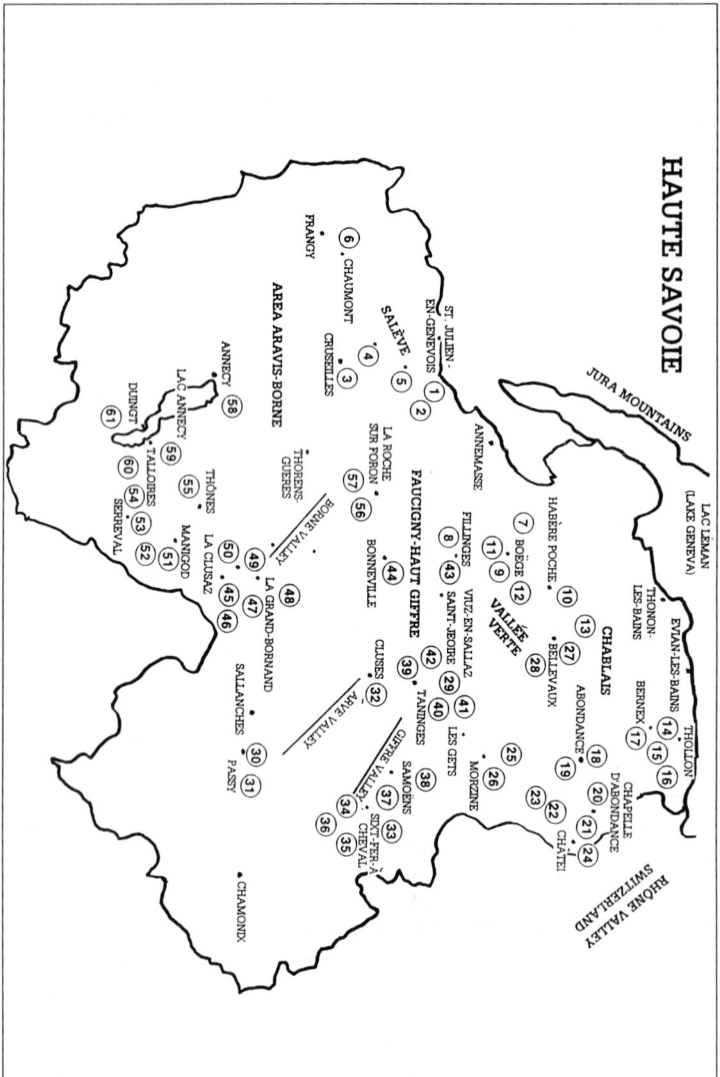
HAUTE SAVOIE
JURA MOUNTAINS
LAC LÉMAN (LAKE GENEVA)
THONON-LES-BAINS
EVIAN-LES-BAINS
THOLLON
BERNEX
CHABLAIS
ABONDANCE
CHAPELLE D'ABONDANCE
RHÔNE VALLEY
SWITZERLAND
HABÈRE POCHE
BOËGE
VALLÉE VERTE
BELLEVAUX
FILLINGES
VIUZ-EN-SALLAZ
SAINT-JEOIRE
ANNEMASSE
ST. JULIEN-EN-GENEVOIS
SALÈVE
CHAUMONT
FRANGY
CRUSEILLES
LA ROCHE SUR FORON
FAUCIGNY-HAUT GIFFRE
BONNEVILLE
CLUSES
TANINGES
LES GETS
MORZINE
SAMOËNS
SIXT-FER-À-CHEVAL
GIFFRE VALLEY
ARVE VALLEY
SALLANCHES
PASSY
CHAMONIX
THORENS-GLIÈRES
BORNE VALLEY
LA GRAND-BORNAND
LA CLUSAZ
MANIGOD
THÔNES
AREA ARAVIS-BORNE
ANNECY
LAC ANNECY
DUINGT
TALLOIRES
SERREVAL

INTRODUCTION

When I was two my parents took a holiday by the sea in South Wales and spent all their time running after me across the sand. As soon as we reached the beach I was off on my stubby legs racing towards the water and wouldn't sit still for a moment, make sandcastles or take a nap. I suppose this behaviour is fairly normal for a two-year-old but I like to think that it was an indication of my predisposition to explore the wider world and, above all, my love for walking.

Most of my formative years were spent in an outer suburb of London where the local crazes were gardening, cleaning cars or going to parties, and it was only when I became a representative for a travel agency in Switzerland that the hiking bug caught me. When not looking after my group of English tourists I was away up the mountains with a group of villagers, scaling everything in sight indiscriminately and with no thought of danger. At that stage it was more climbing than walking, and my ignorance of mountain lore now appalls me but at that time I was quite happy, being the only woman in the group, to let the leader make all the decisions and follow without question. I was roped up, told where to place my feet and initiated into triumphant yodelling when the summit was reached. This was followed by a visit to the nearest café (in the Swiss mountains they are never far away), where great quantities of local wine were consumed before lolloping downwards in a hazy stupor. On one occasion we descended hundreds of feet crammed on a primitive platform used for hauling up provisions to the restaurant - the very thought of that hair-raising journey makes me shudder now.

My present sorties appear tame compared to my early hiking adventures, which would probably make more exciting reading, but then the years have made their mark and I am no longer young or naive. I have also learned to have a healthy respect for the mountains and realise that there are dangers of which I had no inkling in earlier times. The fact that I emerged unscathed is thanks to my Swiss hiking friends, who underneath their bravado really knew their mountains and the hidden dangers. Little did I know that I would spend a greater part of my life with the Alps on my doorstep and so have the opportunity to hike in one of the most impressive regions of Europe. Bringing up four children meant that initially expeditions were somewhat curtailed; a child carried on my husband's back and myself dragging along a somewhat unenthusiastic toddler with the two older ones in the rear. Now that they are all young adults they no longer choose to accompany me (were those childhood experiences so traumatic?) but my enthusiasm, rather than waning, has become even greater and with my new-found freedom I can travel further afield.

I often ask myself what I get out of waking up early in the morning, driving an hour or more to my destination, walking an average of six hours and then driving back physically exhausted in the evening. The answer is that it gives me a tremendous feeling of exhilaration and freedom; there is a destination to be reached, the elements to overcome, the knowledge that every place is different, the shape of the rocks, the colour of the slopes and, above all, the diversity and beauty of the flowers and trees. I get a "high" and, in talking to people who are passionately involved in something specific, I find that this is also what they feel.

Living near Geneva the walking possibilities are unlimited. From where I am typing I can see the long ridge of the Jura range, the nearest summit of which is a mere half-an-hour's drive away. If I look out of my bedroom window the glistening jagged peaks of the Mont Blanc range shimmer invitingly on the horizon. Within an hour and a half by car you can reach Italy.

At first my hiking was indiscriminate. I joined a group of women who walked every week in a very relaxed manner, led by a wonderful German lady who knew the Jura terrain like the back of her hand; she never kept to any paths and we followed her happily chatting, not having a clue where we were going. Such walking was great but I could never retrace my steps and was irritated and embarrassed when my husband said "well, you go walking so often you must know where to go".

This is when the idea of a book first sprung to mind, though at that stage I had not formulated any ideas as to what region I would concentrate on. I simply wanted to record the walks I had done so that I could do them again. At first I had no sense of direction and was a bad map reader. It took me a long time to discover that the closer the contour lines are the steeper the slope is, and to acquire other basic map reading skills such as working out how long it would take to climb a certain hill and where the path changed direction. As I am completely unmechanical it took me even longer to learn to use a compass, a pedometer and an altimeter, and to appreciate that they are only aids and not always necessary. I bought a number of guidebooks in the local shops which were a great help in giving me ideas of areas to walk in, but their descriptions were often uninteresting, vague and even confusing. Perhaps there is a basic element of the French tongue that escapes me; certainly, with detailed directions at hand I occasionally got my family hopelessly lost!

I am really writing this book for myself, although if it helps others appreciate walking so much the better. What I hope it does is to make people realise that we can all hike successfully if we learn a few basic rules, and that it is fun. Every walk described in the following pages has been a personal experience which I will always remember - the type of weather, the time of year, whether we found it tough or the path difficult to find and, the most important factor of all, the people I shared it with. For myself one of the most important joys of hiking are the friends who accompany you; there is an intimate atmosphere about walking. Perhaps it is the feeling that you are out there far from the "madding crowd" and that anything could happen. I have got to know my walking friends in a far deeper way than any others, through getting soaked, windblown, hungry and lost together and at other times sitting quietly enjoying fabulous scenery, a gloriously sunny day, a rare flower, or the satisfaction of a difficult walk accomplished. And we've shared lots of laughs.

A few years back I puffed up the volcanic peak of Stromboli behind a lean, energetic 75-year-old man, trying very hard but unable to catch up with him. At the summit I asked him the secret of his tremendous energy. "No secret", he said, "I have been walking nearly all my life and it keeps me physically and mentally alive. When I go walking I find I can shed all my cares and just enjoy the feeling of being away from the turmoil of civilisation. The mountains are about the only unspoilt places left in the world and I intend to spend many more years exploring them."

How right he was. His words have encouraged me to put down on paper some of my favourite walks so that I and others can enjoy them again and again.

WALKING IN THE HAUTE SAVOIE

If you look at a detailed map of France you will see that the Haute Savoie region is in the south-eastern area, south of Lake Léman (also called Lake Geneva). To the east is the mountainous Valais area of Switzerland and to the west the Rhône valley. The gentler mountains of the pre-Alps to the north give way to the massif mountain ranges of Mont Blanc in the south-east and the beautiful mountain-ringed stretch of water called Lake Annecy to the south-west. The Chamonix/Mont Blanc area has long been known for its immense walking possibilities, especially for the classic week-long tour round Mont Blanc which is done by thousands of tourists every year, however the rest of the region has tended to be overlooked by the English hiker. Until recently many of the local paths (as opposed to the long Grande Randonnée walks) were badly signposted, but this has changed in the last few years as many towns and villages have marked out local walks and in many cases issued maps to attract the summer visitor. The Haute Savoi is a more challenging area to walk in because it has not yet caught up with the Swiss predilection for little yellow signposts at strategic intervals, with destination and time required to get there. There are places where, even on a Sunday in mid August, you can hike all day and not see more than one or two people.

The walks are split into four areas (see map on page 8).

North-west Haute Savoie - the Salève and Vallée Verte region.

North-east Haute Savoie - known as the Chablais, which is just south of Lake Léman (also called Lake Geneva).

Central and east Haute Savoie - the Faucigny and Haut Giffre area.

South-west and central Haute Savoie - Lake Annecy and the Aravis Borne region.

Walks in the Mont Blanc region are not included, even though they are impressive and worth doing, as excellent guidebooks in English have already been written.

When describing each area more fully I have given the names of the towns and villages nearby where overseas visitors might want to stay. The Haute Savoie region is quite small, however, and most walks are within easy reach of a central base. Under "accommodation" I have given a description of the different choices available but no specific names are given as each town and most larger villages have a well documented tourist office or syndicat d'initiative (see list of tourist offices) where up to date information can be found. The choice is usually wide-ranging, from first class hotels to camping sites in the bigger towns, though the smaller villages may have only one hotel. For years the Haute Savoie region has been a tourist area, so there are usually plenty of restaurants and cafés with no lack of good shops and supermarkets.

WALK EXPLANATIONS AND SIGNPOSTING

None of the walks described in this guide is at very high altitude (usually below 2,500m) and all are practicable during the summer months, many even low enough to tackle in the springtime. It is worth remembering that the snow lingers on the higher northern slopes until the beginning of June and sometimes longer, so it is wise to watch the weather forecast or obtain information from the tourist office before you set off. It is very difficult to estimate how tough a walk is, but I have tried to give an honest assessment with extra details, such as "steep and over scree" or "not for those who suffer from vertigo", etc. There are a few walks included which are only for those hardy souls who are in good physical condition and don't mind a bit of scrambling in rather airy places!

One important indicator of the walk difficulty is the overall gain in altitude. With a light rucksack (6 to 7kg) you should be able to climb 400m in one hour (250 to 300m with a weight of 15kg). The descent is quicker, namely 500m in one hour. It is not so much the length of time that a walk takes, although this should be taken into account, but the amount of height to be gained and a steep uphill path can rapidly tire you if you are not used

WALK SIGNS TO BE FOUND ON TREES, ROCKS, WALLS, POSTS ETC.

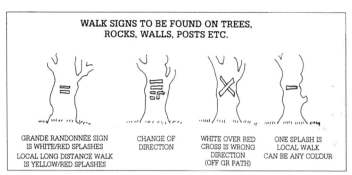

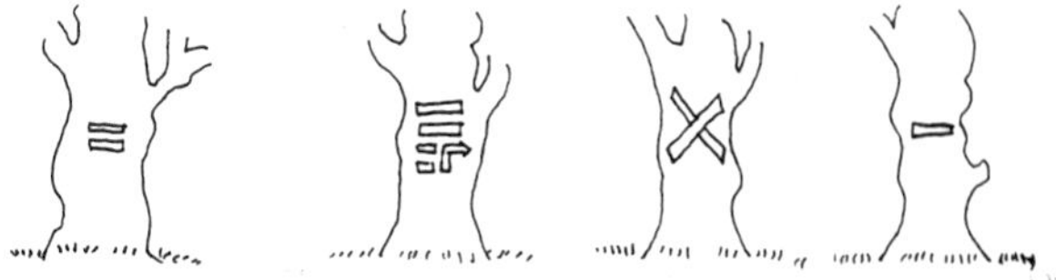

GRANDE RANDONNÉE SIGN IS WHITE/RED SPLASHES
LOCAL LONG DISTANCE WALK IS YELLOW/RED SPLASHES

CHANGE OF DIRECTION

WHITE OVER RED CROSS IS WRONG DIRECTION (OFF GR PATH)

ONE SPLASH IS LOCAL WALK CAN BE ANY COLOUR

to it. The timings given are the average walking pace of a reasonably fit person but everyone has a different rhythm; if you do not know what yours is allow yourself an extra hour or so. My comments on each walk at the end of the directions should give you a good idea as to whether or not this one is for you. Don't forget that the more walking you do the faster you get, and fitter, too!

The "how to get there" always starts from Geneva, but I have also given the nearest village or town from the start of the walk to help those coming from other directions.

Signposting: The whole of France is criss-crossed by the long distance paths of the Grande Randonnée. For example, the GR.5 starts from the small town of Gingolph on Lake Léman and travels all the way to Nice. The GR.4 starts from Nice and goes all the way to the east coast south of La Rochelle, and so on. Said to be the finest walking network in all Europe, it consists of over 40,000km of footpaths. If you see white and red horizontal paint flashes on trees, rocks or posts, this means you are on a long distance GR path (Sentier GR). However there are also long regional walks such as the Balcon du Léman, a path round the mountainous crests of Lac Léman, which are coloured yellow and red. Local regions also have their own, often circular, walks splashed with paint of a different colour - I will not say a specific colour as I have been on hikes where there have been such a variety of different coloured paint splashes that I have been completely confused!

Many local tourist offices now have excellent maps for sale outlining the walks that can be done in their immediate area. Often the coloured splashes indicate different hikes and if you start following a blue splash then stick to it - unless, of course, you are following one of my hikes and I tell you something different. In some areas you will see trees which have a red stripe in a white square painted on the trunks or numbers. This can sometimes confuse you into thinking they are different GR signs, but they are only indications to the foresters that the tree has to be cut down, or serve as boundary marks. One useful sign to remember, when following a GR route, is a white/red cross which means you are about to go in the wrong direction. See page 13 for illustrations of signs to look out for.

All the hikes included in this guide have been done at least twice and some even more. However, routes and paths do alter, mainly through the constant foresting that goes on in many of these mountain areas so it could be that some of the signs or paths have been altered since this guide was written. The Haute Savoie is also becoming more popular as a holiday area, especially for walking. With this in mind the tourist offices are putting up more signposts and in some cases re-routing walks completely, as in the Manigod region. If you are walking late in the season it is worth remembering that in the ski areas the walking signs are taken down in mid-September.

MAPS

The maps used in this guide are as follows:

Maps 1:25,000 (1cm = 250m)

Carte Touristique du Salève (with booklet) by Pierre Bossus (published by the Club Alpin Suisse - Geneva Section 1984).

Promenades en Vallée Verte (published by Boëge Tourist Bureau).

Cartes IGN 3429 ET Top 25 Bonneville/Cluses.

Cartes IGN 3428 ET Top 25 Thonon/Evian/Le Léman.

Cartes IGN 3528 ET Top 25 Morzine Massif du Chablais.

Cartes IGN 3530 ET Top 25 Samoëns/Haut Giffre.

Cartes IGN 3430 ET Top 25 La Clusaz/Grand-Bornand.

Cartes IGN 3531 OT Top 25 Megève Col des Aravis.

Cartes IGN 3431 OT Top 25 Lac d'Annecy.

Cartes IGN Serie Bleu 3430 Annecy (nord-est) Thorens-Glières (Walk No.58 only) - these series are being phased out and replaced by Top 25 series.

Maps 1:50,000 (1cm = 500m)

Editions Didier & Richard IGN No.3 Massifs du Chablais Faucigny & Genevois.

Editions Didier & Richard IGN No.2 Massifs des Bornes-Bauges.

Editions Didier & Richard IGN No.8 Massifs du Mont Blanc/Beaufortain.

Details of the maps you need are given under each walking itinerary. It is wiser to have the 1:25,000 size as these give much more detail. The 1:50,000 maps are adequate but only show the main walking paths. A good map which will give you an overall picture of the Haute Savoie region is the Cartes IGN No.45 Annecy/Lausanne-Parc Naturel Régional du Haut-Jura, Série Verte 1:1,000. Bear in mind that things are changing rapidly in this region and you may find that there are ski-lifts, new roads and jeep tracks which may not be on the maps.

Most large English bookshops with a travel section should sell these maps as it is more interesting to plan your walking holiday before you leave. (Stanfords, 27A Floral Street, London WC2E 9LP, tel: 0171 836 1321. The Map Shop, 15 High Street, Upton- upon-Severn, Worcs WR8 OHJ, tel: 01684 593 146.) However, if not, most bookshops and newsagents in the larger Haute Savoie towns have the maps in stock. They are also usually available in Geneva but are more expensive. The Salève map and booklet is only available in Geneva and the Promenades en Vallée Verte from the tourist office in Boëge.

SOME IMPORTANT WALKING RULES

- Read the walk description carefully and look at the map before you go.
- Give yourself plenty of time by setting off early.
- Listen to the weather forecast and do not set out if there is a danger of fog, storms or snow.
- Never deviate from the marked path - if there is a short cut it is usually shown. If you are lost go back the way you came if possible. Avoid going across patches of scree or snow and watch out for slippery grassy slopes.
- Be careful not to dislodge stones or boulders - they can gather momentum as they roll down the mountain and hit other walkers.
- Be sure that you have enough warm clothes and food, especially water if it is a hot day.
- If you are not used to the sun at altitude remember to put on a high protection sunscreen and also wear reliable sunglasses.
- Never walk alone even if you know the route and always tell someone where you are going.
- If you get caught in a thunderstorm, get off high exposed ground immediately and take shelter, but not under an isolated tree or rock. When lightning strikes, remove any metallic objects you might have on you and if necessary curl up on the ground to avoid being struck.
- When there is an accident, wrap the person concerned in a survival blanket (see equipment list). Use your whistle - six short blasts means you need help (three short ones means you are all right) or six flashes from your torch if it is dark. If you have to leave to get help, make sure you know where you are located and leave as much warm clothing and food with the victim as possible.
- Take all your litter home with you and do not pick the wild flowers but leave them for others to enjoy.
- Remember that these mountains are a cultural heritage and should be left unspoilt for future generations - happy walking!

HOW TO GET THERE AND WHEN TO GO

Air, train, bus and car are the choices, unless you want to get into training and walk!

BY AIR:

The nearest airport to the Haute Savoie is Geneva as many of the walking areas described in the guide are within an hour's drive of this city. You could also fly to Lyon which is about 2hrs away. All the big car hire firms operate out of Geneva and Lyon. You can also fly to Paris and then continue your journey by train.

BY RAIL:

The English office of the the French Railways (SNCF), French Railways House, 179 Piccadilly, London W1V 0BA, tel. 0171 493 9731, fax 0171 493 1621 will, on request, send a very informative brochure outlining all the different ways to get to France by train, including timetables, cost, car hire, travel insurance information, special hotel/rail packages for short and medium breaks, cross channel fares, Interrail information for the under 26s, etc.

One possibility is called Motorail, a shuttle service which consists of putting your car on the ferry at Folkstone and then on the train from Calais. This does save the hours of driving through France and gives you more holiday time. However, the destinations listed do not include any in the Geneva/Haute Savoie region, but this could change. As from summer 1994 a new Eurostar (passengers only) train service was inaugurated. You catch your train in London, Waterloo and, via the Eurotunnel, get to Paris in 3hrs. You then catch the famous TGV fast train and arrive in Geneva in 3hrs or Annecy in 4hrs. For all train information including tickets to British and European destinations, instant reservations, special fares for under 26s, senior citizens discounts etc, tel. 0891 515477 and for bookings only call 0345 300003.

Also worth asking for is the free booklet entitled *TGV Sud-Est - Grandes Lignes. Horaire et guide pratique.* This gives all destinations, timings and costs of trains leaving from Paris to the south-east, including the Haute Savoie area, and also trains within the region.

One tip for travellers taking the TGV fast trains is that you have to have a seat reservation and before boarding you must validate your ticket by punching it into an orange unit (composteur) which you will see before you reach the platform. Also the price indexes in the booklet are outlined in different colours which means that different departures are more expensive or cheaper than others. This is rather complicated for a non-French speaker but the prices are clearly marked.

BY BUS:

The most economical way to come from England is by bus from Victoria Station but of course it takes longer. There is a bus to Chamonix, via Grenoble, Chambéry and Annecy which leaves London at 15.30 and arrives in Annecy at 09.05 (Chamonix 10.25) the next day. Alternatively you can go to Geneva, via Lyon, leaving London at 15.30 arriving Geneva at 10.45 the following morning.

Contact your local National Express agent for further details or Eurolines, 52 Grosvenor Gardens, Victoria, London SWI, tel. 0171 730 0202 for an up to date timetable with prices.

Local bus transport: If you intend to rely on local bus transport I suggest that you plan your walking programme before you leave home by writing or telephoning the Annecy tourist office (see list) for a free copy of their Haute Savoie bus timetable (Indicateur des Transports Routiers). There is a General Information page in English which gives the meanings of the various abbreviations and signs. There are 20 different bus companies serving the region (names, addresses and telephone numbers included in the book) and the timetables are easily understandable. Bear in mind, however, that many of the walks do not start from the towns or villages themselves so read the departure explanations carefully. A number of the walks will be difficult to do simply because there is no public transport to the departure area and taxis are expensive.

BY CAR:

Car is the easiest choice as you will have transport when you arrive. Cross the channel by boat (or the new Eurotunnel). As an example, from Le Havre take the A.15 and then the A.13 to Paris. Then follow the signs clockwise round the "boulevard péripherique" to the A6, direction south to Lyon and Marseille. At Maçon (north of Lyon), branch east on the A40 to Bourg-en-Bresse/Geneva/Annecy/Chamonix.

Once you are in the vicinity of Geneva there are various exits depending on your chosen destination. For Annecy you should get off at Bellegarde (exit No.11) and take the N.508 via Frangy, the shortest route and also very pleasant, or leave at St. Julien-en-Genevois (exit No.13) and take the N.201. Alternatively stay on the A40 beyond Geneva and take the A41 to La Roche-sur-Foron/Annecy/Grenoble/Lyon, but you will see from the map that this is a longer way round. Once round Geneva you are on the way to Chamonix and the possible exits you might want are as follows: Exit 14 Annemasse (for Thonon/Evian/Abondance valley/Morzine). Exit 15 Boëge/St. Jeoire (for Vallée Vert/Taninges/Samoëns). Exit 16 Bonneville (for Borne valley/La Clusaz/Grand-Bornand/Thônes). Exit 18 Scionier (for Cluses/Taninges/Samoëns/Les Gets/Morzine Avoriaz). Exit 19 for Cluses (centre) and Flaine. Exit 20 Sallanches (for Praz d'Arly, Cordon, Combloux, Albertville, Mégève) and Exit 21 St. Gervais-Les-Bains (for Plateau d'Assy, Passy, Le Fayet). After this exit you are in the Chamonix valley.

Don't forget that there are motorway tolls. For example the cost of going from Le Havre to Annecy (a total of 735km of which 688km is motorway) is FF.479 in an average car.

WHEN TO GO

The Haute Savoie climate is more continental than temperate Britain which means the winters are colder and the summers hotter. The major rains come in springtime and the snow can cling to the higher altitudes and the northern slopes well into May. With the recent changes in climatic conditions there has been a trend towards little snow in winter months and then a ton in April! The first snowfall of the winter at high altitude may also arrive at the end of August (though it usually melts), when the hot, sticky weather tends to break with heavy thunderstorms.

Since many of the walks in this guide are at lower altitudes they can be done in late spring though the weather can be fickle at this time, one day beautiful sunshine and the next cold and rainy. The main advantage is that there are few tourists and the flowers are magnificent. Summers (July/ August) are often hot and humid, though the higher you get the fresher it is! There is often a heat haze which obscures the view and sometimes heavy thunderstorms. The main disadvantages are the crowds of people and the difficulty of getting accommodation. With the growing ecology movement the mountain areas are becoming more popular than ever. Some of the better known walks should be avoided during high summer weekends. In my opinion, the best period is September and October when the school holidays are over, there are very few tourists and the days can have a balminess and clarity which makes every rock and stone stand out in sharp relief. Although the glory of the flowers is over you are compensated by the different mushrooms, berries and the trees turning an autumn gold (the mountain rowans with their bright red berries are particularly striking).

Around the start of October, the fog sometimes gathers in the valleys, particularly near Geneva where the lake makes it humid, and the weather at low altitude is grey and miserable. You drive up into the mountains and suddenly you pop out of the fog into brilliant sunshine! There is something awe-inspiring about walking at altitude and looking down on to a sea of cotton wool where the valley should be; other peaks stick up out of the plain like islands, and the permanently snow covered higher ranges such as Mont Blanc look even more impressive with their lower slopes cloaked in fog. If you are walking at this time be careful to find out what the cloud level is (sometimes it can be quite high and you can be walking all day with the sunshine just a few metres above if you but knew it). Also remember that the rocks can be a bit slippery in the morning if the sun has only just reached them and the days are drawing in so there is less walking time. Many of the higher refuges tend to shut around mid-September.

ACCOMMODATION INCLUDING REFUGES

There is plenty of accommodation all over the Haute Savoie ranging from first class hotels to primitive mountain refuges; it is all a matter of choice and how much money you want to spend. It is worth remembering that many of the hotels in the large ski resorts are shut in the summer season. July and August are the high season months so it is advisable to book in advance if you plan to walk at this time, otherwise it is not essential. Below is a short explanation of the different types of accommodation available.

Logis de France: This is a nationwide network of small hotels which offer comfortable accommodation and excellent food at very reasonable prices. The hotels are graded from one to three-star according to their degree of comfort and there are some 200 Logis de France in the towns and villages of the Haute Savoie region (look for their distinctive logo which consists of a yellow fireplace on a green background). For a free booklet in English listing these hotels with all relevant information, contact the French National Tourist Office (address and tel. no. below).

Gîtes de France: Much beloved by the English, these are country cottages which are available for a weekly rent all over the French countryside and are very good value. They can vary from being extremely comfortable to quite basic. It is a good idea to rent a gîte in a central position and then go to a different area every day, none of the walks in this guide being a great distance apart. For a free handbook contact the Gîtes de France office in London (address and tel.no. below) or the French National Tourist Office.

Gîtes d'étape: This is a type of youth hostel, usually without a warden, but open to people of all ages. They can be reasonably comfortable with good beds, showers and a well equipped kitchen but they can also be quite basic and are mainly intended for cheap overnight stops by walkers and cyclists. If you prefer not to cook your own meals there is often a café/ restaurant in the vicinity. In the high season they can be uncomfortably full but are a wonderful way to get to know fellow travellers and share a convivial evening. Out of season you often have the place to yourself. The only snag is that you may have to hunt for the person responsible in the village or nearby (usually posted on the door) to get access to the gîte.

A complete guide to the Gîtes d'étape all over France costs £7.50 (including postage) from the London Gîtes de France office, 178 Piccadilly, London W1V 9DB, tel. 0171 493 3480 or 0171 408 1343/fax 0171 495 6417 or 0171 495 6418. You can also become a friend of the Gîtes de France for £3, which entitles you to various travel benefits. Other publications available are:

Gîtes de Neige (places close to ski resorts) in French only.

French Country Welcome (bed & breakfast) in English.
Chambres d'Hôtes de Prestige (top range b/b) in English.
Camping à la Ferme (Campsites on farms) in French only.
Gîtes accessibles à Tous (accommodation for the disabled) in French only.
Gîtes d'Enfants (catering for children with special activities) in French only.
Gîtes de Pêche (close to rivers for fishing enthusiasts) in French only.

Chambres d'Hôte: This is the English equivalent of bed and breakfast though often the breakfast is not included and it may be limited to coffee and bread (croissants if you are lucky). The number of these establishments is increasing in the French villages (look for the Chambres d'Hôte sign or enquire in the local café or shop). The degree of comfort varies tremendously but, unlike British establishments, you will rarely get a TV or beverage making facilities in your room. Most rooms do have their own shower and toilet. If you can speak some French it is a wonderful way to get to know the local people. A list is available at the French National Tourist Office or see Gîtes de France above.

Youth hostels (auberges de jeunesse): These are rare in France outside the main towns but for a complete list called *Guide des Auberges de Jeunesse en France* contact the Youth Hotels Association, Trevelyan House, 8 St. Stephen's Hill, St. Albans, Herts AL1 2DY, tel. 01727 855215, fax 01727 844126. There are only five youth hostels in the Haute Savoie, namely in Annecy, Evian, La Clusaz, Les Gets and Morzine Avoriaz. Don't forget you have to be a member of the Association to stay in a hostel (reductions in membership fees for under 18's).

Camping: Camping sites are graded from one to five star and range from those offering shop, hot showers and swimming pool to sites with basic washing facilities. Camping à la ferme is cheap and popular though the facilities are minimal - remember some toilets in France, especially on camping sites, are still of the squat variety! The local tourist offices have a complete list of camping sites. See information above in the booklet *Camping à la ferme*.

Naturefriends (Amis de la Nature): This is a non-profit organisation, founded in 1895, which has hostels all over Europe offering accommodation to members at reasonable prices. There are branches in most European countries.

There is a joining fee plus a membership fee which varies according to age and status. Members receive a booklet with lists of all the hostels in Europe.

For further information concerning the English branch contact:

Mrs. Lorna Iden, 43 South Way, Lewes, East Sussex BN7 11LY, tel. 01273 475516.
French Branch - 197 Rue Championnet, 75018 Paris, tel. (1) 46.27.53.56.
Geneva Branch - Claudine Pidoux, Av. Gros-Chêne 27, 1213 Onex, tel. (022) 792.98.78.

Refuges (mountain huts): Details of the refuges on specific walks are given at the end of the walk descriptions. Some are run by the French Alpine Club but many are privately owned. These refuges are usually above 2,000m and are mainly occupied by serious walkers and climbers as a base for tackling local peaks. They can be great fun provided you don't mind communal living, such as sleeping in dormitories (men and women in the same room) and often primitive cooking and washing facilities. One thing to remember is that they are not cheap and food is relatively expensive for what you get, as it has to be hauled up on a mountain pulley or dropped by helicopter. Don't forget your own sleeping sheet as only blankets are provided (see equipment & clothing chapter for other information). For a list of Haute Savoie refuges telephone the local FAC Club in Annecy: 50-45.52.76 (no English spoken). There is no list of private refuges but the local tourist office can often help.

For information concerning the Haute Savoie, contact:
French National Tourist Office, 178 Piccadilly, London WlV 9DB, tel. 0891 244 123
Gîtes de France, 178 Piccadilly, London WlV 9DB, tel. 0171 493 3480.

If you write or telephone they will send the following documentation free of charge:

The Traveller in France Reference Guide which has a wealth of interesting information such as: Dates to note - How to get there - Maps of France - Helpful hints - Motoring in France - Where to stay - Hotel groups - Packaged holidays in hotels - Special interest holidays - Weekends, Short breaks, Day trips - Caravanning and Camping - Self-catering holidays - Maps and Guides - Addresses.
Hotels - a brochure which gives a complete list with telephone numbers, prices and other relevant information in the Isère, Savoie and Haute Savoie regions.
Campings - a complete list of all camping sites in the above areas.
Available locally:
Logis de France (Haute Savoie) - booklet from the Annecy tourist office, tel. 50 45.00.33, Maison des Gîtes de France, 35 Rue Godot-de-Mauroy, 75439 Paris Cedex 09, tel. (1) 49.70.75.75.
(Gîtes d'étapes, Chambres d'hôtes (available in English),
Camping à la Ferme

Haute Savoie Gîtes de France: 3 Rue Dupanloup, 74000 Annecy, tel. 50 52.80.02. Booklet of local chambres d'hôtes, gîtes d'étape, gîtes de groupe, gîtes d'enfants et campings - free.

Guide des Gîtes ruraux (1,000 described)

Accueil à la ferme en Haute Savoie: Campings, auberges, goûters, produits fermiers, visites - free.

LIST OF TOURIST OFFICES AND SYNDICATS D'INITIATIVE IN THE HAUTE SAVOIE (relevant to places named in the guide)

Meaning of symbols for tourist offices:

**** A main tourist office offering a wide range of information. Normally employs qualified personnel able to speak several languages. Open all the year round. Last minute hotel reservations possible.

*** As above but without hotel reservations.

** Offers regional and local information with a bilingual employee (usually English). Open all the year round.

* Local information only with no guarantee of someone speaking English. Open in season only but with answering service all the year round.

Syndicats d'Initiative are the equivalent of tourist offices but are situated in the smaller villages. They are only open in the season - some of them have an answering service but this is not guaranteed.

** Abondance (Chablais), 74360 Haute Savoie. Tel. 50.73.02.90

** Annecy, Bonlieu, 1 Rue Jean-Jaurès, 74000 Haute Savoie. Tel. 50.45.00.33

* Bellevaux (Chablais), 74470 Haute Savoie. Tel. 50.73.71.53

* Bernex (Chablais), 74500 Haute Savoie. Tel. 50.73.60.72

* Boëge (Vallée Verte), 74420, Haute Savoie Tel. 50.39.11.28

* Bonneville (Faucigny/Haut Giffre), 23 Rue de Carroz, 74130 Haute Savoie. Tel. 50.97.38.37

* Brasses (Les), (Faucigny/Haut Giffre), 74490 Haute Savoie. Tel. 50.35.91.83
includes villages of Bogève, Megevette, Onnion, Viuz-en-Sallaz and Saint-Jeoire-en-Faucigny.

*** Carroz (Les), (Faucigny/Haut Giffre), 74300 Haute Savoie. Tel. 50.90.00.04
includes villages of Araches and La Frasse.

** Chapelle d'Abondance (Chablais), 74360 Haute Savoie. Tel. 50.73.51.41

** Châtel (Chablais), 74390 Haute Savoie. Tel. 50.73.22.44

*** Clusaz (La) (Chablais), 74220 Haute Savoie. Tel. 50.32.65.00

** Cluses (Faucigny/Haut Giffre), Chalet Savoyard, Place des Allobroges, 74300 Haute Savoie. Tel. 50.98.31.79

* Cruseilles (Salève), 74350 Haute Savoie. Tel. 50.44.10.21

Duingt (Annecy region), syndicat d'initiative in the mairie, 74410 Haute Savoie. Tel. 50.68.67.07

**** Evian-Les-Bains (Chablais), Place d'Allinges,74502 Haute Savoie. Tel. 50.75.04.26

*** Flaine (Faucigny/Haut Giffre), 74300 Haute Savoie.Tel. 50.90.80.01

Frangy syndicat d'initiative (Salève), 74270 Haute Savoie. Tel. 50.32.26.40

*** Gets (Les), (Chablais), 74260 Haute Savoie. Tel. 50.75.80.80

*** Grand-Bornand (Le), (Aravis/Borne), 74450 Haute Savoie. Tel. 50.02.20.33

* Habère-Poche (Vallée Verte), 74420 Haute Savoie. Tel. 50.39.54.46

** Manigod (Aravis/Borne), 74230 Haute Savoie. Tel. 50.44.92.44

* Marignier (Faucigny/Haut Giffre), 74970 Haute Savoie. Tel. 50.34.60.22

* Menthon-Saint-Bernard (Aravis/Borne), 74290 Haute Savoie. Tel. 50.60.14.30

* Mieussy/Sommand (Faucigny/Haut Giffre) 74440 Hte. Savoie. Tel. 50.43.02.72

* Montiond-Le-Lac (Faucigny/Haut Giffre), 74110 Hte. Savoie. Tel. 50.79.12.81

* Mont Saxonnex (Faucigny/Haut Giffre), 74130 Haute Savoie. Tel. 50.96.97.27

*** Morzine & Morzine-Avoriaz (Chablais), Place de la Cruzaz, 74110 Haute Savoie. Tel. 50.79.03.45

** Passy/Le Plateau d'Assy/Plaines Joux: Av. du Dr. Arnaud, Le Plateau d'Assy, 74480-74190 Haute Savoie. Tel. 50.58.80.52

* Petit-Bornand (Le)/Les Glières (Aravis/Bornes), 74130 Haute Savoie. Tel. 50.03.50.99

* Reposoir (Le) syndicat d'initiative (Faucigny/Haut Giffre), 74950 Haute Savoie. Tel. 50.98.18.01

** Roche-sur-Foron (La) (Aravis/Borne), Place Andrevetan, 74800 Haute Savoie. Tel. 50.03.36.68

* Saint-Jean-d'Aulps (Faucigny/Haut Giffre), 74430 Hte.Savoie. Tel. 50.79.65.09

** Saint-Jean-de-Sixt (Aravis/Borne), 74450 Haute Savoie. Tel. 50.02.70.14

Saint-Jeoire-en-Faucigny (Faucigny/Haut Giffre) - see Les Brasses.

Saint-Sigismond including village of Agy, syndicat d'initiative, (Faucigny/

Haut Giffre), 74300 Haute Savoie. Tel. 50.34.82.50

*** Samoëns (Faucigny/Haut Giffre), Gare Routière, 74340 Haute Savoie. Tel. 50.34.40.28

* Sixt-Fer-à-Cheval (Faucigny/Haut Giffre), 74740 Hte.Savoie. Tel. 50.34.49.36

** Talloires (Annecy region), Place de la Mairie, 74290 Haute Savoie. Tel. 50.60.70.64

* Taninges/Praz de Lys (Faucigny/Haut Giffre), 74440 Haute Savoie. Tel. 50.34.25.05

** Thollon Les Mémises (Chablais), 74500 Haute Savoie. Tel. 50.70.90.01

*** Thônes (Aravis/Borne), Place Avet, 74230 Haute Savoie. Tel. 50.02.00.26

*** Thonon-Les-Bains (Chablais), Place du Marché, 74200 Haute Savoie. Tel. 50.71.55.55

* Thorens-Glières (Aravis/Bornes), 74570 Haute Savoie. Tel. 50.22.40.31

* Val d'Hermone (Chablais) - includes villages of Lullin, Revroz and Vailly, 74470 Haute Savoie. Tel. 50.73.82.05

* Villards-sur-Thônes (Les) (Aravis/Bornes), 74230 Haute Savoie. Tel. 50.02.07.88

* Yvoire (Chablais), 74230 Haute Savoie. Tel. 50.72.80.21

Note that, after the name of the town or village, the applicable area (as indicated in the guide) has been inserted.

The names and addresses of the above tourist offices have been taken from a booklet called *Annuaire Officiel des Offices du Tourisme et Sydicats d'Inititatives Savoie-Dauphiné* and published by the Fédération Nationale des Offices de Tourisme et Syndicats d'Initiative, 2 Rue Linois, 75015 Paris, tel. (1) 40.59.43.82, fax (1) 45.75.27.93. Cost FF.54 (English spoken).

This book contains a wealth of additional information about each town and village including names, addresses and telephone numbers of hotels, caravan and camping sites, gîtes etc. and also places of interest to see in the region. It is a good investment provided you can read French.

REGIONAL SPECIALITIES

The Haute Savoie is not the most gastronomic area of France. Nevertheless, it has a reputation for high-class dried and smoked meats, a variety of mushrooms, berries and fruits, and more especially the succulent Abondance, Chevrotin and Reblochon cheeses. There is an abundance of freshwater fish, such as trout, pike, crayfish, perch and the omble chevalier, a species of arctic char, found mainly in deep mountain waters such as Lake Annecy but now also artificially farmed near Thonon. The region of Frangy and Seyssel in the north-western area produces various white Roussette wine, from a type of vine originating from Cyprus at the time of the Crusades in the 12th century. There are also vineyards in the region of Lake Léman and also near Bonneville which produce Crèpy, a dry white wine with a smell of hawthorn and a bubbling white wine called Ayse. And last but not least are the renowned mineral waters from the towns of Thonon-Les-Bains and Evian-Les-Bains.

Since the 14th century Abondance cheese has been made in the farms of the Abondance valley. Based on the milk of a well-known breed of cow it is a slightly cooked, pressed and salted cheese which is produced in the alpine chalets in summer and in a laiterie (dairy) during the rest of the year. It takes 3 months to ripen and consists of a round and flat slab like a millstone weighing from 7 to 12kg.

Chevrotin cheese is made from fermented goat's milk and has been made in the Aravis mountains for generations. It is a round cheese, about 10cm wide by 8cm high and weighs about 350gm. It only takes 3 weeks to mature in a cellar after which it is ripe and ready to eat.

Reblochon also comes from the Aravis region around Thônes and Grand-Bornand. It has an interesting history dating back to the time when all the land and cattle in the area belonged to the Catholic church. The peasants used to trick the monks by pretending that they had finished milking the cows and then, as soon as the monks were out of sight, they would do a second milking (called la Rôblosse) which was the richest and creamiest. The first mention of this cheese was in the 16th century when it became recognised and much appreciated by the Sardinian/Piedmontese court as it could travel all the way to Turin without getting spoilt. Reblochon cheeses, made from milk which has been slightly warmed till it curdles, are then pressed into a wooden mold and a weight put on top. After a while they are taken out of the molds, salted, washed, brushed and put in a dry cellar where they are turned every few days until ripe. The finished product is about 6 inches in diameter with an orange rind; it has a very distinctive taste which you either like or you don't!

You will find the regional produce in local markets which are great fun to wander round even if you have no intention of buying. Below are the market days in some of the main towns and villages in the Haute Savoie. Most markets start fairly early in the morning and continue till about 13.00:

Monday: La Clusaz, Cluses (town centre), Seyssel, Thonon, Viuz-en-Sallaz.

Tuesday: Annecy - food only in the old quarter and general market, Place des Romains. Annemasse, Boëge, Bonneville, Evian.

Wednesday:	Annecy Le Vieux, Châtel, Frangy, Grand-Bornand, Morzine, Plateau d'Assy, Samoëns, Thorens.
Thursday:	Annecy (Novel), Cluses-Sardagne (afternoon), Cruseilles, Les Gets, Lullin, La Roche-sur-Foron, Taninges, Thonon.
Friday:	Annecy (old quarter), Annemasse, Chapelle d'Abondance, Bonneville, Evian, Marignier (afternoon), St. Jeoire-en-Faucigny, St. Julien-en-Genevois.
Saturday:	Annecy (Bd Taine), St. Pierre-en-Faucigny, Reignier, Sixt (summer only), Thônes, Mieussy (afternoon).
Sunday:	Abondance, Annecy (old town).

EQUIPMENT & CLOTHING

This is a very personal thing and experienced walkers have their own preferences as to what is important to take and what is best left at home. There are people who, even on a hot day in summer, feel it is essential to take a complete change of clothes, raingear, lots of food, flares in case they are lost, etc., and others who are willing to take a chance for the benefit of a lighter rucksack; there is of course a sensible compromise to these two extremes.

Footwear: Sturdy boots are essential for mountain walking, preferably with plenty of ankle support and serrated rubber soles which give a good grip on the rocks. Some people prefer the more traditional leather boots but others like the lighter synthetic models which have made their appearance in recent years. There are dozens of different makes of boot on the market and any good sports shop will give advice as to what to buy, depending on the individual person and how much walking they are planning to do. If you can afford the extra cost, buy boots which are guaranteed waterproof (preferably Gore-Tex): this makes a big difference as walking along with wet feet is no fun! It is not really practical to walk in training shoes as the feet tire more easily and most of them do not have the required ankle grip. It is very important to break your boots in before you start hiking so it is a good idea to walk around the house with them on and suffer the blisters at home rather than on a mountainside. It is amazing how socks can make a difference to foot comfort - make sure they are proper walking socks which are usually a mixture of 65% wool and acrylic combinations with reinforced cushioned heel and toe areas (avoid cotton as it absorbs moisture and can cause blisters).

Rucksack: Again this is very much a matter of choice and there is now a wide range of shapes and sizes to choose from which can sometimes be bewildering. Go to a good sports shop and explain what you need it for and they will advise you. If you are doing day walks only then a smaller, lighter model is sufficient; the ones with a padded fitted back and strap to go round your waist (which means that the weight goes to the hips rather than the back) are to be recommended. Make sure you try it on first and even take a short walk with it if possible because comfort is essential. There is a tendency now, especially with the larger trekking rucksacks, to eliminate the side and top pockets which are so useful for essentials, such as snacks, first-aid kit, money etc. They tend to be narrower with an assortment of straps for fastening a sleeping bag, pick-axe etc. which can sometimes be a nuisance. Some also have a large top pocket which can be unfastened from the rucksack and used as a day pack; this latter feature is very useful if you are doing day sorties from a base camp. The larger, wider rucksacks with the light metal frames are also out of fashion as the frames tend to catch on bushes or get wedged between rocks. Another essential factor to look for is that the rucksack is waterproof; the secret, if you are trekking for a number of days, is to wrap up each individual item in a plastic bag to keep it dry. The rustle of plastic bags is the constant noise you hear when staying overnight in a mountain refuge.

Clothing: Experienced walkers dress in layers which they can put on and take off depending on weather and altitude. It is not really practical to take a bulky down jacket or a heavy sweater as these two items take up a lot of room in a rucksack.

For summer walking, a T-shirt which should be a combination of cotton and acrylic (cotton alone absorbs moisture rather than taking it away from the skin, causing a cooling effect when you need warmth), a long sleeved shirt and a medium weight sweater, would be quite adequate. There is now a wide range of Polartex type sweaters available which give you warmth without weight (thermal insulation) and are quick drying when you sweat; more important, they are light and roll up easily to stuff into your rucksack. One of the most important items is a lightweight, wind and waterproof jacket - again there is a wide choice on the market but it is worth the extra cost to buy one made of a Gore-Tex type material as it will keep you dry for hours and a good jacket can last a lifetime; avoid the lightweight nylon type jacket which does not breathe as there is nothing worse than walking along in the rain hot and sweaty! As for trousers, lightweight, quick drying baggy type trousers are the most comfortable for walking in (ones you can roll up if it suddenly gets hot); or knickerbockers which arrive at the knee and then socks you can roll down. Avoid wearing heavy clinging trousers or jeans as they take a long time to dry properly.

Compass and altimeter: These are not essential for the walks in this guide though they are invaluable in bad weather if you get lost; but find out how to use them before you start. An accurate and reliable altimeter can be expensive but is fun to use. There are various types of pedometer on the market which record the distance walked, but these must be regulated to your stride and are not very accurate for mountain climbing.

For those walking for the first time, below is a suggested list of essentials for your rucksack on a day walk:

Maps (1:25,000 as stipulated in walk explanation).
Basic first aid kit - these can be bought in good sports shops and should include plasters, bandages, antiseptic and insect repellent. Also include moleskin for blisters.
Survival blanket - this is a thin aluminium sheet (takes up minimum room in your rucksack) which you wind round you if you are lost or hurt. It will keep you beautifully warm. Available in good sports shops or in the larger Geneva Migros supermarkets.
Sun cream and lip salve (especially if you are not used to sun at altitude).
Sun hat.
Sunglasses.
Woolly hat and gloves.
Energy tablets i.e. Vitamin C - useful if you begin to flag and refreshing too.
Mixed dried fruit and nuts - packets available from most supermarkets.
Swiss Army knife with as many attachments as you can get (scissors and a tin opener are useful).
Nylon cape/poncho - this goes over everything including your rucksack when it is really pouring. Useful for sitting on when having your picnic!
1 extra lightweight sweater (over and above what you have on).
I lightweight wind and waterproof anorak.
Shorts (if hot).
1 extra pair of socks.
Water bottle - it is better to take lots of water, especially if it is hot. It is not always wise to drink from mountain streams, especially if there are animals around. Many mountain chalets have drinking troughs.
Picnic - buy one of those delicious crusty baguettes at the local bakery before you set off and eat it with fresh cheese or small tins of meat or tuna. So much nicer than soggy sandwiches!
Compass and altimeter (useful but not essential in stable good weather).
Camera, binoculars and reference books (optional).
Whistle - (six blows indicates you need help).

If you are staying overnight in a refuge, add the following:
Washing things, small towel plus change of clothes (it is not always possible to dry wet things if there are lots of people in the refuge).

Sleeping sheet (available at good camping shops or in some Geneva supermarkets). Alternatively just sew up the sides of a wide sheet. All the refuges in the Haute Savoie provide blankets.
Torch - if you are staying in a refuge, a miner's type lamp you fasten round your head is very useful, especially if there is only an outside toilet!
Track suit for relaxing in the evening (use also as pyjamas).
Lightweight tennis shoes (some refuges have slippers available at the door but this is not guaranteed).
Playing cards and/or paperback book - you never know when you will be holed up by bad weather.
Small repair kit with needles, thread, string, buttons etc.
Check that the refuge supplies meals (most of them do) - if not bring your own. Hot water is available for soup and often you can use the kitchen.

FLORA AND FAUNA

FLORA

One of the joys of walking in the mountains, especially in the springtime and early summer, is the abundance and variety of the flowers growing in the alpine pastures, among rock crevices and in places where you would think no plant life could possibly take hold. For many it is sufficient to admire and appreciate the blaze of colour, from deep purple to bright yellow, depending on the region and the time of year. If, however, you are interested in

Alpine anemones (Pasque flowers) - Poite de Ressachaux. (Walk 26)

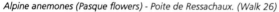

identifying and knowing the names of the individual species buy a good flower book and a magnifying lens and keep them permanently in your rucksack (see below for suggested books). Remember to leave extra time for the walks as flower identification is a time-consuming pastime. The advantage of alpine walking is that you can enjoy the spring flowers on the lower slopes and then, as the months go by, enjoy them again as you gain height! All species are very influenced by the type of mountain terrain, for example some thriving on granite while others prefer limestone.

Some of the first flowers that you will see in the year, pushing through the melting snow, are members of the bulb and corm family; thousands of little white and purple alpine crocuses, scillas, snowdrops, blue gentians and soldanellas (snowbells). These are closely followed by wild daffodils, sweet smelling narcissi, anemones, violets, rock roses and the striking purple trumpet gentians.

In May and June come the small, delicate orchids which, although unlike the large showy specimens you find in tropical countries, are in a certain way more beautiful. The most common in the Alps are the early purple (which flowers in April), the green-winged, the fragrant, the vanilla (it actually smells of vanilla), the fly, the round-headed pyramidal and the soldier or military orchid, but there are others, such as the rare lady's slipper, which can be found in isolated places. Most orchids have a spike of flowers, often with a sort of helmet behind and the lower petal is in the shape of a lip.

The yellow cowslips, oxlips and primroses are also in abundance; watch out for the pretty lilac-pink bird's-eye primrose which looks as if it should be growing in a suburban garden rather than in the wild. The prolific creamy and yellow pasque anemones with their attractive yellow centres strike a vivid note on the dun covered alpine slopes, and the banks of the swollen rivulets cascading down the mountainsides are sprinkled with yellow marsh marigolds. Brightening up bare crevices and clinging to inaccessible rock faces are dozens of different creeping, cushiony rock plants which have lots of tiny blooms, such as the pink and white saxifrages and the yellow, white and lilac rock jasmines. The false helloborine, a delicate tall yellowish-green starred flower with six petals is frequently found around alpine chalets as it likes the nitrogen enriched soil. The cattle never touch its poisonous leaves though they were formerly picked and made into a potion to be used against lice and horseflies. These are just a fraction of the hundreds of different flowers which burst into bloom when the slopes are warmed by spring sunshine and the snows start to melt in earnest.

July, August and September is the time for the taller plants such as the majestic purple delphiniums (larkspur), monkshood, graceful bell-shaped columbines and the varied types of carrot family including cow parsley and the star-like astrantia. There are an endless variety of daisies, from the orange splash of the golden hawksbeard, the purple asters and the fluffy lilac adenostyles, to dozens of different white and purple thistles with their prickly, silvery leaves and the blue willow gentian which favours moist woodland areas (see Walk No. 34). Common on high altitude moorland is the famous alpenrose (alpine rhododendron) which is a bushy evergreen shrub with clusters of pale pink to deep pinkish red flowers, and of course every walker hopes one day to come across the rare edelweiss (I have seen clusters of them in the Swiss Valais but none in the Haute Savoie).

In many of the tourist offices and mountain refuges there are posters indicating which alpine flowers are rare and therefore protected. In the réserves no flowers may be picked. There is nothing more beautiful than a meadow of wild flowers, especially the alpine daffodils or narcissi which can cover an entire mountainside and nothing more heartbreaking than to see people walking along with bunches of wilted flowers in their hands. It is far better to leave the flowers to be admired by others rather than pick them.

Many butterflies can still be found in the meadows and even at higher altitudes, some of which are now rare in Britain such as the graceful creamy yellow and brown swallowtails and the purple camberwell beauty with its striking cream border. Among the commoner species there are plenty of red admirals, tortoiseshells, yellow brimstones and tiny meadow blues.

In autumn the flowers die away but instead there are wild raspberries and bilberries for the picking. In the wooded areas there is also a fascinating range of mushrooms, the edible ones being a real French delicacy. Some of these are quite unlike any found in Britain; they are white, black, grey, purple and even a chilling green and can normally be seen clinging to the roots of trees or hidden under mounds of dead leaves. There are also the big comforting round red mushrooms with white spots which remind one of childhood fairy tales. Many of these fungi are highly poisonous and they should never be eaten without checking first at a local pharmacie (chemist), where there is usually an expert who will do this willingly.

Suggested books:

The Alpine Flowers of Britain & Europe by Greg Wilson & Marjorie Blamey - published by Collins. Paperback edition. The most comprehensive book on the market.

The Hamlyn Guide of Wild Flowers of Britain & Europe by D. & R. Aichele & H.W. & A. Schwegler. Paperback edition.

The Macdonald Encyclopedia of Alpine Flowers by Guido Moggi. Beautiful photographs and good descriptions but since the book spans alpine regions worldwide it covers only the more common species. Paperback.

The Mitchell Beazley Pocket Guides including Birds of Prey, Trees, Mushrooms & Toadstools, Butterflies, (Their wild flowers guide does not include alpine species.).

FAUNA

Thanks to the ecology movement and the recent creation of nature reserves, the animal population of the Alps has increased in recent years which is a welcome sign. The various species which can be glimpsed, if you are lucky and there are not too many people about, are deer, ibex, chamois, mouflons, mountain hares, wild boar, marmots, grouse, buzzards, eagles, ptarmigan and bearded vultures. There are also the more widespread rodents such as foxes, dormice, stoats, weasels, pine martens and squirrels. Bears and lynx may also soon be reintroduced to the Alps, though the alpine farmers are uneasy about the future of their livestock. A wolf has already been spotted recently as far north as the Vanoise National Park (southern Alps), which is a sign that they are moving in from the Italian mountains.

Ibex (bouquetins in French) are mountain goats which were hunted to extinction and only reintroduced to the Alps fairly recently. They have readapted themselves remarkably and are less shy than the nervous chamois, often regarding the mountain climber with disdain from a near distance as though knowing they are a protected species; they have been known to knock stones down from above to deter intruders. Sturdy, passive animals, the ibex has no natural enemies although the babies have been known to make an eagle's meal; they are usually to be seen in small family groups at an altitude of about 2,000m. The males have beautiful long curved serrated horns which they use during the rutting season (December to mid January) to chase away other contenders for their females.

The chamois is a daintier, lighter and more agile animal than the ibex, being the alpine representative of the antelope family. With a pretty striped brown and cream face, the males having two small curving horns, they are often to be seen in large groups leaping from rock to rock in the most inhospitable places but you will rarely get near them as they are timid and nervous. Their speed and agility is due to their hooves which, like small cushions on normal terrain, have the ability to widen and become like crampons on precipitous rocky slopes. The chamois population was greatly reduced by continual hunting after the second world war, but since 1989 hunting quotas have been strictly controlled and there are now around 40,000 in the alpine areas.

The mouflon is a species of mountain sheep, originating from Corsica, Sardinia and Cyprus which was first introduced to the alpine regions in the 1950s so that it could be hunted and solve a food problem. In 1969 about 60 animals were installed in the Roc d'Enfer, Col de Foron region (Faucigny/Haut Giffre) and Mont de Grange National Reserve (Chablais region) and in 1978 a herd were let loose on the Tournette mountain near Annecy. The males, which weigh around 50kg, have huge curled horns and are also characterised by a white saddle across their backs during the winter season.

They are passive, slow animals who spend at least eight hours per day peacefully grazing on the upland slopes. There are at present about 300 in the Haute Savoie although I have personally not seen any. Many ecologists are against animals being introduced into a region where they were never endemic and there is a certain controversy concerning these alpine mouflons.

If you come across a large patch of meadowland where the grass has been churned up and the earth turned over, then you know that there are wild boar in the vicinity. They are not an animal one would choose to come face to face with (fortunately unlikely) since they can weigh as much as 150kg and can be very aggressive if cornered. They are really wild pigs which like to live in small bands, mainly in forest areas (they are more numerous in the wooded Jura mountains than the Alps) and have no enemies other than hunters; their meat, rich and gamey, is considered a great delicacy.

The most charming of all the alpine fauna is the cuddly looking marmot. If you hear a piercing whistle echoing across the slopes, stop dead in your tracks and keep your eyes peeled for one of these enchanting creatures which are usually to be found in rocky grasslands. The whistle is the cry of alarm from the marmot on sentry duty to tell his fellows that there is danger in the vicinity so they can rush back into their holes. But they are not really shy creatures and if you stay quiet curiosity will overcome their fear and you will see a furry head pop out again to look around and survey the slopes. During the winter months the marmots hibernate in their deep grass lined holes living off accumulated fat until they emerge thin and hungry in mid-April. The marmot has few enemies except for eagles who like to snatch the babies; they have never been seriously hunted for food. They are prolific in the Alps and the walker has a good chance of seeing them on many occasions.

Of all the alpine birds of prey, the most impressive is the golden eagle which has been protected now for a number of years and can be seen more frequently. The more recent newcomer is the bearded vulture (gypaète barbu in French) which was reintroduced into the Alps in 1978 where there are now around 100 couples. Since 1987, 19 young birds have been introduced into the Haute Savoie region where they are heavily protected. With a wing span of 3m they are an awe-inspiring sight as they circle majestically amongst the high peaks (see Walk No. 47).

One of the most interesting of birds to be found at around 2,000m is the shy ptarmigan. The size of a pigeon, the ptarmigan can only fly for short bursts, preferring to stay on the ground pecking around for grass and berries. In summer its plumage is brown, a perfect camouflage against the rock and scree where between May and July the females will raise from 4 to 8 chicks in a nest, in rocky hollow or long grass. In winter ptarmigans turn white, merging with the snowy environment and they protect themselves against the arctic cold by building an igloo in the snow with their claws where they can remain for days without food. Unfortunately, their numbers have been much reduced as they are often disturbed by skiers or caught in the overhead wires of ski-lifts. The alpine grouse is another bird which is fast disappearing due to ski installations and being hunted for the pot; it prefers bushy areas at altitudes between 1,400 and 2,600m.

Big black crows are to be found at the top of many a mountain, especially those frequented by picnickers. You will also find the more interesting chough and alpine chough which look completely alike except that the former has a long curved red bill and the latter a shorter yellow one - they make a sinister high pitched screech which is in complete harmony with the rocky precipitous summits they favour. Look out too for falcons, buzzards, hawks, larks and the smaller birds such as the dipper who loves to run along the bottom of rushing alpine torrents at high altitude.

RESERVES

There are four main nature reserves in the Haute Savoie, all in or near the Mont Blanc region. Each has a centre with relevant information about the reserve and a summer programme consisting of conferences, slide shows and guided tours. The three following ones, although each operated by different communes, are connected and are really one large National Park.

The Aiguilles Rouges in the Chamonix-Vallorcine area, facing the Mont Blanc peak, consists of 3,300 hectares (1 hectare is approximately 2 acres) of high mountains and includes forests, alpine pastures, perpendicular cliffs and glaciers. The information centre is at the Col des Montets, Nr. Argentière, open from 1 June to 15 September, tel. 50.54.02.24.

The Réserve de Sixt, near Samoëns (Walk Nos. 33, 35, 36) is an area of 9,200 hectares covering three-quarters of the Sixt commune. It incorporates the Fer à Cheval region, a dramatic horseshoe of peaks with dozens of cascading waterfalls and underground caves hidden in the limestone cliffs, the Lake d'Anterne, the corrugated rock wall of the Rochers de Fiz and the rock fissures in the lunar landscape of the Desert de Platé. The information chalet, in the Fer à Cheval (near Sixt), is open from 15 June to 15 September. There is another museum in the village of Sixt itself which includes the history and the growth of tourism and climbing in the region. Maison de la Reserve Naturelle de Sixt Fer à Cheval: tel. 50.34.91.90.

The Réserve Naturelle de Passy (Walk Nos. 30 & 31) is situated between the Aiguilles Rouge and Sixt Reserves and is a plateau area facing the Mont Blanc mountain range. It was created in 1980 and consists of 2,000 hectares (about 4,000 acres) of alpine pasture including part of the Rochers de Fiz, the Desert de Platé and the marshy area around the Lac de Pormentaz. It is a fascinating geological region consisting of layers of granite, limestone, slate and peat. The presence of such a diverse range of minerals (copper, lead and silver) led to small mining activities in the 18th century and the underground galleries still remain. There is an abundance of wild flowers and butterflies and you can see marmots, chamois and ibex (I have also seen a golden eagle in this region). The information chalet is situated at Plaines Joux (start of Walk No. 31) and is open from 1 July to 30 September, tel. 50.58.80.17.

Réserve Naturelle des Contamines Montjoie (west side of Mont Blanc), near the villages of Les Contamines on the B.902 south of St. Gervais Les Bains. It consists of 5,500 hectares of high mountains (part of the the famous Mont Blanc circular walk), including alpine lakes, pastures, forests and glaciers. The information centre is in the mairie of Les Contamines. Open from 14 June to 12 September, tel. 50.47.00.75.

There are also five smaller reserves which do not have information centres (phone the local tourist office for documentation). These are:

Réserve Naturelle de Carlaveyron in the commune of Les Houches, Nr. Chamonix.
598 hectares of high mountains, lakes and glaciers.

Réserve Naturelle du Vallon de Bérard in the commune of Vallorcine, Nr. Chamonix.
539 hectares of high mountains characterised by a high valley terminating in a ring of glaciers.

Réserve Naturelle du Roc de Chère which is near Talloires on Lake Annecy. It is a massive rock which rears impressively out of the lake itself and has a special Mediterranean climate encouraging the growth of special plants including Spagnum moss.

Réserve Naturelle du Bout du Lac d'Annecy - This is a marshy area of 84 hectares at the southern end of Lake Annecy which has been preserved for its special vegetation and the breeding of innumerable water fowl which also winter here. There is a camping site in the vicinity.

Réserve Naturelle du Delta de la Dranse - the smallest reserve of them all, consisting of only 45 hectares of shifting gravel banks where the Dranse river empties into Lac Léman (Lake Geneva) between Thonon and Evian in the Chablais.

A SHORT HISTORY OF THE HAUTE SAVOIE

The department of the Haute Savoie did not become a definite part of France until 1860 when Napoleon III crossed the Alps with an army of 130,000 and defeated the King of Sardinia, Victor-Emmanuel. At the ensuing treaty on 24 March 1860 the King ceded the Savoie area to the French and it was split into the Haute Savoie (high or north region) and the Savoie (the southern region).

Since then the Savoyards have been ardent members of the Republic. In the 1914-1918 war they lost 10% of the population and were, in the second world war, the fiercest fighters during the Resistance movement, using centuries of mountain knowledge to harass and evade the enemy.

The first traces of human habitation were found on the Salève mountain near Geneva (see chapters on the Salève) in 1833 and date from about 12,000 BC.

These were primitive hunters who killed the local ibex, marmots and hares with rudimentary weapons. It was only around 1,000 BC, when the climate became milder, that the tribes multiplied and started growing cereals on the plains and raising domestic animals. The Romans had difficulty in conquering the Savoie area, mainly because of the mountainous terrain and vast forests. Hannibal had already crossed the Alps with his troop of elephants 150 years before the emperor Augustus gained control of the mountain passes in 16-14 BC. Augustus built the main highway from Aosta (now in Italy) to Vienne with two branches, the first from Conflans to Annecy and the second from Aosta through Seyssel to Geneva. In fact the Roman road still runs along the foot of the Jura mountains in the Geneva plain!

The real history of the Savoie (or La Sapaudia as it was then called) began in AD 443 with the arrival of a Germanic people called the Burgondes who originated from the Bergen region in Norway. They created the first regional monarchies and the Burgundy kingdom which stretched roughly from St. Maurice in the Valais in the east, as far as Geneva on Lac Léman in the west, and southwards to St. Jean de Maurienne. About 100 years earlier the emperor Constantine had made Christianity the state religion. However, it was not until the last king of Burgundy, Rudolphe III, died in 1032 to be succeeded by Humbert aux Blanches Mains who founded the Kingdom of Savoy, that the Cistercian, Benedictine and Chartreuse monasteries were installed in many Savoie villages such as St. Jean d'Aulps, Abondance, Vallon and Le Reposoir.

For the next few hundred years the Savoie was ruled by a series of counts, dukes and petty kings who divided up the territory into little kingdoms and constantly fought amongst themselves. The famous 13th century plague, the Black Death, which ravaged Europe, halved the population of the region. In 1416 Amadée VIII (called the peaceful) became the Duke of Savoie and established good relations with the Geneva nobles who had been constantly warring until then. This peaceful cohabitation lasted until the start of the 15th century when the evangelist Calvin arrived and preached a new doctrine of revolt against the Catholic church. He converted the Geneva people to his new way of thinking, known as Calvinism or later Protestantism, and the reformation, soon to sweep other areas of Europe, was born. The powerful Geneva bishops fled to Annecy and in 1536 the Bernoise (the people from the Berne area of Switzerland who had just joined the Swiss Confederation) invaded the Geneva and Chablais areas. In 1564 the Chablais was returned to the reigning Duke of Savoy, Emmanuel-Philibert, but Catholicism had been outlawed and there was cultural and economic poverty. It was a young priest, François de Sales, born in 1567 in the Château de Thorens near the village of Thorens-Glières who, at the Duke's request, went into the Chablais and after four years managed to convert the population back to the Catholic faith. He became a great saint and is particularly revered in the Haute Savoie region (see chapters on the Chablais). In 1602 he was made Bishop of Annecy where he established the Visitation Order in 1610. He died in Lyon in 1622. His tomb can be seen in the basilica of the Visitation monastery in Annecy. In 1589 war broke out round Geneva and at the Treaty of Lyon, the Pays de Gex (the area between the city and the Jura mountains), the Bugey and the Bresse regions were ceded to France.

The next interesting event was the famous Escalade on the night of 11/12 December 1602 when the Savoyards, led by Charles-Emmanuel the Duke of Savoy, tried to scale the ancient fortification walls encircling Geneva to win back the city. The legend goes that a fierce old lady called Mère Royaume was woken by the noise and sounded the alarm while emptying a bowl of hot soup over the soldiers. Suffice it to say the assailants were routed and never again tried to attack Geneva. Escalade is now a traditional Geneva celebration in December when the entire event is re-enacted in the old town with patriotic speeches and of course the drinking of the traditional hot vegetable soup and breaking of the marmite, the symbolic cauldron which is now made out of chocolate decorated with the red and yellow colours of the city and containing vegetable sweets made out of marzipan!

The Savoie was frequently a battlefield as it hung between the great European powers of France, Austria and Spain, each country coveting the area as part of their empire. Later In the 16th century Savoie again came under French influence, successful campaigns being launched by both Louis XII and Louis XIV. However, in 1713 Victor Armadée II shook off this foreign influence and reclaimed the Savoie in the Treaty of Utrecht in 1713. He also became king of Sicily which he was obliged to exchange 5 years later for the royal command of Sardinia. This was the first of two periods when the Haute Savoie came under Sardinian authority. The village of Carouge (now an attractive part of Geneva) was constructed in 1780 and made the chef-lieu (capital) of the Province. Clock and watch making developed in the Arve valley (see Cluses) but the area was still very poor and many of the peasants emigrated to France and Germany. A notable achievement at this time was the first ascent of Mont Blanc in 1786 by Balmat and Paccard!

In 1792 France invaded yet again and the Savoie (including Geneva) became part of the county of Mont Blanc with Chambéry in the south as the county town. This region was transferred to Geneva in 1798 and became known as the Département du Léman. After the defeat of France in the Napoleonic wars the Sardinians came back into power in 1815 and this time the Geneva people decided to join the Confederation of Swiss States (Switzerland) and cut themselves off irrevocably from the Haute Savoie.

This was followed by a relatively prosperous economic and cultural period known as the Buon Governo (from 1815 to 1847). Many churches and buildings were built at this time and the clock making industry and agriculture became firmly established. During the Sardinian era the French culture and language continued to flourish and in 1860 Napoleon III crossed the Alps and Savoie history changed again!

And what about the region today? Covering an area of 828km with a population of 518,000 people spread over 292 villages, the Haute Savoie is one of the richest and most expanding areas of France, yet a hundred years ago it was one of the poorest. Tourism has grown tremendously in the last 50 years, especially since the 1960s when skiing became popular and new ski resorts were built, such as Flaine and Morzine Avoriaz, opening up hundreds of kilometres of skiable slopes. In 1962 the important Mont Blanc road tunnel was finished, thus linking France with Italy and placing the Haute Savoie on one of the greatest trade routes in Europe. Industry has also expanded, the Arve valley being well-known for its precision and mechanical engineering, with 1,200 enterprises in a 30km radius! There are many other businesses such as sports equipment (the production of skis and mechanical ski-lifts) and wood related industries, such as forestry and furniture making.

But it is the incredibly natural beauty of the Haute Savoie that is its greatest asset, drawing more and more tourists every year to enjoy the freedom of the mountains, lakes and forests. Hopefully it will be realised that the ecology of the region should not be tampered with to excess and that more nature reserves and protected areas are needed rather than ski resorts with their numerous ugly installations.

THE REGIONS OF THE HAUTE SAVOIE

This chapter explains the different areas of the Haute Savoie and suggests some of the towns and villages where the walker may like to stay. From the map you will find many others but it is impossible to mention them all and the author has picked out those she prefers or considers centrally situated. By necessity the explanations are short, but give the reader an impression of the type of countryside and the typical towns and villages they will be walking in.

SALÈVE REGION INCLUDING THE VALLÉE VERTE (North-west Haute Savoie)

The Salève - Walk Nos. 1-5

Although it is situated in France, the people of Geneva consider the Salève their own personal mountain. This is not surprising as it dominates the international city which is isolated at the extreme eastern end of Switzerland, with the French region of the Haute Savoie to the south and the department of Ain, including the Jura mountain range, to the north. In fact it was only in 1815, when the city joined the Swiss Confederation and the Salève region remained in the Haute Savoie, that it was politically severed from the mountain that overshadows it. Whether it is in the same country or not, no picture of Geneva is complete without its lake, the dramatic jet d'eau fountain rising in a powerful spout 130m high from the end of a long jetty, overhung by the brooding cliffs of the Salève with a range of glistening alpine peaks on the distant skyline.

Oriented north-east/south-west, the Salève is a long limestone hump stretching 19km from the village of Etrembières in the north to Cruseilles in the south. There are three distinct areas; first the Petit Salève (little Salève) which, seen from Geneva, is a distinct triangular prism on the left-hand side (north-eastern end); second is the precipitous long rock face of the Salève itself pitted with narrow gorges, caves and grottoes; and third is the southern, mainly wooded area characterised by Les Pitons and the Pointe de Plan lookout points, the terrain resembling the Jura mountains across the lake to the north.

There are a variety of walks in all three regions, though shorter ones on the Petit Salève. This mountain, however, because of its popularity and proximity to Geneva, has claimed more lives than others in the region and it is to be walked over with precaution. You are perfectly fine if you stick to the defined paths and you will not be alone, especially at weekends, but avoid going off the beaten track down the front of the mountain as you could find yourself on the edge of a gorge or falling into a narrow, rocky crevasse. The Salève was the pioneer of escalade rock-climbing as its sheer cliffs, some of them over 200m high, are a great sporting challenge, together with the hundreds of hidden caves and grottoes to be explored, but by experts only! A more recent sport, to which the Salève lends itself perfectly, is parapenting and most afternoons in good weather you will see a flotilla of colourful parapenters drifting down from the top of the mountain like a cluster of butterflies.

The Salève was also the pioneer site for one of the first cable-cars ever built (1894), which went up the steep north face by the side of the immense quarries, from the small village of Le Pas de l'Echelle. It functioned until the mid seventies (apart from the war years because of its proximity to the frontier) and was then closed for security reasons. In 1984 it was completely rebuilt with Swiss participation, thus guaranteeing the Geneva people easy access to their favourite Sunday outing! Before the cable-car there was a train which snaked up from Etrembières to Monnetier and the traces of its tracks can still be seen though most of the route has been quarried away.

If you visit the Museum of Art and History in Geneva you will see the ancient tools and eating utensils of the first inhabitants of the Salève thousands of years ago which were discovered in 1833. Unfortunately the huge quarries, which have steadily eroded the north side of the mountain, have destroyed much of the past and also disfigured the mountain itself. Horace Bénédict de Saussure, the well-known Geneva naturalist, was one of the first people to explore the Salève in depth and the fantastic view of the Alps he saw from its summit inspired him to go further afield and climb higher mountain peaks such as Mont Blanc.

The Vuache - Walk No. 6

A lesser known landmark in the Geneva region, the Vuache is geographically a continuation of the Jura range to the north of the city which dips dramatically at its western edge to let the Rhône river flow through a narrow defile called the Ecluse. A fort of the same name clings to the rocky cliffs which formerly guarded against marauders entering the Geneva plain from beyond. Look to the west on a sunny evening and you will see the impressive Ecluse gap (locally called the Bellegarde gap) and the long low ridge of the Vuache to the left outlined against the setting sun. A mountain like any other you would think, except that it isn't. This limestone saddle which is 1,100m at its highest point, with imposing cliffs dominating the Savoyard plaines of La Semine and Les Daines, has a special micro-climate attracting a Mediterranean-type vegetation and a multitude of flowers, which blossom long before others in the region. The climate is the result of a large vertical fault which crosses the south-western side of the mountain, creating occasional local regional quakes, the most recent being in the nearby village of Chaumont in 1936. The wooded ridge of the Vuache is dotted in early spring with the rare dogstooth violet (not really a violet at all but a delicate pink flower, its solitary white bulb resembling a dog's tooth) and later on there are carpets of daffodils, violets and periwinkles (see Flora and Fauna).

La Vallée Verte (The green valley) - Walk Nos. 7-12

This beautiful southern sloping valley is the most northerly in the Haute Savoie. Because of its proximity to the French town of Annemasse and Swiss Geneva it has become a popular place for weekend retreats, walking and skiing. Despite this influx the valley remains remarkably unspoilt with its green hillsides, eight small villages and numerous farms. Formerly named the

Mènoge valley after the river running through it and creating the frontier between the Chablais region to the north and the Faucigny region to the south, it spills into the Giffre valley at the Pont de Fillinges. On its northern side is the brooding flank of the Voirons mountain which separates the valley from the Geneva plain and to the south is the Mont de Vouan with further up the valley the Pointe de Miribel, the ski area of the Hirmentaz ridge and the Mont Forchat. There is a path right round this valley called Tour de Vallée and you will follow the red/yellow splashes indicating this on some of the walks. The better known Balcon du Léman walk, which goes over the mountain crests fringing Lac Léman, also goes along this valley on the Voirons ridge.

In a region once deeply Catholic, it was fashionable in the 18th century to build stations of the cross, statues and churches on mountain summits, not too high of course, so that the local population could make pilgrimages and gain indulgences (remission in Purgatory). In this tradition the Vallée Verte includes the Pointe de Miribel with its Stations of the Cross and statue of Our Lady, the Mont Forclaz with its figure of St. François de Sales, as well as dozens of little wayside shrines and chapels.

Where to base yourself

To explore the Salève it is not necessary to stay in Geneva which is an expensive city. Annemasse, the French extension of Geneva, is also not recommended and the little villages on and at the foot of the mountain are not especially attractive. The Vallée Verte region, however, is not far away and the old town of La Roche-Sur-Foron (see Faucigny/Haut Giffre area) is about half an hour. Even Annecy is within striking distance, especially as none of the walks is long or arduous.

The little town of Frangy (1,544 inhabitants) on the N.508, at the northern end of the tranquil Val des Usses and 25km north-west of Annecy, is off the tourist track but has a couple of modest hotels, two camping grounds and chambres d'hôtes. The Vuache mountain is nearby and the Salève walks are about 20mins by car. It is a good peaceful spot to choose though the town itself is not particularly exciting, its main claim to fame being the frothy dry white wine produced locally and called La Roussette de Frangy.

The Vallée Verte is an excellent base but has a limited choice of accommodation of all levels. Although popular with the nearby Geneva population it does not swarm with tourists, who tend to congregate in the higher alpine mountains to the south. Boëge is the chef-lieu of the region (1,300 inhabitants) with all the usual amenities including a lively market on Tuesday mornings in the old covered market hall which still stands near the main square; you will also find a friendly reception at the tourist office who are happy to answer all enquiries (they speak English). The villages of Habère-

Lullin, Habère-Poche and Bogève also have hotels though some are shut during the summer months, as they are the nearest places to the Hirmentaz and Les Brasses (Faucigny) downhill and cross-country ski areas. Camping sites, gîtes and chambres d'hôtes are also available in the region.

CHABLAIS REGION (North-east Haute Savoie)

The Chablais region stretches from the southern shores of Lac Léman (called Lake Geneva by the Swiss and most English speakers) to Morzine and the well-known Portes de Soleil ski area to the south. On its eastern edge is Switzerland and the Rhône valley and to the west are the Vallée Verte (technically part of the Chablais) and the Faucigny/Haut Giffre. The Chablais can really be broken up into three distinct areas - the lake shore (La Côte) and pre-Alp area, the Val d'Abondance and the Morzine region.

The lake shore (La Côte) and the Pré-Alps - Walk Nos. 13-17

The flat, green countryside of the lake shore with its many pretty villages and two elegant towns of Thonon-les-Bains and Evian-les-Bains (called Thonon and Evian for short) is called La Côte. Behind this fertile coastal plain rise the rocky white limestone cliffs of the pré-Alps, from which the walker is dazzled by uninterrupted views of the lake, the largest in western Europe, with the Swiss towns of Lausanne, Vevey and Montreux standing out clearly on the opposite shores and on the skyline the long straight line of the Jura mountains. To the east are the impressive high peaks in the Swiss cantons of Vaud and Valais. This area has the most extensive views of the entire Haute Savoie and the contrast of the white limestone cliffs and the deep green of the woods and grassy slopes is magnificent.

Where to base yourself

Thonon, the capital of Chablais, is a bustling town of 30,000 inhabitants, situated on a terrace above the lake shore and linked to its port below by a rather old-fashioned funicular railway. For those who prefer a town atmosphere, lively interesting shops, little squares and pavement cafés in a pedestrian precinct, then Thonon is the place for you. You will not find ancient winding streets as the centre of town has been tastefully renovated by the famous architect Novarina. This does not mean the town lacks history as it was an important commercial centre, even in Roman times, and was the residence of the Dukes of Savoy. Interesting historical places to visit include the Château de Sonnaz built in 1668 and now the Chablais Museum, the Visitation Monastery and chapel, built in the 18th century and the church of Saint Hyppolyte (17th century). In common with neighbouring Evian, Thonon is a spa town, where people come for cures, and it also produces its own increasingly popular brand of mineral water.

Further along the lake and in complete contrast to Thonon, is the smaller town of Evian. While Thonon bustles with life, Evian has a staid, genteel, almost Victorian atmosphere which is more conducive to the hundreds of people who come to "take the waters" for a number of complaints. Since 1860 Evian has been famous for thermal cures and also for its mineral water from natural springs discovered at least a hundred years earlier. Many of the bigger hotels fringing the lake date from the turn of the century and offer the sumptuous comfort needed for convalescing, rather than that required by the ordinary tourist, but there is plenty of alternative accommodation including camping sites. Evian is a pleasant place to wander round as, like Thonon, the main shopping streets are for pedestrians only; the Jardin Anglais (English garden) overlooking the lake has many rare plants and shrubs and there are other beautiful gardens in front of the town hall and old thermal buildings. The architect Novarina was also busy in Evian, creating a new buvette to the baths in 1959, to which was added a completely new thermal centre in 1984. Other places to visit include the church, Notre Dame de L'Assomption, which has some wall frescos, uncovered when renovation work was done in the 1980s, and the building of the Cachat mineral water association built in 1903 (the actual water bottling factory is in the village of Publier, 3km away). Another obvious attraction of both Thonon and Evian are the boat trips which can be made round the lake, getting off and on where you fancy, but don't forget your passport as you will be entering Switzerland!

About 13kms south-east of Evian is the village of Bernex which has a striking church built in the Sardinian style. It nestles in an attractive open valley with the jagged peaks of the impressive Dent d'Oche mountain (alt. 2,225m), in the background (Walk No. 17). A ski centre in winter, it is a calm, restful spot to stay in summer, yet offers swimming and tennis as well as lots of lovely alpine walks.

The name Bellevaux comes from the latin Bella Vista, meaning Belle Vallée (beautiful valley). The village is on the D.26 south of Thonon and linked to the Vallée Verte by the Col du Terramont and to St. Jeoire by the Col de Jambaz. It is one of my favourite places, probably for the reason that it has esçaped complete conversion to tourism. As far as anywhere can be "far from the madding crowd" in the Haute Savoie, the little village of Bellevaux has achieved this, despite its proximity to the skiing regions of the Hirmentaz in the Vallée Verte and La Chèvrerie. Nearby are two delightful walks, the Rochers de Nifflon and the Pointe de la Gay (Nos. 27 and 28) and 6km south is the very attractive Lac de Vallon with its ancient Carthusian abbey. The hamlet of La Chèvrerie at the end of the lake is the start of many walks, including the Pointe de Chalune (see Walk No. 29) - the Roc d'Enfer can also be walked from this side.

The Vallée d'Abondance

Follow the N.902 road south from Thonon, down a winding gorge following the Dranse river, which hurls itself over rocks and through narrow gullies and is popular for rafting and canoeing, till you take a left-hand turn and enter the Val d'Abondance. "The Valley of Abundance" is the English translation and the name is merited. It is the home of the distinctive Abondance cattle with their heavy elaborate bells. White faced with brown rings round their eyes and chestnut coloured bodies, they are renowned for their excellent milk and a regional cheese of the same name. Cross-bred from Swiss and local species, the cattle became a recognised breed in 1891 and can now be seen all over the Savoie region - the farmers are very proud of their individual cattle and there are yearly contests to select the best examples of the race.

Most valleys in the Haute Savoie have their own characteristic style of architecture and the Abondance farms are particularly magnificent; standing in rich pastureland, they are beautifully decorated with long wood sculpted balconies from which drip a blaze of red geraniums all summer long. They are constructed out of local wood, many with a concrete foundation where the stores are kept. The living quarters face south and the hay is stacked under the roof in enormous lofts which one would imagine to be a considerable fire risk. Large extended families lived together, the grown up sons bringing their wives into the family home. The roofs are perhaps the most striking aspect of these farms; some are of slate squares from the nearby quarries in Châtel and Morzine and others of tavaillons, which are small squares of fir wood 30 to 40cm long, placed on slats of timber in a perpendicular fashion - a long meticulous job but the result lasting at least 50 years! Unfortunately, many of these roofs have now been replaced by galvanised iron. The mountain slopes of the valley are particularly abundant in woodland which, happily, have not been entirely denuded by the many sawmills situated along the Abondance river.

Since the fifties life in the valley has changed considerably as tourism and skiing have become the main source of income, at least for those who have not already left to work in the nearby towns or emigrated. The valley is now connected to the Portes de Soleil skiing area, one of the most extensive in the Alps, linking a number of villages in France and Switzerland. Despite this progress and the building of appartments and hotels to house the influx of tourists, much of the valley has remained unspoiled and retained its charm and tranquillity.

Where to base yourself

Abondance, 16km down the valley, is the first village you reach. The historical and municipal "capital" of the region, it is perhaps the prettiest of the three main villages. It is renowned for its abbey and cloisters. Founded in 1080 by the monks of St Augustine who came from the nearby Swiss abbey of St. Maurice, it is the only abbey in the Haute Savoie still intact. Buildings include the abbey church with its choir and trompe-l'oeil statues, the paintings and stained glass windows dating from the Sardinian occupation between 1839 and 1845; the cloisters which have some striking 14th century frescos done by the Italian artist Jacquerio Giacoma representing the holy mysteries; and the Monastery. The latter houses an interesting museum with ancient religious objects, including a model of a 13th century monk's cell and a number of ancient books. From 1978 to 1986 the frescos and buildings were restored. If your French is up to it and you are there in the summer months, the parish priest Père Defollin will show you round and bring the history of this ancient abbey alive. Abondance, slower to adapt to the tourist scene with its first major ski-lift not built until 1964, still retains a village charm. At the foot of the Jorat mountain, with the jagged peaks of the formidable Cornettes de Bise behind, it is the centre of the some of the loveliest walks in the Alps (see Walk Nos. 18 to 20).

Further along the valley is the smaller village of Chapelle d'Abondance which has also evolved successfully from an agricultural community to a tourist resort, expanding rapidly in the eighties with the building of ski installations linking it with the Portes de Soleil. (Walk No. 24).

Châtel is the last village in the valley before you go over the pass to the Swiss village of Morgins and was agriculturally the poorest of the three communities, due to higher altitude and less fertile pasture land. To compensate, it was a great smuggling centre as the wily peasants were able to outwit the customs men by using their own secret paths over the mountains (see Walk No. 24). Châtel was also known for its slate mines (each peasant having his own small gallery) which were worked in the winter months when the fields were under snow. The slates were heaped onto a sledge and dragged down the slopes but later on they were laden on to wooden skips attached to overhead cables. The last slate mine closed as recently as 1986 when it collapsed, sending an avalanche of stones and mud and cutting off the road up to the end of the valley.

Châtel is now the most prosperous of the three villages as it is a major cross-roads in the Portes de Soleil and very popular as a ski resort. Unfortunately, rapid expansion in the 1960s when the farmers were encouraged to build large tasteless chalets to house French schoolchildren coming en masse for their state subsidised annual ski holiday, has resulted in some loss of character. Nevertheless, its alpine surroundings make up for this, dominated by the Mont de Grange mountain, alt. 2,433m, the second highest peak in the Chablais (see Walk Nos. 22 to 24).

Valley d'Aulps, Morzine - Walk Nos.25 and 26

The third area is the Valley d'Aulps round the ski resorts of Morzine and Les Gets. Many of the slopes in this region are criss-crossed with ski installations. Since I have a strong aversion to walking over ski slopes in summer I have only included two walks (Nos.25 and 26), one near the beautiful Lake Morillon and the other up the Pointe de Ressachaux which gives you a bird's-eye view of Morzine-Avoriaz.

If you continue on the D.902 past the turnoff to the Val d'Abondance, you will go through the village of St. Jean d'Aulps where you will see the famous Cistercian ruins of Notre Dame d'Aulps, founded in the 12th century, of which all that remains are the facade and part of the northern wall. A few kilometres further on is the lively ski resort of Morzine. Above it, built into the precipitous cliffs of Les Hauts Forts in the 1960s, are the rock like wooden buildings of Morzine Avoriaz, with its privileged position as the centre of the Portes de Soleil ski complex. It has a well-known film festival every winter which attracts many personalities from show business. Situated at the centre of converging valleys and easily reached by a number of different roads, Morzine is unashamedly given over to tourism; it is interesting to note that at the end of World War I so many people had been killed or emigrated that the village was almost dead. Luckily one of the villagers had the courage to build a hotel and from then on the village prospered and 15 other hotels had been opened by the beginning of World War II. Now there are 52 hotels and a number of camping sites. The old chalets are still intact on the right bank of the river, facing the hotels and buildings of the ever expanding modern town.

Both Les Gets and Morzine have hotels, camping sites, gîtes and chambres d'hôtes which are open in the summer, though check first concerning the hotels. Personally I find staying in ski resorts in summer rather depressing though they do offer tennis, swimming pools, mini-golf and other holiday resort activities. Morzine tourist office issues a free booklet (in French) with local walk itineraries.

FAUCIGNY/HAUT GIFFRE REGION (Central & East Haute Savoie)

Sandwiched between the Chablais region to the north, the Aravis/Borne region to the south, Geneva to the west and Mont Blanc to the east, it is difficult to describe where this region really begins or ends in terms of exact geographical boundaries. It basically comprises the two main valleys of the Giffre and the Arve and is the most populated and industrialised of the Haute Savoie regions.

The Arve valley

The Arve river starts in the glaciers of the Mont Blanc range and flows northwards for 105km before emptying itself into the mighty Rhône in Geneva. There is now a motorway all along this valley which goes through the Mont Blanc tunnel, an important link between north and south Europe. Bonneville is the administrative capital of the Faucigny region and is situated at the entrance to the valley; further south are the towns of Cluses and Sallanches. Despite the advancing industrialisation of this wide valley, the towns still retain their character and the mountains through which the river winds are some of the most impressive in the Alps.

Enough has been written about the Mont Blanc and Chamonix area which is where the valley starts, but east of Sallanches, where the westward flowing Arve turns north toward Cluses, is the Plateau d'Assy. This is a natural plateau of great beauty where the walker can appreciate more extensive views of the Mont Blanc range across the Arve valley than if you were walking round the mighty mountain itself.

Due to its high sunny position facing south, this plateau was once a tuberculosis treatment centre and its many sanatorium buildings are still used as convalescent homes for people being treated for depression, alcoholism and other disorders. The commune of Passy stretches from the Arve valley to the Chaine des Fiz and includes the Aiguilles Rouges and Tête Noire mountain ranges. A nature reserve was created in this region in 1980 consisting of 2,000 hectares between altitudes 1,347m and 2,723m (see separate chapter on reserves).

To the north the peak of the Aigle du Varan and the desolate rocky ridges of the Désert du Platte separate the Plateau d'Assy from the extensive skiing area of Flaine. Built during the sixties in a natural bowl in the mountains by Marcel Breurer, a well-known architect, and also housing a modern art centre, its serried ranks of lego-like concrete apartments can only be appreciated by connoisseurs and ski enthusiasts. The 140km of superb ski slopes called Le Grand Massif link the ski resorts of Les Carroz, below Flaine on the same access road, Morillon and Samoëns. Undeniably the scenery is magnificent but the walker would do better to base himself in Samoëns or Sixt (see below) in order to explore the region.

Where to base yourself

Passy, Plateau d'Assy and Plaines Joux - Walk Nos. 30 and 31

The commune of Passy consists of four hamlets; Les Plagnes on the west slopes, Chedde (in the plain), Passy and the Plateau d'Assy, with the ski station of Plaines Joux 300m higher. The latter three villages are the more convenient places to stay as they are geared to tourism and offer eight hotels, two campsites, and plenty of apartments. In Plateau d'Assy there is the modern church of Notre Dame de Toute Grace, constructed by the local architect Novarino between 1937 and 1945 (see Evian and Thonon) with a vividly painted facade by Fernand Léger. Inside the church there are stained glass windows by Chagall, Matisse, Lurcat, Léger and Bercot. Also on the road from the village of Passy to Plaines Joux you will see modern sculptures by well-known artists. Many walkers may find this area too crowded for their liking in the high season though it is amazing how quickly people melt away in the mountains!

Cluses

This town is situated where the Arve valley narrows and is dominated by the Pointe de Chevran, one of the author's favourite walks (No. 32). The first references to Cluses were in the 13th century when it was already an important communications centre. In 1844 a fire destroyed much of the town which was completely rebuilt on Sardinian lines. Recent modernisation has made an attractive pedestrian centre with easy parking facilities and good shops. Cluses was formerly renowned for its watch and clock making (it houses a watch museum), but this has been replaced by precision engineering and other small industries. Historical buildings include the 15th century Eglise des Cordieliers, an ancient convent chapel, with its particularly striking 17th century font, the 18th century church of St. Nicholas, parts of the old town and the fountain in the Place Allobroges (1791). Cluses is more of a town to visit than to stay in although it does have hotels and an all year round caravanning/camping park. The walker might prefer the villages in the vicinity and between the two valleys (nearer other walks) such as Châtillon sur Cluses (on the D.902 which goes north to Taninges), St. Sigismond, La Frasse and Arâches and Marignier on the D.26 where the Giffre flows into the Arve. These villages are small, however, and accommodation is limited.

Bearing west of Cluses and through the satellite town of Scionzier, the D.4 takes you to the alpine village of Le Reposoir which has a flourishing 800 year old monastery called La Chartreuse du Reposoir, taken over from the Carthusian monks in 1932 by the Carmelites. The D.4 winds over the Col de la Colombière to Grand-Bornand facing the Chaine des Aravis.

Giffre valley region

The River Giffre, springing from glaciers beneath the mighty Buet in the Fer à Cheval mountain region near the village of Sixt, flows through a softer less commercialised valley with spectacular mountain scenery. It passes through the pretty villages of Samoëns, Taninges and Mieussy before bearing south at the Pont de Giffre and spilling into the Arve north of Cluses. The valley continues northward passing by St. Jeoire with the distinctive peak of the Môle mountain to the left, and through Viuz-en-Sallaz before reaching the Pont de Fillinges and later Annemasse on the outskirts of Geneva. On both sides of this main artery are extensive walking areas and subsidiary valleys worth exploring. From the 15th century, the people of the Giffre were well-known as stone engravers and builders and the local grey stone houses, churches, fountains and wayside shrines are a testament to their craft. Many of the buildings in Geneva, Lyon and other big towns were built by these stalwart valley people who were forced to practise their craft further afield in order to earn a living.

Where to base yourself

Sixt - Walk Nos. 33-36

Voted one of the most beautiful villages in France, Sixt is at the head of the Giffre valley and 6km from the larger resort of Samoëns. The region is a walker's paradise; drive a few kilometres further up the valley and enter a breathtakingly dramatic amphiteatre of rock walls which rise straight out of the flat valley floor; you are looking at the Fer à Cheval (horseshoe) mountain peaks which must be visited if you are exploring the Haute Savoie region. At the end of the road there is a huge car park, with picnic areas, a café and a very interesting exhibition explaining the geological phenomena of the Fer à Cheval. This is an extremely popular spot so it is wise to avoid weekends in summer when there are literally hundreds of people. Take time to walk down this horseshoe to the Bout du Monde (end of the world) and admire the dozens of rushing streams which course down the gigantic slopes to end in magnificent waterfalls (see Walk No. 33). This area became a nature reserve in 1977 covering three-quarters of the Sixt commune (see chapter on reserves). The village itself is grouped around an ancient abbey built in the 11th century by the same monks who founded the Abondance abbey (see Chablais). It is now a hotel with a classified 17th century dining room! The church has an interesting 13th century nave and houses Les Trésors des Moines (valuable monastic chalices, etc) which can be seen on request. On a wall is a plaque dedicated to Jâcques Balmat, the first person to conquer Mt. Blanc in 1783 and who died mysteriously in the Fer à Cheval mountains while looking for gold in 1831 at the age of 72; many days were spent searching for his body, which was never found.

If you turn left in the village of Sixt you will pass through the hamlet of Salvagny (see Walk Nos. 34 and 35). Further up is the start of the two day walk to the Lac d'Anterne and the Refuge de Sales - this area connects with the region around Flaine, mentioned above, and the impressive Désert de Platté (see Walk No. 36).

Samoëns - Walk Nos. 37 & 38

Inspite of the fact that Samoëns is full of tourists in summer and winter and has a wealth of hotels, apartments to rent, two gîtes d'étapes and two camping sites, it manages to retain a certain charm with its ancient stone houses and streets, the centre of the village now being restricted to pedestrians. The inhabitants are called septimontains in memory of the seven alps which were given to the people by Amadée VIII (the local chief) in 1438; and since then the septimontains have gone to all corners of Europe as stone-engravers and masons. The village was well known in Napoleonic times as Bonaparte said that he would not visit it without a boat! - referring presumably to the hundreds of waterfalls in the region. Samoëns also had its patron in the name of Louise Jaÿ who, born of a modest family in a nearby hamlet, made her fortune in Paris. Not forgetting her roots she came back to Samoëns in her old age and created an alpine garden, restored the 17th century church in 1917 (restored again in 1975) and built a house for the local doctor!

There are many beautiful little villages and hamlets to explore around Samoëns such as Les Vallons (Walk No. 37), Les Moulins, Le Bérouze, Verchaix and Mathonex. Samoëns connects with Morzine by the winding D.354 over the Col de Joux Plaine. If you start up this road and branch off at the sign Les Allamands you reach the walking area of the Dentes Blanches (see Walk No. 38).

Taninges/Praz de Lys - Walk Nos. 39-42

Taninges, situated 12km down the valley from Samoëns, is a pleasant small town, its distinctive feature being the Pointe de Marcelly a mountain which juts out above the town and has a cross at the summit (Walk No. 39). The places to see are some quaint old streets, the Chapel of St. Anne (1583) which is now a private house but has retained its old bell tower, the 18th century Sardinian style church of St. Jean Baptist and the Chartreuse de Meylan, built in 1283, which has some interesting 16th century cloisters. Taninges boasts four hotels, a camping site, and the usual apartments to rent and is connected to the ski resorts of Les Gets and Morzine by the D.902.

Praz de Lys, alt. 1,518m

If you turn left 7km up the D.902 at the Pont des Gets, you will arrive at the ski resort of Praz de Lys 6km later. Praz de Lys has a beautiful setting, sitting in a wide open plateau surrounded by the jagged peaks of the Pointe de Marcelly, Haute Pointe, Pointe de Chalune, Le Roc d'Enfer and Pointe D'Uble (Walk Nos. 39 to 42) and with lovely views of the Mont Blanc range. However, it is not an original alpine village and the buildings, dating from the

1960s, are a scattered hotchpotch of apartment blocks and chalets. In the winter there is a lot of life as the plateau is a perfect cross-country ski area, but in the summer it is all rather dead. There are four hotels, one youth hostel, numerous appartments for rent but no camping ground.

The village of Mieussy, not far from Taninges, which connects with the cross-country area of Sommand and, by the Col de Ramaz, to Praz de Lys, is a more attractive choice for a base though accommodation is limited.

St. Jeoire - Walk Nos. 43 and 44

Continuing down the Giffre valley, you come to the pleasant village of St. Jeoire (also called St. Jeoire-en-Faucigny). Set back from the road at the confluence of the Risse and Giffre rivers, St. Jeoire is dominated by the beautiful small château de Beauregard (now in private hands). If you go into the village itself and take the D.26 up the Risse valley you will be driving through one of the most unspoilt valleys in the region, despite the relative nearness to Geneva. It takes you to the popular cross-country ski area of Les Brasses; there are six villages in the Les Brasses area apart from St. Jeoire; namely Megevette and Onnion (two hotels, one open in summer), both on the D.26 which continues to Bellevaux and the Hirmentaz skiing region (Chablais) and Viuz-en-Sallaz, Bogève and Villard (Vallée Verte).

ARAVIS/BORNE REGIONS (South-west haute Savoie)

As with the other three areas, there is no well established definition of this region and enquiries in various tourist offices and other information centres have resulted in maps with conflicting boundaries. For example, on one map Annecy is in the Genevois region, on another in the Lac d'Annecy region and on the third it is in the Aravis/Borne!

Georgraphically, the Aravis/Borne is the area east of the Arve valley, bordered to the north by Geneva and the Salève, to the west by the Rhône valley and to the south by the Savoie. For convenience I have included Lake Annecy.

Aravis

The Chaine des Aravis is a jagged line of peaks, 25km long, stretching south/west north/east, starting at the eastern end of Lake Annecy with Mt. Charvin, alt. 2,407m and culminating in the distinctive Pointe Percée, alt. 2,752m, west of Sallanches in the Arve valley. The Aravis pass, alt. 1,486m, cuts through the range south of La Clusaz and was formerly an important link between the Annecy and Mt. Blanc regions.

Places to visit and base yourself

La Clusaz - Walk Nos. 45 and 46

La Clusaz is a bustling and popular ski resort at the foot of the northern end of the Chaine des Aravis on the D.909 coming from the town of Thônes and the last village before the road goes over the Col des Aravis. The origin of the name La Clusaz comes from Via Clusa meaning "road confined between two mountains", and it was a tiny unknown agricultural hamlet before the Col des Aravis was opened in 1902 when it became a fashionable spot for the Annecy people to spend their summers. Somewhat overbuilt with numerous apartment blocks which straggle over the slopes, the only structure worthy of note is the church with its tall onion style steeple which is worth a visit as the interior has been strikingly renovated in the 1970s. Although the village already had a skating rink, the first sophisticated ski-lifts were not built until 1945 after a primitive toboggan type lift had crashed killing six tourists. Two local ski champions, Guy Perillat and later Edgar Grospiron, helped to put La Clusaz on the map. The village is also full of life in the summer (market day Monday morning) which is not always the case with ski resorts, and offers a wide variety of sporting activities as well as a good selection of mountain paths. There are plenty of hotels, apartments to rent, a youth hostel and a caravanning park (no camping). Just up the road is the very pretty Lac des Confins and the start of some tougher walks in the Chaine des Aravis.

Le Grand-Bornand - Walk Nos. 47 and 48

Bridging the Borne river in the valley of the same name, Le Grand-Bornand is the last village on the D.4 before the road goes over the Col de la Colombière towards Cluses. Although it is also a well-known ski station (a cable-car links the ski slopes which are further up the valley towards the pass), it has not lost its traditional agricultural activities such as the raising of Abondance dairy cattle from whose milk the famous Reblochon cheese is made (see Regional Specialities). Every week there is a lively market (Wednesday morning) which used to be held in the ancient covered market hall but has now moved to the central square in front of the church with its classic onion shaped steeple. If you follow the sign Vallée de Bouchet keeping to the Borne river out of the village, you will come to a cross-country skiing area, and at the end of this road is the departure point for the popular walk up to the Pointe Percée. Worth visiting is the old hamlet of Chinaillon just off the road up to the pass which has some traditional old chalets and a charming little chapel. Le Grand-Bornand has all the attributes of a tourist resort, namely 15 hotels, flats to rent and two camping sites.

St. Jean-de-Sixt - Walk Nos. 49 and 50

Down the D.909 towards Thônes, and on the crossroads between Le Grand-

Bornand and La Clusaz, is the smaller village of St. Jean-de-Sixt. This is a much quieter place to stay and there are only two hotels and a camping site. Although the village does not have much to offer architecturally the surrounding valley countryside has some splendid old chalets and farms (Walk No. 49), many with the roofs made out of the traditional tavaillon style tiles (see under Abondance valley). There are numerous sawmills on the Non torrent which runs all the way along the valley bottom to join the larger Fier river south of Thônes. It was a sawmill owner, Jean Marie Favre Lorraine, who as well as building many traditional chalets, built two architecturally different farms in the hamlet of Les Lombardes south of the village, for himself and his brother in 1903 and 1907. They are beautifully embellished with intricate wood carvings but, more extraordinary for those days of no central heating, they have enormous windows, indoor toilets (unheard of then) and separate bedrooms for the children!

Thônes - Walk Nos. 51-55

Thônes sits at the entrance to the Aravis region in a junction of three valleys: the Non coming in to the east, the Fier to the west and the Sulens to the south. This big village (hardly a town) has always been strategically important; in 1889 a tramway was built (subsequently closed in 1930) linking it to the town of Annecy which helped the economic development of the area considerably. Thônes has managed to retain its quaint stone bridge over the Non river and its arcaded shops looking on to a pleasant square with the parish church of St. Maurice opposite. If you appreciate baroque interiors, this church has the best example of such work in the whole Savoie area, the altar having been sculpted and decorated by the Italian Pierre Jacquetti in 1721. There is also a fascinating museum, Le Musée du Pays de Thônes, which gives an interesting insight into the life of the local people past and present. On the D.909 towards Annecy is the Musée de la Résistance, which is dedicated to the Resistance Movement during the second world war. It commemorates the battle of the free-French army in March 1944 in the nearby Plateau des Glières, when a few hundred men held out for two months against a German army of 7,000 trained alpine troops. The battle became the symbol of the French resistance against the Germans and the survivors were able to play an important part in the liberation of the Haute Savoie a few months later (see Thorens-Glières). Thônes has other claims to fame as the "capital" of Reblochon cheese which is made in the adjacent valleys ; you can visit the cheese co-operative on the road to Annecy. It is also, due to the nearness of so many wood-mills, the site of the Mobalpa fitted kitchens factory.

Thônes has four hotels and there are another six in nearby villages, plus four camping sites in the region and various gîtes. It is a centre to be recommended. The local walks in this guide start from the beautiful valleys south of Thônes: the Manigod valley running south-west along the Fier river which goes over the Col de Fry and joins the D.909 south of La Clusaz, the Sulens valley behind the mighty Tournette mountain (see Annecy region) which joins the Manigod valley south of Thônes and the narrow valley to the hamlet of Montremont along the Mainant river. These valleys, until recently victims of the rural exodus to nearby towns, are breathtakingly unspoilt with bright green fields, beautiful old farms and lots of chapels and wayside shrines. They are still mainly agricultural, the large farms producing cheese and milk from their extensive herds of Abondance cattle. Of course times are changing and the ageing population are selling their unprofitable land to larger enterprises. The farms, which have often been in the same family for hundreds of years, are then sold and renovated into holiday homes - all in the name of progress! Manigod is the only village in these valleys which has a syndicat d'initiative (see list of tourist offices) and has four hotels; there is skiing further up at the Col de Fry which is linked with La Clusaz.

Borne is the plateau area south of the Salève mountain (including the Plateau des Glières) and includes the pre-alpine mountains of the Sous Dine, La Roche Parnal and the Chaine du Bargy; in fact all the countryside south-east of the Annecy region and bordered by the Chaine des Aravis. Flowing from the snows of the Pointe Percée the Borne river passes through the village of Le Grand-Bornand before swinging north and cutting a sinuous gorge-like passage through the mountains, to empty itself into the Arve at Bonneville 33km later.

La Roche-sur-Foron - Walk Nos. 56 and 57

West of the Arve valley on the River Foron and almost opposite the town of Bonneville, La Roche-sur-Foron is situated on the Plateau de Borne under the shadow of the first range of mountains (pre-alps). La Roche (as it is called locally) has long been an important regional centre second only to Annecy in its historical heritage, but far less known. Despite industrial development the centre has retained a medieval aspect, with picturesque cobbled streets and old houses from the 15th and 16th centuries. The ruins of a tower perched on the top of a tall rock are all that remain of the château/fortress of the Counts of Geneva built in the 12th century and destroyed in the 15th during the Savoyard wars - hence the name La Roche-sur-Foron (Rock over the Foron). Somewhat off the general tourist route, La Roche is a delightful place to stay in and has four hotels, apartments for rent and four camping sites. There are another ten hotels in the surrounding villages of La Chapelle-Rambaud (1), St. Laurent (1), St. Pierre en Faucigny (4) and St. Sixt (4). Orange is the nearest village to the start of the two walks in this guide and has one hotel and a camping site.

Thorens-Glières, on the D.2 road going south-west towards Annecy from La Roche, is famous as the birthplace in 1567 of the famous Saint François de Sales who is still venerated throughout the region and is responsible for the extreme Catholicism of the entire Savoie area - in contrast to the Calvanism of Geneva to the north. The 12th century château was restored in 1873 by Count Eugène de Roussy de Sales and is still owned by the de Sales family. The Château Museum was opened to the public in 1960 (visits in season only). 14km from the village is the historic Plateau des Glières with an impressive white stone monument dedicated to the men who fell in the Resistance during the second world war (see Thônes). The monument, which symbolises two arms in the air with one cut in half, was designed by the Italian sculptor Emile Giglioli and inaugurated in September 1973 by André Malraux, the well-known French writer. There are three camping sites in the vicinity, several restaurants and one hotel; in winter the Plateau is a popular cross-country ski area. The village of Le Petit-Bornand in the narrow winding Borne valley is 7km by road from the Plateau and has one hotel, a gîte d'étape and a camping site.

Annecy area - Walk Nos. 58-61

Annecy is unashamedly beautiful, situated between the Bornes and Bauges pré-alps with the Parmelan mountain as a back-drop (Walk No. 58) and at the end of the cleanest lake in Europe. Pretty little ports and villages hug the lake shore and a diversity of mountain scenery rears behind culminating in the grandiose Tournette peak at the southern end (Walk No. 60). Annecy must be visited, preferably out of season, but is only a place to stay if you appreciate a very touristy environment. Capital of the Haute Savoie region with a population of around 120,000, Annecy has a rich historical past and was an important centre even in Roman times. The castle was built by the Counts of Geneva in the 12th century and still dominates the old town which has remained almost intact with its narrow cobbled streets, bordered with deep arcades alongside the flower lined Thiou canal and lock. The Palais de l'Isle, said to be one of the most photographed places in France, is an old building jutting out into the fast flowing canal like the prow of a ship. Originally constructed in the 12th century, and used later as an administration centre, it was only saved from demolition at the eleventh hour in 1952 by the people of Annecy who purchased it for a symbolic sum of 1,000 French francs.

There is much else to see: the basilica of the Visitation, built in 1922, which is the Mother House of the St. François de Sales order also overlooking the town and beautifully illuminated at night; the cathedral of St. Peter, built originally as a chapel by the Franciscans in the 15th century but afterwards to become the cathedral for the Bishop of Geneva when he took refuge in

Annecy during the Reformation; the churches of St. Maurice (dated 1422), Notre Dame de Liesse (16th century) and St. François (16th century), to name but a few.

The Annecy tourist office has a brochure in English with descriptions of places of interest and a map of the old town. It also has full documentation on hotels, camping sites (most of these are round the lake) and a youth hostel. If you are going to stay in the Annecy lake area in high season it is advisable to book your accommodation well in advance.

The lakeside is swarming with people in the summer months of July and August but in spring and autumn it is reasonably peaceful. There are lots of sporting possibilities including swimming, sailing, water-skiing, wind-surfing and the hiring of peddle-boats. You can also relax and take a boat trip round the lake calling in at the various lakeside villages; the first tourist paddle steamer was built in 1839 as Annecy was a popular tourist town even then!

Talloires - Walk No. 59

An ancient village with lots of charm on the western side of the lake where it begins to narrow, Talloires has a 17th century abbey, which can be visited but is now a hotel and a 13th century priory (now an international centre). Talloires is rather up-market with a well-known restaurant and numerous hotels. There are eight camping sites in the vicinity and all the usual sports facilities on offer. North of the village is the Roc de Chère nature reserve and a lovely easy waterfall walk (Walk No. 59). Just before the village you turn off on the D.42 for the Col de Forclaz (worth going to see for a fabulous view right down the lake) and the start of the walk up the splendid Tournette peak (Walk No. 60).

Duingt - Walk No. 61

Almost facing Talloires on the opposite shore is the equally ancient but unspoiled village of Duingt with its beautiful old houses and château jutting out into the water. Just off the busy lake road and therefore protected from the mainstream traffic, it has been inhabited since Roman times and the church was originally built in 1370, though it was newly constructed in 1831 and again in 1900. The château dates from medieval times and was the seat of the local overlords; in the 1400s it belonged to the Count of Geneva. The present building with its tower dates from the 18th century and houses some beautiful Italian paintings. It is privately owned by the Certeau family. Duingt has seven hotels and three camping sites.

Salève and Vallée Verte

1: SALEVE - ORJOBET/GRANDE GORGE - Alt.1,285 metres
(Salève - Geneva region)

Difficulty:	Medium; steep up and down.
Time:	3hrs 30mins.
Height gain:	619 metres.
Maps:	Editions Didier & Richard IGN No.3 Massifs du Chablais Faucigny & Genevois 1:50,000. Carte Touristique du Salève 1:25,000 (published by the Club Alpin Suisse - Geneva Section).
Depart from:	Le Coin - 666 metres.
Signposting:	Could be clearer.

How to get there (from Geneva)

Go through Vernier or Troinex customs and turn right towards Collonges sous Salève. Watch for the filter on the right to Bossy/Salève which goes back left over the motorway and upwards to Le Coin (this is the better road). ALTERNATIVELY go through the customs at Croix de Rozon and straight on across the main road, signposted Collonges sur Salève. At the cross-roads take the road up the Salève signposted La Croisette which leads to Le Coin. At Le Coin there is a restaurant/buvette on the left and then a corner - leave your car in the car park opposite this corner.

Directions

Take the narrow, tarmac road which goes up on the left of the road to the Salève, across from the car park. There is a signpost saying CAS (Club Alpin Suisse) Orjobet. The road soon becomes stony and on the left-hand side there is another parking lot with an orientation map which gives information about the geological and botanical terrain of the region (in French only).

The path narrows and goes upwards through woods. Go right at the first fork where there is no indication then follow the sign which says Orjobet and stay on the main path. This is a well defined sunken track, often quite steep, through woods. There are intermittent GR signs (red/white splashes) and also local blue/white stripes on the trees.

The path becomes rocky (20mins) and you get your first superb view on the left of the Geneva countryside below with the Jura on the horizon. You come to a green sign on the path which points straight ahead to Chavardon/ Grotte de la mules/Les Etournelles. Do not take this but bear to your right on a path which goes along the edge of the mountain. You will see blue and white signs on a rock. Later on you pass under a rock on a narrow path, where there is a cable to hang on to and a fence on the other side.

The path bears round to the left and you climb around an overhanging rock face on natural rocky steps with another iron cable for security (60mins). About 5mins later there is an opening in the rock face which is the entrance to a large, impressive grotto. A plaque on the wall says "Sentier d'Orjobet crée 1905 par la Section Genevoise du Club Alpin Suisse". First you climb across a long wooden plank with steps and then walk up large steps cut out of the natural stone with another iron rope for safety. Looking back there is a magnificent view of the wooded slopes of the Salève and the mountains framed in the rock - it takes about 5mins to climb through and out on to the other side. At the exit you will see blue & white stripes on a rock. The path bears round to the right - if you go straight you will go over the edge but this is evident!

Historical note: This grotto was discovered in 1799 by the well-known Geneva scientist H.B. de Saussure who named it Orjobet after his guide who was a peasant from the village of Le Coin. In 1905 the Geneva section of the Swiss Alpine Club made the path through the cave and has been responsible for the upkeep ever since. They became the official "guardians" of the path from 1955.

For most of the way from here to the top you get sweeping views over the Geneva countryside, the lake and the Jura mountains. You come to a rock with an arrow pointing upwards to Etournelle and another pointing left to La Mule (this goes to the Grotte de la Mule and is very steep so should be avoided). Go on upwards keeping right ignoring turning to left marked La Tine and other paths which converge in. The track undulates and curves round the side of the mountain. When you arrive at a T-junction go right; the path to the left is an interesting cliff walk along a shelf to La Corraterie - here you can watch the more intrepid souls rock climbing.

When you come out of the woodland onto the shoulder of the mountain, go immediately to the left (1hr 15mins) through an opening in the fence (if you follow the path straight up you will reach the road along the top of the Salève). This is a narrow, grassy stretch going upwards medium steep through open meadowland with some bushes. Keep to the path along the mountain edge with the fence on your left-hand side. Back on your right you can see a big TV aerial and what used to be a jump-off area for parapenting but is now used for model aeroplanes. Go through another opening and now the fence is on your right as you skirt a gorge cutting into the mountain. As

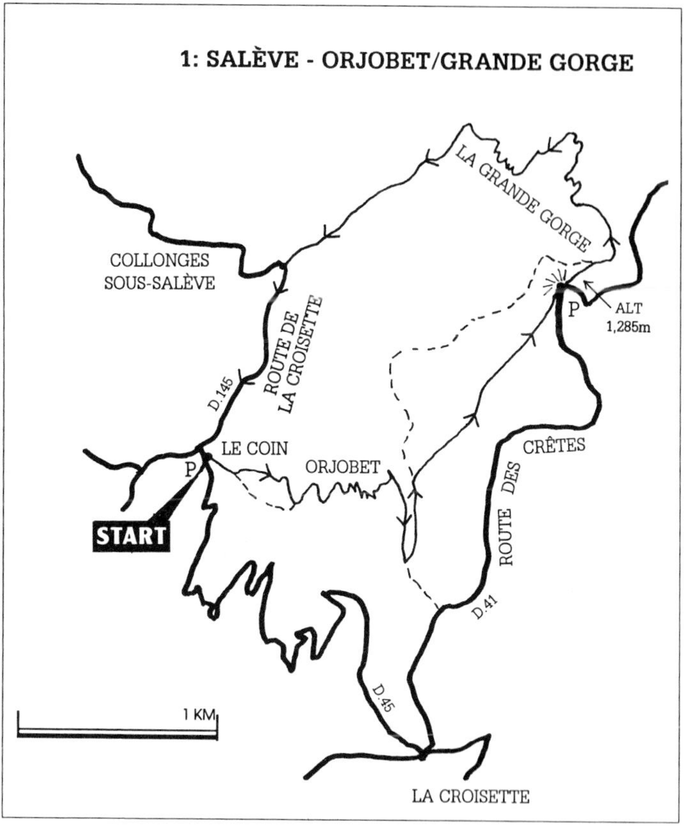

you leave the gorge look up to your right for a defined break in the fence with a short iron post on the other side; go through this break and cut left (eastwards) across the open meadowland, or if you want a good view of the Alps, make for a fence on the horizon ahead and follow it along to the left. You will see an observatory tower with round dishes on it, a stone balustrade (concrete blocks which mark the side of the road across the top of the Salève) and a hut. Make for these landmarks, going through another break in a fence which divides the meadowland. At the balustrade (2hrs) there is a sign on the road saying Grand Gorge, alt. 1,282m.

The path goes briefly between the wall, the fence and the gorge and is fairly well defined. Beyond the wall is the road, curling round on the right, as you walk straight across the meadow keeping the fence on your left. Before long you come to an iron gate (GR signs on your left) which leads to the road. Just after the gate, however, take the small path to your left which goes down the Grand Gorge (2hrs 5mins). At the first T-junction go down left. You come to a rock face on your left, where there is a plaque saying Grande Gorge 1854 to 1954. Don't go straight here but down right. At first you curl round the mountain (red/white splashes on trees) and then the path becomes steep and stony; in one place there are rough stone steps and a chain to hang on to. The path actually goes down the side of the Grand Gorge and there is a look out on the way down with a magnificent view of the precipitous grey cliffs with trees on the summit. *Historical note: You come to another plaque on a rock face which says "Sentier de la Grande Gorge" looked after since 1868 by the Section Genevois, Club Alpin Suisse - also carved in the rock is 1854 G which is the date the path was made, the money being donated by the public of Geneva. No wonder it is a well defined path as it has been used for over one hundred years!*

When you come to a yellow arrow on a rock which says Buis/Petite Gorge, do not follow this but keep going down. The path skirts the Grande Gorge for a short while and then goes steeply down through a ravine; though it is rather vertiginous, it is well-trodden and there are steps and cables to help you on the more difficult patches. The path goes back down the side of the Grande Gorge and becomes less steep as you get lower.

You come to a cross-roads in the woods (3hrs); the first time I did the walk there were signposts, but the second time they had disappeared! Go left (which was marked Collonges). This is a flat, defined path following the contour of the hill and is a welcome relief after the steep stony descent of the last hour. On the left is the steep rock face of the Salève looking even more dramatic from below. Keep straight for 10mins till you arrive at a wide jeep track where there is a sign on the tree in front indicating left Le Coin/ Collonges and right Veyrier/Bossy. Turn left and after 5mins you reach the road. (If you want to cut off some of the road take the first turning left just before the iron barrier and then first right. This takes you on a path alongside the road till you come out at tennis courts.) From here you walk along the road for about 15mins (Route de la Croisette). You pass the café and then round the corner is the car park (3hrs 30mins).

Remarks: Though steep in places, this is a lovely half day walk up the Salève within easy reach of Geneva and is very popular. It is better to do the walk when the leaves are off the trees as you have magnificent views on the way up and down as well as on the summit; bear in mind though that you are walking up the north side so the snow may linger here in the spring.

The Salève is pitted with grottoes and its sheer rock faces are well-

known for rock climbing and abseiling. If you are interested in learning more about the Salève there is an interesting booklet with 53 walks and a large map (in French), called Randonnées au Salève *by Pierre Bossus, available at most good Geneva bookshops. It also contains interesting historical and geographical details of the region.*

2: ALONG THE TOP OF THE SALEVE - Alt. 1,285 metres
(Salève - Geneva region)

Difficulty:	None - this is an easy walk along the top of the Salève.
Time:	2hrs.
Height gain:	None.
Maps:	Editions Didier & Richard IGN No.3 Massifs du Chablais Faucigny & Genevois 1:50,000. Carte Touristique du Salève 1:25,000 (published by the Club Alpin Suisse - Geneva Section).
Depart from:	La Croisette - 1,175 metres.
Signposting:	Sporadic but the way is evident.

How to get there (from Geneva)
Go through the Vernier or Troinex customs and turn right towards Collonges-sous-Salève. Watch for the filter on the right to Bossy/Salève which goes back left over the motorway and upwards to Le Coin (this is a better road). ALTERNATIVELY go through the customs at Croix-de-Rozon and go straight on across the main road signposted Collonges-sous-Salève. At the cross-roads take the road up the Salève to La Croisette (8km) and park your car in the car park on the top at a T-junction, opposite a restaurant.

Directions
Facing the line of Alps, turn left (signpost says Téléphérique 6km/Monnetier 11km), walk by the Auberge des Montagnards and bear right up a jeep track. This is wide and grassy, passing a house on the left and undulating along the top of the mountain parallel to the road. To the left is a fantastic view of the valley below and the town of Geneva with the Jura mountains on the horizon. Behind is the Bellegarde Gap with the Fort Ecluse one side and the Vuache ridge (see Walk No. 6) on the other. Regain the road after 10mins (it goes all the way along the top and you meet it again later on).

Follow the road (D.41) for about 10mins and watch for a narrow path off to the right where there is no sign (20mins); up on the left is an ugly building and the TV aerial of Les Crêtes. The path becomes a jeep track

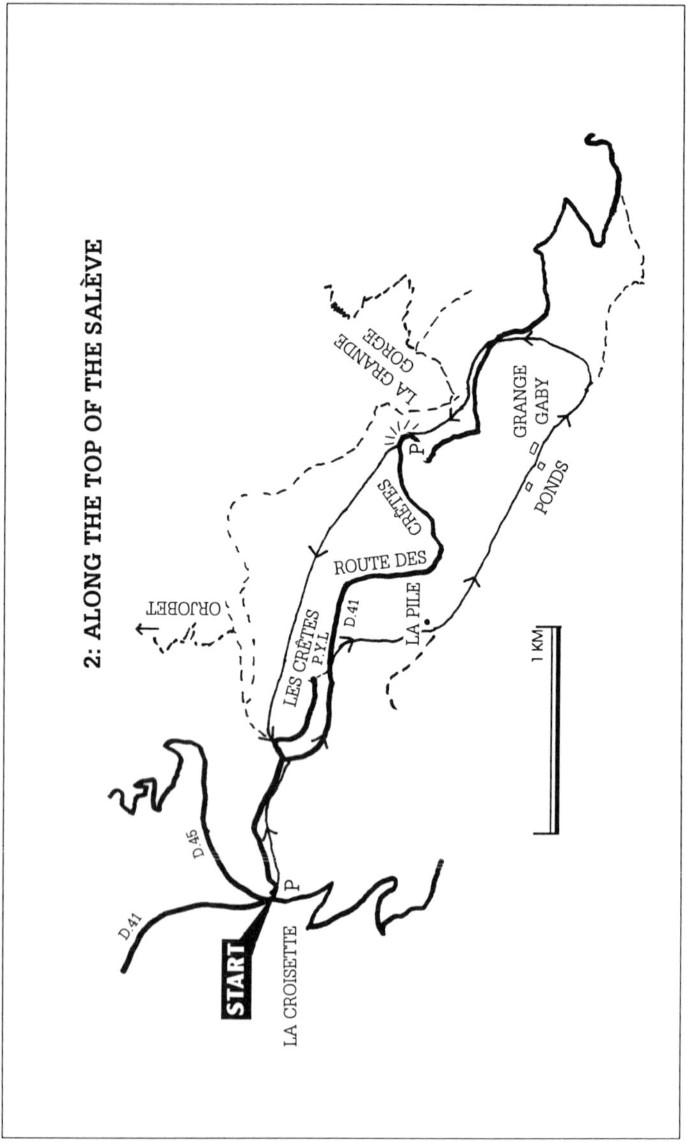
2: ALONG THE TOP OF THE SALÈVE
START
LA CROISETTE
D.41
D.45
P
LES CRÊTES
P.Y.L
ORJOBET
D.41
ROUTE DES
CRÊTES
LA PILE
LA GRANDE
GORGE
P
GRANGE
GABY
PONDS
1 KM

initially losing height as it traverses round the mountain with the Alps on the right. You come to a large barn and house called La Pile, alt. 1,230m. The jeep track becomes a wide, flat, grassy path as it goes through an attractive old gnarled beech wood, passing two stagnant ponds, the second one opposite a burnt out house called Grange Gaby (45mins). The view of the Alps and Mont Blanc along this path is considered the finest in the Geneva region and inspired the famous 18th century Genevese naturalist H.B. de Saussure to explore the Alps further.

5mins later take a turning to the left (there is a GR red/white splash on a tree), and continue slightly upwards through woods towards the road; there are carpets of white crocuses all along here in springtime. Where the path forks, bear right (although if you bear left you get to the road anyway) towards the television tower and a green barrier which borders the fenced road. Go through a stile in the fence by a sign which says Restaurant/Bar l'Observatoire and cross to the other side of the road (1hr).

The grassy path leads along the top of the Salève, parallel to the D.41 on the left. There are detours to the right which are worth taking to get good views of the dramatic gorge (La Grande Gorge, see Walk No. 1) which dissects the north face of the mountain and the lake and town of Geneva in the valley below. After 10mins you meet the road again briefly before bearing off to the right and, still keeping near the road, going round the top of the Grande Gorge. Ignore a path to the right which goes down the mountain by the Grande Gorge (see Walk No. 1) and almost immediately after you go through a green gate where there are GR signs (1hr 15mins) and up to a stone balustrade (concrete blocks which mark the side of the road) and a hut beyond (1hr 20mins). Follow the grassy path across the open meadowland on the top of the mountain, through a stile and keeping the fence on your left; further over on the left is a TV aerial and a windsock - *in springtime watch for the many skylarks hovering in the air, recognisable by their melodious cry, streaked brown plumage, long wings and white edged tail.*

As you draw parallel to the windsock the path starts to descend and then levels out. Continue straight when you meet the road (1hr 45mins) which is going to the TV aerial called Les Crêtes and 5mins later you regain the original D.41. Retrace your steps to La Croisette (2hrs).

Remarks: A classic, easy walk along the top of the Salève giving magnificent views of Geneva and the surrounding countryside with the Jura in the background on one side and the whole range of the Alps on the other. In early spring the top of the mountain is carpeted with small white and purple crocuses, followed later by a blaze of dandelions. See Walk No. 1 and chapter on Salève for more information on this region.

3: CRUSEILLES TO L'ISELET

(Salève - Geneva region)

Difficulty:	Easy with little height gain.
Time:	2hrs 45mins.
Height gain:	336 metres.
Map:	Editions Didier & Richard IGN No.3 Massifs du Chablais Faucigny & Genevois 1:50,000. Carte Touristique du Salève 1:25,000 (published by Club Alpin Suisse - Geneva Section).
Depart from:	Cruseilles - 784 metres.
Signposting:	There is only one sign half way round and some yellow splashes.

How to get there (from Geneva)

Take the N.201 direction Annecy which goes through the new Bardonnex customs post (by-passing St. Julien-en-Genevois). Take the first exit (signposted St. Julien-en-Genevois/Cruseilles) and at the roundabout follow the road signposted Cruseilles/Annecy. You are now back on the original N.201 to Annecy which reaches Cruseilles after about 20km. Park your car in the parking at the entrance of the village on the right, just before the main traffic lights.

Directions

Walk up the "ancien route de Salève" which you will find by crossing the main road and then going up to your left on a small road called the Rue de Pontet, just before the D.15 signposted La Roche-sur-Foron. The path goes upwards between oldish houses and after a few minutes meets the D.41. Cross the road and go up right on the other side at a sign saying Les Coudrets. After about 50m turn left at a red and white sign Trail interdit (trail bikes not allowed) between two houses. Follow a wide grassy path, going round and up, with stations of the cross on the right-hand side - the first one is dated 1927. These are rather plain stone crosses with round wooden pictures in the centre. Follow the stations of the cross path (ignore the path going off to the right) until you reach the first right-hand hairpin. Leave the hairpin on a narrow path which goes straight on just before a bench.

Detour: It is worthwhile to follow the stations of the cross to the right, leading to an open air altar where mass is celebrated from time to time. Written on the altar is "Année Mariale 8 Décembre 1953 - 1954. En reconnaissance des Coudrets pour la protection accordée au Parroise de

Geneva from the top of the Salève with Jura range in background
La Grande Gueule cave, Mont de Vouan

The Hirmentaz ridge, Vallée Verte

View Alps (Dent d'Oche) from Notre Dame, Mont Hermone

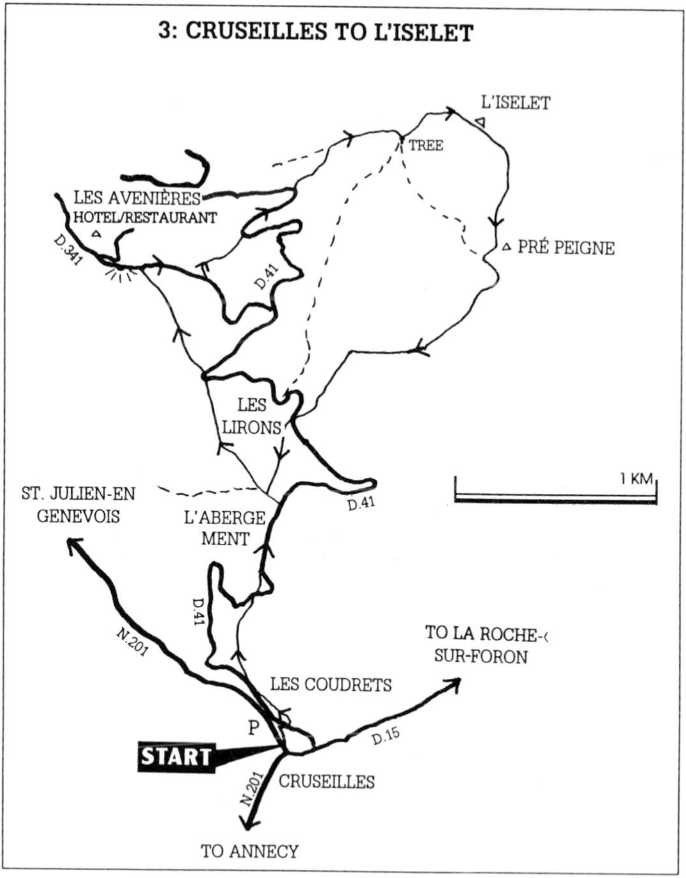

Cruseilles pendant les années 1939 - 45". Surrounded by railings is a grotto with a shrine and a statue of Our Lady. At the top is a cross. Dotted about the rock are plaques put there in thanksgiving by people who have successfully petitioned to Our Lady. Then go back down the road onto the narrow path at the hairpin bend.

This path goes through shrubs and then out at the side of a new garage at the entrance to someone's garden (obviously built after the path was made). Go straight along this road and then bear right, going upwards.

Continue on the road (there is an evident short cut at the first bend) where you can see big electricity pylons in front. When the minor road (called Les Coudrets), hits a bigger road, turn right, still going up (20mins). You are now on the D41 (you can cut the corner again here). Continue on the road till you get to the sign to a little village called L'Abergement. The road continues round a bend to the right signposted Salève/La Croisette, but walk straight up into the village. In the centre of the village there is a cross. At this cross bear up left, with houses on each side, till you see a little road on your left called Chemin de chez La Crimée.

Follow this road to the left for a few minutes until it leads on to a jeep track. Keep right (ignore tracks to the left, one saying Chemin Privé). Then keep right again down a sunken, bushy lane (do not go straight). There are lovely open fields down on the left and up on the right is an old stone wall covered in grass. This must have been an old mule track at some stage. The lane goes into sparse fir and beech wood and then narrows into a ditch full of leaves (may be damp or muddy depending on the season). You are slowly gaining height. Keep straight at a cross-roads and then bear left, ignoring all paths off to the right.

You can see the railing of the main road up on the right as you walk through the wood which takes you out into a magnificent open field with some lovely solitary trees. Keep going straight hugging the wood on the right until you reach a grassy jeep track which continues to the top of the field, where you meet the D.41 again opposite a house (this is the hamlet of La Chenaz). *If you look back there is a lovely view of the Alps and in front is a "Victorian style" château called the Château des Avenières., constructed in 1907. This has recently been turned into a hotel/restaurant. If you want to visit it turn left on the D.41 till you reach the entrance.*

Turn directly right on the D.41 into an avenue of trees and then woods. On the first right-hand bend, take a very sharp turning back to the left, opposite an old wall (yellow arrow on telephone pole) onto a wide path through woods (1hr). There is an immediate fork but keep left and at the next fork go right. Continue until you see a small marker stone with a red splash on it and a yellow arrow on a tree. Turn left here and do not go downwards. Shortly, you reach the D.341 on a hairpin bend, where you should go up left.

On the next hairpin bend to the left take the path right (1hr 15mins), signposted L'Iselet dep. circuit 2 (the one and only signpost you see on the whole walk!). This wide jeep track goes through coniferous woods until you come to a tree with arrows on the trunk; circuit 2 to left and circuit 1 to right. Go left and through a fence; you are walking along the bottom of an attractive shallow valley with woods set back to the right and left. After 10mins you pass an isolated farm on your left which is L'Iselet, set in a sort of dip in the hills (1hr 30mins). This is the highest point of the walk at alt. 1,094m and a good spot to stop and have a picnic as there is a lovely view of the Alps.

Go through a stile in the fence and bear up right across open meadowland. Then follow a path which goes down through woods with a fence on your right for part of the way. It takes you through a clearing and briefly into the woods again before reaching a larger clearing with, down on your left, a path to a large pile of stones. This is all that remains of the farm of Le Pré Peigne. Go down the path beyond the pile of rubble and you will see a lovely overgrown pond on your right with a cliff behind. Just beyond the pond bear left on a defined path which becomes sunken and goes down through woods. Stay on the main track downwards until you reach a road. Careful here as the path forks just before you meet the road; take the left fork as otherwise you miss the turning on the road.

Turn right on to the road and almost immediately left down a path before a hairpin and road railings (2hrs 15mins). This is another shallow valley; the village of Les Lirons is up to the right. Go down till you meet a road again and then bear left. Shortly you will be on the outskirts of L'Abergement and you pass, to the right, the road you took on the outward journey. Retrace same route you took on the way up.

Remarks: A nice, easy half-day walk on the western edge of the Salève mountain with glorious views of the Alps. It is a good winter walk when the snow is on the higher slopes, but it is also lovely in early springtime when the woodland flowers are out. The only drawback is that there is some road hopping and only one sign all the way round.

At first glance Cruseilles is a rather ugly large village but it has some quaint old streets if you explore off the main road. It is situated where five roads meet, hence its ancient name Crusillia meaning cross-roads. Once a small fortified town it was destroyed by the Genevese troops in 1590 .

4: POINTE DU PLAN FROM ST BLAISE - Alt. 1,348 metres
(Salève - Geneva region)

Difficulty:	Easy up but medium steep descent through woods on return. Note: alternative route back is steeper.
Time:	3hrs 30mins or (alternative route) 3hrs 45mins.
Height gain:	457 metres.
Map:	Editions Didier & Richard IGN No.3 Massifs du Chablais Faucigny & Genevois 1:50,000. Carte Touristique du Salève 1:25,000 (published by the Club Alpin Suisse-Geneva Section).

Depart from: St. Blaise on the road to Annecy - 891 metres.
Signposting: Not at all clear (the occasional GR sign and yellow splashes).

How to get there from Geneva

Take the N.201 direction Annecy which will take you through the new Bardonnex customs post (by-passing St. Julien-en-Genevois). Take the first exit (signposted St. Julien-en-Genevois/Cruseilles) and at the roundabout follow the road signposted Cruseilles/Annecy. You are now back on the original N.201 to Annecy. Before Cruseilles, at the hamlet of Le Mont Sion, branch left at a signpost to St. Blaise on the D.223. Continue to the village and park your car beside the church.

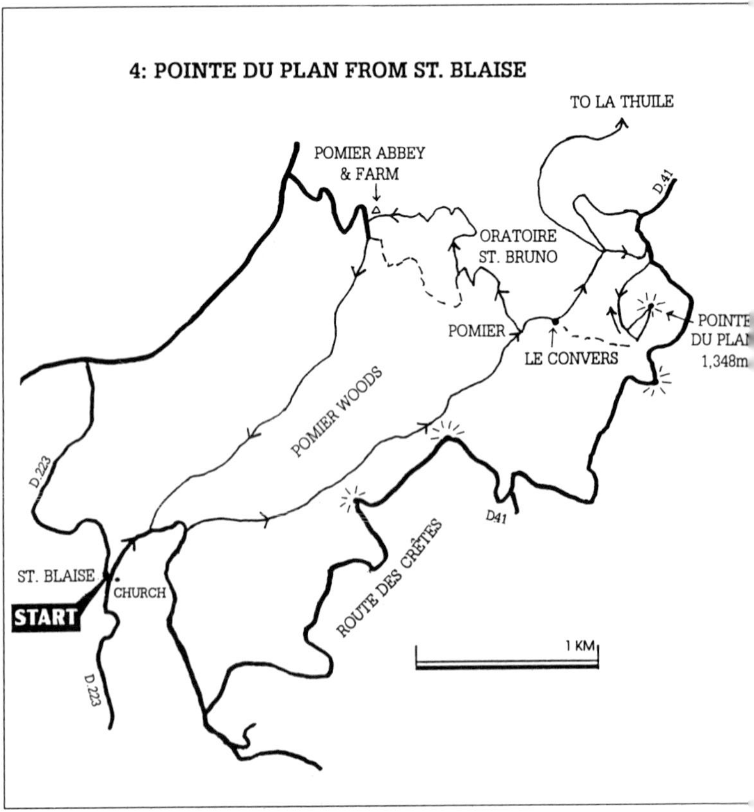

Directions

Walk up the road from the church on the D.223. After the second bend (5mins) there is a GR splash on the left and a wooden sign saying Grand Piton 1hr 45mins. This is difficult to see so be careful. You go up a sunken lane and after about 5mins the path branches to the left by a GR sign (10mins) - both ways meet up further on. Follow the GR splashes and when you come to a T-junction, turn left. The path is steep at first and then levels out, undulating around the mountain through pleasant woodland called the Bois de Pomier, with attractive views down to the left over Geneva through breaks in the trees.

Leave the woods at the bottom of an open hill (50mins) and go through a fence. Ignore the GR sign pointing upwards and turn right, skirting the bottom of the hill until you reach a small red sign to Pomier going down through the woods (1hr). This is the way back but it is easier to locate it on the way up. From here go straight up the hill to the farmhouse which you can see at the top, called Le Convers (1hr 5mins).

As you are facing the farm, go left; you will see a faded GR splash on a big, ancient beech tree which looks as if it has been struck by lightning, to the left of the wide, grassy tractor path. This path takes you over a dry river bed (GR signs on tree) to a stony jeep track at a hairpin bend (lhr 15mins). Do not go on to this jeep track but bear up right in a sort of wide grassy gully. There is no defined path but make your way to the top of the low ridge in front when you will find another grassy track with the Pointe du Plan hump up on your right. Follow the grassy track to the left until it meets a tarmac road, the D.41, and a parking area. Turn right on the road for about 10m and then through an opening in the fence onto a path going along towards another farm called the Chalet du Plan, which is visible from the top of the Pointe. This path seems to be going backwards, but higher up, for about 5mins. Just before a clump of trees, branch off to the left to get to the top of the grassy hump (no defined path).

At the top of the Pointe du Plan, alt. 1,348m (1hr 40mins), there is a stone trigonometric point and a glorious view right across the Alps, including Mont Blanc and down towards Lake Annecy with its surrounding peaks - an ideal picnic spot! You can see the Chalet du Plan down on your right. Make for this farm and then turn right along the grassy track back to the road retracing your steps to Le Convers farm. From here go down the hill till you get to the sign marked Pomier. ALTERNATIVELY, take a short cut from the Chalet du Plan down the hill directly to Le Convers but there is no defined path.

From the Pomier sign (2hrs) go down the side of the mountain through attractive woodland. The path is wide at first, and there is a wooden hut on the left. After this hut go straight (there are yellow splashes on the trees). The path narrows and is quite steep and stony. After 15mins you come to a stone cairn on the path and a green stripe. Bear left; on the right is a little red signpost with a cross to Sentiers des Petites Croix (see alternative way back below). Keep going down this steep slope through the woods; you can see Pomier far beneath you.

Ignore a turning to the left, cross a clearing and keep going until you arrive at a T-junction at the bottom of the slope (2hrs 45mins). Take a look here at the huge white cliff back to the right of where you have been clambering down (this is the south-western end of the Salève). You can see the path you have taken which is in a sort of gully in the woods. At the T-junction turn right (the way back to St. Blaise is to the left) and walk along for a few minutes to have a look at Le Pomier which is a lovely big old working farm with an attractive small château type house nearby which used to be a restaurant but is now shut (originally an Abbey- see alternative below).

Retrace your steps and continue along a very attractive jeep track (take no notice if there is a sign which says Chemin Sans Issue). This path goes along the bottom of the hillside through scattered woods and open fields and is a welcome relief after all the climbing you have done. You pass a wooden chalet on the right and join an old mule track to St. Blaise. After 30mins (3hrs 45mins) you come to a yellow borne (marker) and a track going off to the right. Ignore this and keep straight. Soon after you come out on to the D.341. Turn right and in 5mins you are back at the church.

ALTERNATIVE WAY BACK via Sentier des Petites Croix: This is a steeper, rockier route which zigzags down underneath the steep cliff face at the end of the Salève; follow the green/yellow stripes. After 15mins you reach the Oratoire de St. Bruno, which is a small grotto dug out of the rock face. Behind a grill is a primitive, but rather beautiful, old wooden statue of St. Bruno (unfortunately not dated). *St. Bruno was the founder of the Chartreuse order of monks and he built the small abbey in the hamlet of Pomier in 1179 (recently a restaurant, see above) which was also a hospice. The monks tilled the land on the Salève and made the road which went from Cruseilles to Geneva, replacing the old Roman route which went over the top of the Salève. When the Bernese invaded the monks were thrown out and the abbey library was burnt; a series of arches is all that remains of the cloisters.* From here downwards there are occasional red crosses painted on the trees marking a pilgrimage up to the statue. The path continues down steeply; follow the yellow/green signs on the main path. At a T-junction (2hrs 40mins) turn right before going through denser coniferous wood for about 5mins and to another T-junction, where you go straight across. You have now come to a Parcours Vita (numbered athletics course) in a delightful beech wood. When you get to Parcours Pomier No.1 go right onto a more defined path and then left at Parcours No.22 which will take you round the back of Pomier and out behind the large farm. Take a look at the lovely old farm and former abbey before bearing left to join the previous return route.

Remarks: A very pleasant walk with lovely sweeping views over Geneva on the way up and back, plus a glorious view of the Alps from the Pointe. The alternative return route is more interesting (shrine of St. Bruno), but somewhat steeper. It is a little known area of the Salève; I have walked there on a Sunday in springtime and hardly seen anyone, though there is a road which takes you within 10mins of the Pointe itself.

5: LE GRAND PITON - Alt. 1,379 metres

(Salève - Geneva region)

Difficulty:	Medium, though steep in places.
Time:	3hrs 30mins.
Height gain:	627 metres.
Maps:	Editions Didier & Richard IGN No.3 Massifs du Chablais, Faucigny & Genevois 1:50,000. Carte Touristique du Salève 1:25,000 (published by the Club Alpin Suisse - Geneva Section).
Depart from:	Village of Beaumont - 752 metres.
Signposting:	Sporadic some yellow splashes and GR signs.

How to get there (from Geneva)

Take the N.201 direction Annecy which will take you through the new Bardonnex customs post (by-passing St. Julien-en-Genevois). Take the first exit (signposted St. Julien-en-Genevois/Cruseilles) and at the roundabout follow the road signposted Cruseilles/Annecy. You are now on the old N.201 to Annecy. Just after the village of Chable (6km along the road) turn left on the D.177 and almost immediately take the right fork signposted Jussy/ Beaumont. You reach the village of Beaumont about 5mins after the turn-off. Park your car beside the church where, if you look upwards, you will see your destination, the Bastian Tower of the Grand Piton, on the skyline.

Directions

Go up the road behind and to the left of the church, signposted Marmoux, passing through fields with scattered houses. At the hamlet of Les Traverse, just after an attractive old crooked stone cross dated 1831 on the right, take a jeep track left which goes to a modern house and then continues as a wide grassy track going gently upwards to join the road again. Branch left to the farm called Marmoux (15mins) where there is a stone fountain, then bear right at the side of the building and right again when the path forks. The path is broad and stony going upwards through meadows, houses and woods to another farm which you can see over on the left called Les Molliets. Turn left towards the farm, following a yellow arrow, and just before the gate there is a path up to the right, signposted Les Pitons (25mins). A few minutes later turn left at a cross-roads, following yellow splashes. This is a wide, defined path which seems to be curling round the bottom of the hill (ignore any paths branching off). After 5mins turn right at a T-junction and a few metres on take a right fork signposted Les Pitons (left says Chavanne).

The path zigzags up through the woods but there are open spaces with lovely views of the valley and the Jura mountains behind. The track is steep and becomes rocky, before curling round a tall cliff face called Sur la Grande Roche. Be careful when it is wet as it is often covered with slippery beech leaves. There are yellow/red signs on the trees. Soon after the cliff and a yellow Sentier de Piton sign (1hr 15mins) you cross a wide forest track, leading on to a narrow ascending path. 5mins later you cross a jeep track and emerge onto the open hillside.

Go through a stile and straight up the hill till you come to a grassy track (ALTERNATIVE: turn right here and continue to the D.4. Then turn left and follow signs to Les Pitons). Cross the track and continue straight up the hill (there is no defined path), keeping the wood on your right (you will see a faint red arrow on a rock), till you see a stone trough and a path. Go briefly on the path left and then bear up right where there are three big fir trees and you reach a shallow depression in the mountains. Make for the jumble of rocks up on your left and a pleasant picnic place (1hr 40mins). *The view is breathtaking - to the north is the silhouette of the Jura from the Bellegarde Gap to the Vaudois Alps with Geneva and the lake below in the foreground; to the south, is a jagged line of Alps, with Mont Blanc towering above the peaks, and over to the west the shimmer of Lake Annecy dominated by the Tournette peak.*

There is no defined track to the Grand Piton, alt. 1,379m, which is hidden in trees, but you can see the tower clearly. Make your way across to the right (if you are facing the Alps - left if you are facing the lake!) and it is only about a 5mins scramble among trees and rocks to the tower which stands on the edge of the Salève looking towards the Jura. It is known by two names, La Tour Bastian and La Tour des Pitons and was constructed in 1860 (the reason why is unclear), then badly renovated in 1982. Just in front to the right is a strange rock, seemingly detached from the summit; you feel you could push it and the huge mass would roll down the mountain. This rock is called La Sorcière (witch) though there is no interesting legend to explain this name.

With the tower behind you go through a fence and straight onto a rocky track (there is a red concrete survey stone to the left) with GR signs and white

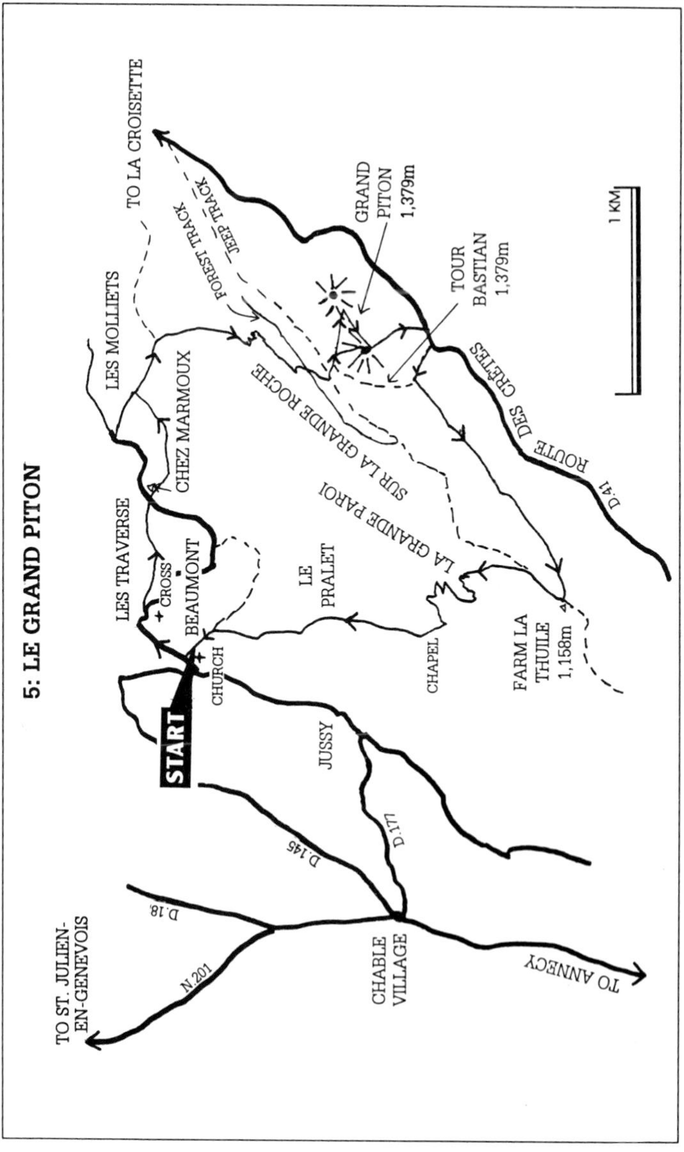
5: LE GRAND PITON
TO LA CROISETTE
FOREST TRACK
JEEP TRACK
GRAND
PITON
1,379m
TOUR
BASTIAN
1,379m
1 KM
LES MOLLIETS
CHEZ MARMOUX
SUR LA GRANDE ROCHE
LA GRANDE PAROI
ROUTE DES CRÊTES
D.41
LES TRAVERSE
CROSS
BEAUMONT
LE
PRALET
START
CHURCH
CHAPEL
FARM LA
THUILE
1,158m
JUSSY
D.145
D.177
D.18
TO ST. JULIEN-
EN-GENEVOIS
N.201
CHABLE
VILLAGE
TO ANNECY

flashes; 5mins later you go through a stile onto the road (1hr 55mins); here there is a sign back the way you came saying Les Pitons. *On a fine day in summer there will be masses of tourists here who come up by car and then make the 5mins walk to the tower. However, if you go during the week out of season, you will probably see nobody.*

Turn right and walk down the road for a few metres till you see GR red/white splashes and a sign down to the right to St. Blaise (difficult to see as it is on the wrong side of a tree). Take this narrow path which goes down initially beside a fence. It is a defined track going down left round the side of the mountain, never too steeply, through woodland and clearings with lovely views. After 20mins you arrive at the jeep track which leads (right fork) to the big, old farm of La Thuile (2hrs 15mins). If you walk through the farm there is an old round fountain dated 1893. The place looks deserted but what a view it has, perched near the edge of the mountain with a sweeping panorama of the entire Geneva valley and the Jura mountains beyond.

The path goes past the front of the farm, through a stile, across a meadow and through another stile before entering woods. Where it forks, take the left-hand side and zigzag down steeply - keep straight on where it crosses a wide path and straight again across another 5mins later. It is a good route down through woods with quite a drop one side and curls round just before you come to the high cliff of the Grand Paroi. You pass a big jumble of rocks where there must have been a dramatic landslide in the past. Shortly after this do not take a tempting path to the right but keep straight (actually if you do go right it is a short cut, but you miss the chapel).

You reach scattered chalets and come to a cross-roads where there is a clearing to the left which looks recently made (3hrs). Here there is a newly built, small stone chapel called Notre Dame de l'Espérance. Inside are benches and a big statue of the Virgin Mary with a stained glass window behind. Take a look at the visitor's book which is full of rather touching messages and don't miss the beautiful crucifixion at the side of the clearing; Jesus is made out of very modern black pincers and wire clippers and the crown of thorns is a small piece of barbed wire - a really dramatic piece of artistry.

Go back to the cross-roads and then straight on from where you came out originally. This is the start of a wider track which takes you past the houses of Le Pralet and the beautiful old farm of Chez Bellot. You eventually get back to the road at Préma Queue (the sign back where you have come says La Thuile). Turn left to get back into the village and the church (3hrs 30mins).

Remarks: This is a lovely half-day walk on the southern end of the Salève mountain. Although the way up is steep it is not difficult and the views from the Grand Piton are superb.

6: LE VUACHE DE CHAUMONT - Alt. 1,070 metres
(Salève - Geneva region)

Difficulty:	Easy once you are on the ridge - the climb up is a medium steep gradient.
Time:	3hrs.
Height gain:	461 metres.
Maps:	Cartes IGN No.45 Annecy/Lausanne Serie Vert 1:100,000. Editions Didier & Richard IGN No.3 Massifs du Chablais Faucigny & Genevois 1:50,000.
Depart from:	Chaumont village - 640 metres.
Signposting:	Adequate - follow red/white GR signs.

How to get there (from Geneva)
Take the N.201 direction St. Julien-en-Genevois/Annecy. From St. Julien take the N.206 signposted Bellegarde. 5km later turn left at the village of Viry onto the D.992 direction Frangy. Continue on this road for about 12km and then at Le Malpas take the right fork to Chaumont. Drive into the village and park your car opposite the church (take a look inside if it is open as it has been tastefully renovated).

Directions
Go behind the church where there is an orientation map showing the area. Opposite is the Auberge de Pralet (a peaceful spot for an inexpensive lunch or a drink, preferably after your walk). On the left is a sign to the Sommet du Vuache, 1hr 30mins. Also look for the red/white GR splashes as this is part of the long-distance Balcon du Léman path. There is a small gîte (meaning a refuge) up on the right for overnight trekkers.

Walk up a steep, stony lane with a crumbling wall covered with ivy to the right; in spring the banks are covered with blue periwinkle flowers, violets and primroses. Ignore a sign to the right which says Vuache par Cortagy and continue straight up following the GR splashes. *In early March the upper slopes are a mass of the rare dogstooth violet; the word violet is misleading as it does not resemble a violet at all, although its single white bulb does look somewhat like a dog's tooth. It has a small striking pink flower, the narrow petals pointing backwards with the stamen and style projecting; its leaves are fleshy, flecked with black spots.* The path comes out of the woods as you pass under the wires of a pylon (35mins); you are now on the open slope of the mountain with an interrupted view down the Usses valley with the Jura on the other side. There are holly and juniper bushes and in early spring the slopes under the trees are covered in delicate blue scillas.

The path comes to a sign which indicates left to Chaumont par Vovray (this is the way back) and continues past the ruins of a house, essentially a wall and a heap of stone (50mins). Keep straight along the ridge, eventually going back into woodland. *These woods are renowned for their flowers in springtime; after the pink splashes of the dogstooth violets mingling with the blue of the violets and scillas come the alpine daffodils which make brilliant patches of yellow in the undergrowth, against the fierce green leaves of wild garlic. Unfortunately people come and pick the daffodils and on one springtime visit I passed two people with enormous bunches, the beautiful blooms already looking tired and faded.*

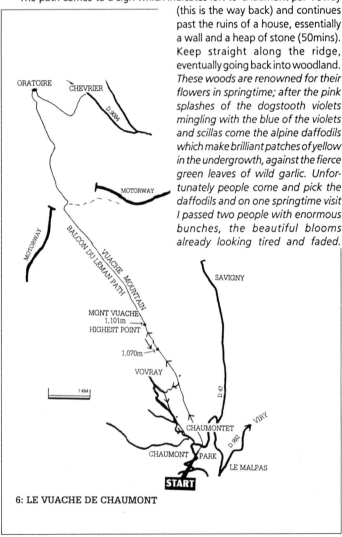

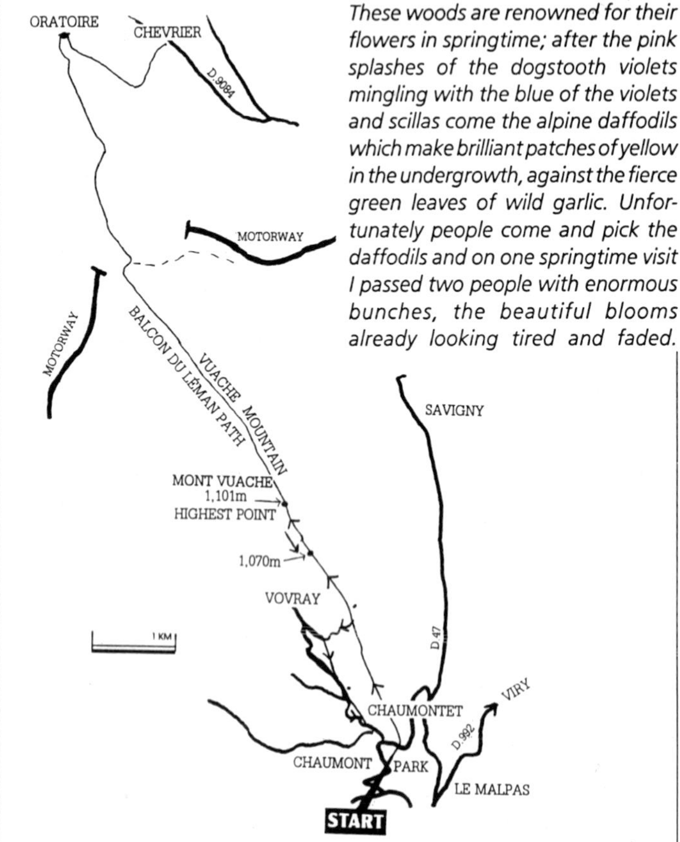

6: LE VUACHE DE CHAUMONT

When we got to the woods all we could see were the green daffodil leaves and the occasional bloom - they had picked the lot!

5mins after entering the wood the path goes to the left (look for the GR indication on a rock). You are now on the ridge proper picking your way amongst rocks, many of them covered with interesting creeping plants. From here you get sweeping views on both sides; to the left the Usses valley and Jura again and to the right the Rhône valley and Geneva with its Jet d'eau (the water fountain which is a well-known landmark of Geneva), the lake and Vaudois mountains in the background; if you look back along the ridge there is a glistening row of jagged snow covered peaks dominated by Mont Blanc.

Keeping to the well trodden path which goes back into the woods you will come to a primitive wooden cross, a borne (concrete boundary marker) and heap of rocks (1hr 15mins). Under the trees here in early March are hundreds of white snowflake (also called snowbell) flowers, which are like snowdrops only larger with yellow tipped petals. 15mins later you come to a wooden sign which says Mont Vuache, alt. 1,101m and is the highest part of the ridge (1hr 30mins).

ALTERNATIVE: If you have two cars and can leave one in the village of Chevrier, you can continue on the GR Balcon du Léman which is an easy undulating path towards the Defile de l'Ecluse (Bellegarde Gap) where the Rhône cuts through the mountain. You can see the new motorway which tunnels right under the Vuache. Before you reach the end of the ridge bear right by the Oratoire Ste. Victoire and continue down the slope to the village of Chevrier (this has not been walked by the author).

From Mont Vuache retrace your steps to the signpost which says Chaumont par Vouvry just beyond the ruined house (2hrs). Bear down right across a meadow to a sort of spring (there are usually some horses here and an old bath). Turn left along the side of the wood until you see another sign to Chaumont. The path goes down medium steep through woods where there are more dogstooth violets and daffodils in springtime. It is rocky in places, but not difficult, passing through the occasional clearing. You come out of the woods into a field where there is a small summerhouse up on the right. Cross the field to a jeep track where you turn left and continue through trees and fields for about 10mins until you meet the tarmac road (2hrs 45mins) in the pretty hamlet of Chaumontet.

Bear left and left again at a T-junction where there is a cross. At the first bend, just before an isolated wooden chalet, there is a path bearing down to the left. Here there is a lovely view of Chaumont with the church tower and the ruins of an old château on the hill to the right - beyond is the sharp outline of the Parmelan mountain near Annecy with the snow covered Alps in the background. Keep on this path, passing the cemetery on the left, till you come to another road. Turn left and walk up into the village (3hrs).

Remarks: My favourite springtime walk and a yearly ritual to see the carpets of flowers, especially the dogstooth violet. The best times to go vary from year to year, but it is normally in early March when the first spring sun warms the slopes and then go two weeks later when the violets fade and the bright yellow alpine daffodils take over. This mountain is protected - please don't pick the flowers! (For more information see Vuache).

The village of Chaumont is strategically situated between the Vuache ridge and Mont Chauve, where you can see the sparse ruins of an ancient château on the Mont de Saint Jean (worth a visit). Built in the 12th century it changed hands between the Counts of Geneva and the Dukes of Savoie, was partially dismantled by Francois I and reconstructed by the Duke Emmanuel-Philibert, before being destroyed by Louis XIII. Formerly on the Roman road linking Vienne to Geneva, Chaumont used to be a small bustling commercial centre with its own market but fell into decline in the 17th century when the town of Frangy grew more important. After the second world war the village stagnated as the exodus to the cities started and the old houses and farms started to crumble. Happily the village has recently been brought back to life and the houses lovingly restored.

7: SIGNAL DES VOIRONS - Alt. 1,480 metres
(Vallée Verte Region)

Difficulty:	Moderate.
Time:	4hrs 45mins.
Height gain:	681 metres.
Maps:	Editions Didier & Richard IGN No.3 Massifs du Chablais Faucigny & Genevois 1:50,000. Cartes IGN 3429 ET Top 25 Bonneville/Cluses 1:25,000 and/or Promenades en Vallée Verte 1:25,000.
Depart from:	Le Penaz - 864 metres.
Signposting:	Follow the white splashes to the monastery - dark blue from the monastery to the Signal des Voirons - then red and white splashes.

How to get there (from Geneva)

Take the motorway direction Chamonix and exit at No.15, Boëge/St. Jeoire. Turn left briefly on the D.903 and watch for the D.9 right signposted Fillinges, Samoëns and Vallée Verte. Follow this road to the Pont de Fillinges and then turn left on the D.907 and after almost immediately right into the Vallée

Verte, signposted Boëge. (ALTERNATIVELY go through Annemasse and take the D.907 to Taninges. Just before the Pont de Fillinges turn left on the D.20 into the Vallée Verte, signposted Boëge.) In the centre of Boëge continue left on the D.20 towards Saxel. Just after the Boëge end of village sign, turn left on the V.7 to Perriers and follow this road round to the left where it says Auberge du Chalet (if you go straight you end up in a farmyard). Keep left at the next junction and then bear up right following signpost Penaz (about 2km from Boëge) - drive up till you can go no further and park just beyond a farm. If there is not enough parking space behind the farm, leave your car in the parking area on the way up to Penaz on the right and walk up the road.

Directions

Start at the signpost Les Lillettes 40min/Tour de Vallée on a wide, grassy

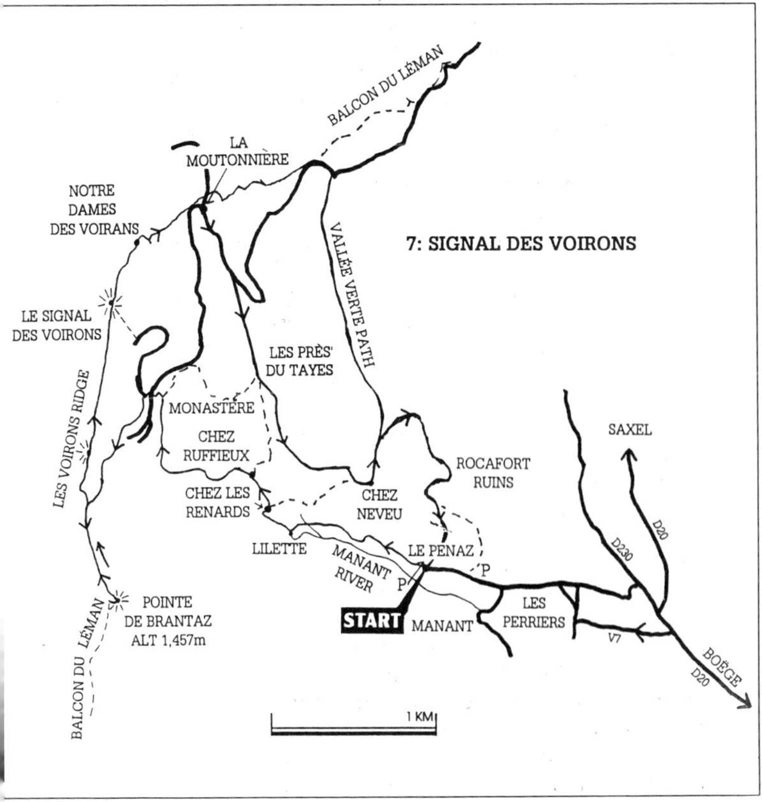

uphill path with periwinkles flowering on the banks in springtime. Down on the left there is a narrow stream (Nant de Manant) and the sound of rushing water is delightful company for the first part of your walk upwards through woodland. The path is defined and becomes stony; keep on the main path, ignoring others coming in, including one to the left saying Cascade (5mins) and follow the white splashes on the trees. You go over a stone bridge crossing the stream (20mins) where the stream divides, one part going off up to the right under another old bridge and the other still gurgling beside you on the left, level with the path. Now you see the red/yellow signs of the Tour du Vallée Verte but ignore them and stick to the white signs all the way.

You come to a grassy clearing with a farm called Les Lilettes, alt. 1,080m (30mins). Here there are various signs: left Monastère lhr and right Chez Neveu, Chateau Rocafort, Chez Les Baud (this is the Tour de Vallée path which you do not want). Keep left following the white arrows which go up to Chez les Renards, another farm and house with various outbuildings. Be careful here to follow the signs left and then almost immediately round to the right by the house (do not go straight on). Follow the white splashes carefully as there are a number of path crossings and you could take a wrong turning.

The path climbs up medium steep and joins a jeep track at a sign pointing back to Chez les Renards (45mins). Turn left - there is an old chalet in front with a small modern statue of the Virgin Mary high on the outer wall and a ruin on the right (this is an old priest's house and called Chez Ruffieux, but there is no marker). Look back here for a magnificent view of the valley below. After the house bear to the right at a fork - lots of trees have been cut down at this spot.

The path goes upwards through close coniferous forest; follow the white splashes carefully as there is quite a profusion of paths going off in different directions. Note that a white cross on a tree indicates the wrong way! You reach a sign which points back to Chez Ruffieux and straight ahead downhill to Près des Thays. However, take the path on the left (you can see the monastery buildings above) which takes you to the parking of the Monastère de Bethléhem (1hr 15mins) - see below for brief history and description. At the top of this path a lot of trees have been cut down but make for the buildings you can see ahead. *It is worthwhile looking round the monastery; they have a church, an interesting audio-visual film describing the history of the place and a shop selling pottery and other religious goods.*

Cross the road with the car park on your right and follow the narrow path going straight up signposted Signal des Voirons 30mins and Pointe de Brantaz 1hr. From now on follow the blue splashes carefully. Cross the road again and turn left; at the first corner you see a track going straight on (marked blue). This is a narrow path through dense coniferous forest; watch carefully all the way for the blue splashes on the trees. You pass a gate on the left saying that the area beyond belongs to the Sisters of Bethlehem but ignore this and go straight with the tall boundary fence on your left. The path curls round the contour of the mountain and even goes down for a short while; you are momentarily on a jeep track before coming to a large red arrow which goes up to the right. Follow this arrow (blue splashes start again) up to the ridge through an area where a considerable amount of tree felling has taken place and you finally reach the wide path going along the top, 45mins from the monastery (2hrs).

Turn left on the path (this is now the Grande Randonnée Balcon du Léman) which traverses the wide ridge, but at this point you cannot see the view over the other side. After a few minutes there is a sign saying Pointe de Brantaz left. Follow this narrow path which takes you up the slope to the Pointe (2hrs 15mins), alt. 1,457m, where there are lovely views into the valley below with the Alps, including Mont Blanc. *This is a good place to have a rest and less crowded in summer than the Signal des Voirons itself.*

Retrace your steps and turn right back along the ridge on the same path passing where you came up from the monastery. It takes about 40mins to the Signal des Voirons which is 30m higher than the Pointe de Brantaz. The path gets nearer and nearer the ridge and just after it becomes sandy (15mins from Pointe de Brantaz) look carefully for a narrow path up to the left - there is a blue splash on a stone. This takes you right along the ridge where you get beautiful views over the Geneva countryside with the lake and the Jura mountains beyond. Look back and you get a good view of the Salève, the ski resort of Les Brasses and the Môle. There are lots of tree stumps and on the hill below new trees have been planted. At one viewpoint there is a bench which is in a perfect spot to have a rest and appreciate the sweeping views. Continue on the defined path to the Signal des Voirons, alt. 1,480m (3hrs), which is marked by an IGN stone survey point and dated 1958. From here you can see the Dents du Midi, to the south, framed by trees.

At the Signal des Voirons the blue splashes disappear and from now on follow the red/white signs of the GR Balcon du Léman path. The path winds downwards for 15mins, sometimes quite steeply through bushes (be careful if it is wet or snowy). Keep looking for the splashes as sometimes the track is not so defined; just before you arrive at the Chapel Notre Dame des Voirons (100m lower than the Signal) there is a slippery rock to clamber down.

The old chapel of Notre Dame des Voirons (3hrs 15mins) is in a grassy clearing where there is also a tall wooden cross. On the chapel there is an inscription saying that "the chapel, dedicated to the Virgin Mary, has been a place of pilgrimage for five centuries. People have come here with their burdens and through their prayers have received grace and benediction". There is also a large old house next door to the chapel. From here turn right signposted La Moutonnière (GR signs on tree). Almost immediately take a narrow path down to the left where there are red/white marks on a tree (do not go straight on; this is where you leave the Balcon du Léman).

The narrow path goes down quite steeply through woods. After a few minutes bear down left at a sign saying La Moutonnière (do not go straight on to the Parking). You continue down quite steeply, still following red splashes, until you hit the road on a hair-pin (this is the road going up to the monastery). Turn left on this hair-pin bend which is La Moutonnière, alt.1,264m (3hrs 30mins). Go down this road for about 10mins and look for a wide jeep track off to the right where a number of trees have been felled. There are signs on the right-hand side saying Monastère/Près du Tayes/ Pointe des Brantaz. Still following red splashes, walk on this muddy, flattish track, past an old building on your right, till you come to a clearing which is Près du Tayes. (There are signs here indicating right to the monastery and straight on Chez les Renards.) Here there is a small logging cabin. Follow the sign further over on the left indicating Chez Neveu and Le Penaz (4hrs).

The path is quite wide and defined, through mixed beech and fir woods, and there are white as well as red splashes. You pass a house on the right with a green gate, before you come to an attractive clearing. Follow the obvious path through the clearing (red splash on tree to right) and you come to Chez Neveu, alt. 1,080m, which is a beautiful old deserted farm with two smaller buildings which have been renovated. Ignore the sign right to St. André 2hrs 20mins and Saxel 1hr 40mins but bear left at the back of the farm, following red/yellow/white flashes. You go down a very attractive short valley where there are some gnarled old fruit trees. The grassy path takes you to a signpost pointing back to La Monastère. Do not go straight on here (the Tour of the Vallée Verte path goes on to La Lilette) but branch to the right towards La Relaz, though there is no sign; you are now following white splashes only (4hrs 10mins).

The path goes into woods again and up over a small hill and medium steep down round the hill with further lovely views of the Vallée Verte below. You reach a signpost saying Le Penaz right and Château de Rocafort left 100m. DETOUR: To visit the château turn left. After 5mins you crest a small hillock and see an old wall which is all that remains of the old castle. *The Château de Rocafort, one of the oldest in the region, was originally constructed in Roman times and added to in the 12th and 13th centuries. It belonged to one of the nobles of the Boëge region and, strategically situated on the east side of the Voirons ridge, dominated the valley from Boëge to the Col de Saxel. Ruined during the 14th century wars with the Dauphinoises it was never rebuilt, but replaced by the Château de Marcossy (near the village of St. André), which in its turn was burnt to the ground in the 15th century.*

Turn right to Le Penaz (4hrs 25mins) on a delightful, wide path through woodland hugging the contour of the hill. 5mins later, when you are amongst tall fir trees, go straight ahead ignoring the white cross on a tree. (There is a narrow path going down left with white flashes, which reaches the road at the parking area below Le Penaz.) The wide path goes down past a wooden chalet and then you are in an open clearing. Continue on past chalets and you will come out at the hamlet of Le Penaz and the farm (4hrs 45mins).

Remarks: Despite rather complicated instructions, this is an attractive, easy hike of about 19km with not too much hard climbing. The walk along the ridge is about 2.5km but relatively flat with lovely views. This is a popular spot in the summer months as it is easily reached from Geneva.

The Monastère de Bethléhem, also called Le Monastère Notre Dame de la Gloire Dieu, has an interesting historical background. In Roman times this was a pagan site, a statue of Jupiter being found here in the 5th century, later destroyed by the Bishop of Geneva. In 1456 the first chapel and monastery were erected by Louis de Langin, who owned most of the land on the mountain, in thanksgiving to the Virgin Mary for saving him from being ravaged by a wild boar. He also had a beautiful statue of the Virgin sculpted in black lebanese cedar (some say it was brought back from the crusades). Louis spent the rest of his life in thanksgiving and prayer together with a small band of followers. These buildings were burnt by the Bernese during the war with the Duke of Savoy in 1536, but rebuilt at the beginning of the 17th century and inhabited by the Dominican community. In 1768 they were destroyed again by fire but rebuilt in 1863. In 1852 the black statue of the Virgin Mary was brought down from the mountain and placed in the newly constructed Boëge parish church. The present community of nuns installed themselves in 1967 and have since made the monastery a place of pilgrimage and spiritual healing, providing accommodation for novices and lay people who wish to spend a period of time in silent worship.

8: MONT DE VOUAN - Alt. 960 metres

(Vallée Verte region)

Difficulty:	Medium - part of this walk is along a wide ridge.
Time:	3hrs 30mins.
Height gain:	320 metres.
Maps:	Editions Didier & Richard IGN No.3 Massifs du Chablais

	Faucigny & Genevois 1:50,000. Cartes IGN 3429 ET Top 25 Bonneville/ Cluses. 1:25,000 or Promenades en Vallée Verte 1:25,000.
Depart from:	Boisinges (Viuz en Sallaz) - 638 metres.
Signposting:	Adequate - yellow/red splashes much of the way.

How to get there (from Geneva)

Take the motorway direction Chamonix and exit at No.15, Boëge/St. Jeoire. Turn left briefly on the D.903 and watch for the D.9 right signposted Fillinges, Samoëns and Vallée Verte. Follow this road to the Pont de Fillinges and then turn right on the D.907 direction Taninges/Samoëns. (ALTERNATIVELY go through Annemasse and take the D.907 direction Taninges.) Take a narrow left turn about 0.5-1km after the Pont de Fillinges onto the D.292 signposted Boisinges. Continue up this road past Chez les Bourguignons until you come to the Boisinges village sign and a T-junction (where the D.292 turns upwards signposted Sevraz) or D.190. Park your car here though there is not much room - if you have lots of cars park as stated below:

Alternative start of walk: Continue up the D.292 road past Chez les Bourguignons till you see a wide jeep track going off to the left (there is a sort of grassy triangle). Drive down here till you come to a large parking area. Leave your car and walk up the wide track to a T-junction where there are signs left to Crêtes de Vouan and back to Source Qui Rit. Turn left to join the main directions below at the point marked (*).

Directions

From the T-junction cross the D.292 but do not continue up the road to Sevraz. Take the narrow tarmac lane facing you with a fountain on the right and a wooden signpost on a tree to the left to Crêtes de Vouan. Walk up this lane for approximately 3mins and take the path going straight on at the first corner. You are on a wide, leafy track going along the edge of the Mont Vouan with open views on your left. Keep to the main path undulating round the hill through coniferous and deciduous woods ignoring all paths to the right and left. There is a wooden sign high on a tree indicating straight to Crêtes de Vouan (just after a path down to the left). After you come to a sign (25mins) pointing down to the left to Source Qui Rit (*) - this is the way you take on your way back.

Follow two further signs to Crêtes de Vouan keeping to the main path. Where you turn a wide right-hand bend (there is another sign here), ignore the path down to the left but continue upwards for about 100m and you will see a narrow track up to the right (it is not signposted). This is a 10min fairly steep detour to a grotto called La Grande Gueule (keep left where it forks

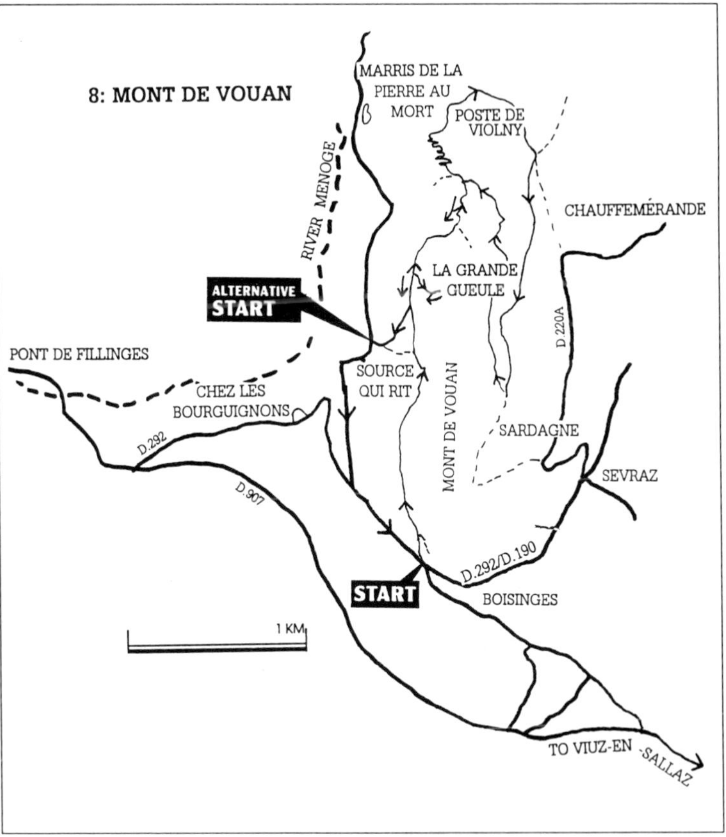

as it is less steep), where you can still see the imprints of the millstones which were cut out of the solid rock (see notes below as to how they did this). La Grande Gueule is an impressive cave-like structure which resembles its name (big mouth). Unfortunately now disfigured with graffiti, it was the scene of great industry a hundred years ago. If you continue along the path at the end of the open area you can see other rocky imprints of enormous meules which were hewn out of the cliff face.

This is an obvious picnic stop as there is a lovely view, though the noise from the road below does tend to echo against the rock wall. I have also seen someone practising rappelling on the jutting out rock face. Retrace your steps to the original path.

From the Grande Gueule junction continue up on the main path following all signs to Poste de Violny, for about 10mins. (After a few minutes be careful to go straight on at the signpost and not go to your right - GR cross on a tree.) At a right-hand hairpin leave the main track, going straight on (there is a signpost here saying Poste de Violny but it is difficult to see). If you look up you will see the tree covered cliffs of the Vouan ridge.Walk for about 60m and take a narrow path upwards to the right, again signposted Poste de Violny (1hr 15mins). There are red/yellow splashes on trees. Keep to the main track as the path winds up the mountain medium steep through stunted beech and oak trees and higher up there are clumps of heather. Look back and you will get beautiful views of the Vallée Verte. In June there are lots of wild strawberries and in summer there are lovely blue harebells on the side of the path.

At the top you reach a clearing with signposts (1hr 30mins) which is the Poste de Violny. Take the sign to the left which says St. André-de-Boëge and Chauffemérande. This is a wide track going downwards round the mountain and then levelling out. After 5mins follow a sign up right to Chauffemérande on a narrow path. You come to a red/yellow sign on a stone in the middle of the path which says go left (you can either take this and then at the top where there is a T-junction turn right) or go straight which is a short cut. At the top there is another signpost left to St. André-de-Boëge and right to Chauffemérande. Go right, along a wide path which curls around the hill, ignoring the wide path going up to the right.

Shortly after, watch out for a sign to the right which says Crêtes de Vouan. Be careful as the sign is hidden in the trees and not very visible. Take this attractive narrow track going along the crest of the Vouan ridge (there are still red/yellow splashes on the trees). To the left, you can glimpse through the trees, the snowy Mont Blanc range and the Dents du Midi while nearer is the solitary Môle peak. To the right are extensive views of the Lake Geneva basin and the southern side of the Salève mountain; you can also see the village of Mijouet in the valley below with the ugly buildings of a holiday centre on the hill behind. There are lots of bilberry bushes on this ridge so it is a good place to come in autumn if you want to gather the berries which make delicious tarts.

Still undulating along this attractive wooded ridge you come to a sort of cross-roads where it says Crêt de Vouan (2hrs). There is a clear view of a hamlet down to your left. Continue straight upwards keeping to the top of the ridge and do not follow the red/yellow flashes which go down right. The ridge path goes up quite steeply to a hump, before levelling out and then going down to a wider path and a T-junction which says Sardagne to the left and Boisinges down to the right (2hrs 30mins). Take the right path to Boisinges which meanders medium steep down the side of the mountain through open woodland (lots of trees have been cut down) and blackberry bushes. On a clear day you can see over to the town of Geneva and the famous Jet d'Eau (fountain). Just before the wide path peters out, take the narrow path left which reaches a sort of promontory jutting out of the hillside where there is a magnificent view. Do not go too near the edge as there is a sharp drop! Go back a few metres and continue on the main track which continues downwards and is eroded in places.

The path finally widens and joins the upward route on a left-hand hairpin (2hrs 50mins). Keep going down following signs to Boisinges passing the narrow path up to the Grande Gueule. Continue on the same path you came up until you reach the track down to the right called Source Qui Rit (3hrs). (OR go straight, retracing your steps to Boisinges.) You go down through woods till you come to a T-junction and a wide jeep track.

Detour: To the right is the Gouille au Morts (the water of the dead), so called because a quarry man got caught up in the ropes of the millstone he was hauling down and fell into a pond and was drowned. At 100m or so above this patch of water is another big quarry with the round impressions of the millstones sculpted on the rock face. This detour takes about an hour walking, but if you have parked your car on the alternative route you can take it and drive along the road till you pass the two stagnant ponds. Just after there is a parking space to the right. Park your car here and then take the narrow path up behind. At a hairpin bend to the left take the track straight up and this will bring you to the quarry. The walk from the parking space takes approximately 10mins.

Turn left at the T-junction (there is a wide space to park cars here) and walk down the road till you see the Source Qui Rit (the laughing fountain) on the left which is a big disappointment as it is merely an iron pipe spilling water out of the hillside into a stream. However, the water from it is delicious and local people come here to get supplies.

10mins later the jeep track bears left round by some recently renovated farm buildings on the right and then comes out into flat fields. After 5mins you meet the D.292. There is no sign here, but turn left and walk up the road for about 10mins till you come to the T-junction in Boisinges where the car is parked (3hrs 30mins).

Remarks: This is a shortish walk but can be made longer if you visit the other quarries. It is well worth doing for its historical value and lovely views. If you have the time pay a visit to the interesting Musée Paysan in Viuz-en-Sallaz (follow signposts), which will give you a fascinating insight into the life of the people in the region up to the last century. Open every day from 9h - 12h and from 14h - 18h (Sundays 14h - 18h 30). Entrance (adults) FF.18.

Of historical interest: *The area around Mont Vouan, which is situated* *at the entrance of the Vallée Verte, was exploited up to 1914. It was famous for its quarries out of which were hewn the millstones and fruit presses for the surrounding areas. In order to make the millstone the workers chipped out a perfect circle in the rock face which they then filled up with wood. The wood was watered till it swelled and forced the stone away from the rock face. The enormously heavy circles of rock were then hauled down the sides of the mountain by means of ropes and pulleys - an amazing and exhausting feat of endurance.*

As well as the fascinating impressions of the millstones left in the rock face there are innumerable shell fossils from the time when this area was under the sea thousands of years ago. When the Alps folded up the imprints of the sea shells and marine creatures remained on the rocks for ever.

9: POINTE DE MIRIBEL - Alt. 1,581 metres

(Vallée Verte Region)

Difficulty:	Easy walk except when climbing up to the statue.
Time:	3hrs.
Height gain:	183 metres.
Maps:	Editions Didier & Richard IGN No.3 Massifs du Chablais Faucigny & Genevois 1:50,000. Cartes IGN 3429 ET Top 25 Bonneville/Cluses and/or Promenades en Vallée Verte 1:25,000.
Depart from:	Ajon (near Bogève) - 1,398 metres.
Signposting:	Good.

How to get there (from Geneva)

Take the motorway direction Chamonix and exit at No.15, Boëge/St. Jeoire. The turn left briefly on the D.903 and watch for the D.9 right signposted Fillinges, Samoëns and Vallée Verte. Follow this road to the Pont de Fillinges and then turn right on the D.907 direction Taninges/Samoëns. (ALTERNATIVELY go through Annemasse and take the D.907 direction Taninges/Samoëns.) When you come to a cross-roads (lights) at Les Brochets, Viuz-en-Sallaz (the next place after Le Pont de Fillinges), turn left on the D.12 towards Bogève. At Bogève take the D.190b to the Plateau de Plaine Joux and then to Ajon, alt. 1,398m (6km from Bogève), where there is a car park, picnic area, a few chalets and glorious views in all directions.

Directions

At the start of the walk you can see the Pointe de Miribel on the left with its statue of the Virgin and stations of the cross. However, take the jeep track

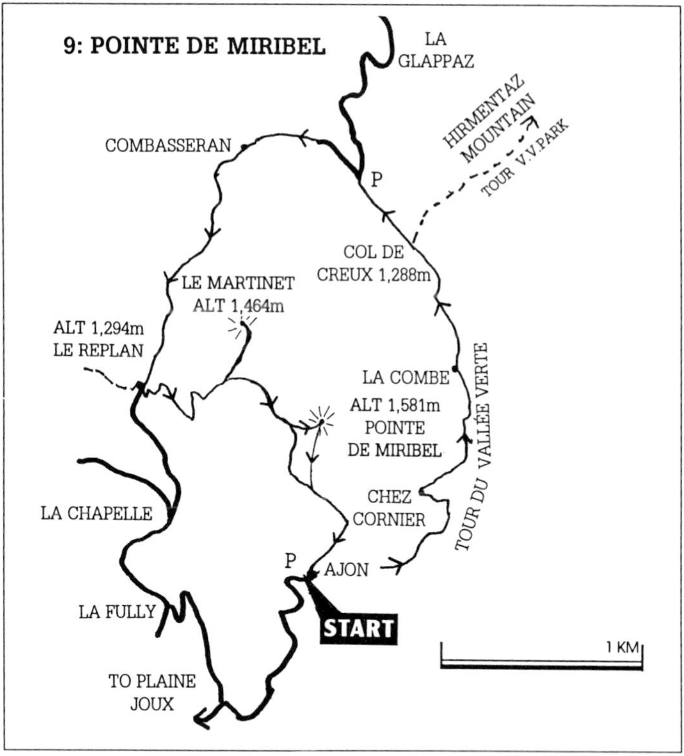

signposted Col de Creux 1hr 15mins and Plaines Joux 30mins, which bears gradually downwards. All around is the classic cross-country ski terrain of Les Brassus, rolling grass covered hills with the main Chablais peaks in the background. There are red/yellow splashes which show you are on the Tour du Vallée Verte, a circular path which goes all round this valley. The track winds round the hill and 10mins from the start you pass a typical "Heath Robinson" type farm, called Chez Cornier, with turkeys and chickens underfoot and scattered outhouses.

Continue on the jeep track until you reach a corner (25mins) where there are some old farmhouses. Here you bear off to the left. There is a concealed signpost saying Tour du Vallée Verte on the side of a farmhouse and on the left is a wooden cross and an old trough. You are off the main jeep track now and on to a wide path. Over on the right is a good view of the peaks of the Roc d'Enfer, Pointe de Chalune and the Haute Pointe. Continue until you come to a tree which has a red and yellow sign (40mins) pointing up to the right with a wooden signpost beyond which says Col de Creux. *Here the Tour du Vallée Verte continues along the Montagne d'Hirmentaz which makes a longer circular walk (see Montagne d'Hirmentaz, Walk No. 12).*

Turn left at the tree and continue on a grassy path through a cutting in the hills - the path goes slightly down and round the mountain. You cross a small stream where there is a sign which points back to the Col de Creux/Crêt d'Hirmentaz and straight on to Habère-Poche par le Repland; here you hit the end of a tarmac road (50mins), with a car park. Just beyond is the Auberge de Miribel (a good place to stop for refreshment if it is open). Bear up to the left following another wooden sign saying Combasseran 10mins/Les Ervines 15mins.

The wide and stony track continues circling round the mountain; look back and there is a beautiful unspoilt view of the Hirmentaz, which is marred on its other side by numerous ski lifts. You walk past a large corrugated iron hut and then through a hamlet of farms called Combasseran, alt. l,297m (1hr 10mins) where there is another signpost. The path is well defined through sparse woodlands and open hillside and starts to narrow as it continues through low shrubs, falling away on the right with glorious open views of the Vallée Verte. Just after a small house there is a sign saying Les Ervines (1hr 20mins) and then the path starts to wind gently upwards. Keep on the main track ignoring the path going off to the left. The track undulates until it meets another paved road (1hr 30mins) which leads to the tiny hamlet of Le Replan, alt. 1,294m (the road snakes down to the hamlets of La Chapelle, La Fully and Plaines Joux).

However, go up left on a wide track and after 50m there is a signpost to Le Repland/La Glappe/Miribel/Ajon. About 20m further on there is another signpost to Le Martinet which is a muddy path up to the right through scattered woods, medium steep. Take this narrow path which forks after about 5mins. Bear right following blue markings on trees. The grassy path zigzags up and in places is not well defined. There are lovely views all round, and if you look behind you get your first glimpse of Lake Léman through the hills. Look for an old stone water trough on your left and continue straight to a low pass just ahead. On the left is the hump of Le Martinet, alt. 1,464m, which is another viewpoint.

From this unnamed pass (2hrs 5mins) you can see the Col de Creux over on the left so you have literally walked round the mountain in a circle! Continue straight along a narrow path and ahead is the Pointe de Miribel on the horizon with its impressive statue. You get another lovely view of the Hirmentaz mountain on the left with higher peaks beyond. On the right is the tree covered hump of the Tête de Cudres. *In early summer look for the many different species of alpine orchids along this path; you will be able to identify*

The Pointe de Miribel, Vallée Verte from the start of walk 9

the early purple, the burnt orchid, the fly orchid and the military orchid amongst others.

Go through a wooden stile (2hrs 20mins) and bear to the left along the ridge up to the Pointe. There is a signpost to Ajon going down to the right (this is the way back if you do not wish to climb up to the statue). It is a steep 10mins scramble up the shoulder of the hill but worth the extra energy for the satisfaction of reaching the statue of the Virgin Mary, built in 1878 (2hrs 30mins). Here is a good place for a picnic if there are not too many people, as the view of the surrounding Chablais mountains is superb.

Start down following the stations of the cross which climb up the hill from the other side, spaced about 50 yards apart. It is a path down a rocky chimney rather like the way up. These stations of the cross, now needing some renovation, were hewn out of red marble in 1804 by a local sculptor called Joseph Marie Felisaz. At that time there was a big oak cross on the summit erected in 1774 which was later replaced by the statue. You can see where the cars are down below so you just follow your nose over the grassy meadows (in fact there is a path) till you reach the car park at Ajon, which takes about 15mins (3hrs).

Remarks: An ideal walk as it is not long or difficult (apart from the last 10mins scramble) and you get maximum views of the Vallée Verte and surrounding Chablais peaks. It can also be done on a rainy day when you cannot go too high. This area is very popular in summer with the local people so you will probably find it crowded at weekends in July and August - in winter it is a frequented cross-country ski area.

10: HEIGHTS OF HABÈRE-POCHE (Le Mont Forchat)

Alt. 1,539 metres (Vallée Verte Region)

Difficulty:	Medium, though the climb to the statue on top of Mont Forchat is quite steep.
Time:	5hrs 15mins.
Height gain:	500 metres.
Maps:	Editions Didier & Richard IGN No.3 Massifs du Chablais Faucigny & Genevois 1:50,000. Cartes IGN 3428 ET Top 25 Thonon, Evian and/or Promenades en Vallée Verte 1:25,000.
Depart from:	Habère-Poche - 1,039 metres.
Signposting:	Good - splashes all the way.

How to get there (from Geneva)

Take the motorway direction Chamonix and exit at No.15, Boëge/St. Jeoire. Then turn left briefly on the D.903 and watch for the D.9 signposted Fillinges, Samoëns and Vallée Verte. Follow this road to the Pont de Fillinges and then turn left on the D.907 and after almost immediately right into the Vallée Verte, signposted Boëge. (ALTERNATIVELY go through Annemasse and take the D.907 direction Taninges. Just before the Pont de Fillinges turn left on the D.20 into the Vallée Verte, signposted Boëge.) In the centre of Boëge turn right following the sign to Col de Cou (D.22/D.12) which goes through Villard and Habère-Lullin to Habère-Poche. In the village of Habère-Poche park your car opposite the Tionnolet Restaurant.

Directions

Go straight along the main road from the restaurant in the direction of Col de Cou, which takes you through the hamlet of Le Vernay. After 15mins turn up right, on a narrower tarmac road signposted Doucy 0.5. There are also wooden signposts here saying Grange Michaux/Mont Forchat/Col des Arces. You pass a renovated farm on the left called Etoile des Cimes which is rather twee with green and red shutters. Go round the first bend and after 100m there is a path going hard back to the right signposted Granges Michaux 35mins/Mont Forchat 1hr 45min/Col des Arces 50min/Le Mont 2hrs. This is an easy, wide path on the edge of woods, becoming leafy and sunken as it climbs the hill. Follow the yellow splashes and when the path seems to go round to the left continue straight (yellow splash on tree on left). The narrow, leafy track reaches an open glade where there is an old barn (45mins); you are now at Les Granges Michaux, alt. 1,120m. There are three

10: HEIGHTS OF HABÈRE-POCHE

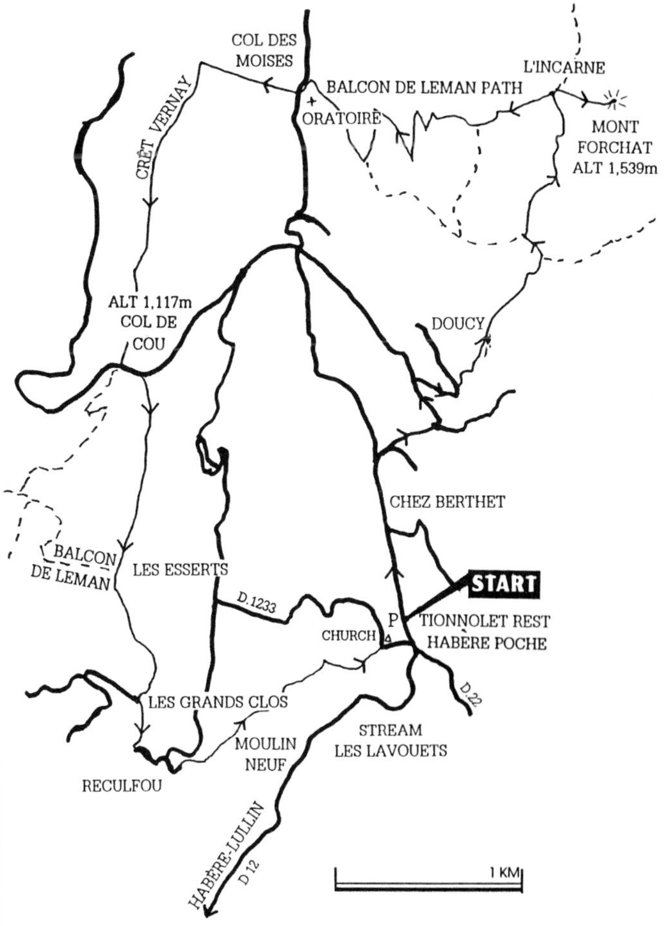

COL DES MOISES
L'INCARNE
BALCON DE LEMAN PATH
ORATOIRE
CRÊT VERNAY
MONT FORCHAT ALT 1,539m
ALT 1,117m COL DE COU
DOUCY
CHEZ BERTHET
BALCON DE LEMAN
LES ESSERTS
START
D.1233
P
TIONNOLET REST
HABÈRE POCHE
CHURCH
D.22
LES GRANDS CLOS
STREAM LES LAVOUETS
MOULIN NEUF
RECULFOU
HABÈRE-LULLIN
D 12
1 KM

sets of signposts here but you continue straight ahead following the direction to Mont Forchat.

Stay on the main path which goes round to the left with yellow circles to guide you (you can go straight up but it is much steeper). Keep straight on, climbing fairly steeply, and you come out into the open at a pass between two hills which is called L'Incarne, alt. 1,429m (1hr 25mins). Here there is a lovely view down into a grassy valley below where you can see the track winding down to a group of chalets called Très Le Mont. The sign points left to Col des Moises and on the right you can see the statue on the top of the Mont Forchat which is where you are making for. The track climbs 100m from the pass; it is steep and in places quite stony, so care should be taken both going up and down, especially if it has been raining.

20mins later and rather puffed you reach the top of Mont Forchat (1hr 45mins) where there is a large white statue of St. François de Sales, the famous saint born near Annecy in 1567. The statue was erected by the Parroise (Parish) de Lullin in 1828 in the days when it was fashionable to build statues on top of mountain peaks! From the summit, which is a cosy, grassy knoll, there is a magnificent view of the rolling hills of the Vallée Verte with the mightier surrounding peaks of the Chablais area of the Haute Savoie, including the Dents du Midi and the Mont Blanc range in the background, on one side, and on the other, Lake Geneva with the Jura mountains on the horizon. Another perfect picnic spot!

Walk back to the Col l'Incarne and take the path straight on signposted Col des Moises. You are now on the Grande Randonnée Balcon de Léman which is indicated by white/red splashes. This is a wide, pleasant path through spaced out fir trees, reasonably level. There is a signpost announcing that you are entering a Réserve de Lièvres (hare reserve). When you come to an attractive grassy clearing (2hrs 25mins), carpeted with crocuses in springtime, look carefully across the clearing, almost straight ahead, for the red/white and yellow splashes on a tree.

You pass through woods of oak, beech and fir losing height gradually with magnificent views through the trees of Lake Geneva on the right. The path becomes narrow in places and winds down towards the Col des Moises amongst bushes and young fir trees with a lovely view to the left. Turn down right towards Col des Moises at a T-junction where there are a number of signs, and left 5mins later at another T-junction (2hrs 40mins) - (to the right are red/white warning crosses). Stay on the main path where there has been quite a lot of clearing of trees and logging.

You come to yet another T-junction with a Tour du Vallée sign indicating that you have rejoined the the Tour du Vallée Verte. Bear down right through the woods till you arrive at a tarmac road (D.246) by more signposts. This is the Col (pass) des Moises, alt. 1,121m (3hrs). *Take the time to look at the*

Oratoire des Moises, a small shrine just down the road on the left-hand side, which is a little square building with a roof and a cross on it. Behind the grill is a primitive statue of Our Lady; 1160 is scratched on the wall but I find it hard to believe that this is the date of the shrine.

Walk back 20m from the shrine and follow the sign on the left-hand side to Col de Cou 45 min/Reculfou 1hr 20min (you are still on the Balcon de Léman). The path is not so well defined initially and you cross a marshy area with willows to the right; there are lots of yellow marsh marigolds here in springtime. Follow the fence posts on the right as you go up the field and straight towards the trees.

The path enters the woods and climbs up steeply following GR red/white splashes and also yellow signs. Bear left when you are almost at the top - it is well signed (3hrs 15mins). You are now walking along the wooded Crêt Vernay, with lovely views through the trees, particularly to the left where you can see the path down to the Col des Moises clearly. For part of the way along this ridge there is a sharp drop to your right. You come to a clearing, called L'Aiguille, alt. 1,225m (not signposted) where there is a good view to the north over the lake with the Jura on the horizon.

Continue along the ridge which is well marked with splashes. Many of the trees here have been felled in a long swath across the ridge and it is now covered with low bushes including wild raspberries. The path finally comes out into the open at the end of the ridge by a gold painted statue of the Virgin Mary (3hrs 40mins). This statue was erected in 1879 and pilgrims are offered an indulgence of 40 days if they say three Hail Marys at this spot! Before you is a long grassy path which goes down a slope, (careful, it is slippery after rain), past two round cement water covers, which meets the road at the Col de Cou, alt.1,117m. You can see the continuation of the Balcon de Léman going up again but you do not take this.

At the Col de Cou (4hrs) there are a few chalets and a hotel/restaurant straight ahead. Turn left on the road downwards and then first right towards Les Grands Clos 20mins/Reculfou 40mins/Habère-Poche. You are still following the yellow/red Vallée Verte signs. This is a wide, jeep track curling round the side of a wooded slope with lovely views all around, including the Mont Forchat to the left. After 50m ignore the path to the right with a white sign left saying Saxel and continue on the main track.

You come to a 4-way junction at Les Esserts, alt. 1,150m, where there are lots of signposts. This is where you leave the Tour du Vallée Verte. Go down left following the yellow splashes and signs saying Les Grands Clos/ Reculfou/Habère-Poche. Keep to the main path which becomes sunken and defined, going through woods, medium steep, until you come to a large, ugly building on a tarmac road which looks like a colonie de vacances (children's holiday home). This is Les Grands Clos (4hrs 25mins), and from here you can see the hamlet of Reculfou down on the left. Look for another signpost off the road to your left which says Reculfou; follow this path which goes down fairly steeply beside a fence, initially with a field on your left, then into a beech wood and an attractive shallow ravine with a stream gushing down on the right. You reach the tarmac road and the hamlet of Reculfou, alt. 920m (4hrs 35mins).

Follow the road down into the village. At a fork by a cross go either left or right round a beautiful old farm in the bend with a row of beehives in the garden. Continue down to the main road by another cross on the right, erected in the Jubilee Year of 1885. Cross the road and take a turning on the right with a yellow splash on an electricity pole and a sign Tour du Vallée/ Habère-Poche (actually this path is no longer on the Valley Tour so someone has bungled!). You are now on the valley floor and walking through fields - you can see the Hirmentaz ridge straight ahead with the Mont Forchat to the far left and the Pointe de Miribel on the right. Keep to the open flat jeep track over the fields and you come to a sewage plant on the right.

Go straight past the sewage plant and cross the Lavouets stream just beyond an old house called Moulin Neuf. You enter woods again, going upwards with another rivulet flowing down on the right. Leave the woods by a jeep track and shortly after the church of Habère-Poche is visible in front on the right. Make for the church which has a very tall spire continuing on the jeep track and taking no notice of a path going off to the left. Continue gently uphill towards the village passing the graveyard and church on the left and then the Mairie on the right. You meet the main road where you turn left and make for the Restaurant Les Tionnolet and much needed refreshment! (5hrs 15mins).

Remarks: Although there is one stretch of tarmac road,which can be done either at the beginning or the end, this is an attractive walk; a sort of switch back as you go up and down over two cols (passes) with lots of lovely views of the Vallée Verte and the surrounding Chablais peaks. Habère-Poche is the highest village in the valley and is a centre for both downhill (on the nearby Hirmentaz mountain) and cross-country skiing.

11: WALK AROUND VILLARD - Alt. 1,338 metres
(Vallée Verte Region)

Difficulty: Easy low walk.
Time: 3hrs 30mins.
Height gain: 542 metres.

Village of Bellevaux, Chablais
Author with Château d'Oche behind

Walking along ridge of Pointe de Ressachaux

Refuge de Vogealle

Maps:	Editions Didier & Richard IGN No.3 Massifs du Chablais Faucigny & Genevois 1:50,000. Cartes IGN 3429 ET Top 25 Bonneville/Cluses 1:25,000 and/or Promenades en Vallée Verte 1:25,000.
Depart from:	Village of Villard - 796 metres.
Signposting:	Good, look for wooden signs and red, then later blue splashes.

How to get there (from Geneva)

Take the motorway to Chamonix and exit at No.15, Boëge/St. Jeoire. Then turn left briefly on the D.903 and watch for the D.9 right signposted Fillinges, Samoëns and Vallée Verte. Follow this road to the Pont de Fillinges and then turn left on the D.907 and after almost immediately right into the Vallée Verte signposted Boëge. (ALTERNATIVELY go through Annemasse and take the D.907 direction Taninges. Just before the Pont de Fillinges turn left on the D.20 into the Vallée Verte signposted Boëge.) In the centre of Boëge turn right on the D.22 to Villard. Park your car in the car park in Villard opposite the mairie, which is a big grey building on the right at the start of the village (it says Mairie on the door).

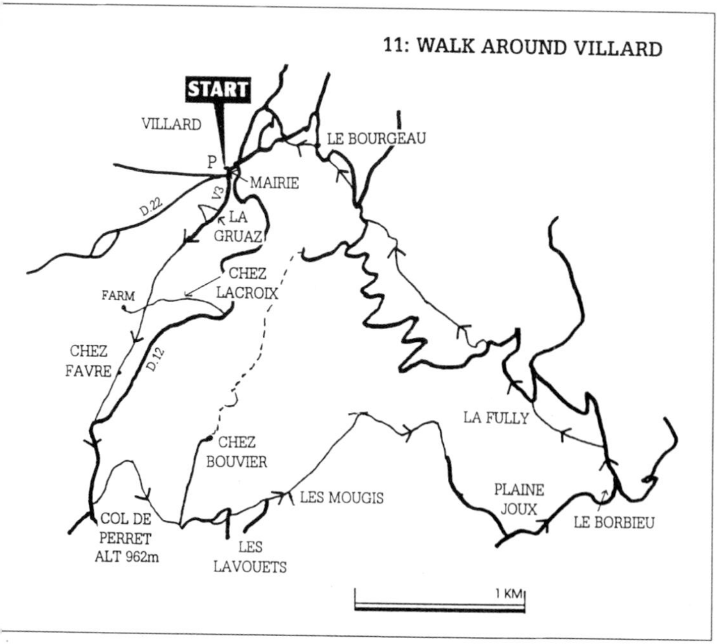

Directions

With the Mairie behind you, and a wooden cattle trough on your right, cross the road and take the V.3; there is an attractive stone plinth here with a modern iron crucifix on top. This narrow road takes you immediately through the hamlet of La Gruaz, where you should keep straight, and after about 5mins the road peters out by a stream on to a wide track. Here there are wooden signs saying Col de Perret/Les Lavouets/Plaine Joux/Tour de Vallée Verte (10mins). This is a wide path through attractive open meadowland and beech wood. Follow red splashes.

Cross a narrow paved road (20mins) which goes to a farm on the right. Continue upwards following what looks like an ancient mule track and you see another old farm on your right called Chez Favre, built 1869. You are walking gently upwards through lovely beech woods with a stream in a small ravine down on your right. The track becomes tarmac again and a few minutes later you hit the D.12 and signs to Col de Perret. Turn right and walk up to the the col, alt. 962m. This is disappointing, hardly qualifying the name col (pass), and has a few nondescript buildings, but far worse, disfiguring electricity wires - my private bête noir (35mins).

At the col follow the wooden signpost left indicating Les Lavouets/Les Mougis/Plaine Joux. Keep following the red splashes which take you up a lane and then over fields with lots of wide open views of the valley. You walk by some new houses and then meet the road at the hamlet of Les Lavouets (50mins). Turn left then right following the sign to Les Mougis 1.3km. There is also a wooden signpost saying Les Mougis/Les Pointes/Plaine Joux. Take a short cut on a corner, beside a small stone shrine to St. Joseph, built 1848. 5mins later you cross the same road and cut up again through the woods, medium steep, following the red splashes *(OR you can keep to the road all the way up which takes about 10mins longer).*

The short cut arrives at a farm where you go straight across the road and up to another road by a crucifix on a stone plinth, dated Jubilee 1901. You are now at Les Mougis, alt. 1,073m (1hr 5mins). There is a clear wooden sign on the opposite side of the road indicating left Les Pointes/Plaine Joux. From here you are on the GR du Pays Vallée Verte which is a circular walk right round the valley. Pass through Les Mougis which is a scattered hamlet with some lovely old farms. Turn left again by an old farm (1hr 10mins) where there are more signposts to Les Pointes/Plaine Joux and another iron crucifix, dated 1902. This is a lovely wide path through coniferous and beech woods. Follow the red splashes carefully and keep to the main path which goes up steadily round the mountain and is quite muddy in wet weather as there is a lot of logging being done in these woods. At one point the woods slope down quite steeply on the left.

You reach a delightful open clearing with wooden signs (there is one

War memorial in Villard, Vallée Verte

indicating Les Pointes on the right). Follow the sign to Plaine Joux (1hr 40mins) which takes you through the clearing with fir trees to the right and a chalet on the left. You meet a road (1hr 50mins) where there are some houses, and then turn right downwards past a café on the right called Chez Monique. You are now in the cross-country ski area of Plaine Joux; a rather desolate open area with a big restaurant and ski hire place etc. *Here you can appreciate how even cross-country skiing disfigures the landscape.*

At the T-junction in Plaine Joux turn left (you can see the Pointe de Miribel straight ahead). Walk up the open road (ignore the road off to the right), following the sign to Ajonc/Col de Creux. This takes you to Le Borbieu, which consists of two adjacent farms on the left, and shortly after to a T-junction (2hrs 5mins). Bear left at the T-junction which says Villard 7km and walk down the road (you are now leaving the GR du Pays Vallée Verte and the red splashes) for about 5mins until you see a wooden sign on your left to La Fully.

Follow blue splashes from here to the end of the walk. After passing through a fence the path is poorly defined and you are mainly walking in a stream bed. Go straight down past an old farm on your right and continue till you reach a road at La Fully opposite an old barn, with signposts. Keep left down the tarmac road following blue flashes till you get to a hairpin bend in dense coniferous wood. At this bend look for a sign to the right saying Le Bourgeau/Villard (3hrs) and continue downwards on a delightful leafy path keeping to the main track. There is a stream on the left and you then cross a rivulet coming down from the right (3hrs 10mins). Follow the continuing blue splashes which lead you down the slope of the hill with a drop on the left and the stream running through a ravine.

You reach a road and cross it three times, taking short cuts which are evident, following the blue splashes all the way arriving at an old public wash-house, dated 1902. There is also a shrine here on a wall with a statue of the Virgin, dated 1799, and two curious oriental heads below it; this is the pretty hamlet of Le Bourgeau. Continue straight down from here across the road (there is a worn blue flash on a concrete pylon) and turn left towards the church of Villard which is visible ahead.

There is an interesting inscription on the memorial in front of the church - "in memory of the children of Villard killed and burnt by the Germans in the Château of Habère-Lullin on Christmas Day 1943". Underneath are four names. Apparently there was a dance at the château and someone tipped off the Germans that members of the Resistance were present. They surrounded the château and shot four of the young people. When trying to get more information concerning this memorial, I encountered a certain reticence on the part of the locals. Many people in the Vallée Verte were part of the Resistance during the second world war (see Thorens-Glières). Feelings still run high, amongst the older inhabitants, between those who collaborated with the Germans and those who did not and certain families still do not speak to each other.

Take the turning left in front of the church and you come right out opposite the Mairie where your car is parked (3hrs 30mins).

Remarks: A lovely hike, even though there is some walking on roads, combining strolling through delightful Savoyard hamlets with some beautiful old farms, open fields and woods. It is an easy walk with no stiff climbing and not too long.

It is best done in springtime when there is still snow on the higher slopes.

12: MONTAGNE D'HIRMENTAZ - Alt. 1,598 metres
(Vallée Verte region)

Difficulty:	Medium - part of this walk is along a ridge.
Time:	3hrs 30mins.
Height gain:	404 metres.
Maps:	Editions Didier & Richard IGN No.3 Massifs du Chablais Faucigny & Genevois 1:50,000.

	Cartes IGN 3429 ET Top 25 Bonneville/Cluses and/or Promenades en Vallée Verte 1:25,000.
Depart from:	Col de Terramont - 1,096 metres.
Signposting:	Good - follow the red/yellow splashes.

How to get there (from Geneva)

Take the motorway direction Chamonix and exit at No.15, Boëge/St. Jeoire. Then turn briefly on the D.903 and watch for the D.9 right signposted Fillinges/Samoëns and Vallée Verte. Follow this road to the Pont de Fillinges and then turn left on the D.907 and after almost immediately right on the D.20 into the Vallée Verte, signposted Boëge. (ALTERNATIVELY go through

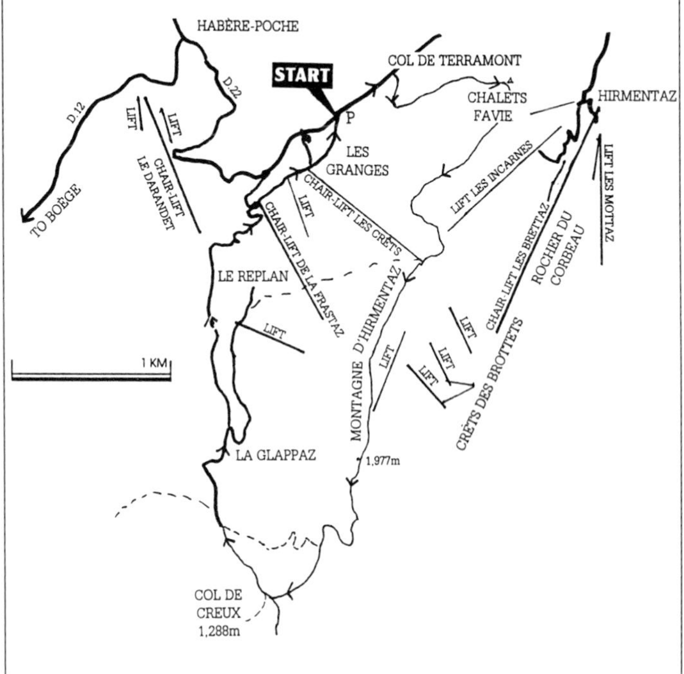

12: MONTAGNE D'HIRMENTAZ

Annemasse and take the D.907 to Taninges. Just before the Pont de Fillinges turn left on the D.20 into the Vallée Verte, signposted Boëge.) In the centre of Boëge, turn right on the D.22 towards Villard/Habère-Poche (8km). In Habère-Poche take the D.22 right to the Col de Terramont. Before you get to the col look for a parking area on the right-hand side just after the second road right signposted Les Granges (careful - there are two roads signposted Les Granges!) beyond a sign for the Habère-Poche Télésiège; park here as there is not much room at Les Mouilles (Col de Terramont) itself.

Directions

Walk up the road to the Col de Terramont, alt. 1,096m. At the last house on the right, which is a gîte de France, turn up right at a signpost saying Chalets Favie/Crêtes d'Hirmentaz/Le Replan. The path is not well defined but you can see a yellow/red splash on a tree further up (these are the signs for the Tour du Vallée Verte which you follow to the Col de Creux). It goes briefly up through a field into a sunken ditch and skirts the edge of the wood. Bear up to your left (10mins) where there is a warning cross on a tree straight ahead and then a minute later bear up left at a T-junction. Follow the red/yellow splashes and ignore any paths coming in. You are climbing a medium steep gradient through lovely woods with tall beech and coniferous trees; as the path starts to level out in light woodland, look out for a path up to your right, indicated by red/yellow splashes but with no sign (20mins).

This is a narrow path going up steeply through intermittent woodland; there is a lovely view down into the Vallée Verte. The path comes out into the open and you see signs up on your right. Beyond these, over a rise, are some rather ugly chalets called the Chalets Favie, alt.. 1,270m. Bear up to the right following the sign to the Col de Perret. Take the grassy path bearing straight round the foot of the hill which takes you into a shallow valley; you can now see the Hirmentaz mountain to the left and a long chair-lift on the higher ridge beyond (Crêt des Brottets). The undefined grassy path joins a wide muddy path, passing a stone trough with red/yellow splashes on it, heading towards a fold in the mountain. Go through a rather tumble-down fence (sometimes open to let the cattle through) where there is a sign pointing ahead to Crêtes d'Hirmentaz (45mins) and continue on the muddy path, past rocks with yellow/red splashes, making for another signpost you can see in front saying Crêtes Hirmentaz 25mins left/Col de Creux/La Glappaz. At the signpost there is a lovely view down into the Vallée Verte and in springtime the slopes are dotted with beautiful early purple orchids. Turn left here.

There are lots of little paths going up the slope so choose your own or follow the red/yellow splashes; make for the top of the ski-lifts which are coming from both left and right. The summit is a tumble of rocks, alt. 1,509m

(1hr 15mins) with an arrival hut for the chair-lift coming up from near where you parked the car; a drag lift from the other side also ends here. You can now see along the impressive jagged ridge of the Hirmentaz mountain and the path going all the way along the top, clearly marked with yellow/red splashes.

As you walk along this ridge you get dramatic views on both sides; to the right down into the Vallée Verte and beyond the lake with the Jura range in the background; to the left you look down into a dip where there are a number of ski-lifts, and over to the chair-lift going up the Brottet ridge; on the horizon is the Mont Blanc range - behind are the peaks of the Chablais mountains. The path is well trodden and undulates along the top - you come to a sign indicating you are at Les Feulattes with another ski-lift arriving from the left; there seem to be ski-lifts converging from all directions! In some places the path is vertiginous with sudden drops, mainly to the right, but there is no need for scrambling. You reach what appears to be the highest spot in the ridge (1hr 30mins) but there is no indication; this is a good place to stop and have your picnic.

Continue straight, past a sign pointing down left to Chemin de Crêts/ Pointe d'Hirmentaz, on a narrow defined path which goes under a fence still following the red/yellow splashes keeping to the ridge - ignore the wider path to the left. The path starts to drop and there is a lovely view of the nearby Pointe de Miribel, with its statue of the Virgin Mary on the summit. As you zigzag down there are lots of narrow converging paths but make for the jeep track on your left with a renovated barn, other chalets dotted about. Walk down the jeep track, passing a signpost at the Col de Creux, alt. 1,288m. *On this side of the hill the early purple orchids are even more magnificent in spring and make a striking contrast against the carpets of yellow dandelions and blue forget-me-nots.*

Just beyond the col (2hrs 15mins) where the jeep track bears left, turn right on a path through a sort of crease in the hill. This track takes you slightly down and round the mountain beside a shallow, grassy combe. You cross a small rivulet (signposts) reaching a small parking area and the road coming from Le Replan (2hrs 30mins).

Walk down the road, past the Auberge de Miribel on the left (a good place to stop for refreshment if it is open) and some lovely old farms. At a T-junction, alt. 1,174m, turn right following a sign to Le Replan/Habère-Poche. Walk down this narrow tarmac road, attractively dotted with chalets and renovated farms, mostly holiday homes; in springtime the verges are a riot of fluffy cow parsley and forget-me-nots. For a while the road goes through woods with a steep drop to the left as you wind back round the bottom of the Hirmentaz mountain. Continue down, turning up right at the T-junction by the Frastaz chair-lift and passing the Auberge Les Granges on the left and Les Crêtes chair-lift. At a fork in the road, go straight on following the sign Col de Terramont (left is indicated Les Lavourets/Habère-Poche) which will take you to where you parked your car (3hrs 30mins).

Remarks: The views from the Hirmentaz ridge are spectacular as it is the first range of hills rising from the lake; it is a pity that the the area is criss-crossed by numerous ski installations. The best time to do the walk is in springtime to appreciate the flowers, especially the abundance of early purple orchids. This walk can be combined with the Pointe de Miribel (Walk No. 9) which would make a very agreeable day's hike of about 5hrs.

Thistle

Chablais Region

13: MONT HERMONE - Alt. 1,412 metres
(Chablais region)

Difficulty:	Easy, though some uphill walking.
Time:	3hrs 30mins.
Height gain:	571 metres.
Maps:	Editions Didier & Richard IGN No.3 Massifs du Chablais Faucigny & Genevois 1:50,000. Cartes IGN 3428 ET Top 25 Thonon, Evian 1:25,000.
Depart from:	Reyvroz - Alt. 842 metres.
Signposting:	Good in parts.

How to get there (from Geneva)
Take the N.37/N.5 road to Thonon-Les-Bains. In Thonon take the D.26 direction Bellevaux. This takes you through the village of Armoy and then Reyvroz. ALTERNATIVELY take the motorway direction Chamonix and exit at No.15 Boëge/St. Jeoire. Then turn left briefly on the D.903 and watch for the D.9 right signposted Fillinges, Samoëns and Vallée Verte. Follow this road to the Pont de Fillinges and then turn right on the D.907 till you get to St. Jeoire. (ALTERNATIVELY from Annemasse take the D.907 direction Taninges until you reach St. Jeoire.) At St. Jeoire take the D.26 through the villages of Onnion, Megevette, Bellevaux and Vailly. Turn left to Reyvroz on the D126.. Park your car in front of the church where there is a big white statue of the Virgin Mary.

Directions
As you face the church go straight up a road which has a dead-end notice on it. There is a GR red/white splash on an electricity pole nearby (though we are not following the GR signs but the Balcon du Léman path). The road soon becomes a jeep track, briefly between old stone walls and comes to a charming little shrine called L'Oratoire des Pas, dated 1723. *Like many of the shrines in this region it is a small stone edifice with a primitive statue (usually of the Virgin), in a niche in the stone with a grill in front; this one even has a wooden roof on it.*

Go up to the left following a wooden sign saying Notre Dame de

Hermone and G.G. Hermone. This is a wide jeep track going up medium steep through bushes and light woodland; down on the left there is a lovely view of Reyvroz and the church. Keep straight on this jeep track following red/white splashes and ignore the path off to the right marked 524 with an orange arrow (15mins). You come into coniferous trees and later there is a fork right (there is a red/white warning cross to the left). The track winds upwards, through a fence and into a clearing with a big barn called Le Saut on the right (35mins). Keep going across the clearing, through intermittent woodland, and shortly afterwards you come onto the open pastureland of the Mont Hermone. *On the map this is called the Montagne des Soeurs (mountain of the nuns). I can find no explanation for this name except that in the 11th century it was called the Chemin des Chartreux as the monks used to cross here when they were going from their monastery near Lac Vallon to their establishment in Thonon.*

Do not go off to your right but keep straight; there is a cross on the top of the hill to your right and then you see two big, shabby barns which are the Granges d'Hermone, alt. 1,217m. Make for the signposts up on the right just past these barns (45mins) and follow the sign Notre Dame d'Hermone par la Crêt, a wide grassy track to the left going along the hill, shortly joining a muddy jeep track which takes you into coniferous wood (1hr). Take the left fork here, where there are white/red and yellow splashes and a sign saying Notre Dame d'Hermone 1hr (a little further on the left there is a narrow path signposted Vailly/La Côte).

You are now climbing up and along a very wide ridge through woodland and bushes, but with some open spaces where you get magnificent views. To the right you see over Lake Léman with the Jura mountains on the horizon. To the left, beyond the valley, are the Chablais peaks of (from left to right) the Dent d'Oche, Les Cornettes de Bise, Mont Chauffé, Mont Billiat, Pointe d'Ireuse and the Rocher de Nifflon. In the foreground, over to the right, is the Montage d'Hirmentaz in the Vallée Verte. The defined path undulates across the top of this wooded wide ridge, dropping down through tall pine forest at one stage and then up again. You come to some more signs (1hr 30mins); Notre Dame d'Hermone is still straight on while Les Combes/Vailly is down to the left. Further on go past another left branch to Les Combes/Reyvroz / Chevroz/Vailly (1hr 45mins) - this is the path you take on your way back. 5mins after go by yet a third fork left to Le Plan Suet/Vailly.

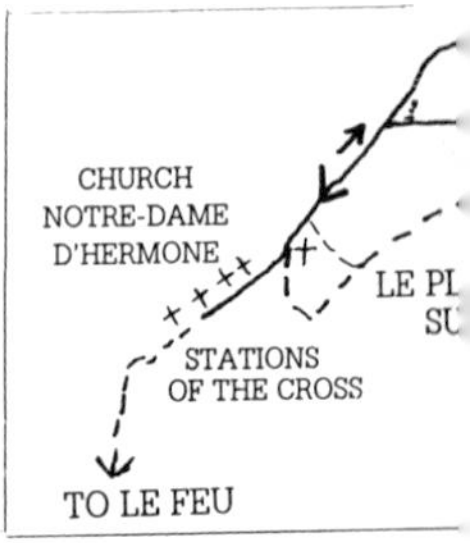

Shortly after a wind-sock for parapenting, the Chapel of Notre Dame d'Hermone is visible on your left, and you can go directly up a grassy path (2hrs). ALTERNATIVELY you can continue for a few minutes into woodland, until you hit a path going sharply up left with stations of the cross. Follow them (the path joins at the 10th station) up to the chapel. *These stations of the cross, which now look rather run-down, were put up in 1840 and are stone plinths with an iron crucifix on top. Each station was donated by one or more members of a neighbouring village, and the names of the contributors are carved on the stones. The church itself is quite austere with a galvanised iron roof, but it has a steeple with a cross and on top an impressive weather-vane in the shape of a cockerel - rather a pagan finish but typical of many churches in this region. On the roof of the church is an imposing white statue of Our Lady and at the side a more modern cross with "1975 Année de la Reconciliation" marked on it. There is also an outside stone altar. It is still the custom at Pentecost, the Feast of the Assumption (15 August) and on Our Lady's Birthday (8 September) for people to follow the stations of the cross up to the church and then hear open air mass. For*

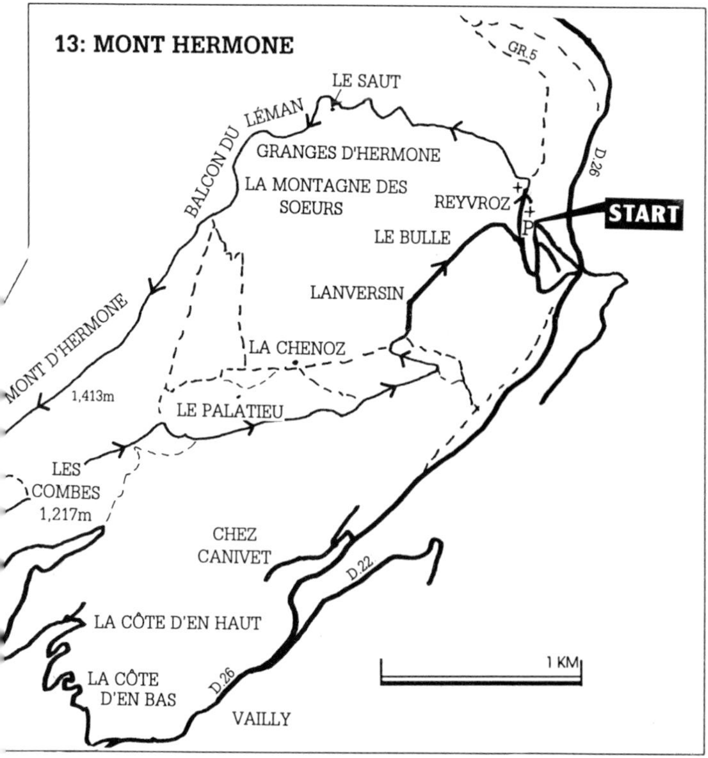

500 years a chapel has stood on this spot. Over the centuries it has suffered many vicissitudes, including being burnt down and turned into a dwelling in 1792 when the Bernese invaded the Savoie and Catholicism was outlawed. It was later rebuilt but fell into disrepair in the early 18th century and was rebuilt again in the late 1800s. More recently it was renovated in 1979 and the old doors were replaced in 1989, the year of its centenary. The church is situated on an open spur at the end of the Mont d'Hermone ridge and has a beautiful uninterrupted view of the surrounding Chablais peaks, as well as Lake Geneva.

Retrace your steps back along the ridge and take the second turning down on your right to Les Combes/Reyvroz. This is a lovely path winding back round the contour of the mountain; follow the occasional yellow spots carefully. The track goes through bushes, mainly raspberries, alder and hawthorn, though there is some juniper. These are then replaced by coniferous woods alternating with delightful open spaces where you can appreciate the wonderful views again. Pass in front of an abandoned chalet (note the lovely old trees around it - they are often planted by isolated dwellings to protect them from the wind), before reaching a junction left to Les Combes, alt. 1,200m, and straight on to Reyvroz (2hrs 20mins). It is worth going up to have at look at Les Combes which consists of three tumble-down old farm dwellings and some ruins. It is situated on a lovely open shelf in the hillside and must have once had cultivated fields around it and animals grazing. There is something rather sad in seeing what was once a thriving tiny community (they obviously only came up here in the summer) fall into neglect and disrepair, though one presumes it will not be long before someone comes along and renovates the buildings for holiday homes.

Go back down to the signpost and take the direction to Reyvroz. The path gets a bit steeper from here on and there are bare patches of hillside where the trees have been taken for logging (all replanted with tiny fir saplings), followed by sombre, dense patches of coniferous wood. You come to another signpost (2hrs 40mins) at a sort of cross-roads. Be careful to follow the sign Reyvroz par les Deux Sapins onto a small grassy path going straight on (avoid the wider one round to the right). The path is narrow and not always clear; follow the occasional yellow dots. It is still winding round the mountain through patches of dense, young coniferous wood. At another set of signposts (2hrs 50mins) go down right (Reyvroz 30mins). You join a logging track for a few minutes and then go down through beech wood to a fence on your right beyond which are open fields and a big old barn (3hrs).

Do not bear right into the field but continue straight following the ridge down through the beech wood; the path descends rather steeply and is not very obvious so look out for the yellow circles. 5mins later you emerge onto a wide track which leads to the meadow and barn up on the right. However, go down to the left and a few minutes later follow the signpost straight on to Reyvroz (left Chenoz/right Les Combes). Continue following the signs to Revroz. As you go down this jeep track, you have a lovely view of the little village, dominated by its church down below on the left, with beyond the serrated grey ridge of the Mémise with the Pic Boré alongside. There is also get a magnificent view of the two peaks of the Dent d'Oche.

When you come to a little wooden chalet (constructed by the farmer below so that he can enjoy the view), you are at Les Deux Sapins, alt. 895m, aptly named after the two big fir trees on your right. Continue down on the wide path and bear right at the bottom by the last lot of signposts (3hrs 15mins). You pass through the lovely old farm buildings of Lanversin and then meet the tarmac road. Walk through the hamlets of Le Bulle and Chez le Gaud before arriving at the village of Reyvroz (3hrs 30mins).

Remarks: Hermone is the French translation of the ancient name of this mountain which was Armonna. It is a delightful ridge walk, 3.5km long, which is not difficult and which gives extensive views of the surrounding Chablais countryside and peaks, as well as the lake with the Jura mountains on the skyline. This is one of my favourite areas of the Haute Savoie as it is relatively unspoilt, though it is near the towns of Thonon and Evian. The director of the local syndicat d'initiative very kindly took me round the route after I had lost my way on a first attempt. At the same time he cleared the track which had become rather overgrown and promised me that he would repaint the yellow circles!

14: PIC DES MÉMISES - Alt. 1,677 metres
(Chablais region)

Difficulty:	Medium steep up and down. Easy ridge walk.
Time:	5hrs 15mins.
Height gain:	750 metres.
Maps:	Editions Didier & Richard IGN No.3 Massifs du Chablais Faucigny & Genevois 1:50,000. Cartes IGN 3528 ET Top 25 Morzine Massif du Chablais 1:25,000.
Depart from:	Church just before village of Thollon - 922 metres.
Signposting:	Sporadic - lots of yellow/blue/green splashes in places.

How to get there (from Geneva)

Take the N.37/N.5 road through Thonon-Les-Bains to Evian-Les-Bains. From Evian follow the signs to Neuvecelle/Thollon. This becomes the D.24 which you should follow towards Thollon. Just before you come to the village, after the hamlet of Chez Cachat, park in front of the church which you will see on your right-hand side.

Directions

Take the narrow, tarmac road which goes to the right of the church (as you are facing the church from the road), through scattered chalets until you meet a T-junction. Turn right and continue to the hamlet of Chez Les Vesins (10mins). In the middle of the hamlet by a fountain there is a sign on a tree, marked Creusaz. Turn left and there is another sign to Col de Pertuis/Col de Creusaz further on as the tarmac road becomes a wide defined path. Follow the green splashes you will see on the rocks; the path is stony but pleasant going up through woodland. Ignore all pathways branching off and at a 4-way junction (25mins) take the path straight on where there is a green arrow and a signpost to Col de Creusaz.

Ignore all paths going off to the right or left and continue straight up. When the track enters a meadow be sure to take the right fork going up through the trees. You come out into attractive open fields (45mins), carpeted with flowers in springtime, and the going becomes flat. Continue till you reach the first large chalet, which is the Col de Creusaz, alt. 1,160m. Be careful, do not continue down the road here but turn sharp left at a dilapidated wooden sign where there are yellow/blue/green splashes (55mins). The path is well defined through open fields and woods and you get your first view of Lake Geneva down on your left. Watch for the multi-coloured splashes on the stones. Ignore the path branching off to your right and go straight. At a fork (1hr 10mins) bear left and a few minutes later go through a metal gate.

Shortly after the gate there are markings on a tree to the right, but continue towards a signpost you can see ahead in the open meadow. Careful here, do not follow the defined path which goes on from the signpost, as this curls round the bottom of the mountain, but follow the sign right saying Col de Perthuis. There is no clear path initially but strike up the hill for a few metres (there are signs on a fir tree) until you meet the well-defined higher track going up the mountain by the side of a fence. This is steep and narrow with blue/yellow/green splashes on rocks. Continue up the hill, past a water trough (1hr 45mins), winding steeply up the mountain (ignore paths branching off, but there are some obvious short cuts). Appreciate the beautiful open views of the lake behind you as you get nearer and nearer the impressive rock face of the Pic des Mémises (1hr 50mins). Pass through a stile

14: PIC DES MÉMISES
15: PIC BORÉ

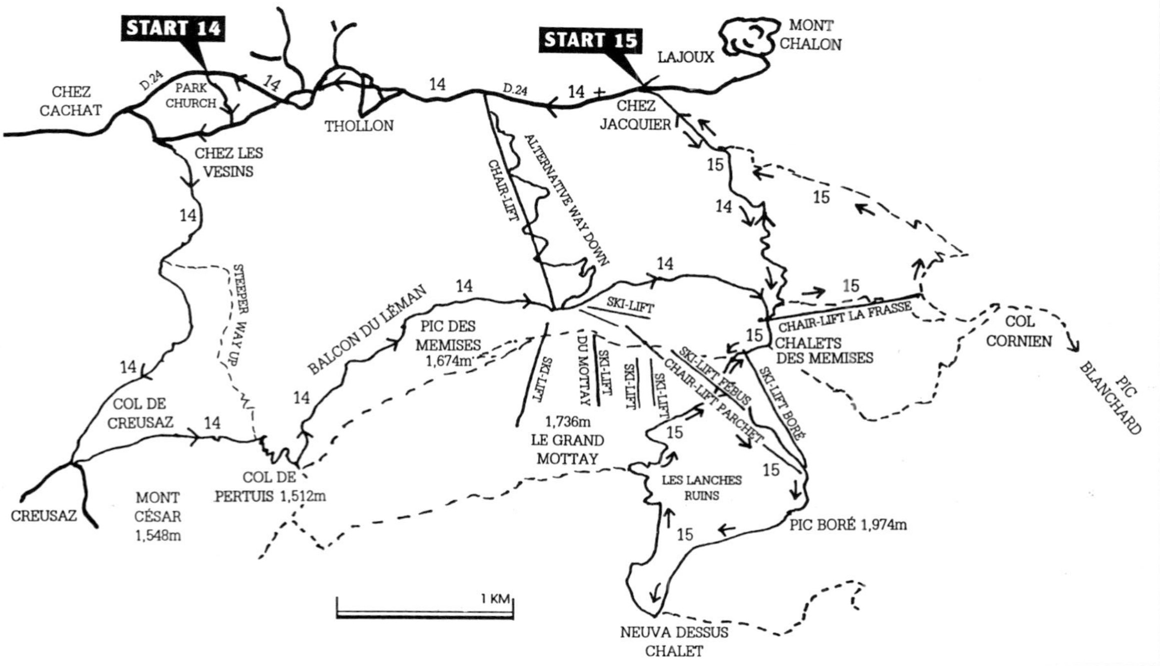

and, shortly after, go up to your left at a T-junction. The path gets steeper and stonier as you approach the Col de Perthuis, alt. 1,512m, where you get your first breathtaking view of the mountain ranges on the other side, dominated by the rearing peak of the nearby Dent d'Oche, alt. 2,221m.

Turn left at the next signpost (2hrs 20mins) towards the Pic des Mémises left (right to La Rasse, straight on to Chalets des Mémises). This is a steep open path up to the first peak, called the Perthuis, alt. 1,632m (2hrs 35mins). *After this short, steep climb it is worth stopping for refreshment as further along the ridge, in summertime, you risk meeting the crowds coming up in the chair-lift.*

The big climb is now over! At the Perthuis carry on up left along a wide ridge path to the Pic des Mémises, alt. 1,682m, which is marked with a cross. You are now on the Grande Randonnée Balcon du Léman which goes all round the lake. The views on both sides are extensive; to the left you see right over the lake with the Jura mountains beyond and to the right the sombre looking Pic Boré, alt. 1,974m, with the Dent d'Oche behind. Continue along the ridge, passing an ugly, tall electricity pylon with a GR sign on it (2hrs 5mins), two chalets and finally the cable-car station which also has a restaurant (3hrs 15mins).

(ALTERNATIVE: It is possible here to take the path going down from the cable-car, signposted Thollon, but it is steep, stony and rather boring.) At this point this lovely mountain ridge has been spoilt by several ski installations which have not been tastefully built and mar the landscape.

Just after the cable-car building the path forks - take the left upper fork as this continues along the ridge and there are better views. Follow the signposts to Chalets des Mémises. You pass by a parapenting jump-off area and then a second cross (3hrs 30mins). From this point you have a different but equally impressive view of the Swiss Vaudois alps with the massive Diablerets peaks and the town of Montreux nestling below on the other side of the lake. Continue till you see the Chalets des Mémises over on your right and, nearer, the top of the Télésiège de la Frasse. Make for the signposts which are visible just beyond the chair-lift. Turn left towards the Col de Corniens. This takes you down a jeep track, under the ski-lift again and past a slope of reddish rock to your left. Just after this rock and before you go through a turnstile, take a narrow path on your left (3hrs 45mins) where there are red and white marks on a rock and a signpost to Chez Jacquier. Careful, this is easy to miss!

The path drops steeply down the front of the mountain, snaking down into a wide cleft in the hillside. Be careful to watch out for the red splashes on the rocks or you could land up in a dry river bed. Take care in wet weather as the path is slippery and you have to watch your footing sometimes as you pick your way down. There are magnificent views of the lake in front and you

The Chablais peaks of (L to R) Pic des Mémises (Walk 14) Pic Boré (Walk 15) La Dent d'Oche (Walk 17)

feel you could almost jump into it! As you lose height the vegetation becomes denser (watch for nettles) and there are lots of wild raspberry bushes. The path goes through young coniferous trees for a few minutes before joining a wide jeep track (4hrs 45mins). Here there are signposts. Go left towards Lajoux and a few minutes later you hit the D.24 at Chez Jacquier. Turn left towards Thollon. Not long after there is an attractive grotto with a statue of Our Lady on the right.

Take the obvious short cut to the right. You arrive in the centre of Thollon (4hrs 55mins) having passed the cable-car station. There are a number of cafés, shops and modern chalets but it is not very pretty, most of it having been purpose-built for the skiing trade. Walk through the modern village and take another short cut on the right when the road turns left. Note the exceptionally large stone trough, no doubt formerly used as the village laundry, and the curious house opposite with wooden carvings of the local fauna. Cross the road at the bottom and continue on down with the church now visible in front of you. When you join the D.24 again turn right to get back to the car park in front of the church (5hrs 15mins).

Remarks: This walk is a must as the Mémises ridge is the first high mountain south of Lake Geneva, so has the most incredible views of the surrounding countryside; you can see right over the lake to the Jura and Vaudois mountain ranges and back to the main peaks of the Chablais region. If you are tired at the top you can avoid the steep path down by taking the cable-car (open during the skiing season and in July and August).

15: PIC BORÉ - Alt. 1,947 metres (see map p111)
(Chablais region)

Difficulty:	Medium steep - the walk along the summit is airy and not for anyone who suffers from vertigo.
Time:	5hrs 45mins.
Height gain:	877 metres.
Maps:	Editions Didier & Richard IGN No.3 Massifs du Chablais Faucigny & Genevois 1:50,000. Cartes IGN 3528 ET Top 25 Morzine Massif du Chablais 1:25,000.
Depart from:	Chez Jacquier (Nr. Lajoux, Thollon) - 1,052 metres.
Signposting:	Good new signposting most of the way plus red/ white splashes.

How to get there (from Geneva)
Take the N.37/N.5 road through Thonon-Les-Bains to Evian-Les-Bains. From Evian follow the signs to Neuvecelle/Thollon. This becomes the D.24 which you should follow all the way to Thollon and then to Lajoux. Just before you enter Lajoux, at Chez Jacquier, look for a blue signpost on the left which says Lajoux/Grand Roche du Mont Chalon. Park on the grassy verge behind the sign and take the jeep track going up the hill opposite. There is a no entry sign at the start and a signpost saying Col de Corniens/La Frasse/Nordevaux.

Directions
Take the wide stony jeep track which is flattish at first and then starts to climb gradually through beech and coniferous wood with some open country. After 10mins follow the sign to the right indicating La Frasse. This is a narrow path which goes through dense dwarf fir trees for about 5mins and then comes out on to the open hillside. The uphill gradient is steep and winding, through wild raspberry and alder bushes, at first through a wide cleft in the hillside and then becoming more open as it goes higher. Follow the occasional red splashes and take time to look back and appreciate the wonderful view of Lake Geneva with the town of Vevey on the Swiss shore, the gentle Vaudois countryside and the Vaudois peaks beyond.

This climb is tiring and you are thankful to reach the top at a jeep track by the chair-lift of La Frasse (1hr 15mins). Follow signs right to Crêts de Memises on the jeep track and then under the chair-lift towards the signposts at La Frasse, alt. 1,620m heading for the Chalets des Mémises which you can see in front of you. This area is a wide valley which is criss-crossed with ski-lifts of various kinds. To the right you can see the long shoulder of the Mémises mountain and the top of the télécabine which goes down to Thollon; ahead are the sombre cliffs of the Pic Boré. As you approach the chalets make for a new wide, muddy jeep track which you can see behind on the right following sign Boré 1hr. Pass underneath the Téléski du Boré and keep it on your left as you walk up, with the Téléski Fébus on your right and another chair-lift (Télésiège Parchet) beyond.

The track doubles back underneath the Téléski and chair-lift as you come to the top of the first hill, where there is a small hut (the top of the Téléski Fébus). Keep between the two ski-lifts making for the path you can see ahead which goes to the bottom of the Pic Boré. Continue up fairly steeply over open pasture towards the little hut which is the end of the chair-lift Parchet (2hrs 15mins). Beyond the hut the path becomes fairly steep and exposed; at this stage there are orange splashes which you should follow. This leads into a wide, steepish, grassy chimney in the rock face of the Pic Boré, which requires some clambering but it is short and not technically difficult.

The chimney only takes 10mins followed by a short final climb to a further hump which is the Pic Boré itself, alt. 1,974m (2hrs 25mins). This is a good spot to stop if the weather is fine and there is no wind, while you admire the vast panorama of the entire lake, the towns and countryside of the Swiss shore and the Vaudois, Valais and Jura mountain ranges; just behind the ridge are the magnificent rocky slopes of the Dent d'Oche, alt. 2,221m. Walk along the ridge on a defined path which is rather narrow and airy, making for the cross you can see at the end, alt. 1,938m (2hrs 40mins).

At the cross you can see the Chalets de Neuva Dessus as you look towards the village of Bernex in the valley below. Make your way down through a fence across the open alpine pasture; there is a track but it is not very clear. The chalets consist of one big, unused cow barn and a shepherd's hut (3hrs).

On the side of the barn there is a red/white GR sign as you have now joined a variant of the Balcon du Léman (you can see the main track going off to the left up the Dent d'Oche). Go down the open path, following the GR sign on a rock to the right, and make for the woods further down the slope (do not go round towards the fence which is following the contour of the hill); at this stage the path is badly defined. As you enter light coniferous wood you can see the GR marks clearly. Go through a stile and the path improves as you see it ahead winding round the bottom of the mountain down to the valley and then becoming a jeep track, climbing up again to a ski-lift on the horizon.

The path is narrow and in places rather grown over with bushes and long grass; at times there is quite a drop on one side. Follow the GR signs all the way till you come to the ruins of Les Lanches, a large square wall about a metre high which must originally have been a barn (3hrs 20mins). Look for the GR sign on the wall to the right and follow the path down till you cross a stream at the bottom of an unspoilt valley. Ahead is Le Grand Mottay and behind the Mémises ridge with Mont César to the left. Continue on the path till you reach the muddy jeep track. Follow sign Chalets de Mémises (3hrs 35mins) up right towards the ridge leaving the GR path which goes down left (a variant of the Balcon du Léman). There are yellow splashes all the way up this rather tedious track. Go past another ruin on the right before tackling the last steep gradient up to the crest and under the chair-lift Parchet again (3hrs 55mins).

You are now back in the wide Mémises valley dotted with lifts; make for the path you took from the Chalets des Mémises and continue from there to the chalets and the signposts beyond (4hrs 5mins). Follow the sign to Col de Cornien, on a wide jeep track with a medium gradient down the mountain following the Frasse chair-lift; there are blue splashes all the way (on the left at the top you will see the start of the steep path you took on your way up beside curious red mud banks probably caused by erosion). At the bottom is the Frasse chair-lift hut (4hrs 30mins) near a stream. Follow the road round (or take a narrow path ahead which is a short cut through the woods) crossing two streams, till it connects with the path going up to the Pic Blanchard marked by blue and orange splashes.

Bear down left onto a wide jeep track, winding through coniferous forest where a lot of logging is being done. Cross a stream by a beautiful waterfall before going under a rusty pylon and past the signpost to the Chalets des Mémises taken on the outward journey, to arrive at Chez Jacquier (5hrs 45mins).

Remarks: Although this walk is not long it is quite challenging, incorporating a steep upward climb at the start, the scrambling through the wide chimney to the summit and the ridge walk. If you are reasonably fit and not afraid of heights it is worth doing. There are lots of ski installations but somehow the dramatic views offset this disadvantage.

16: PIC BLANCHARD - Alt. 1,526 metres
(Chablais region)

Difficulty:	Medium; some gully crossings to negotiate.
Time:	4hrs 30mins.
Height gain:	474 metres.
Maps:	Editions Didier & Richard IGN No. 3 Massifs du Chablais Faucigny & Genevois 1:50,000.

	Cartes IGN 3528 ET Top 25 Morzine Massif du Chablais 1:25,000.
Depart from:	Chez Jacquier (Nr. Lajoux, Thollon) - 1,052 metres.
Signposting:	Adequate - orange splashes most of the way.

How to get there (from Geneva)

Take the N.37/N.5 road through Thonon-Les-Bains to Evian-Les-Bains. From Evian follow the signs to Neuvecelle/Thollon. This becomes the D.24 which you should follow all the way to Thollon and then to Lajoux. Just before you enter Lajoux, at Chez Jacquier, look for a blue signpost on the left which says Lajoux/Grand Roche du Mont Chalon. Park on the grassy verge behind the sign and take the jeep track going uphill opposite. There is a no entry sign at the start and a signpost with Col des Corniens/La Frasse/Nordevaux.

Directions

Take the wide stony jeep track which is flattish at first and then starts to climb gradually through beech and coniferous wood with some open country. After 10mins go straight past a sign to the right which says La Frasse and then walk underneath a rusty pylon. The track winds on a balcony path round the north-eastern base of the Mémises mountain with a steepish drop to the left. There are glorious views of the lake all along this path getting more extensive as you go higher; you can also see the towns of Vevey and Montreux on the Swiss side with the charming little Vaudois lake (Lac de Bret) nestling in the hills across the water with the Vaudois alps beyond. You pass a waterfall (25mins) where the water streams across the track if it has been raining after which the gradient begins to steepen.

Keep on the main jeep track snaking upwards, following the orange markings on trees and rocks. For some of the time there is a stream running down on your left. Eventually, through the fir trees to the right, you can see the hut which is the start of the Frasse chair-lift up to the Mémises ski complex (50mins). Pass over a cattle grid and into a wide, open dell called La Plaine with the rocky Pointe de Corniens dominating the skyline. Keep straight at a wooden sign to the right indicating La Frasse (55mins). The path seems to be going straight for this rocky peak but then skirts up to the left out of the dell; you can see another téléski way over in the woods on the other side.

The path goes through a crease in the mountains at the Col de Corniens, alt. 1,426m, where there there is a pulley for hauling logs. Here you join the white/red GR splashes of the Balcon du Léman path. You are now in another open dip with the téléski de Corniens spoiling the landscape. Keep going gently downhill on the open jeep track with the Chalets des Corniens visible ahead, which consist of a large tumble-down barn and a small wooden chalet (1hr 10mins); behind are the rocky crags of the Pointe de l'Aiguille, alt.

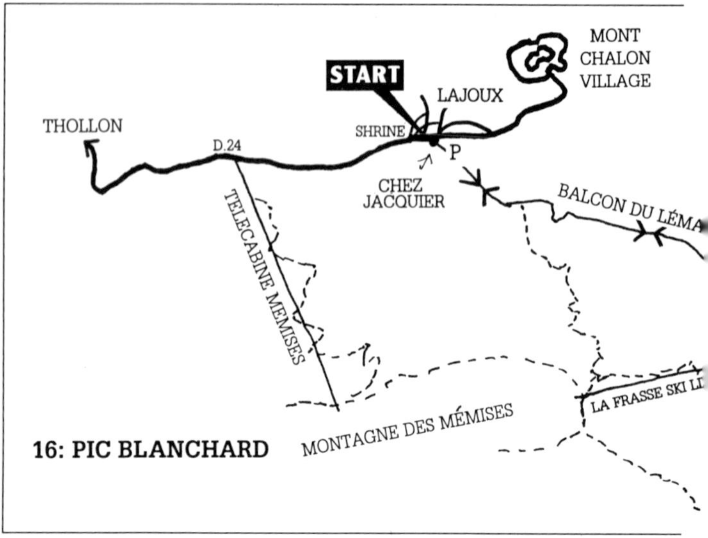

1,716m. Go by the stone fountain in front of the barn. There is a sign saying Novel on the wall and further on orange marks and red/white splashes on rocks to the right. Continue on the narrow path towards Novel, past a sign up to the right to Nordevaux. Go straight on (1hr 20mins) over a little stream.

The steep stony path flattens out before going down again and undulating round the side of the mountain in a sort of circle through scrub, wood and open areas. There are more beautiful views over the lake and you can see the tower of the radio station above Montreux. You traverse some narrow, muddy gullies with streams running through them and quite a drop to the left, so be careful, especially if it has been raining.

Still following the GR splashes and orange markings, fork right at a T-junction,. towards the Col de Blanchard/Novel (1hr 55mins). The path becomes a jeep track here but then narrows again; up in front are the grassy alpine meadows of the Pic Blanchard. Still in woodland, cross two more tricky gullies and ignore the path up to the right signposted Novel (2hrs 5mins) where the Balcon du Léman continues over the Col de Blanchard down to the village of Novel. Continue straight and 5mins later there is an abandoned hut on the left; look above this hut for a good view of the Pointe de l'Aritte, alt. 1,626m. Shortly after there is an unusual perspective of the lake in the V between two plunging hillsides. The path becomes easier before entering long waving grassland, which looks as if it has never been grazed. Note, the orange markings disappear here.

Follow the crushed path through the long grass along the middle of the hillside and then up to the crest (there may be no defined path over this section in high summer). From the crest of the hill (2hrs 20mins) there is a fantastic view down to the end of the lake and the start of the Rhône valley, with the alpine peaks beyond, dominated by the Diableret. Behind are the main Chablaiš summits of the Dent d'Oche, Cornettes de Bises, Pic Boré and the Pic des Mémises. Go left along the wide crest of the hill on a defined path, till you reach the stone marker (borne) of the Pic Blanchard, alt. 1,472m, on a grassy hump (2hrs 30mins). From here you look down onto the village of St. Gingolph, which has the Swiss/French border running right through its

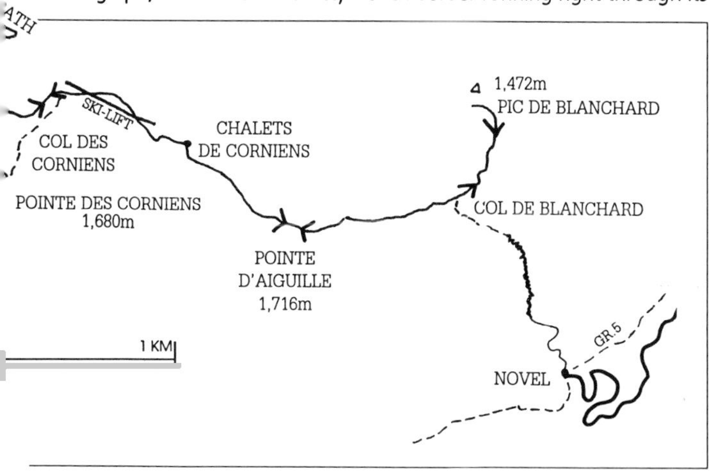

centre.

Go back along the crest of the hill and follow the path down, or take a short cut diagonally across the hill, to catch the defined path back through the woods. Retrace your steps to where you parked the car (4hrs 30mins).

Remarks: There is a lot of logging in this area so it may be muddy, especially after rain. However, the views of the lake, the Vaudois mountains and towns on the Swiss side of the lake as you are climb up are magnificent, only surpassed by the overall panorama at the summit. You will not find crowds of people at any time of the year so it is an ideal walk in high summer; there is also plenty of shade and water.

17: LA DENT D'OCHE - Alt. 2,221 metres

(Chablais region)

Difficulty:	Difficult - this walk is steep and has chains in some places. Not for anyone afraid of heights.
Height gain:	1,120 metres.
Time:	5hrs 15mins.
Depart from:	La Fétiùre (near Bernex) Alt. 1,286m.
Maps:	Editions Didier & Richard IGN No.3 Massifs du Chablais Faucigny & Genevois 1:50,000. Cartes IGN 3528 ET Top 25 Morzine Massif du Chablais 1:25,000.
Signposting:	Adequate - red splashes on the way up only though path is obvious.

How to get there (from Geneva)

Take the N.37/N.5 (lake road) through Thonon-Les-Bains towards Evian. Where the road crosses the Dranse river take the D.32 right signposted Bernex/St. Paul-en Chablais. Follow this road through Publier (D.11) towards St. Paul-en-Chablais (D.21) and then follow the D.52 to Bernex. (ALTERNATIVELY go to Evian and take the D.21 signposted St. Paul-en-Chablais and then D.52 to Bernex.) At the entrance to Bernex do not turn down right but carry on straight along a narrower road (not well signposted) through the hamlets of Trossy and Charmet. After Charmet you come to a bridge. Go right across the bridge and past a large café/restaurant on the right and continue for about 2km till you come to a small parking area with the chalet (café in season) of La Fétiùre on the left.

Directions

Follow the wooden sign post indication La Dent d'Oche 2hrs 30mins, past La Fétiùre on a wide rocky path which goes steeply up through widely spaced woods with a stream on the left; in parts the path has curious rocky ridges which makes walking uncomfortable. Cross the stream on a wooden bridge called Pont des Bures, constructed in 1990 (20mins), where the path comes out onto alpine pasture. There is a magnificent view of the formidable looking Dent d'Oche rock in front but do not get discouraged!! It has an unusual formation; a rocky peak rearing up in front, the Château d'Oche, alt. 2,197m, which sweeps down to a grassy ridge called the Col de Planchamp and then up the long rocky ridges of the Dent d'Oche itself (dent means tooth).

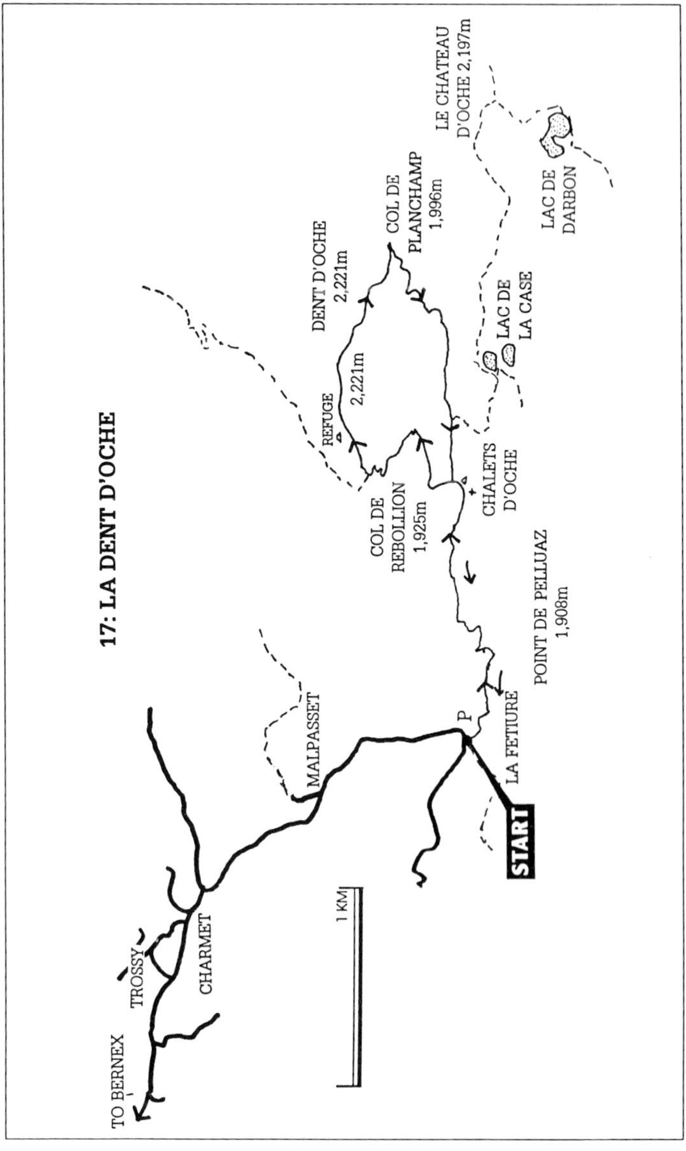
17: LA DENT D'OCHE
LE CHATEAU D'OCHE 2,197m
LAC DE DARBON
COL DE PLANCHAMP 1,996m
DENT D'OCHE 2,221m
2,221m
LAC DE LA CASE
REFUGE
CHALETS D'OCHE
COL DE REBOLLION 1,925m
POINT DE PELLUAZ 1,908m
P
LA FETIURE
START
MALPASSET
1 KM
CHARMET
TROSSY
TO BERNEX

Continue on this defined path which climbs gently along the bottom of the mountain, past a low ruin with coniferous woods set back on the right and the rearing slopes of the Dent d'Oche on your left. Re-cross the stream, which has now become a rivulet, and follow the intermittent yellow, orange or mauve markings (I wish they would be consistent with their colours but they seem to choose a different one each year!). On a grassy knoll up on the left is a wooden cross.

Crosses, statues and stone plaques in a mountain setting always send a shiver of apprehension through me as they are usually erected in memory of someone who died at that spot and there is a ghoulish thrill in reading the details - was he/she young or old and did they fall or were they flattened by an avalanche? In a certain sense they are timely reminders of how vulnerable we are in these mountain areas and how careful and vigilant one must be - and yet what a wonderful way to go! - suddenly, in the most beautiful surroundings and forever immortalised in stone or wood for countless walkers to contemplate.

At the Chalets d'Oche, alt. 2,150m (1hr), you have already climbed 400m. Here they house the flocks of sheep to be seen on the surrounding slopes and there is a large water trough which makes a refreshing stop on a hot day. Look back for a magnificent view of Lac Léman and surroundings before following the Dent d'Oche sign on the side of the building on a path round the hut and straight up the slope. On the right you can see the narrow valley you will come back down and a beautiful high waterfall. The path goes up steeply and then bears right along the side of the mountain, as if you are making for the cleft between the two peaks which is the Col de Planchamp - there is a dramatic view of the Château d'Oche ahead and, across the valley on the right, the interesting grassy mountain ridge of the Pointe de Pelluaz with the silhouettes of two crosses. However, the track winds round to the left instead of continuing towards the ridge where you can see two attractive little lakes on the other side - one green and the other brown - which, after discussion, we decided was mainly bog covered with weed.

You come to a signpost (1hr 40mins) which indicates right to the Refuge de la Dent d'Oche 30mins and left to the Col de Rebollion/Novel 4hrs. From the Chalets d'Oche you have been on the GR.5 which goes from Lake Léman (Lake Geneva) to Chamonix and eventually to Nice. It is worth a detour to the Col de Rebollion, alt. 1,925m (5mins), to appreciate the magnificent view in front of Mt. César and the Pic des Mémises ridge with the lake beyond and Jura mountains on the horizon; to the right is the serrated crest of the Pic Boré.

Retrace your steps to the signpost (1hr 40mins) and take the path going up steeply to the Refuge de la Dent d'Oche. When it forks round a jutting rock it is better to take the left-hand side which is rockier and has chains to hang

Young ibex on La Dent d'Oche

on to (the right side has more scree). You are climbing into a sort of rocky funnel and it becomes a hands and feet job as you scramble up steeply with the help of chains (be extra careful in wet weather when the rocks are slippery). Follow the yellow arrows up this chimney where there are three lots of chains before you reach the refuge at alt. 2,113m (2hrs 30mins), perched rather grimly on a rocky mound.

Refuge de Dent d'Oche, tel. 50.73.71.53 or 50.73.60.53
owned by the French Alpine Club. Guardian: M. Begain.
Dormitory accommodation for about 80 people.
Evening meals - fondue, snacks and soup available.

Continue on the path going round and up the mountain at the back of the refuge. This is another steep scramble over rocks following yellow arrows - you need to use both hands and there are cables provided which is a great help! You climb onto a rocky shoulder - airy is the word for it, but it is not as bad as it looks from below! Continue along this ridge to a new iron cross dated 1981 (blessed in September 1982). From the cross it is a few minutes to the real summit, alt. 2,221m (3hrs). The views are breathtaking, especially of the nearby Cornettes de Bise *(this is hearsay as every time I have done this part of the walk the clouds have obscured the view!).*

The path continues along the ridge, going down from the summit - be careful here as this is the north side and snows hangs around late in the season. There is a helpful chain at one place as you pick your way carefully through scree and rock, watching where you place your feet! The path is obvious but curiously there are no yellow flashes here. At an imposing expanse of wide flat rock there is a 20m cable for support as you feel your way across, but again it looks more difficult than it actually is as there are numerous footholds. A few minutes later there is another chain where you climb in and over a rocky gully. After these tricky bits are over, you come off the rock onto grassy mountainside, heading towards the Col de Planchamp with views of the narrow valley on the right, and the two small lakes over the mountain ridge beyond.

Keep a watch out for bouquetins (ibex) and chamois as this mountain has quite a colony. They are used to walkers and are curiously tame, not leaping out of sight when you approach them. In early summer the young ones are overcome by curiosity and almost bound towards you! Listen also for the marmot's whistle of alarm as you pass through the rocky meadows - this is perfect marmot territory!

After negotiating a steep grassy slope you reach the Col de Planchamp (4hrs); behind it is the huge cliff of the Château d'Oche with an intriguing looking cave opening at the bottom (but too far up to reach!). There is a magnificent view from both sides of the col - to the north the valley drops down to the village of Novel with the lake beyond; across the lake is Montreux with the motorway snaking behind and the Vaudois alps in the background.

The defined path curves downwards into the top end of the valley towards the Chalets d'Oche which you can see in front. There are various branches off to the left in the direction of the two lakes seen from above, and near the chalets there are signs to Lac de la Case 20mins/Les Portes d'Oche 1hr 20min/Point de Pelluaz 1hr 30mins. The path is pleasantly undulating through the valley floor until you come back to the Chalets d'Oche (4hrs 30mins). From here you retrace your steps to the Buvette de la Fétuière and the car (5hrs 15mins).

Remarks: This is a lovely walk and another Chablais classic. I have done it three times and the summit has always been enveloped in cloud so there is a strange mystical feel about it. The unusual shape of this mountain, which is really two distinct ranges, can be recognised from afar and resembles two spaced out teeth (hence its name). Unlike the Roc d'Enfer or the Cornettes de Bise, it does not inspire me with fear though it is just as hard to climb! This is not a mountain for anyone who hates heights or clinging to chains over steep slopes but it is a wonderful experience and a must for the more intrepid explorer of the Haute Savoie peaks.

18: ROUND MONT CHAUFFÉ - Alt. 1,693 metres
(Chablais region)

Difficulty:	Three steep up and down gradients, but not difficult.
Time:	5hrs.
Height gain:	873 metres (in three climbs).
Maps:	Editions Didier & Richard IGN No.3 Massifs du Chablais Faucigny & Genevois 1:50,000. Cartes IGN 3528 ET Top 25 Morzine Massifs du Chablais 1:25,000.
Depart from:	Le Mont 1,166 metres.
Signposting:	Very good in parts.

How to get there (from Geneva)

Take the N.37/N.5 to Thonon-Les-Bains and then the D.902 direction Morzine. This takes you along the Dranse river gorge which is popular for rafting and canoeing. At Bioge turn left on the D.22 into the Abondance valley. In Abondance village, either take the small road behind the abbey or continue on till you see a sign saying Le Mont to the left (these roads converge). It is about 2km to Le Mont where you can park at the end of the road behind a big chalet and by a stream (there is not much room).

Directions

Take the wide, stony jeep track upwards following signposts to Col de la Plagne du Mont 45mins/Autigny 1hr 15mins; on the left is a rushing stream and if you look behind there is a lovely view of the snowy peak of Mont de Grange. Cross the stream (5mins) ignoring first path to the left, keep straight up through coniferous forest; there are red splashes on rocks. When the track forks (10mins), bear left following the red splashes. There is a lovely view of the Abondance valley through the trees as the path curls round to the left of the Mont Chauffé rising not too steeply.

5mins later you come to Les Raffours, alt. 1,319m. Follow the sign to Autigny 1hr and shortly after walk through La Plagne du Mont, which consists of an open glade with two typical Abondance style chalets (see Vallée d'Abondance). Afterwards you start climbing again and cross over a stream in and out of coniferous woods and open meadowland. Continue following the red splashes. *In spring there are carpets of flowers in these meadows, including the birdseye primrose which has a cluster of attractive pink five petalled flowers on the end of a long stalk, the marsh marigold and the yellow oxlip (I counted a record number of 17 heads on one oxlip here).*

At a T-junction on a pebbled road (25mins) follow the signpost left towards Autigny up to the Col de la Plagne du Mont, alt. 1,546m, where there is a cross dated 1983. Do not continue on to the Chalets d'Autigny but branch right to Ubine on an attractive grassy path with scattered firs and in spring masses of flowers, especially the trumpet gentians and large purple pansies. This is a wide grassy undulating path with a fence on the right. After 15mins you leave the fence and start to go down quite steeply through woodland. In places there is quite a steep drop to the left. If you are doing this walk in spring, you realise, when you come out on to the bare mountainside, that you are on the north side of the mountain as the vegetation is way behind and the snow has only just left the slopes. There are carpets of little white and purple crocuses and anemones which are the first flowers to bloom after the snow. You are now following the long distance footpath of the Portes de Soleil but there are no red splashes. At the bottom of the hill cross the river before arriving at Ubine.

Ubine (1hr 30mins) is a hamlet with some attractive old chalets, many with their original wooden roofs (see Vallée d'Abondance). There is a beautiful old chapel built in 1611, renovated in 1852 and then again in 1971. It is incredible to think that this remote spot was inhabited so long ago. Go inside the chapel and admire the ancient stone altar and some primitive stained glass windows. The steeple has an attractive weathervane in the shape of a cockerel and the stone tiles of the roof have been stuck straight on to the rafters. In Ubine there is also a large modern chalet belonging to the Amis de la Nature (Friends of Nature) organisation, where you can stay the night (see Accommodation). You can see the path going up towards the col, but it is very eroded so difficult to follow. You are walking up the side of a shallow valley with the massive cliffs of the Mont Chauffé over on the right and Ubine down below in a sort of amphitheatre; the gradient becomes quite steep as you get nearer the pass.

At the Col d'Ubine, alt. 1,633m, which is your second col of the day, there is a sign ahead to Chevennes 45mins and left to Chalet de Mens 15mins. The direct way to Chevennes is down a couloir (corridor) of steep scree, often covered with snow in spring. It is wiser to take the left route to Chalet de Mens which traverses the mountain and is less difficult. The path is fairly precipitous as the hill drops away steeply at first; lower down it gets rocky in places and you have to pick your way carefully. You can see below where the path meets the road going to the Chalet de Mens. There is a good view of the Cornettes de Bise mountain rearing up straight ahead and the cliffs of

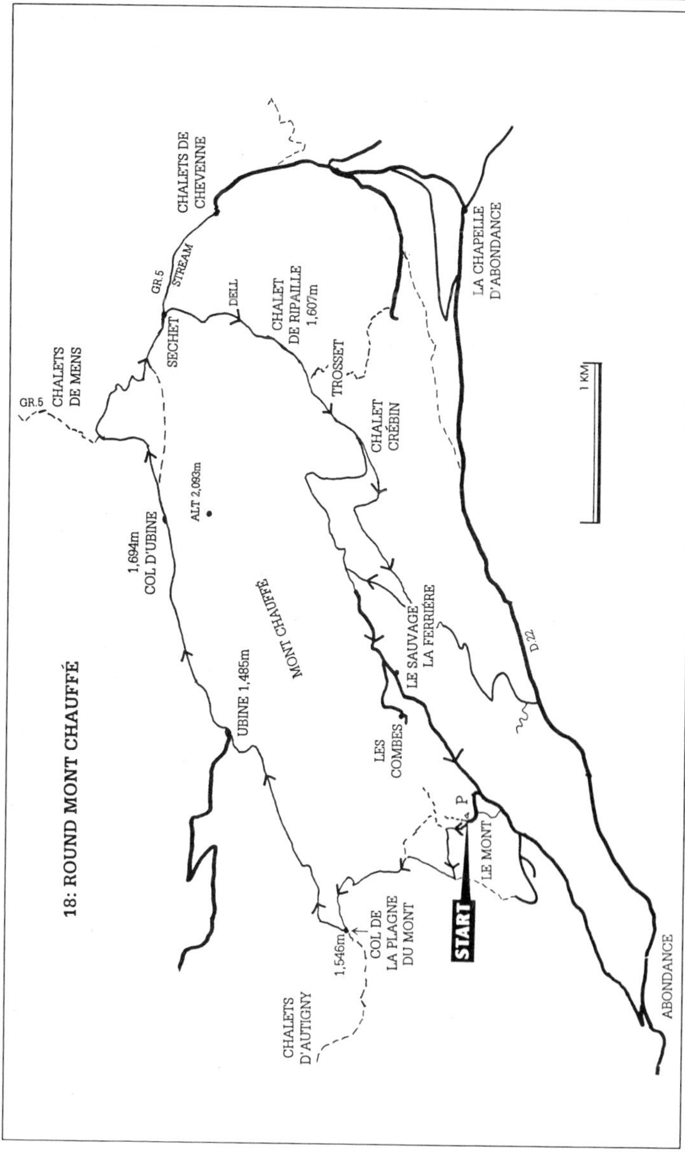

18: ROUND MONT CHAUFFÉ
CHALETS DE CHEVENNE
LA CHAPELLE D'ABONDANCE
GR.5
STREAM
DELL
CHALET DE RIPAILLE 1,607m
CHALETS DE MENS
SECHET
TROSSET
CHALET CRÉBIN
1 KM
ALT 2,093m
1,694m COL D'UBINE
MONT CHAUFFÉ
LE SAUVAGE
LA FERRIÈRE
D.22
UBINE 1,485m
LES COMBES
P
LE MONT
START
1,546m
COL DE LA PLAGNE DU MONT
CHALETS D'AUTIGNY
ABONDANCE

the Chauffé behind you. *On this hillside there are spring snowflake flowers which are a very distinctive white with a dot of yellow at the end of each six petals and lovely yellow stamens.*

When you reach the jeep track (2hrs 20mins), do not turn up left (which goes to the Chalet de Mens, a huge refuge and one tumble-down chalet, and eventually to the Pas de la Bosse) but turn down right towards the Chalets de Chevenne (the popular start for the ascent of the Cornettes de Bise). Keep to the main jeep track down following the red splashes, crossing a walled alpine pasture and a stream and then through coniferous forest with the stream below on your right and lots of felled trees.

Cross the stream at a signpost (3hrs) which indicates the direct, steeper path to the Col d'Ubine. Keep going for about 10mins but look very carefully for a red star on a rock to the right and a new signpost saying chalet La Raille (there is a field with chalets further on and a dry stream down on left so if you reach the chalets you know you have gone too far).

The path is narrow and winds up steeply with a dramatic view of the path down from the col and the Chalet de Mens. The going is steep and precipitous in places and winds up for 200m (you notice the drops less in summer because of the long grass). 25mins later you finally come to a wooded dell surrounded by slopes (3hrs 35mins), which is very attractive in summer with numerous species of butterfly, such as swallowtails, red admirals, meadow blues and tortoiseshells. Take the path winding up the open hillside to the right which you can see quite clearly from the dell.

15mins later you reach the Chalet de Raille, alt. 1,607m (3hrs 50mins), and a wooden cross. On the left is a lovely view of the Abondance valley with the Mont Grange beyond. You are walking on a lovely balcony path with the rock wall of the Mont Chauffé on your right which is delightful after all the previous ups and downs, passing the typical, old Abondance style farmhouses of Trosset and the Chalets de Crebin. The track goes down fairly gently through woods and open spaces and then more steeply to the road going up to Le Mont (4hrs 50mins). Retrace your steps to the big chalet (5hrs).

Remarks: This walk adds variety as it makes a change to walk round a mountain rather than to the summit (there is a path to the top but it is steep and dangerous). The Mont Chauffé is an impressive hunk of rock with some similarity to Ayers rock in Australia as it dominates the surrounding countryside. This is certainly a three star walk in terms of beauty and scenery, but you have to be fit to do the three ups and downs. Although the meadows are abundant with flowers in spring, the snow tends to hang about, especially on the north slope, so it is more of a summer walk with the advantage that the long grass hides the somewhat precipitous slopes!

19: ROC DE TAVANEUSE - Alt. 2,156 metres
(Chablais region)

Difficulty:	Medium to the lake - after it is a steep climb and for the final ascent to the Roc you must have a head for heights.
Time:	5hrs 15mins.
Height gain:	1,026 metres.
Maps:	Editions Didier & Richard IGN No.3 Massifs du Chablais Faucigny & Genevois 1:50,000. Cartes IGN 3528 ET Top 25 Morzine Massif du Chablais 1:25,000.
Depart from:	Prétairié, Abondance valley - 1,131 metres.
Signposting:	Adequate, but after the Col de Tavaneuse there are no signs.

How to get there (from Geneva)
Take the N.37/N.5 to Thonon-Les-Bains and then the D.902 direction Morzine. This takes you along the Dranse river gorge which is popular for rafting and canoeing. At Bioge turn left on the D.22 into the Abondance valley. In the centre of Abondance village turn right over the bridge and go up the main street past shops until the road forks. Take the right fork signposted Lac de Tavaneuse which goes alongside the Edian stream, passing the Essert cable-car, to the hamlet of Charmy. At Charmy follow the signs onto a narrower road to Prétairié which consists of a large parking area and a few houses - you are 4km from Abondance.

Directions
At the entrance to the car park there is a signpost to Serranants/Lac de Tavaneuse/Pic de la Corne. Follow this sign straight through the parking area onto a wide jeep track. The mass of the Roc de Tavaneuse towers above you as you walk along and you wonder how you are ever going to get up there! After 20mins go left at the signpost to Lac de Tavaneuse (the jeep track continues to the Chalets de Serranants and to the Pic de la Corne).

The path narrows and winds steeply up the mountainside through stunted trees and scrub, and then into the open. There are occasional red markings on stones. It is rocky in places and you have to watch your footing, especially near the top where there are cables trailing across the path; there is also a cable overhead. This is a well-used route and it can be slippery if it has just rained. Turn left upwards where the path goes straight ahead along the rock face. This is the way you take on the return, an alternative and less steep path down.

The path gets rockier and steeper with the Ruisseau (stream) de Tavaneuse on the left and waterfalls in spring and early summer - there is an imposing view backwards to Prétairié and the Cornettes de Bise mountain on the right. You come to a plateau at the Chalets de Tavaneuse (1hr 20mins) which consists of a few tumble-down huts and scraggy vegetation. Take the path you can see winding up the mountain in front.

After a hard short grind by a little stream on your left you arrive at the col and a picturesque little lake, alt. 1,805m, with high mountain slopes all around it (1hr 50mins). A signpost indicates left Entre Deux Pertuis and Chalet d'Ardens, but keep to the path going round the lake heading for another col where you can see a signpost on the top. The path goes up quite steeply with a stream flowing down to the right. This is bare, open mountainside with not a tree in sight and looks very austere. Keep your eyes on the path as it is easy to wander off it. There is a higher path coming in from the right which is another way down.

When you arrive at the Col de Tavaneuse, alt. 1,990m and not 1,850m as wrongly stated on the signpost! (2hrs 30mins), there is a spectacular view, particularly of the Pointe de Nanteaux 2,170m straight ahead. You can see a path down to the Chalet de Lens which eventually leads to the Lac de Montriond, and another to the left over a crest which looks very airy. There is a signpost right to the Roc de Tavaneuse.

Of the two paths on the right, take the one that goes up the ridge (not the well defined path that skirts round the side of the mountain). It is airy and precipitous but certainly not dangerous. In autumn the slopes are carpeted with heather. When you reach the end at a big rock, climb up right to the Roc de Tavaneuse itself, alt. 2,156m - the way is exposed but not technically difficult (2hrs 50mins). From the roc you get magnificent views of the surrounding alpine peaks including Mont Blanc, Dents du Midi, the Valaisan alps, the Matterhorn and even down to the Vanoise on a clear day.

Go back to the col and continue down. Five minutes later take the left fork which is easier and gives you different views down to the lake, where you rejoin the original path (3hrs 30mins). ALTERNATIVE FROM THE ROCK ITSELF - I am told that there is a way round if you take a path off to the left about 20 metres down from the summit. This path circles round the summit and then joins the ridge; apparently it is not difficult though rather airy.

From the lake, retrace your steps and keep on the same track down till you see a plaque on the rock wall commemorating a 12 year old girl killed in an avalanche in 1967. 10mins further on you come to the alternative return path mentioned on the upward journey (4hrs 25mins).

It is recommended to take the path which goes along the side of the rock face which joins the jeep track by the Chalets de Serranants. This is easier but longer than if you take the direct route down. There is a good view up to the Roc d'Enfer col, the route you would take on the walk to the Pic de la Corne. Take the jeep track down till you reach the car park at Prétairié (5hrs 15mins).

Remarks: The walk as far as the Lac de Tavaneuse is a classic and in high summer you risk finding a crowd going the same way - the climb higher to the roc itself is only for those with a head for heights! This is not one of my favourite walks as the slopes are steep and the mountain rather overpowering for my taste - however, the lake is very beautiful. Avoid doing this walk if it has been raining.

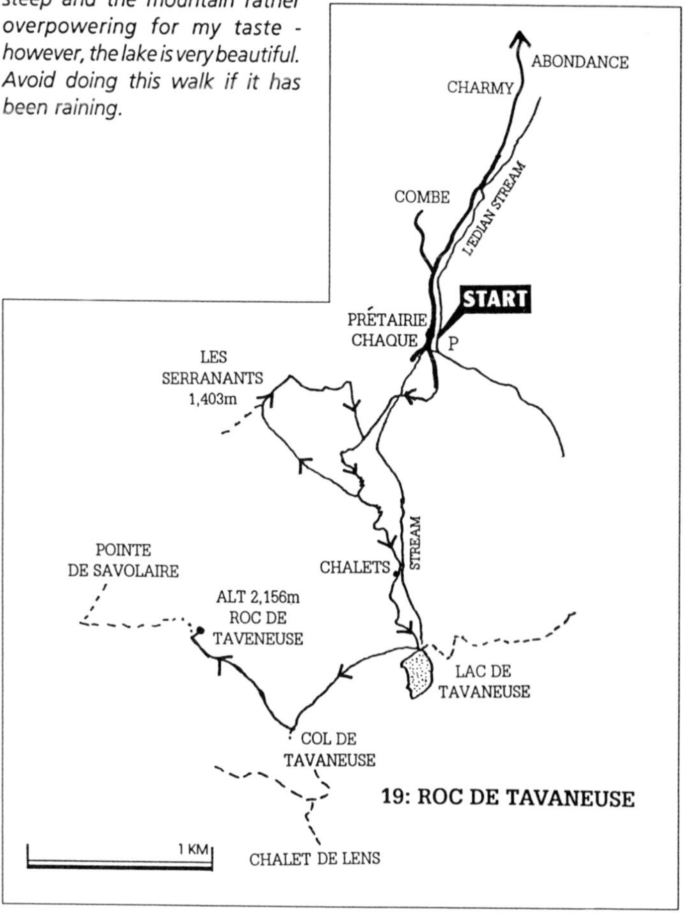

20: LES CORNETTES DE BISE - Alt. 2,432 metres
(Chablais region)

Difficulty:	Difficult - only for walkers not afraid of steep slopes. One particularly tricky spot.
Time:	6hrs 15mins.
Height gain:	1,217 metres.
Maps:	Editions Didier & Richard IGN No.3 Massifs du Chablais Faucigny & Genevois 1:50,000. Cartes IGN 3528 ET Top 25 Morzine Massif du Chablais 1:25,000.
Depart from:	Chevenne (Chapelle d'Abondance) - 1,250 metres.
Signposting:	Good - red splashes most of the way - where you start clambering there are heads of bouquetins painted on the rocks to guide you (we counted 37 to the summit).

How to get there (from Geneva)
Take the N.37/N.5 to Thonon-Les-Bains and then the D.902 direction Morzine. This takes you along the Dranse river gorge which is popular for rafting and canoeing. At Bioge turn left on the D22 into the Abondance valley. Chapelle d'Abondance is about 16km along this road. In the village, turn left just before the Hôtel Montfleury on the B.3 signposted Chevenne. Go up this narrow road which goes through woods beside the Sechet stream to a clearing where there are lots of signs and plenty of room for parking.

Directions
Follow the sign Col de Vernaz/Lac d'Arvouin/Cornettes de Bise 3hrs 30mins. This is a wide jeep track alongside a stream going gently upwards with a big GR sign on a rock to the right (this is the well-known GR.5 track going all the way from Hook of Holland to Nice). There is a beautiful, rather daunting, view of the entire Cornettes de Bise mountain in front. After about 8mins look for a wooden sign to the left which says Chalets de Chevenne. Turn left and follow the GR signs (ignoring the path lower down to the left). The path narrows as it climbs up through scattered coniferous wood. There is another signpost to the right to La Cheneau 35mins/Pas de la Bosse 1hr 10mins/Col de Vernaz 1hr.30mins. Shortly after, where the path splits, take the upper branch (there is a sign on a tree).

The path comes out of the woods onto an open grassy slope where it bears left of the Cornettes de Bise towering above. Look back for a beautiful

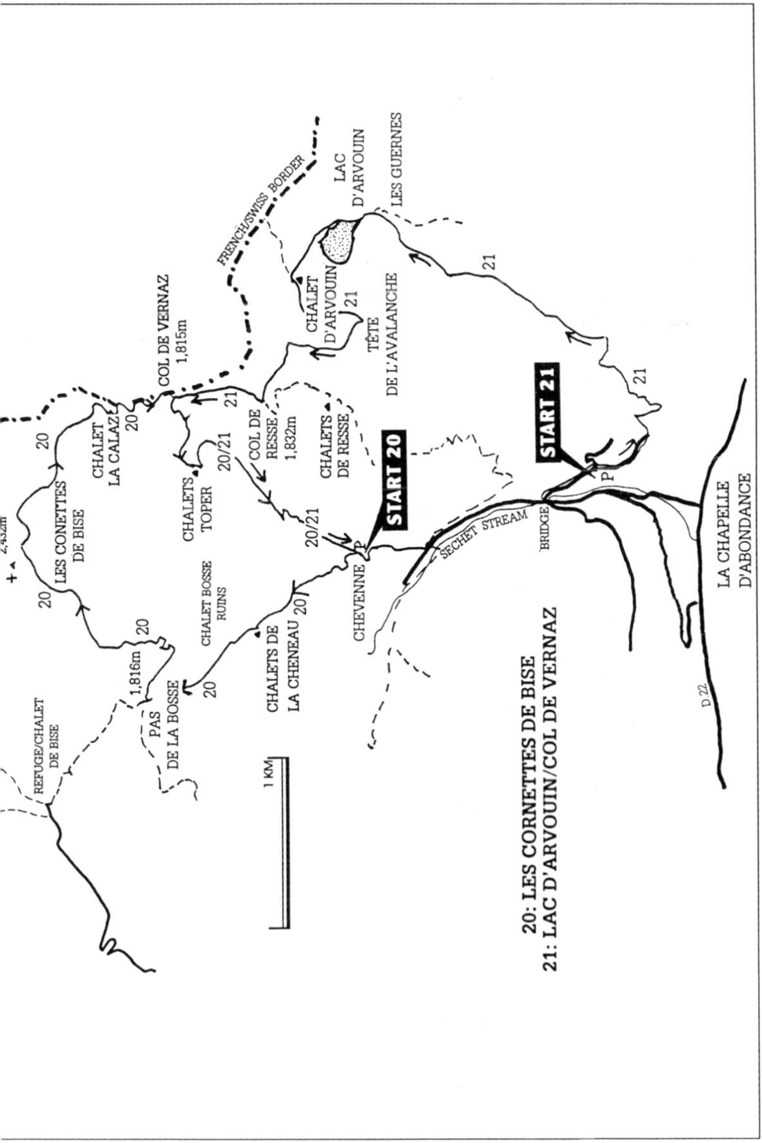
20: LES CORNETTES DE BISE
21: LAC D'ARVOUIN/COL DE VERNAZ
FRENCH/SWISS BORDER
LAC D'ARVOUIN
LES GUERNES
CHALET D'ARVOUIN
TÊTE DE L'AVALANCHE
COL DE VERNAZ 1,815m
CHALET LA CALAZ
COL DE RESSE 1,832m
CHALETS DE RESSE
CHALETS TOPER
LES CONETTES DE BISE
2,432m
CHALET BOSSE RUINS
CHALETS DE LA CHENEAU
CHEVENNE
START 20
START 21
SECHET STREAM
BRIDGE
P
LA CHAPELLE D'ABONDANCE
D.22
1,816m
PAS DE LA BOSSE
REFUGE/CHALET DE BISE
1 KM

view down the unspoilt Chevenne valley with no ski-lifts in sight and the Dents du Midi over on the left. At a water trough just before the Chalets de la Cheneau, alt. 1,590m (50mins), turn right over a muddy stream and follow the GR signs on rocks up past the chalet, to a signpost, by a large rock, to Col de la Bosse 35mins.

The path is well defined with GR red/white splashes and leads to the ruins of the Chalet de la Bosse in a shallow combe and then continues up to the col at alt. 1,816m (1hr 25mins). Go left for a couple of minutes for a striking view down into the valley the other side with the path coming up from the Chalets de Bise (here there is a French Alpine Club refuge). At this point you have gained 600m - half the height gain of the entire walk. However, the next part is the difficult bit!!

From the signpost bear right on a path which winds along the side of the mountain and from where you have a good view of the path you came up. This is a pleasant stroll for about 10mins until you start clambering up the side of the rock called the Serrauquin couloir (corridor). The path becomes rocky with some scree where you should proceed cautiously to avoid slipping. The gradient is steep and you need to keep constant watch for where to put your feet. Start looking for your first bouquetin (ibex) painting and red splashes as it is better to take the indicated path.

The path bears round to the left of the rock - to the right is too precipitous! At the 15th ibex painting you reach the first ridge where you can see down to the Chalets de Bises and then you climb up a wide grassy shoulder at the top of the corridor (2hrs 35mins). Take a rest here and enjoy the even more extensive views of the valley behind. Traverse round to the right where you have to climb up the side of a rock. The path then winds round to the left and resumes its ascent, crossing a rocky sector to another ridge. Bear right along this ridge and climb up another rocky outcrop. Up ahead you will see a large red arrow on the rock pointing up to the right and also "Bise" painted in yellow underneath (21st ibex). Here you climb up an impressive rocky face, but there are lots of good hand and foot holds.

You are now on the other side of the mountain with views down into the Abondance valley to Chatel and further over into the Rhône valley and Switzerland (3hrs 10mins). You can see the path ahead running along the side of the mountain and across on to the top. There are two exposed passages here and the second one requires some agility as you are climbing round a rock and the slope below is rather precipitous but the remainder of the ascent though rocky in places is relatively straightforward. About 10mins before the summit look to your left through a gigantic hole in the rock which gives a dizzy view of the slope below. Bear right along a defined path on the Abondance valley side of the slope and then bear left before bearing sharp left again (30th ibex) for the final ascent to the summit alt. 2,432m (4hrs) which has a cairn on it marking the boundary between France and Switzerland. This is one of the highest and most dramatic of the Chablais peaks so the panorama is exceptional. On a clear day you will see Mt. Blanc (due south) with the jagged black peaks of the Dents du Midi on the left and further left the snow-covered Grand Combin. To the north is Lake Léman with the long line of the Jura in the background.

Follow the same path you took up down to the 35th ibex and then bear left. The path is clear, rocky and quite steep, but not technically difficult. It descends fairly rapidly to the Col de Chaudin where there are yellow Swiss signposts. Left indicates to Tanay/Montagne de Loz but go straight following the sign to the Col de Vernaz (4hrs 20mins). As you bear left round the flank of the mountain you can see the way you have come up and also the north-eastern side of the Mont Chauffé. There is a further rocky descent and then a grassy path. Where it divides take the lower path which brings you to the two buildings of La Calaz, alt. 2067m, built 1983, perched on the bare hillside (4hrs 45mins). They consist of two big cowsheds and an unlocked small room with a bench inside - presumably a refuge for anyone caught on the mountain in bad weather. From here the path snakes down to the Col de Vernaz, alt. 1,815m, which is visible from the La Calaz (5hrs 30mins). At the col you can look back up and appreciate how you came down the mountain in big zigzags. You are again on the Swiss border where a yellow signpost says Verne 40mins/Tanay 1hr 40mins/ Chevennes 1hr 20mins Lac D'Arvouin (see Walk No.21). Note, there is a short cut you can take before you reach the signpost.

Take the path down to the right which leads to Les Chalets de Chevenne. This is steep in places and also rather tiring as there is a lot of erosion where you have to pick your way down. It follows the Chevenne stream, only a trickle in summer, and then levels slightly passing the Chalets Topfer which has horses, cows and sheep grazing. The path deteriorates again as the descent continues, always in the open with no shady trees to give relief on a hot day. About 5mins from Chevenne there is a turning to the right onto the GR.5 which you took on your outward journey (6hrs 15mins).

Remarks: This walk is a classic as the Cornettes de Bise (meaning horns of cold wind) is one of the highest and most dramatic of the Chablais peaks. However, it is challenging and only for those not afraid of heights and some scrambling. It should not be climbed too early in the season as the snow takes time to melt in the crevices; it is a popular hike for more experienced walkers and at weekends in high summer you will not be tackling it alone!

21: LAC D'ARVOUIN/COL DE VERNAZ - Alt. 1,815 metres

(see map p133) (Chablais region)

Difficulty:	Medium with two short scrambles on the way to the Col Vernaz.
Time:	4hrs.
Height gain:	675 metres.
Maps:	Editions Didier & Richard IGN No.3 Massifs du Chablais Faucigny & Genevois 1:50,000. Cartes IGN 3528 ET Top 25 Morzine Massif du Chablais 1:25,000.
Depart from:	Chevennes (Chapelle d'Abondance) - 1,248 metres.
Signposting:	Good and where there is no signposting the way is obvious. Some orange/red splashes.

How to get there (from Geneva)

Take the N.37/N.5 to Thonon-Les-Bains and then the D.902 direction Morzine. This takes you along the Dranse river gorge which is popular for rafting and canoeing.

At Bioge turn left on the D.22 into the Abondance valley. Chapelle d'Abondance is about 16km along this road. In the village, turn left just before the Hôtel Montfleury on the B.3 signposted Chevennes. Go up this narrow road and take the first turning to the right at a green bridge over the Sechet stream, and continue (not far) until you see a jeep track coming down from the left. Park the car opposite in a small parking area.

Directions

Walk along the tarmac road which winds round the hill with a few chalets dotted about. Down on the right there is a glorious view over the Abondance valley and the village of Chapelle d'Abondance with the three main Chablais peaks of Les Cornettes de Bise, La Dent d'Oche and Le Mont Chauffé behind; ahead is the impressive Mont de Grange. After a large chalet on the left called Haute Cime, the road turns into a wide track and goes slightly down through woods and over a stream.

After 10mins and 50m beyond the stream turn up left where there is a sign on a tree indicating Lac d'Arvouin. The path is narrow and climbs quite steeply through coniferous woods. At a little chalet on the right, continue upwards through the forest (orange/red splashes on trees) crossing the end of a wide jeep track (parking area here) and keep going till you reach a wide stony road where you turn left (30mins). Stay on the jeep track until a cross-roads (45mins) and then go right, following the sign to Lac d'Arvouin. This is another wide jeep track through very attractive widely spaced coniferous trees, steep at first and then flattening out before rising again. There is a beautiful view of the nearby Mont Chauffé.

You come to an attractive deep bowl in the mountains which must have once contained a small lake. The path goes up round the right side of the bowl and through a wide gorge with large serrated rocks on the right called Les Guernes. Beyond you can see another green slope with white rocks behind like a row of teeth, strikingly unusual and beautiful. Cresting the top of the slope you suddenly discover the delightful Lac d'Arvouin, alt 1,669m in front (1hr 30mins) with a small stream flowing out. A typical alpine lake, round and deep green, its shores fringed by tall reeds, it nestles amongst the surrounding mountains like a magic puddle; you feel you want to linger at this spot, dip your feet in the icy water and go no further! Signs point ahead to Col de Serpentin 45mins/Col de Resse 1hr 10mins/Col de Vernaz 1hr 20mins.

Take the path you can see going round the lake to the right and curling up the mountain. This leads to two large cow sheds called the Chalets d'Arvouin, alt. 1,770m, where there is a beautiful view overlooking the lake with the peak of Le Lineu, alt. 2,093m, rearing up beyond. Behind the cowsheds there are two paths winding up to the mountain pass; you can take your choice, the one to the left is longer but less steep! (1hr 45mins).

After a 15min climb (by the left-hand ascent) you reach the top of the ridge which is covered with low alder bushes (2hrs). To the right is the peak of the Tête de l'Avalanche. This is the perfect spot for a rest to admire the full range of Chablais peaks all around including the nearby Vaudois alps. The path follows the summit, but turn right and shortly after you come to a signpost which says Col de Serpentin alt. 1,850m.

Ignore the path which goes straight up to another ridge and take the left which curls round the hill. It snakes down over alpine pastures and levels out for a while before the two tricky bits of the walk where you have to pick your way down over small rocks, but the path is well defined and not technically difficult. ALTERNATIVE: If you prefer you can take a path down to the left which goes past the Chalets de Resse and is a shorter way back meeting the road going up to the Chalets de Chevenne.

After 20mins you reach the Col de Resse, alt l,781m (2hrs 20mins), where there is an even closer view of the precipitous cliffs of the rocky Mont Chauffé. Turn right on a narrow path which goes round the side of the mountain and up to the Col de Vernaz, alt. 1,993m (2hrs 40mins). *Along the banks there are lovely flowers, especially in July when a riot of purple cornflowers, monkshood and adenostyles is offset by contrasting white cow parsley and frilly, pink tinged astrantia.*

Here you are on the Swiss border and there is a yellow signpost down to the right saying Verne 40mins/Tanay 1hr 40mins).*There is an amusing confusion here between the Swiss and French signposts - the Swiss signpost calls this the Col de Verne at 1,814m but the neighbouring French one calls it the Col de Vernaz at 1,815m!* To the right is the Rhône valley and ahead the towering Cornettes de Bise, where you may see walkers toiling up to the summit and an alpine hut half way up the exposed mountain slope - it looks an impressive climb!

Take the path down to the left which leads to Les Chalets de Chevenne. This is steep in places and also rather tiring as there is a lot of erosion where you have to pick your way down. It follows the Chevenne stream, only a trickle in summer, and then levels slightly passing the Chalets Topfer which has horses, cows and sheep grazing.The path deteriorates again as the descent continues, always in the open with no shady trees to give relief on a hot day. About 5mins from Chevenne the GR.5 joins your path from the right.

The descent takes approximately three-quarters of an hour to 1hr to reach the road at Les Chevennes, alt. 1,250m. There are numerous signposts here as it is the jump-off point for several walks including the Cornettes de Bise (Walk No. 20). Walk down the road till you see the turning on the left with the green bridge - then you are only 5mins from the car (4hrs).

Remarks: This walk gives impressive views of the four main Chablais peaks (Le Mont Chauffé, La Dent d'Oche, Les Cornettes de Bise and Mont de Grange). The contrast between the vivid green slopes and the abrupt white rocks is breathtaking, making this one of the loveliest regions of the Haute Savoie. It is best avoided on a hot summer's day as there is very little shade.

22: POINTE DES MATTES - Alt. 2,010 metres
(Chablais region)

Difficulty:	Medium, though a stiff but short haul over a grassy slope to the Pointe des Mattes.
Time:	5hrs.
Height gain:	850 metres.
Maps:	Editions Didier & Richard IGN No.3 Massifs du Chablais Faucigny & Genevois 1:50,000. Cartes IGN 3528 ET Top 25 Morzine Massif du Chablais 1:25,000.
Depart from:	Très Les Pierres (Châtel) - 1,200 metres.
Signposting:	Sporadic - orange splashes on upward journey.

How to get there (from Geneva)
Take the N.37/N.5 to Thonon-Les-Bains and then the D.902 direction Morzine. This takes you along the Dranse river gorge which is popular for rafting and canoeing. At Bioge turn left on the D.22 into the Abondance valley. Châtel (27km from the turning), is the last village in France before the road goes over the Morgins Pass into Switzerland. Just after the church in Châtel go down to the right on the D.228 which continues along the Dranse valley (straight on leads into Switzerland). Pass a sawmill and then the Lingua Cable-car before reaching Très les Pierres which is a collection of chalets 3.5km from Châtel. There is a car park by the river on the left, next to a ski de fond orientation map and opposite a chalet called Les Airelles.

Directions
Walk down the road for a short distance past a sign on the left saying Très les Pierres and then follow the sign left towards Sur le Crac 40mins/Betzalin 1hr 5mins on a narrow tarmac road between two old chalets. A few minutes later you come to a quaint little chapel, built in 1784, with a GR sign on a huge rock behind. Keep straight past the rock where the road turns into a jeep track. Shortly after, at a number of signs, take the one to the left to Sur le Crac (the one straight on says Châtel 3hrs). You are now entering the Mont de Grange reserve.

The track goes upwards medium steep through woods, across a stream and then becomes somewhat steeper and stonier. There are occasional orange splashes all the way up. You eventually see the top of the Portes de Soleil ski complex above Châtel on the other side of the valley. Keep on the main jeep track following the Sur le Crac sign at a corner (15mins) - do not take the narrower path straight. On one side is a tall rocky cliff and on the other are wooded slopes dropping steeply to the valley floor.

At Sur le Crac, alt. 1,430m (40mins,) continue straight following the sign Sur l'Arête/Cornillon. The path comes out into an attractive open grassy bowl. Keep to the grassy path with fir trees to the left; to the right is a track leading to the farm of L'Arête. You can see the Col de la Corne, alt. 2,159m, on the horizon ahead and the rearing mass of Mont de Grange, alt. 2,432m, to the left. The path crosses a lovely stream (1hr) where there is a chalet up on the right and then crosses it again higher up by a waterfall to the left.

Turn right when you reach a T-junction (no sign) at the end of this lovely mountain ringed amphitheatre (1hr 10mins). The GR.5 comes in from the left at a signpost saying L'Etrye 20mins and you can see the red/white marks going straight up the mountain in front. Do not follow the GR marks but keep right; if you look back there is a lovely view of the Portes de Soleil skiing area. The path gets wider as it curls round the mountain and at one stage even goes downwards before coming out into the open with a chalet down on the right and lovely views of the upper part of the Abondance valley. The path starts rising again medium steep through coniferous woods and you arrive at a big deserted barn called Le Cornillon, alt. 1,780 (1hr 40mins), standing in a large open area on the edge of a dip. On the right there is a rock ridge and scree sweeping down to green pasture and it is here that a herd of chamois can often be seen. Take the path straight on past the barn (not the more obvious one to the right) - the orange markings disappear from now on.

It takes 20mins from Cornillon to the Chalet des Mattes, signposted alt. 1,900m (2hrs), on a path through coniferous trees and then out onto high

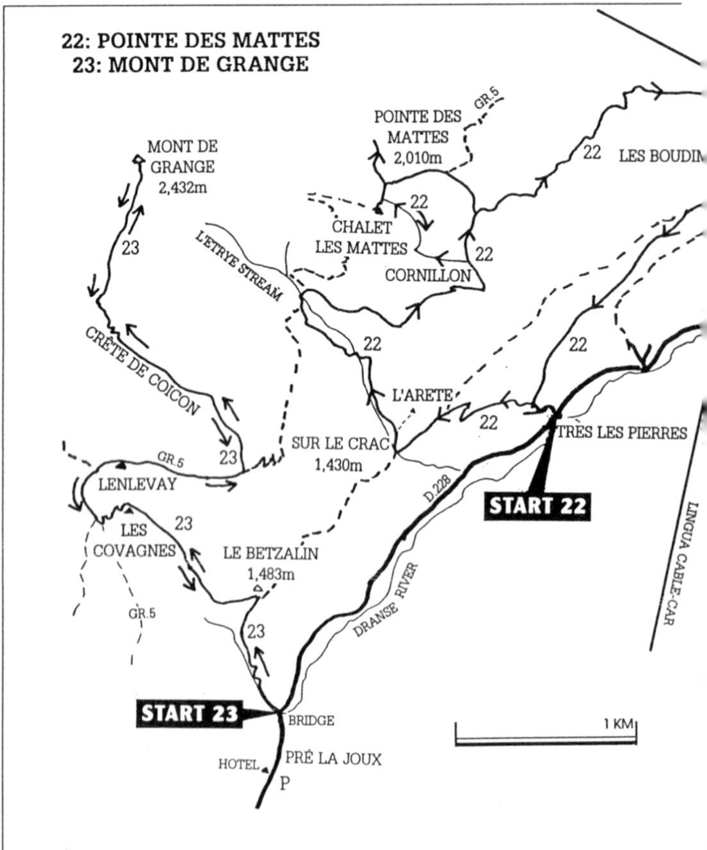

heather covered alpine pasture. The path becomes less well defined on the top but make for the chalet you can see in front. This is quite an exposed spot but an ideal place for a picnic if the weather is good - there are lovely views in all directions, particularly of the Mont de Grange towering above. Leave your rucksack at the barn and climb up the grassy slope of the Pointe des Mattes, another 110m higher but well worth the rather stiff climb (20mins there and back) for an even greater view of the surrounding mountains as well as down into the Abondance valley. Be careful here as the ridge falls away very abruptly. Looking down on the Chalet des Mattes from the slope above you can see two small ponds nearby, presumably watering points for the animals.

Retrace your steps from the Chalets des Mattes to the Chalet des Cornillons and admire the view on the way of the Dents du Midi and, on the horizon, to the left, the Pointe Percée at the end of the Chaine des Aravis. At the Chalet des Cornillons do not continue down the path you came up but go to the left down the dip with the scree and cliff on the left. Take the bottom path (not the top one) which goes along this shallow combe for about 5mins and

Les Dents du Midi from Pointe des Mattes

then into coniferous wood flanking the side of the hill. The wide path seems to go up the mountain before passing through coniferous and alder bushes alternating with open alpine pasture. After approximately 20mins (2hrs 40mins) you start descending over a wide grassy crest. There is a magnificent view over to the Lac des Vonnes on the outskirts of Châtel with the Pas de Morgins winding up and over into Switzerland, the Dents du Midi over on the right, Mont de Grange at the back with the Pointe des Mattes on the left and across the valley, and in front the distinctive Cornettes de Bise. Follow the path down medium steep towards a huge electricity pylon on the left which you eventually go under.

Keep to the main path which goes through some woodland to a T-junction (3hrs 30mins). Go right, signposted Boudimes, and 5mins later you come out through open meadows to the scattered chalets of Les Boudimes, alt. 1,450m (there is a signpost). Keep on the jeep track which drops quite steeply down the side of the mountain through forest and over a number of streams running off the rock face.

After 15mins follow the signpost to Le Betzalin 1hr 45mins, though you do not reach Le Betzalin itself (do not take the little path down to left signposted Villapeyron 20mins/Châtel 2hrs 5mins). You go along the side of the mountain on a balcony path with glorious views into the top end of the Abondance valley and the La Lingua ski-lift on the other side. The track then starts to go down fairly steeply - there are lovely waterfalls spilling over the rock face, and across your path down to the valley below. Continue to the collection of signposts at the start of the walk where you went left to Sur le Crac. Retrace your steps to the road and turn right to the car park (4hrs 15mins).

Remarks: This is a lovely walk in the Mont de Grange reserve where you see herds of chamois if you are quiet! There are also mouflons here though I have not seen them (see Fauna). The views of nearby Mont de Grange are impressive, as are the peaks of the Dents du Midi. Although there is little signposting on the return path, it is not difficult to follow.

23: MONT DE GRANGE - (see map p140) Alt. 2,433 metres (Chablais region)

Difficulty:	Long, but not technically difficult.
Time:	6hrs.
Height gain:	1,223 metres.
Maps:	Editions Didier & Richard IGN No.3 Chablais Faucigny

	& Genevois 1:50,000. Cartes IGN 3528 ET Top 25 Morzine Massif du Chablais 1:25,000.
Depart from:	Pré La Joux (near Châtel) - Alt. 1,160 metres.
Signposting:	Good - purple then GR white/red splashes.

How to get there (from Geneva)
Take the N.37/N.5 to Thonon-Les-Bains and then the D.902 direction Morzine. This takes you along the Dranse river gorge which is popular for rafting and canoeing. At Bioge turn left on the D.22 which goes into the Adondance valley. Châtel (27km from the turning) is the last village in France before the road goes over the Morgins Pass into Switzerland. Just after the church in Châtel bear down right on the D.228 which is a continuation of the Dranse valley (straight on is Switzerland). Drive to the hamlet of Pré La Joux and park opposite the hotel/restaurant La Perdrix Blanche.

Directions
Walk back down the road for a few minutes to where the Dranse goes underneath the road. Turn up left where you can see signposts and some chalets. Follow the sign Le Betzalin 30mins on a well defined path, initially past scattered chalets and then through light coniferous forest, winding up fairly steeply. Continue towards Betzalin at the next set of signposts where there is a junction left to Les Grands Plans/Plaine Dranse 1hr 55mins. Here there are purple splashes (it makes a change from the usual red and white!). Cross a wooden bridge and then up through meadowland to the two lovely old wooden chalets of Benzalin (30mins), alt. 1,483m. Beside the chalets is a bubble type cable-car used to bring up provisions. From here you have an uninterrupted view down into the valley and the ski installations of the Tête de Lingua and the Châtel area are clearly visible.

Go round to the left towards the Col de Grange (straight on leads to Sur le Crac - see Walk No. 22). Continue through coniferous woods on a jeep track, marked by purple splashes, crossing a stile and the occasional stream (the Ruisseau des Rubis is down on the left). You come out into alpine pasture again by an attractive wooden fountain at the chalets of Les Covagny, alt. 1,726m (1hr 30mins). Stop here and appreciate the clear, though somewhat intimidating, view of the majestic Mont de Grange.

Now you join the red/white splashes of the GR.5. Continue past the chalets on an open jeep track and bear right at the next signposts in the direction of Mont Grange par Coicon 2hrs; the left fork says Les Plagnes 1hr 50mins. This leads to another large cow shed called Lenlevay with more GR signs. In season you can buy the local Reblochon cheese here (see Regional Specialities). A few minutes after the shed, bear right at a T-junction (left goes to a small chalet) continuing on a wide track which starts to steepen as it curls up round the mountain. You can see the GR path snaking right down into the valley below. Shortly after the farm of L'Etyre visible down on the right, you leave the GR and take a narrow path bearing up left, signposted Mont de Grange (2hrs).

The path goes up medium steep through stunted alder and raspberry bushes. After 20mins you get your first glimpse of the distinctive Pointe des Mattes on the right (Walk No. 22) and another great view all along the valley to Châtel with the jagged tooth-like peaks of Les Dents du Midi on the horizon. You are now climbing up the long southern shoulder of the mountain, called the Crête de Coicon. *When I did this walk in late autumn the slopes were snow covered; a herd of chamois was gathered on the exposed rocks and they were so busy looking for nourishment that we were able to approach within a few yards.* About 40mins after leaving the GR (2hrs 40mins) you walk along the side of a ridge which falls away quite steeply on both sides for a while before tackling an exposed, steep slope. When you reach the summit of the shoulder (2hrs 45mins), the worst is over though there is still a long but less exacting climb to the top (4hrs). The summit is a long rocky ridge with an iron cross at alt. 2,432m and a "borne" (concrete marker) at the end. Even if you feel exhausted it is worth doing this last 10min stretch so you can savour the incredible panorama in all directions.

This is one of the highest peaks in the Chablais region and the views are literally breathtaking. The field of vision extends from the Gran Paradiso National Park in northern Italy, the entire Mont Blanc range and the Pointe Percée in the Aravis range to the Dents du Midi and the major Swiss peaks in the Bernese Oberland including the Matterhorn, Jungfrau and Eiger.

Remarks: This is a really challenging walk up the second highest peak in the Chablais (Les Hauts Forts above Morzine Avoriaz is about 20m higher) and the views at the summit are the most extensive in the region. It is one of the few walks recorded in this book which goes up and down the same way. There is an alternative route up but it is badly marked and too difficult for the average walker. The Mont de Grange is a National Reserve so you have a good chance to see chamois, ibex and, if lucky, the elusive mouflon.

24: LE MORCLAN - Alt. 1,970 metres
(Chablais region)

Difficulty:	Medium - somewhat airy on the Pointe des Ombrieux.
Time:	4hrs.
Height gain:	801 metres.
Maps:	Editions Didier & Richard IGN No.3 Massifs du Chablais Faucigny & Genevois 1:50,000. Cartes IGN 3528 ET Top 25 Morzine Massif du Chablais 1:25,000.
Depart from:	Above Petit Châtel - 1,250 metres.
Signposting:	Good in parts - red and purple splashes (some signs removed from September).

How to get there (from Geneva)

Take the N.37/N.5 to Thonon-Les-Bains and then the D.902 direction Morzine. This takes you along the Dranse river gorge which is popular for rafting and canoeing. At Bioge turn left on the D.22 into the Abondance valley. Châtel (27km from the turning) is the last village in France before the road goes over the Morgins Pass into Switzerland. In the centre of Châtel, opposite the church, turn up left and then left again at a sign saying Petit Châtel. Drive up this narrow road through scattered chalets till you get to Petit Châtel, alt. 1,250m, and then turn right by the signpost indicating Col de Conches/Morgins. The road goes under the chair-lift before degrading into a stony jeep track. Continue on the jeep track and leave your car in the space on the second hairpin bend (not too near a wooden hut where there is a no-parking sign). Up on the right is a wooden sign indicating right Super Châtel/Lac de Conches and left La Pierre/Barbossine dessous/La Mouet. If there is no space at the hairpin there is plenty of room further up the track.

Directions

Turn right on the wide jeep track following the sign to Super Châtel; ignore other paths branching off. There is a chair-lift over on the right and another visible nearby. After 10mins follow the signpost to Sur le Crêt which will take you under the chair-lift through open meadowland, bearing round the right of the mountain. There is a beautiful view right down the Abondance valley and you can see Sur le Crêt, alt. 1,400m, which is a huddle of huts, over on the right. Take the obvious short cuts as you zigzag up this track, past a new shrine dated 1990, to a bar/restaurant called Les Portes de Soleil and the start of the Téléski Les Coqs.

After the restaurant bear left on the jeep track towards Super Saxel. (Normally there are signposts here, but when we did the walk in mid-September there were none. The tourist bureau said they had been taken down for the coming ski season - rather early I thought!) Look out for occasional purple splashes on the path. You go through intermittent coniferous woods and twice under a chair-lift before arriving at the hideous buildings of Super Châtel (40mins) with lifts in all directions. *This is one of the main liaison areas of the Portes de Soleil ski complex (see below for details).*

BE CAREFUL HERE; continue on the jeep track past the restaurant/hotel Escale Blanche Relais de Gourmand and the cable-car building on the right and after negotiating a stile bear left by a small chalet with a white concrete base and red shutters. Just after going under the chair-lift and before reaching three huts (the middle one is dark wood with a map showing the different ski-lifts on it), take the jeep track bearing up to the right. Keep to the steep jeep track which parallels and goes under the chair-lift to Le Morclan following occasional red splashes. If you look back there is a lovely view down to Châtel and the Dranse valley dominated by the Mont de Grange, alt. 2,432m, the second highest peak in the Chablais area.

You reach the summit of the ridge known as the Morclan at 1,970m (1hr 45mins). To the left is a large TV dish and to the right is the top of the chair-lift. There is a new wooden cross here dated 1993 and two orientation tables giving the names of the surrounding Chablais peaks. This is the border between Switzerland and France and there are old stones marking the frontier; the French one is inscribed 1891. Down on the left, in an attractive bowl surrounded by green slopes, is an old farm with an interesting dark green circle behind it surrounded by walls. It looks strange but is probably a traditional grazing area for sheep and fertiliser may have been sprayed on it. In front of you on this ridge is a spectacular view of the Rhône valley.

Continue to the right along the ridge, passing the top of the chair-lift, on a defined path with red splashes. This is a beautiful walk with fantastic views on each side. To the right is the Mont Blanc range and to the left the Rhône valley with the Valais mountains beyond. The path dips down about 60m to the Col de la Folière (2hrs) - *see below for anecdote about smuggling in this region and also Châtel* - and then climbs up again to the Pointe des Ombrieux at 1,978m. This is a dramatic airy ridge walk for about 20mins but the way is quite clear and not technically difficult. The path follows along the border between Switzerland and France and there are magnificent views of the end of Lake Geneva with the towns of Montreux and Vevey on the far shore and Aigle further up the Rhône valley.

After descending a final slope on the ridge there is a ski-tow coming up from the right and a yellow Swiss signpost (2hrs 30mins) which says Tour de Don 20mins; you can see the green hump of the Don over on the right. Keep

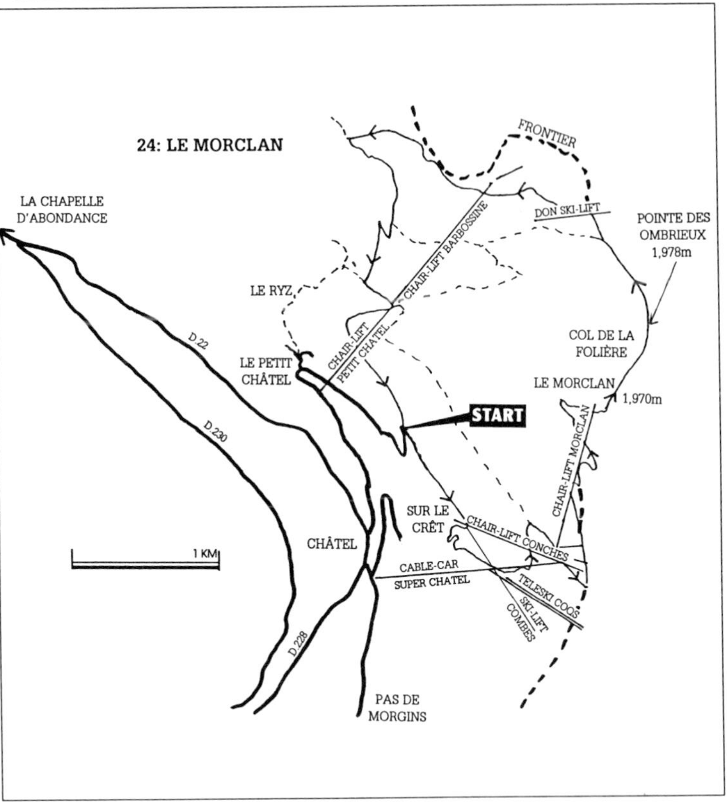

straight on the path which goes round another green amphitheatre with farms down below following the red flashes and the old border stones. There are two huts over on the right: one is Chaux Longe which is the end of a ski-tow coming up from Switzerland and further on you walk underneath another one starting in the dip on the left. Keep to the path following red splashes (there is the end of another ski-tow on the right) over open alpine pasture, climbing up slightly till you meet a jeep track (3hrs). Then bear down left and pass under the Barbossine chair-lift (a long lift which connects with the one coming up from Petit Châtel) and goes to the Tête du Tronchet. At the Col de Reculat, alt. 1,807m (3hrs 15mins) continue straight even through the signpost indicates Châtel left - there is also a path coming up from the Swiss side. The track descends past an ugly new chalet, and then two more buildings before reaching a T-junction and turning left (3hrs 30mins).

Follow the jeep track down to more signposts and another T-junction. Bear left and go by the start of the Barbossine chair where it connects with the end of the Petit Châtel chair-lift. At a further T-junction (signposted left Barbossine 30mins/right Petit Châtel 30mins) turn down right and right again at an immediate fork on the more defined jeep track. Continue on this track through spaced woodland curling back round the base of the mountain till you reach your car (4hrs).

Remarks: Châtel is one of the 12 linked villages in the well-known Portes de Soleil ski area (four in Switzerland and eight in France), which stretches 20km from north to south and 13km from east to west. If you want to see how a really beautiful region can be spoilt by dozens of ski-lifts of all kinds strung haphazardly across the mountain slopes, then this is the walk for you!! But in fairness once you are away from these eyesores, the scenery is breathtaking and this is indeed a wonderful skiing area. Beware that some of the signposts are removed in mid-September to prepare for the winter season.

These mountains used to be a hot-bed of smuggling between France and Switzerland before tourism and skiing took over! Many an old family in Châtel can still recount tales of their grandfather's exploits at outwitting the customs officers (called gabelous in the local dialect). It was at the Col de Folière that one dark night a group of smugglers, laden with haunches of ham bound for Switzerland, heard the sound of the customs men lying in wait for them. They quickly threw their merchandise into holes caused by snow at the foot of fir trees and then convinced their interlocutors that they were simply taking a mountain stroll to enjoy the moonlight playing on the ridge. In the absence of proof, the customs men nevertheless escorted the smugglers back to the village where they were released. When they scurried back to retrieve their hidden contraband the next day, they found to their horror that it had been eaten with gusto by the local foxes - justice had been done!

25: COL DE CHÉSERY - Alt. 1,992 metres
(Chablais region)

Difficulty:	Medium/Easy with no tricky bits at all.
Time:	4hrs 15mins.
Height gain:	525 metres.
Maps:	Editions Didier & Richard IGN No.3 Massifs du Chablais Faucigny et Genevois 1:50,000.

	Cartes IGN 3528 ET Top 25 Morzine Massif du Chablais 1:25,000. Les Lindarets - 1,467 metres.
Signposting:	Good in parts - yellow splashes to the Col de Chésery and then GR.5 red/white stripes to the Col de Bassachaux.

How to get there (from Geneva)
There are three different routes from Geneva to Morzine but this is the way I go. Take the motorway to Chamonix and exit at No.15, Boëge/St. Jeoire. Turn left briefly on the D.903 and watch for the D.9 right signposted Fillinges, Samoëns and Vallée Verte. Follow this road to the Pont de Fillinges and then turn right on the D.907 direction Taninges/Samoëns. (ALTERNATIVELY go through Annemasse and take the D.907 direction Taninges/Samoëns.) In Taninges turn left on the D.902 towards Morzine and just before you get to the village turn left on the D.228 following all signs to the Lac de Montriond. The road goes by the lake and on to Les Lindarets. Drive through the hamlet and turn left at the start of a wide shallow valley which is just round the corner. Park your car on the left beyond Les Marmottes ski-lift (note on the map this is called La Chaux Fleurie!).

Directions
Walk down the big open valley for about 20mins, following yellow splashes on rocks. There are numerous chair-lifts, ski-tows and chalet-style restaurants specially built for the tourist trade, as you are in the well-known Portes de Soleil ski area. Turn left at a sign saying Col de Brochau 1hr 30mins/Col de Chésery 1hr 40mins, just before the chair-lift of La Lécherette which runs parallel to the right of the wide jeep track for about 100m. *Note: at the end of the summer season the sign is taken away so that skiers do not ski into it. A new lift is being built here and machines have messed up the hillside - in the autumn of 1993, when I did the walk for the second time, we watched a helicopter taking buckets of cement back and forth from the cement mixer half way up the track to the top of the mountain where the chair-lift station was being constructed.*

Continue up this fairly steep track following the yellow splashes over alpine pasture until you come to a signpost (50mins). Go left towards Col de Chésery/Lac Vert (straight on is Cubore/Chavanette). This is a narrow, well-defined path, rocky in places, going more steeply up the hillside.

The col (1hr 40mins) sits on the French/Swiss border and is liberally equipped with signposts, not only the French and standard yellow Swiss, but also direction signs for the official Portes de Soleil runs. Follow the sign to Lac Vert/Les Crosets/Champery onto the GR.5, marked by the usual red/white stripes. It is 10mins to the Refuge de Chésery which has the Swiss flag flying above it *(see below for details)* and overlooks the attractive Lac Vert, alt. 1,972m, a small round lake nestling in a bowl in the mountains. You can see the GR.5 snaking round the left side of the lake and over the top of another pass. *The terrace of the refuge is perfectly situated for a drink and a rest to contemplate the lake and surrounding alpine scenery (no ski-lifts to mar the view). It is a very popular spot in summer, especially at weekends.*

Retrace your path back to the signposts and follow the sign to Montriond 2hr 30mins/Col de Bassachaux 1hr 15mins. This is a balcony walk on a well-defined path which undulates along the side of the mountain with the track visible a long way in front (GR signs on rocks). There are numerous ski-lifts in the valley down on the left and you can check that your car is still safely parked. The peaks on the other side of the valley are dotted with the ski-lifts of the well-known resort of Morzine Avoriaz. *In early autumn the slopes are russet coloured from the bilberry bushes - this is the time when you may see the local farmers picking the small blue berries which*

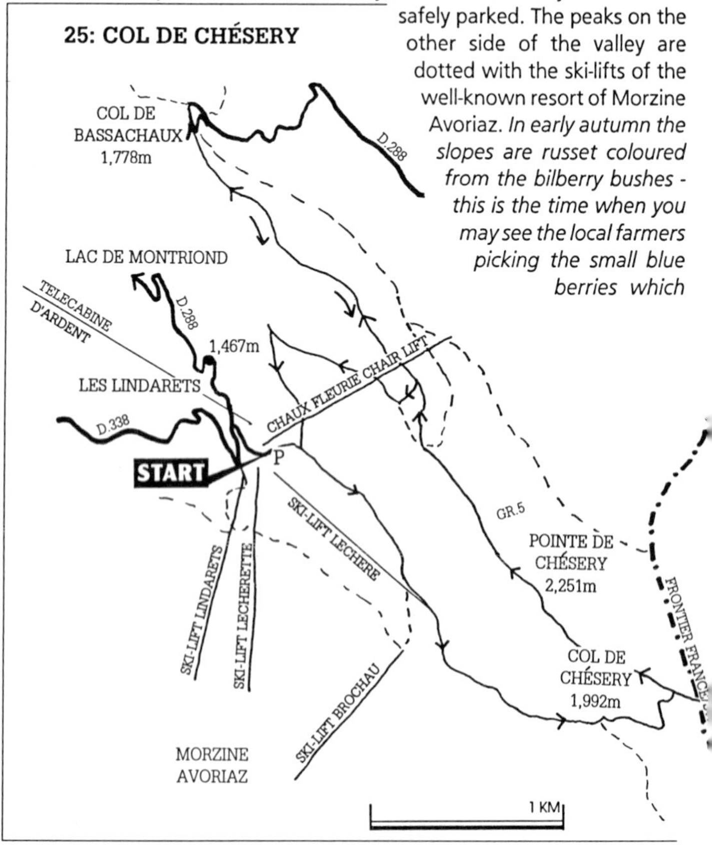

are then made into jam or delicious tarts. They scrape the bushes with a wooden comb which has a box on the end for the berries to fall into - each farmer has his own picking territory and intruders are not particularly welcome! The heather is also in bloom in September giving added colour to the mountainside.

The path goes underneath an electricity line (2hrs 40mins) to a signpost which says Col de Bassachaux 30mins straight/Les Lindarets to the left. (*If you are tired you can return to Les Lindarets from this point.)* Continue straight to Bassachaux. The path widens into a level jeep track going through occasional coniferous trees and crossing rivulets of water if the weather has been wet. There are lovely views to the left of Lac Montriond with the surrounding peaks reflected in its deep green water. Cross under the Chaux-Fleurie chair-lift and past a junction off to the right; this is the higher path from the Col de Chésery over the Crête des Rochassons, which is only for those who do not mind airy places! Continue straight on round the mountain.

There are usually lots of cars and people when you arrive at the Col de Bassachaux (3hrs 15mins) since it is accessible from Châtel in the Abondance valley and boasts a well-frequented restaurant. One is compensated with a wonderful panorama down the Abondance valley to Châtel and one of the best uninterrupted views of the majestic Mont de Grange, alt. 2,432m, the second highest peak in the Chablais region.

Retrace your steps for half an hour until you see a wide ski-run down to the right just before the signpost indicating the path down to Les Lindarets (3hrs 45mins). Walk down the slope and follow another sign to the right, which leads on to a wide jeep track taking you underneath the chair-lift again in the direction of the col, only lower down, before doubling back down to the valley just beyond where you parked your car (4hrs 15mins). *Note: a lot of earth moving is in progress round here and the slope is being flattened for a new ski-run so the track down may well be modified soon.*

Refuge de Chésery, Lac Vert, tel. Switzerland 025/79.14.24.
Famille Jean-Paul Es-Borrat, CH-1873 Val D'Illiez.
Open all summer - dormitory for 35 people - drinks and snacks available.
Fishing permits for the Lac Vert sold here.

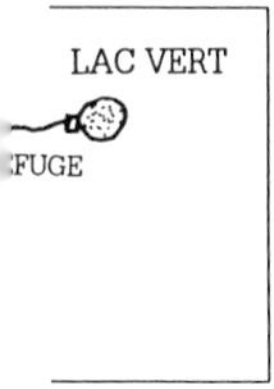

Remarks: Apart from the initial climb up to the Col de Chésery this is an easy balcony walk with glorious views of the Lac de Montriond and (at the Col de Bassachaux) the Abondance valley and Mt. de Grange. About 10 years ago I can remember skiing down into this valley from Switzerland as it was already part of the Portes de Soleil ski complex,

where you can ski from resort to resort for hundreds of kilometres; the place was practically deserted with one little hut and a sole ski-lift to Morzine Avoriaz. Now it has been defaced by more ski-lifts and chalets, making the valley a criss-cross of wires. In summer the valley is swarming with tourists, as is the nearby hamlet of Les Lindarets which specialises in goats and everything relating to them! However, the crowds are mainly static and once away from the valley you meet fewer people. The walk is worth doing, even for the educational experience of how natural landscape can be damaged by human progress!

26: POINTE DE RESSACHAUX - Alt. 2,173 metres
(Chablais region)

Difficulty:	Medium/difficult - a long haul to the top through woods and then a grassy shoulder; keep to the lower path round the summit if you suffer from vertigo.
Time:	5hrs.
Height gain:	1,132 metres.
Maps:	Editions Didier & Richard IGN No.3 Massifs du Chablais Faucigny & Genevois 1:50,000. Cartes IGN 3528 ET Top 25 Morzine Massif du Chablais 1:25,000.
Depart from:	La Grangette (Morzine) - 1,052 metres.
Signposting:	Good in parts - follow yellow circles.

How to get there (from Geneva)
Take the motorway to Chamonix and exit at No.15, Boëge/St. Jeoire. Turn left briefly on the D.903 and watch for the D.9 right signposted Fillinges, Samoëns and Vallée Verte. Follow this road to the Pont de Fillinges and then turn right on the D.907 direction Taninges/Samoëns. (ALTERNATIVELY go through Annemasse and take the D.907 direction Taninges/Samoëns.) In Taninges turn left on the D.902 direction Morzine. Go to the centre of Morzine and cross the bridge making for the church. At the end of the bridge turn right signposted Vallée de la Manche and Télépherique Nyon/ Charmossière. Drive by the start of the télépherique and at La Grangette turn back left (200m after the sign bearing the name of the hamlet). Park on the left about 400m along this road, next to a bench and opposite a wooden signpost saying Pointe de Ressachaux.

Directions

Follow the wooden sign which says Pointe de Ressachaux 2hrs 30mins (this is optimistic) /Le Creux 1hr 30mins. The path is narrow and goes immediately steeply up through tall coniferous trees and beech wood with yellow circles to show the way. A few minutes from the start bear right and keep on the main path which is well trodden with a few tree roots to be negotiated - it is steep all the way! You reach a clearing (45mins) and a large ruined chalet called Les Mernaies consisting of piles of tumble-down wooden beams. From here it is less steep with more open woodland. Keep on the main path where there is a path going off to the left (1hr) (yellow and red marking on a rock and a wooden arrow) - it looks like a T-junction on the map.

The path comes out into open alpine pasture (1hr 10mins) with a good view of the Morzine valley below and the Le Plénay Télépherique up to the ski area on the other side of the valley. There is a little hut with La Piot marked on it to the left (called l'Apiot according to the map!). Continue straight - you will notice a narrow undefined path coming in from the right; this is the way you will return. The path is still well defined going up fairly steeply through wild raspberry and alder bushes. The peak of the Ressachaux mountain is visible ahead and you can see the long steep shoulder you have to go up which looks rather daunting! The path takes you into a combe (shallow valley) with a number of small huts dotted about. This is a place to take a well earned rest before tackling the second part of the ascent.

Make for the huts called Le Creux which you can see over on the left and the path which you can see going up the side of the mountain. After skirting around them, the path climbs up steeply through open meadowland and then some bushes on to the shoulder of the mountain; in high summer there are lots of tall yellow and purple monkshood, the feathery purple adenostyles with their big green leaves, cornflowers, scabious and astrantia; in June the slopes are covered with the attractive creamy pasque flowers (alpine anemones). On the left there is a clear view of the village of Morzine in the valley below.

Now begins a hard ascent up the long grassy shoulder of the mountain - it seems to go on forever! Higher up the slopes are carpeted with trumpet gentians in June. Look carefully as the path divides about 150m below the summit (this is easy to miss); here you need to keep to the left. If you suffer from vertigo take the right fork which curls round the side of the mountain to the col without going to the summit. The left path takes you up to and along a precipitous ridge to the Pointe, alt. 2,173m (2hrs 45mins), which is rocky and rather airy. You have an interesting view over to the ski resort of Morzine Avoriaz built on the edge of an imposing rock face, with its many dark wooden apartment buildings built to blend in with the surrounding mountain and its ski-lifts going in all directions - all rather majestic from this

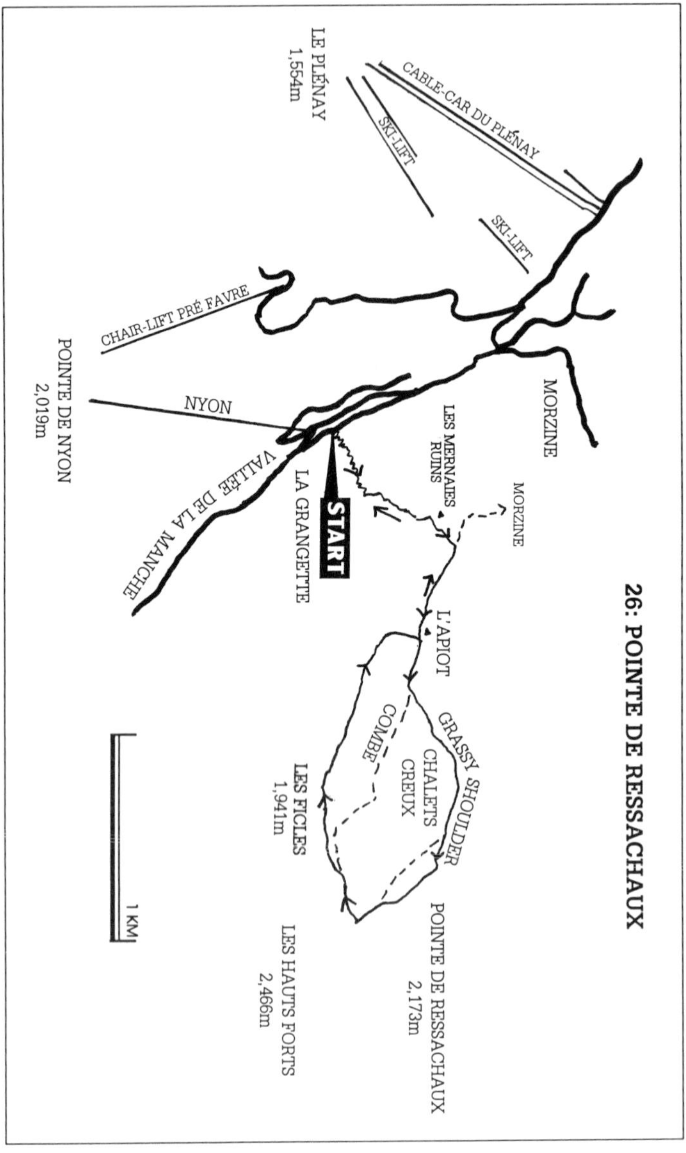
26: POINTE DE RESSACHAUX
LE PLÉNAY
1,554m
CABLE-CAR DU PLÉNAY
SKI-LIFT
SKI-LIFT
CHAIR-LIFT PRÉ FAVRE
POINTE DE NYON
2,019m
NYON
MORZINE
LES MERNAIES
RUINS
MORZINE
VALLÉE DE LA MANCHE
LA GRANGETTE
START
L'APIOT
GRASSY SHOULDER
COMBE
CHALETS
CREUX
LES FICLES
1,941m
1 KM
POINTE DE RESSACHAUX
2,173m
LES HAUTS FORTS
2,466m

angle. Further round are the high peaks of the Les Hauts Forts range.

Retrace your steps about 10m, then clamber down steeply through grass and skirt round to the left below the summit rock onto a narrow but well defined path. It becomes rather rocky at the end but it is not difficult. This leads to a small col called Pic à Talon (3hrs) where just before the col you join up with the easier path going along the south flank of the mountain. From here you can see the path going right down to the huts of Le Creux. There are lovely views straight ahead of the Môle, Pointe de Marcelly and the mountains round Pra de Lys, and nearer left of the Tête de Bostan near Samoëns.

For a more interesting way back do not follow the path with the yellow circles down to a hut you can see below, but keep to the ridge where there is a less defined track which goes round the end of the shallow valley with extensive views both sides. (Author's note: the last time I did this walk which was in high summer, the path seemed to have disappeared altogether but nevertheless we managed to get round and found the path down through the dense alder bushes.) The path skirts round the combe, eventually through alder bushes and shrubs and to the left there is a precipitous rock face which falls to the valley below; luckily the track does not go close to the edge so you are not aware of it! You can see clearly on the other side of the combe the way you took up. The path curls round and down through dense alder bushes and rowan trees and at times is rather undefined - it may be rather muddy after rainfall.

You arrive back at the mountain hut of l'Apiot (4hrs) at the start of the shallow valley from where you retrace your steps down to your car (5hrs).

ALTERNATIVELY: If you do not wish to take the ridge path round, follow the defined path down with the yellow dots. This takes you past a hut built next to a large rock and back down the combe to the L'Apiot hut - this is marginally quicker than going round by the ridge.

Remarks: The Pointe de Ressachaux dominates the town of Morzine and looks rather imposing from afar. It is a strenuous walk but not technically difficult as it is through woods and over a long grassy shoulder where you are rather exposed to the elements. From the summit you get a bird's-eye view of the ski resort of Morzine Avoriaz and the nearby Hauts Forts ridge, the highest in the Chablais area. Despite the proximity of Morzine this is not a well-known walk so your enjoyment is not spoiled by hordes of people.

27: POINTE DE LA GAY - Alt. 1,801 metres
(Chablais region)

Difficulty:	Medium with one short steep descent in woods.
Time:	4hrs 30mins.
Height gain:	789 metres.
Maps:	Editions Didier & Richard IGN No.3 Massifs du Chablais Faucigny & Genevois 1:50,000. Cartes IGN 3429 ET Top 25 Bonneville/Cluses 1:25,000. (NOTE: Bellevaux village is off this map but not Pointe de la Gay).
Depart from:	L'Ermont 1,020 metres.
Signposting:	Adequate till Pointe de la Gay and then nothing indicated for the circular way back. However, it is not difficult to find.

How to get there (from Geneva)
Take the motorway towards Chamonix and exit at No.15, Boëge/St. Jeoire. Then turn left briefly on the D.903 and watch for the D.9 right signposted Fillinges, Samoëns and Vallée Verte. Follow this road to the Pont de Fillinges and then turn right on the D.907 direction Taninges/Samoëns to St. Jeoire. (ALTERNATIVELY go through Annemasse and take the D.907 direction Taninges to St. Jeoire.) At St. Jeoire take the D.26 through Onnion and Megevette to Bellevaux. Turn right into the village square and then take the small road left around the church, signposted L'Ermont. Go along this windy road for about 4km, through the hamlet of Le Frêne and just before the hamlet of L'Ermont, cross a bridge and park on the right-hand side where there are wooden signs saying Les Nants/Col de la Balme/ Nifflon/Pointe de la Gay.

Directions
Up to the Col de la Balme these are the same as for the Grand Rocher de Nifflon.

Go straight up the wide jeep track (ignore the one going off to the left). The woods slope upwards on the left and the Nants river flows through a ravine on the right. After 10mins go past an old chalet on a corner and then keep straight on where another path branches off to the right (20mins) which is the way you will come back. Here the river crosses under the track and is now on your left as you go through an attractive gorge which then

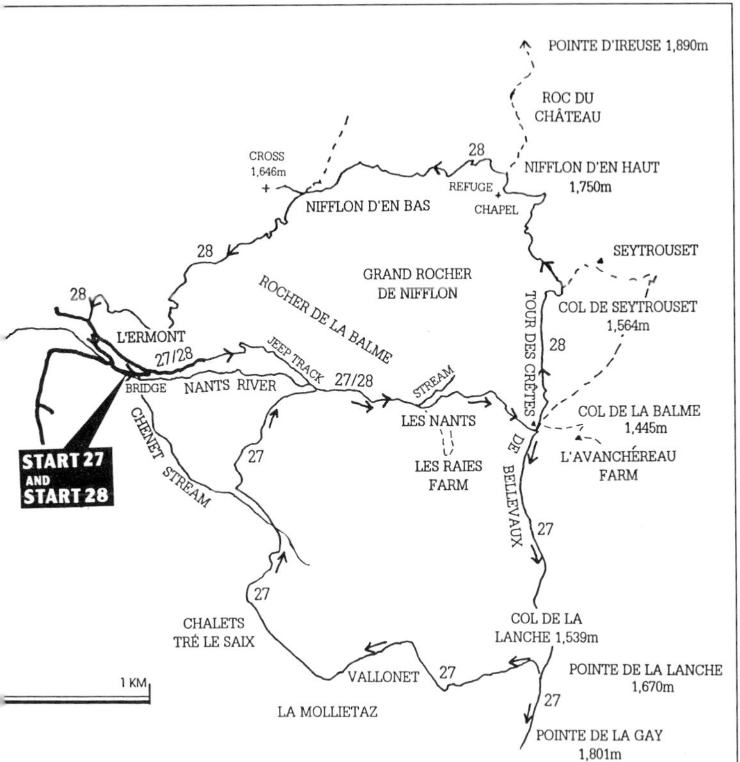

27: POINTE DE LA GAY
28: GRAND ROCHER DE NIFFLON

levels out into a narrow valley with meadows and the large rocky mountain of the Nifflon on the left.

Cross a wooden bridge over a stream (40mins) where there are more signposts and you arrive at the unspoilt hamlet of Nants. Walk right through the hamlet and turn left in front of an old barn just before the road bears to the right to Les Raies Farm. *Note: There should be a sign here saying Col de Balme but it could have disappeared (see Nifflon explanation).* This is a narrow, steepish path, with a row of fir trees on the right, which comes out into an attractive meadow with a quaint old farm on the left. Follow up the slope of the meadow and you will come to a defined path which goes through coniferous trees. The path climbs, steeply in places, for 400m to the Col de la Balme, alt. 1,445m (1hr 15mins), which is an open grassy shelf with a small wooden hut to the left. You can see a large farm below at the end of a narrow valley which continues down to the village of Seytroux. Straight ahead is a magnificent view of the Chablais peaks, including the Cornettes de Bise, Mont Chauffé and Mont de Grange.

Turn right at the sign which says Pointe de la Gay (left goes to the Nifflon). The grassy path climbs upwards and after a short while goes between two fences. It then levels out and you are on the side of a slope which becomes a wide ridge with spectacular views of the Dranse valley to Morzine through fir trees down on the left and of the Nifflon on the right. There are occasional red/yellow signs on trees. Go straight on at signposts in the woods (1hr 30mins) to Col de Lanche; this is a narrow path criss-crossed with tree roots through stunted coniferous trees and mossy, dank woodland where there are lots of mushrooms in autumn. You come to a rocky place which is the Pointe de la Balme, alt. 1,591m, but there is no sign.

Shortly after watch your footing as the path goes down steeply (not to be done on a wet day!) into a sort of dip between two mountains at the Col de la Lanche, alt. 1,539m (1hr 45mins). At the col you join the jeep track coming up from the left (this is the one which goes by the farm you see below the Col de la Balme) and continue straight along it, following the wooden sign to Pointe de la Gay. It goes through tall coniferous trees with lovely views of the Nifflon mountain on the right and becomes narrower before another sign up to the left to Pointe de la Gay (2hrs). Follow this still narrower path up through fir and nut trees (green signs on trees) with a steep hillside to the right. Walk through open pleasant meadowland till you get to the crest of the hill which is the Pointe de la Lanche, alt. 1,670m, with another superb view.

Turn right, following the line of the hill (ignore the path off to the left) and climb about 140m to the top of the mountain (2hrs 35mins). The hill must have been covered with bushes at one time but these have all been cut back and it looks rather shorn and untidy. There are lots of goat droppings on the top which makes picnicking rather hazardous *(though we had ours and were rewarded by seeing an eagle glide by).* From the summit you can see north over to Lake Léman with the Jura on the horizon to the north and looking south all the Chablais range and particularly the jagged ridge of the Roc d'Enfer with the Mont Blanc range in the background; nearby is the brooding dark rock of the Rocher de Nifflon with the hamlet of Nants nestling in the valley below it. The path continues along the crest past the Col des Follys to the Roc d'Enfer. Retrace your steps to the Pointe de la Lanche.

The first time I did this walk we met a dear old man whom we had seen earlier picking myrtilles (bilberries). He very kindly took us down the mountain and showed us the way back as the path is not very clear and there are no signposts. He had two huge buckets of berries with which his wife was going to make jam. He explained that he was a retired labourer but still kept six cows and some hens as well as taking in paying guests in his three spare rooms. On the way down we met two other old men who were also picking berries - it was fascinating talking to them and finding out what life was like in the village of Bellevaux before tourists and ski-lifts invaded this rural mountain region.

At the Pointe de la Lanche go left to the Pointe de la Gay signpost where you took a left turn off the jeep track on the way up. Note: the signpost is not so easy to see on your way back (3hrs). Turn left and keep on the path which becomes less defined though there are green signs on a rock. 5mins later you go through a green turnstile in a fence and then continue down over gentle meadowland dotted with fir trees; there is no clear path over the meadows but go straight.

You arrive at Vallonet which seems to be just a grassy cross-roads in a dip (3hrs 10mins). The path to the right goes back to Les Nants. (This is an alternative, easier way back and takes about 1hr 30mins to the hamlet.) Even though there is no proper track, go straight on over a hill and down the other side. From here you can see the wide grassy path going up to the chalets of Tré le Saix which you can see in the distance over to the left.

BE CAREFUL HERE as there are no signs and you can see numerous cow paths crossing the meadowlands. Make for the wide grassy path going up to the chalets but before it turns the first corner bear down into the combe (shallow valley) on your right. Go down the easy slope, cross the combe and join the path you can see up on the right (do not go through the fence at the end of the combe). Follow this path, now well defined, along the side of the combe (there is a red mark on a tree to the right) and go through a green turnstile at the end of the combe (3hrs 45mins). From here go downwards through open and then later denser woodland; there are the occasional red splashes on trees but keep your eyes on the track as it is not well trodden.

CAREFUL: Look for a card with an A on it nailed to a tall fir tree on the left and shortly after there is a grassy cross-roads (4hrs). Go right here and keep right all the way as you go down through dense beech woods till you meet a logging track (4hrs 10mins). Continue down on this logging track, ignoring any paths branching off, with the Nifflon mountain ahead of you, till you reach the original road to Les Nants. Turn left and walk down to where you left the car (4hrs 30mins).

Remarks: The Pointe de la Gay, although right next door to the rocky Rocher de Nifflon, is a complete contrast. It is a grassy, wooded mountain covered with shrubs and bilberry bushes with open alpine pastures on the way back

- a delightful walk at all times of the year, especially in high summer as this unspoilt part of the Haute Savoie is not invaded by hundreds of tourists. There are dramatic views of the surrounding Chablais peaks, especially the well-known Roc d'Enfer. For part of the return the path is not defined so attention to the directions is needed. Don't forget to look out for the eagle!

Just below the Pointe de la Gay there was an enormous landslide in March 1942 which destroyed about 15 chalets and three saw-mills as it slid down the mountainside. It created a natural dam in the Brevon river in the valley below completely drowning the then existing hamlet of L'Econduit. The very attractive Lac de Vallon, as we know it today, is the result of this catastrophe.

28: GRAND ROCHER DE NIFFLON - (see map p157)
Alt. 1,816 metres (Chablais region)

Difficulty:	Medium - one short scramble.
Time:	4hrs 30mins.
Height gain:	796 metres.
Maps:	Editions Didier & Richard IGN No.3 Massifs du Chablais Faucigny & Genevois 1:50,000. Cartes IGN Top 25 3428 ET Thonon, Evian 1:25,000.
Depart from:	L'Ermont - 1,020 metres.
Signposting:	Good in parts though beware as existing signs tend to disappear - sporadic yellow/red/green stripes. Path is well defined most of the way round.

How to get there (from Geneva)
Take the motorway to Chamonix and exit at No.15, Boëge/St. Jeoire. Turn left briefly on the D.903 and watch for the D.9 right signposted Fillinges, Samoëns and Vallée Verte. Follow this road to the Pont de Fillinges and then turn right on the D.907 direction Taninges/Samoëns. (ALTERNATIVELY go through Annemasse and take the D.907 direction Taninges to St. Jeoire.) At St. Jeoire take the D.26 through Onnion and Megevette to Bellevaux. Turn right into the village square and then take the small road left around the church, signposted L'Ermont. Go along this windy road for about 4km, through the hamlet of Le Frêne and just before the hamlet of L'Ermont, cross a bridge and park on the right-hand side where there are wooden signs saying Les Nants/Col de la Balme/Nifflon/Pointe de la Gay.

Climbing to the Trou de la Mouche. (Walk 46)

Top of the Môle

Scrambling up to the Trou de la Mouche *(Photo by Colin Mitchell)*

Directions

Up to the Col de la Balme these are the same as for Pointe de la Gay. Go straight up the wide jeep track (ignore the one going off to the left). The woods slope upwards on the left and the Nants river flows through a ravine on the right. After 10mins go past an old chalet on a corner and then keep straight on where another path branches off to the right (20mins). Here the river crosses under the track and is now on your left as you go through an attractive gorge which then levels out into a narrow valley with meadows and the large rocky mountain of the Nifflon on the left.

Cross a wooden bridge over a stream (40mins) where there are more signposts and you arrive at the unspoilt hamlet of Nants. Walk right through the hamlet and turn left in front of a barn just before the road bears to the right to Les Raies Farm. *Note: when we did the walk the first time, the sign was being repaired by an old man at the barn and luckily we asked him as otherwise we would have walked right by! - the second time it had completely disappeared. However, the tourist office assures me that the sign will be replaced.* This is a narrow, steepish path, with a row of firs on the right, which comes out into an attractive meadow with a quaint old farm on the left. Follow up the slope of the meadow and you will come to a defined path which goes through coniferous trees. The path climbs, steeply in places, for 400m to the Col de la Balme, alt. 1,445m (1hr 15mins), which is an open grassy shelf with a small wooden hut to the left. You can see a large farm below at the end of a narrow valley which continues down to the village of Seytroux. Straight ahead is a magnificent view of the Chablais peaks including the Cornettes de Bise, Mont Chauffé and Mont de Grange.

Turn left at the sign which says Nifflon 1hr (right goes to the Pointe de la Gay). Beyond the hut take the left fork signposted Nifflon d'en Haut (the right one indicates Pointe de Riandets) which climbs up medium steep through meadows, sparse tall firs, wild raspberries and, in August, masses of tall red fire flowers. The path levels out and curls round the mountain through shady woods, with lovely views through the trees over the Bellevaux valley. Be careful of the fir tree roots which seem to grow out of the path itself.

You finally come out into an open meadow at the Col de Seytrouset with the imposing Nifflon rock formation to your left. Go through an electric fence (1hr 30mins) - there is no signpost here but it is evident you should turn left as you can see the narrow path going up beside the fence. Before turning left it is worth going straight on to take a look at the magnificent view. Below there is a jeep track up to an alpine farm called Seytrouset where you can see lots of cattle. The path climbs fairly steeply up the hillside, joining the path coming up from the farm at a sign back saying Col de Balme and getting nearer and nearer to the rocky surface of the Nifflon. As you climb up the rocky side of the mountain, there is some scrambling where you may need both hands but it is not technically difficult and the path is well defined. If you look back you can see the track all the way back to the Col de Balme.

The summit is a surprise as it doesn't fall down sharply on the other side but into a grassy bowl with a collection of huts and a cute little chapel and another ridge beyond. Behind there is a magnificent panorama which starts with all the Chablais summits, Dent d'Oche, Cornettes de Bise, Mont Chauffé round to the Roc d'Enfer, and in front is Lake Léman with the Jura a dark smudge on the horizon. Take the visible path down into the huddle of huts which is called Nifflon d'en Haut, alt 1,783m (2hrs 15mins). There is a refuge here where you can stay the night but you have to get the key from the syndicat d'initiative in Bellevaux. The chapel is made of stone with a galvanised iron roof and a very attractive iron-shaped steeple with an imposing weather-vane in the shape of a cockerel; opposite the chapel is a tall wooden cross.

This little chapel was originally constructed in wood in 1796 by the Parish Priest of Bellevaux who decided to close the village church because of the Revolution and celebrate mass on the mountain (it must have been a long walk for the parishioners!). He dedicated the chapel to Notre Dames des Neiges (Virgin of the Snows) probably because of the numerous snow crevices from which the shepherds watered their flocks. In 1821 the wood was replaced by stone and a statue of the Virgin and child was sculpted by Emmanuel Gougain. In 1886 the chapel was renovated again and the steeple added.

Take the path through the huts and on the other side there is a sign which says Pointe D'Ireuse (it is a 30m steepish climb to the top). To continue, follow the sign Nifflon d'en Bas and pass between two big rocky depressions. The *mountain is riddled with these big rocky holes which are characteristic of limestone areas. In Savoyard "patois" (dialect) they are called "tannes". In very dry summers the shepherds would lower big wooden barrels into the holes to draw up the snow still lying at the bottom.* At first the path appears to be an old mule track which curls down into a narrow valley. It is a pleasant rocky walk, sprinkled with coniferous and rowan trees, where you will find lots of flowers and butterflies in summer and moss, bracken and various mushrooms in autumn. The path levels out through woodland, winding round the side of the mountain, rather like the path coming up, with a lovely view in front of Lake Léman.

You reach Nifflon d'en Bas in 30mins (3hrs) which is in a sort of bowl open at both ends and consisting of three chalets and a large wooden cross. The path goes down left just before the cross and is signposted L'Ermont. If you want a fantastic viewpoint, go through the hamlet and take the obvious path up to a promontory with another cross on it which is called the Rochers de la Mache, alt. 1,646m. The view from here is breath taking; to the north is a panoramic view to Lake Léman, where the intervening mountains are more gentle and rounded; to the south are the Chablais mountains and Mont Billiat to the east among other peaks, to the south-west is the Hirmentaz ridge and the Vallée Verte. Down in the valley you can see the village of Bellevaux.

Retrace your steps to the wooden cross (3hrs 30mins) and turn downwards through high vegetation and eventually into coniferous woods where the path is more defined. This is a delightful descent through cool beech and fir woods. Later on the woods get denser and the path becomes steeper but never too difficult. You come out of the woods into meadow land and then into woods again with a view below of the village of L'Ermont. After three quarters of an hour (4hrs 15mins) you come to a signpost which says Le Chatelard 10mins/Bellevaux 40mins, (signpost back to Nifflon says 2hrs 30mins). Take the jeep track towards Bellevaux till it reaches a tarmac road. Left says L'Ermont but turn right which goes down the road and round the corner to the car park beyond the bridge (4hrs 30mins).

Remarks: An incredibly beautiful walk with magnificent views in a really unspoilt area of the Haute Savoie where, even in high summer, you will not meet many other walkers. The name Nifflon comes from the latin Nec Fleure meaning area where there is no water, as the mountains in this region are predominantly limestone. There is no open water source on this mountain as all the water filters through the enormous grottoes and into hidden rivulets, soaking the earth. The pastures are therefore very fertile and the butter from here has a special rich flavour.

29: POINTE DE CHALUNE - Alt. 2,113 metres
(Chablais region)

Difficulty:	Medium but long with quite a bit of up and down.
Time:	6hrs.
Height gain:	993 metres.
Maps:	Editions Didier & Richard IGN No.3 Massifs du Chablais Faucigny & Genevois 1:50,000. Cartes IGN 3429 ET Top 25 Bonneville/Cluses 1:25,000.
Depart from:	La Chèvrerie (Lac de Vallon) - 1,108 metres.
Signposting:	Good in parts - yellow and blue markings but not consistent.

How to get there (from Geneva)

Take the motorway to Chamonix and exit at No.15, Boëge/St. Jeoire. Then turn left briefly on the D.903 and watch for the D.9 right signposted Fillinges, Samoëns and Vallée Verte. Follow this road to the Pont de Fillinges and then turn right on the D.907 direction Taninges/Samoëns. (ALTERNATIVELY go through Annemasse and take the D.907 direction Taninges/Samoëns.) At St. Jeoire (before Taninges) turn left on the D.26 and continue through the villages of Onnion and Megevette for about 13km. About 2km before Bellevaux take the narrow road going down on the right, signposted Lac de Vallon, La Chèvrerie. Continue past the very pretty lake and the hamlet of La Chèvrerie and leave your car in a large ugly parking area where there is a big green galvanised-iron snack bar, piles of enormous logs, the Torchon chair-lift, and a notice board showing the different skiing areas.

Directions

There are lots of signs here as it is the starting point for a number of walks. Take the wide track to the right of the chair-lift signposted Pointe de Chalune/Roc d'Enfer. This is a wide muddy jeep track with the Brevon stream flowing down on the right. After 10mins you arrive at Le Finge on your left (signposted with a yellow mark underneath) which consists of one small hut and a fish breeding pond. After Le Finge keep straight with the stream always on the right and ignore the path off to the left. When you reach a fork take either path as they merge again about 50m later.

You reach Les Favières (20mins), which consists of a pretty old stone hut and two other wooden huts; there is a sign on one of the wooden huts and a bright yellow splash. Continue straight on following signs Col de Foron/ Source de Brevon/Lac de Pététoz through dense coniferous forest to an area which has really been messed up by logging; there are mounds of mud, stones and tree trunks. You come to another bevy of signposts showing Cor de Foron 1 hr 20mins ahead (left Col de Graidon/Crêtes de Bellevaux). According to the map you are now at Souvroz d'en Bas. Continue upwards through woods medium steep (there is a sign down to the right indicating the path to Source de Brevon/Lac de Pététoz), on a path which curls round the side of the mountain becoming rockier and eventually going through a green stile. If you look back here there is a glorious view of La Chèvrerie and the Lac de Vallon. There is another little river now on the right which is the Ruisseau de Souvroz.

You come to an attractive bowl in the mountains with the end of the impressive Roc d'Enfer on the left and the Col de Foron visible ahead. There is a sign indicating straight ahead Col de Foron/Roc d'Enfer (1hr 15mins). The name Petit Souvroz is inscribed on a rock and there is a wooden trough with eau potable" (drinking water) which makes a refreshing stop. *This is rocky*

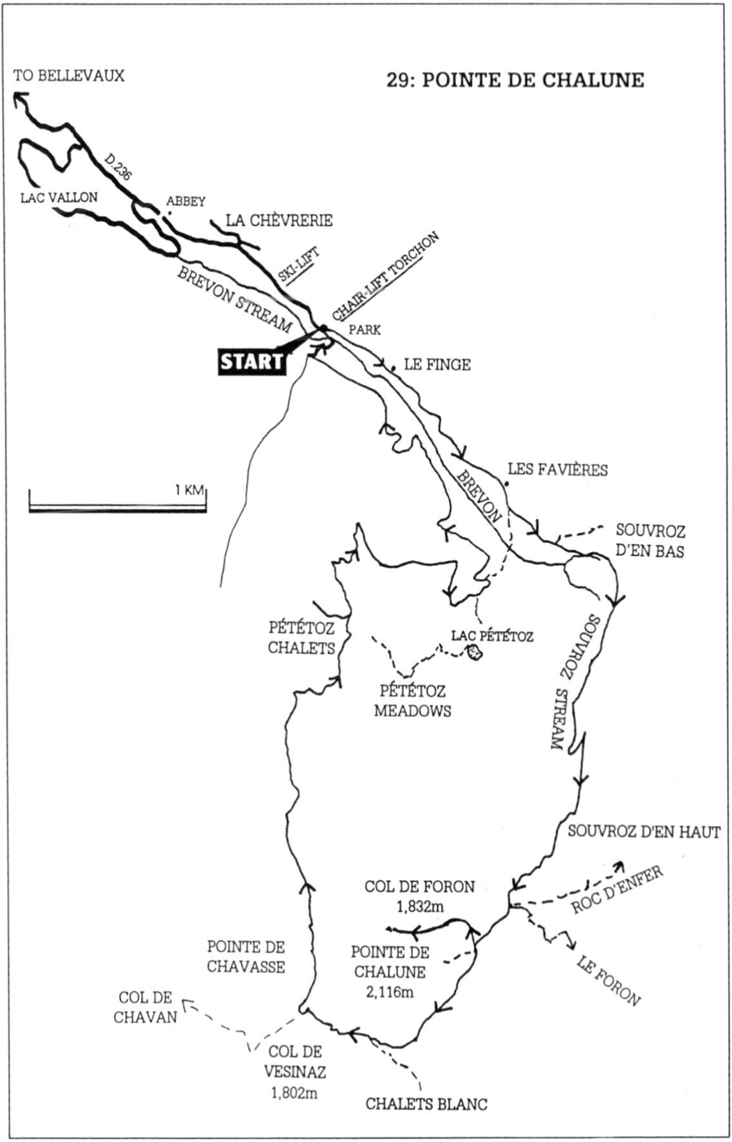
29: POINTE DE CHALUNE
TO BELLEVAUX
D.236
LAC VALLON
ABBEY
LA CHÈVRERIE
SKI-LIFT
CHAIR-LIFT TORCHON
BREVON STREAM
PARK
START
LE FINGE
1 KM
LES FAVIÈRES
BREVON
SOUVROZ
D'EN BAS
PÉTÉTOZ
CHALETS
LAC PÉTÉTOZ
PÉTÉTOZ
MEADOWS
SOUVROZ STREAM
SOUVROZ D'EN HAUT
COL DE FORON
1,832m
ROC D'ENFER
POINTE DE
CHAVASSE
POINTE DE
CHALUNE
2,116m
LE FORON
COL DE
CHAVAN
COL DE
VESINAZ
1,802m
CHALETS BLANC

country so keep an eye out for marmots - they announce their presence by a piercing whistle, which is the sentry's signal to the others that intruders are in the vicinity. The track continues, crossing the rushing stream from time to time in a series of slopes like giant steps, still in the attractive bowl with mountains all round and the col (pass) on the horizon. At the end the path gets much steeper and becomes somewhat eroded; there are blue marks from time to time on the path.

40mins from the start of the bowl turn right at the Col de Foron, alt. 1,832m (2hrs), following the signpost Col de Chalune, alt. 1,896m, following blue splashes. You can see the pass clearly up on the right as you skirt round the mountain. To your left is the airy path along the Roc D'Enfer which is not for anyone suffering from vertigo; there is a clear view of the path coming up from the farm at Foron and, if you look behind, you can see the way you have walked up from La Chèvrerie; on the horizon is the entire Mont Blanc range.

It takes 15mins from the Col de Foron to the Col de Chalune (2hrs 15mins) on a defined path. From here there are extensive views down into the skiing village of Pra de Lys and over to the impressive Marcelly ridge, with the cross at the end which dominates the town of Taninges. You can go straight on here if you do not wish to climb to the Pointe, otherwise double back to the right along a path which goes up to a spur, then round to the left and along a ridge to the top following blue splashes. This is quite an exposed steep path and it takes about 20mins to climb 220m (2hrs 35mins) but is well worth the effort when you get to the top as there are incredible views of the surrounding peaks which include the Pointe d'Uble, the Roc d'Enfer, the Rocher de Nifflon, Pointe de la Gay and the Môle. The Lac de Roy is down below with the Marcelly ridge behind and you can see Lake Léman and the Jura in the distance - there are not many viewpoints where you can see so far in all directions!

Retrace your steps to the col. Avoid the first path to the right which seems to go across the mountain and take the next one which goes down towards some chalets (Chalets Blanc). The path is initially fairly steep and then wiggles around the mountain about 100 metres above the chalets before continuing down. You can see the way right round the mountain which climbs up between two interesting peaks, the one on the right of a curiously pink, streaky colouring but with no name and the other called the Pointe de Chavasse.

At a T-junction just before the Col de Vésinaz, alt. 1,802m (3hrs 30mins) turn right and bear slightly to the left over an ugly green stile through a fence, quite out of place in such a lovely setting (there is a path up to the left to the Col de Chavan which you cross on the Haute Pointe Walk No. 42). There is no signpost here but some blue and yellow markings; you get a lovely view of the rocky west side of the Pointe de Chalune.

Go down the other side on the top path (there are two paths near together), which takes you to the right of a woody hump, following blue markings and then yellow ones. You are now walking in a very attractive hanging valley which takes you over a rise and down again past a little pond. You undulate down the narrow valley and then into a wider one and walk along the side of a hill with woods in the valley bottom (there is a road right across the other side). In spring and summer the flowers here are spectacular. If you look back you can see the path you came down from the Pointe de Chalune and the Chalets Blanc.

You come to a signpost which indicates Col de Jorat (4hrs 25mins), though you hardly feel you are at a col and it is not marked on the map. This takes you out of the wide valley into the Pâturage (meadows) de Pététoz and then down the hill towards another valley. At a T-junction go left or right as they join up later. Make for the chalets you can see below called Pététoz (4hrs 45mins). The chalets are set in beautiful open meadows which are carpeted with yellow buttercups and white anemones in late spring; up over to the right you can see a small cross. Follow the sign on the side of one of the huts on a path across the meadowland and then into woodland by another green stile. You are now on a jeep track walking through spaced coniferous wood marked with red/white splashes! It is a pleasant path as there is no logging here.

Go right when you reach a big open clearing, continuing on the jeep track proper (don't take the path off to the right). There are blue splashes as you wind round the mountainside and continue down through open forest. You can now see over to Les Favières and the path up on the other side of the valley. Keep straight on when you arrive at a T-junction (5hrs 45mins) till you get back to the large parking area (6hrs). Note: if you go to the right at the T-junction, you eventually find yourself crossing the river again back to Les Favières. Then take the same logging track back.

Remarks: This is a long walk which goes over three passes and gives wonderful views of the whole area as far as Lake Léman and the Jura. We saw chamois and marmots on the way. There is a large troupeau (flock) of mouflons in the Col de Foron area though I have not personally seen them (see Flora and Fauna).

Faucigny/Haut Giffre Region

30: WALK ON PLATEAU D'ASSY - Alt. 1,620 metres
(Faucigny/Haut Giffre)

Difficulty: An easy balcony walk with fantastic views of the Mont Blanc range. Please read important note in the text concerning this walk.
Time: 4hrs.
Height gain: 563 metres.
Maps: Editions Didier & Richard IGN No.8 Massifs du Mont Blanc/Beaufortain 1:50,000.
Cartes IGN 3530 ET Top 25 Samoëns/Haut Giffre 1:25,000.
Depart from: Le Coudray 1,127 metres.
Signposting: Good except in one spot where the markings have been painted out.

How to get there (from Geneva)
Take the motorway direction Chamonix and exit at No.21, Passy/Le Fayat. Follow briefly the D.339 and D.39 signposted Passy/Plateau d'Assy before turning left on the D.43 in Passy. Continue on towards Plateau d'Assy for about 4km until you see a chapel on the left. At this point take the signpost left saying Bay and Refuge de Varan. Continue to the hamlet of Le Coudray (Chemin de Coudray) at the end of the road and park in the car park.

Directions
Start up the tarmac road beyond the chalets which soon becomes a wide jeep track through woods follow all signs to Varan (red/yellow splashes). After 15mins look for a sign to the left which says Chalet de Varan. There are a few wooden steps and then a narrow path upwards through woods. This is a short cut, but if you keep to the jeep track all the way up you get there anyway!

At Pertuis d'en bas, alt. 1,367m (45mins), follow the signpost to Chalets de Varan 35mins and Charbonnière 1hr 50mins. On the jeep track to the left there is a rock painted in different colours which looks quite hideous. *At this stage we saw an eagle whirling around above us in the air currents. It looked*

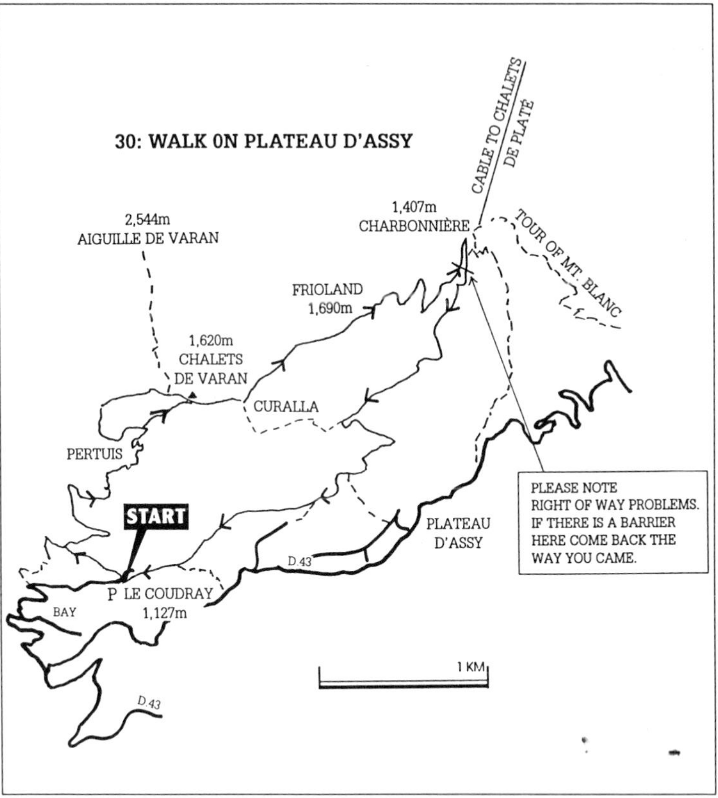

very impressive with the imposing Aiguille de Varan behind. This was the second eagle I have ever seen in the Alps so it was an exciting moment.

The track becomes stonier as it comes out of the woodland into open meadowland. On one side there is a beautiful view down the Arve valley and its little lakes with the entire Mont Blanc range beyond and on the other the dramatic rocky peak of the Aiguille de Varan. Behind is the Chaine des Aravis with the Mont Percée rearing up at the end. Keep on the jeep track or look out for another short cut to the right on a steep narrow track which cuts across a wide corner.

You arrive at the Chalets de Varan, alt. 1,620m (1hr 15mins) where you can stay overnight (see details below). Situated on an open ledge with magnificent views of the Mont Blanc range, it is a convenient place to stop

for refreshment. This is also the start of the walk up the Aiguille de Varan which is a tough climb of nearly 1,000m. Go down to the back of the refuge (the way you came up if you took the short cut) and follow the sign to Charbonnière 1hr 15mins (Tour du Pays de Mont Blanc) - this is not the official Mt. Blanc circuit but an offshoot. The path is defined and at first goes down through scattered woodland before levelling out. After 15mins and just before some shale the path divides and you can see the hamlet of Curalla down on your right. Continue straight but keep a sharp eye out for the red/yellow stripes. Where there is a red arrow on a stone go left upwards and over open hillside rather than straight into the woods. The path curls up and round the mountain and the views across to the Mont Blanc range are spectacular.

35mins later you come to Frioland, alt. 1,690m (1hr 45mins). This is a dip in the mountain side and the highest point of the walk. The grassy hump to the left is an ideal place for a picnic. Still defined the path, eroded in many places, winds medium steep down the hillside. To the right is the impressive rock wall of The Desert de Platé and the Derochoir (see Walk No. 36) with the Rochers des Fiz beyond. You come into

"La Porte du Soleil", sculpture by Albert Feraud - Plateau d'Assy

scattered and then dense woodland where there is an old mule trail with a wall on one side. You arrive at Charbonnière, alt. 1,407m (2hrs 15mins). This used to be a hamlet where they made charcoal (Charbonnière means charcoal burner in English) but is now just a sad, lonely huddle of little huts. There are all sorts of splashes on rocks, including yellow/red ones (the variant of the Mont Blanc circular walk goes straight on).and a long cable platform used to haul food to the Refuge de Platé which is visible on the skyline (the past tense is appropriate as most foodstuffs are now taken up by helicopter).

BE CAREFUL HERE - do not take the path signposted Plateau d'Assy 1hr but go back up the path you came down and at the first corner you will see a wooden sign left indicating "sans issue" with a walker painted on it. This part of the walk is an enigma as the Tourist Office obviously do not wish people to pass this way and the red/yellow splashes have been painted out with silver or look rather old. However, according to my map it is the only way back to Le Coudray so follow the still defined path across a field (there are signs still visible on a rock in the middle of this field) which lead up and to the left. In either case the path goes through the wood at the top end of the field.

IMPORTANT NOTE (as from summer 1995) there is a right of way problem here as the owner of this field wishes to build a chalet. The Tourist Office has assured me that they are trying to solve the problem and create another path through. **However, if the field is fenced off please go back the way you came.**

At the edge of the wood the path is not obvious but do not be discouraged as after a few minutes it becomes defined. Continue on an easy leafy path through woodland (there is a big cliff to the left which is difficult to see through the trees) and it is sometimes quite steep on the left. The splashes are indistinct and have been partly obliterated by silver paint. There are lovely open spaces with tantalising views of the valley below. After a rocky area where the path starts to descend you come to a seismograph station, with its own solar panel for power, consisting of boxes and gadgets on a tall iron pole (apparently to check the movement of the mountain).

About 1hr from the charcoal huts (3hrs 15mins) you reach the path going off right to the alpine chalets of Curalla. You are now on a wide stony jeep track for about 15mins which goes down towards the village of Plateau d'Assy. Ignore sign on left saying Balcon d'Assy by a concrete bunker but continue on past a nasty man-made yellow concrete waterfall and after 15mins take the path up right signposted Le Coudray (3hrs 30mins), on an attractive narrow stretch through woods and clearings. You get a good view of Plateau d'Assy through the trees.

15mins later go straight on at a cross-roads, still on a pleasant narrow wooded path with a huge cliff back to one side. At a T-junction follow the signpost right to Le Coudray through open meadowland and what looks like a private garden (though this is the official path), back to the car park (4hrs).

Remarks: This walk is ideal for a fit visitor who wants to do some hiking but has never really been in mountain country as you get magnificent views of the Mont Blanc range across the valley for a moderate effort! There is an added attraction in the world famous modern church in Plateau d'Assy called Notre Dame de Toute Grâce. Here there are dramatic stained glass windows by famous artists such as Chagall, Matisse, Lurcat, Léger and Bercot. There are also modern sculptures by well-known artists on the road from Passy to Plaine Joux. Beware, this is a well-known part of the Chamonix region and on weekends in high season you risk meeting a lot of people!

St Bernard's lily - Plateau d'Assy

31: REFUGE DU MOËDE D'ANTERNE - Alt. 2,003 metres
(Faucigny/Haut Giffre region)

Difficulty:	Easy up to the refuge but the way back along the gorge is tricky (marked with dots on map) so if you are not used to heights go back the way you came.
Time:	From Plaine Joux 5hrs 30mins/Le Chatelet 4hrs 30mins. Detour to Lac de Pormenaz 20mins.
Height gain:	748 metres (to refuge).
Maps:	Editions Didier & Richard IGN No.8 Massifs du Mont Blanc/Beaufontain 1:50,000. Cartes IGN 3530 ET Top 25 Samoëns/Haut Giffre 1:25,000.
Depart from:	Plaine Joux 1,360m or Le Chatelet 1,418m.
Signposting:	Excellent - this is a very popular walking area.

How to get there (from Geneva)
Take the motorway direction Chamonix and exit at No.21, Passy/Le Fayat. Follow briefly the D.339 and D.39 signposted Passy and Plateau d'Assy before turning left on the D.43 in Passy to Plateau d'Assy. At Plateau d'Assy follow the signposting to Plaine Joux. You can park your car at Plaine Joux which is a large open area and the start of various ski-lifts.

ALTERNATIVE: From Plaine Joux continue along the upper road marked Anterne/Chatelet for 2km (the last 400m unpaved) and park by the restaurant at Chatelet d'Ayere. This saves 1hr on the overall walk but you will miss the Lac Vert on the return path to Plaine Joux.

Directions
If you park at Plaine Joux walk along the paved road (signposted Col d'Anterne), which degrades into a jeep track and is fairly flat, for about 20mins to the alternative parking at the restaurant at Chatelet d'Ayere. On the left are the impressive white limestone cliffs of the southern end of the Rochers des Fiz and to the right incredible views down the valley to the Col d'Aravis with the Mont Blanc range on the other side. After the restaurant there is a big board saying Réserve Naturelle du Passy. There is no sign to the Col d'Anterne but continue straight on the wide jeep track. The yellow marks on the trees means that this is an easy walk. You come to another small parking area (you could leave your car here and save another three-quarters of an hour!).

Shortly after there is a sign to Le Gouet, alt.1,430m, a small yellow sign to Anterne and another one, further up by two chalets, to Ayent en Bas. This is an attractive way with pine trees on the left and behind the impressive rock wall of the Rochers des Fiz. Continue on the wide jeep track till you come to the Chalets de Souay on a corner. There is a signpost here indicating straight to Lac de Pormenaz/La Chorde (this is the narrow path you will return on). Keep to the main track which is fairly steep and completely exposed. When you reach lots of signposts saying Réserve Naturelle, Lac d'Anterne etc, follow the one which says Chalets d'Anterne. You are still on the jeep track climbing steadily through open alpine pastures, but there are several obvious short cuts you can take.

On the right there is a shallow valley and you can see a path along the other side which you will take on your way back. Keep going towards the chalet/hotel and do not take a path up to the left indicated Col d'Anterne - this goes over the col and down to the Lac d'Anterne on the other side.

You arrive at the Chalet/Hotel du Col d'Anterne, alt.2,003m (2hrs) - *in various guidebooks this is called the Refuge de Moëde d'Anterne so as not to confuse it with the other refuge beyond the col and the lake which has a similar name.* It is a pleasant, privately owned refuge built at the turn of the century with an almost Victorian look about it (further details below). There is now a new refuge alongside which was being built when I did the walk in 1992. *I can recommend the delicious bilberry tarts they serve here in the*

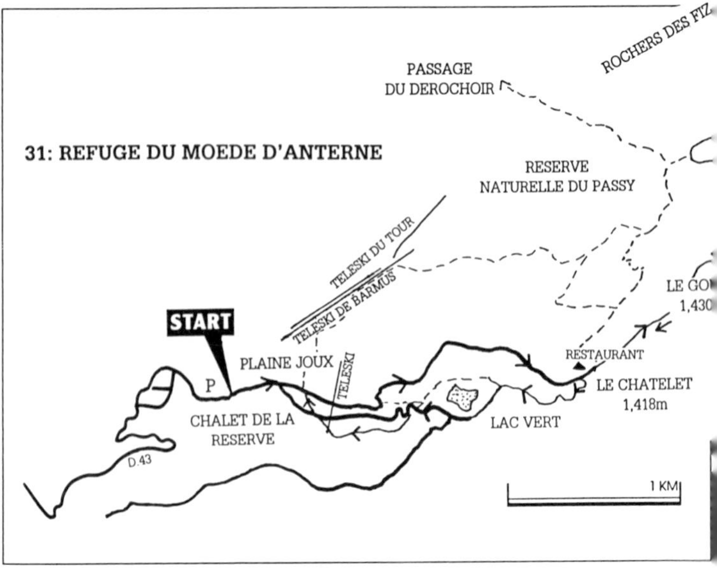

season, amongst other tempting dishes. Don't be surprised if you hear English spoken, as they employ British students as waitresses during the summer.

For the return, take the path on the other side of the valley which is easy to see from the refuge. Go right where it forks (left is the Tour de Mont Blanc which goes eventually to Le Brevent) on a narrow open path past the Lac Laochet, a tiny patch of water fringed with incredibly flat white plants. This is a lovely undulating walk over a grassy mound with the lake to the left and lovely view of the Rochers des Fiz to the right. After 20mins you come to more signposts (2hrs 20mins). Go right in the direction of Ayers/Plaine Joux.

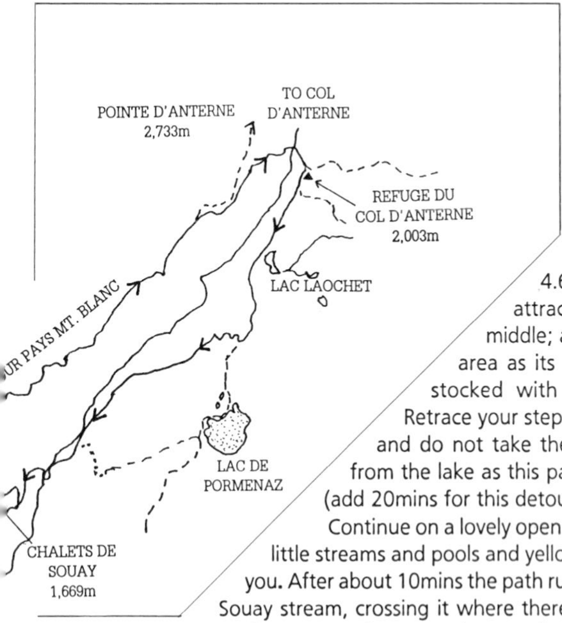

ALTERNATIVELY, you can go straight on to the very pretty Lac de Pormenaz, alt. 1,945m, situated in a rocky glacial depression of 4.6 hectares with an attractive island in the middle; a popular fishing area as its pure waters are stocked with rainbow trout. Retrace your steps to the signpost and do not take the short cut right from the lake as this path is precipitous (add 20mins for this detour).

Continue on a lovely open grassy path with little streams and pools and yellow signs to guide you. After about 10mins the path runs parallel to the Souay stream, crossing it where there are stones and scree (in summer there may be very little water) before climbing up quite high above the stream in a rocky gorge. This is a rocky, twisty section, quite steep in places and you have to watch your feet. At one place there is a drop on the right but there are chains on the rock to the left to give support if necessary. *This part of the walk is marked on the map with little dots meaning tricky and is not for anyone suffering from vertigo.* After half an hour you meet the path coming down from Lake Pormenaz, marked Passage Difficile. The path eventually winds down out of the narrow gorge back to the river and then up to the jeep track at the Chalets du Souay where you come out of the reserve. Retrace your steps back to the restaurant at Le Chatelet (4hrs 30mins).

If you have left your car in Plaine Joux, continue past the restaurant and then follow the sign down to the left to the Lac Vert, 25mins. This is a wide steep path through tall pine trees and has been eroded by continual use. There are interesting rocks covered with lichens in the woods on the left. The path comes out of the woods and Lac Vert is in front. It is a beautiful little deep green lake nestling in the woods with five rocks in the middle. It is somewhat spoiled by a large restaurant and car park on one side and in high season there may be crowds of people as it is accessible by road.

Long ago, according to legend, this lake was frequented by beautiful fairies who liked to play on the shore and bathe in the transparent water. The bad spirits who lived in the mountain caves higher up observed them at play and decided to come down and seduce them. However, the fairies repulsed their advances which made the spirits very angry. In revenge they sent down an avalanche of rocks which blocked the lake and the fairies had to leave.The lake became silent and sinister. Years later some young girls from Passy were laughing and singing in the region. Their joyful sound reached the mountain spirits who thought the fairies had returned and sent down another avalanche of rocks. However, the fairies were watching and managed to send the rocks in another direction. Above the Ayeres chalet there is to this day a round green fairy circle called the Pré des Dames (circle of women). It was here that the girls escaped a tragic death.

Start on the road back to Plaine Joux but look for a short cut on the left through the woods back to the large parking area. Follow signs saying Plaine Joux and ignoring other paths branching off (5hrs 15mins).

Chalet/Refuge du Moëde Anterne, tel. 50.93.60.43.

Open from 20 June to end September.

Remarks: This is a magnificent area for walking not far from Mont Blanc, but it tends to be crowded with tourists in summer so should be avoided at weekends. However, the further you walk the less people you find! The jeep track up to the Chalets d'Anterne is eroded and does seem to go on and on, but the exciting way back along the narrow ravine makes up for it!

The word Moëde means "between two waters" in Patois - the waters being the Souay stream and the Diosaz to the south. The name Anterne was given to the area by the inhabitants of Sixt who owned it until 1313 and could come from the Latin word "internus" (insular) .

Don't forget to visit Notre Dame de Toute Grâce in the village of Plateau d'Assy (see Walk No. 30).

32: POINTE DE CHEVRAN - Alt. 1,150 metres
(Faucigny/Haut Giffre region)

Difficulty:	Medium, except for a 30min steep climb.
Time:	3hrs 35mins (4hrs on official map).
Height gain:	675 metres.
Maps:	Editions Didier & Richard IGN No.3 Massifs du Chablais Faucigny & Genevois 1:50,000. Cartes IGN 3430 ET Top 25 La Clusaz/Grand Bornard 1:25,000.
Depart from:	Cluses - 485 metres.
Signposting:	Good - follow green/red splashes.

How to get there (from Geneva)

Take the motorway direction Chamonix and exit at No.19, Cluses centre. Turn left and make for the centre of Cluses. Turn right immediately before the Mairie onto the Rue de l'Hôtel de Ville. Continue straight on this street, crossing the railway and passing the cemetery on the right. Here the name of the street changes to Blvd. de Chevron. You will see the Gyro Television store beyond and there is a small parking space before it to the right where there is a narrow road.

ALTERNATIVE START: If you go slightly further on the Blvd. de Chevron you will see a wider road to the right with a small notice board showing a map of the walk - this is the official start with the red/green splashes and it says 4hrs.

Directions

Walk up the jeep track between the store and the parking area passing some rather shabby tin shacks on the right with houses down on the left before the path narrows and becomes stony. After 10mins you come to a cross-roads. Turn right through an iron gate, as indicated by the red/green splashes (for the alternative start go straight in the direction shown until you reach the iron gate). From here on there are red/green direction indicators for the entire walk on rocks, trees and wooden arrows.

Continue along the wide track; on the right there is a beautiful view over the town of Cluses with its surrounding peaks, including the dramatic Pic de Marcelly way back on the right which dominates the town of Taninges. The path passes under a small grey limestone cliff called Fontaine aux Oiseaux (fountain of the birds) before curling round the left of the mountain. Just before the track starts to descend, bear up left (30mins) - the splashes are a short way up this path. 10mins later turn up left on a narrower, winding path, going up steeply through tall coniferous forest till you reach the ruins of a house on the right (1hr).

From here the path becomes steep and zigzags through the woods for approximately 30mins. *In late April and early May there are some magnificent specimens of the early purple orchids and in the autumn you can see the flowers of the delicate pink cyclamen.* You may get a glimpse through the trees (if they are not in leaf) of the motorway snaking through the valley on its way to Chamonix. Continue until the path reaches a high shoulder and levels out at 1,150m. For the best view, bear up right through trees (there is no defined path) until you come to the edge of a sheer cliff face called Rochers de la Maladière, where there is a metal chain used for rappelling (it says Le Grand Cric on the rock). This is a good picnic spot while you contemplate the wonderful view down the Arve valley with the motorway and river running through it. On the other side you can see the road winding up the slopes to the little villages of La Frasse and Nancy sur Cluses. Retrace your steps to the track, which starts to go down before emerging into a clearing with a number of signposts (1hr 50mins). *Optionally you can go straight on and then up a path to the right (not signposted) which takes you nearer the cliff edge and eventually to a lookout spot called La Dent, alt. 1,196m. Before the look-out there is a path down to your left through the forest, which eventually joins up with the path which has come through the combe (see below).*

Follow the sign left to La Croix Verte on a grassy path, down the centre of an attractive combe (shallow valley) with woods at the edge of the slopes. This takes you by Chevran d'en Haut and then 5mins later Chevran d'en Bas. These are lovely old barns with some ancient gnarled fruit trees nearby. In springtime the surrounding fields are covered with yellow dandelions and other meadow flowers.

After Chevran d'en Bas continue along the combe for a few minutes before entering the forest again and going down, gently at first and then on a somewhat more steep and stony path, to a cross-roads with signposts (2hrs 10mins). The way you've come is marked Pointe de Chevran and to the right Chevran via La Fôret *(this is where the alternative path mentioned above comes out).* Go straight, though there is no signpost, following the usual red/green splashes.

You reach a road (the D.6) and can see the attractive villages of La Frasse (not the same one you saw from the cliff) and Treydon nestling in the valley to the right. At the side of the road is the Croix Verte, which is a tall wooden cross inscribed with the date 1976 (2hrs 30mins). Turn left on the road towards St. Sigismond (another good view here of the cross on the top of the Pointe de Marcelly straight ahead) and a few metres along there is a path

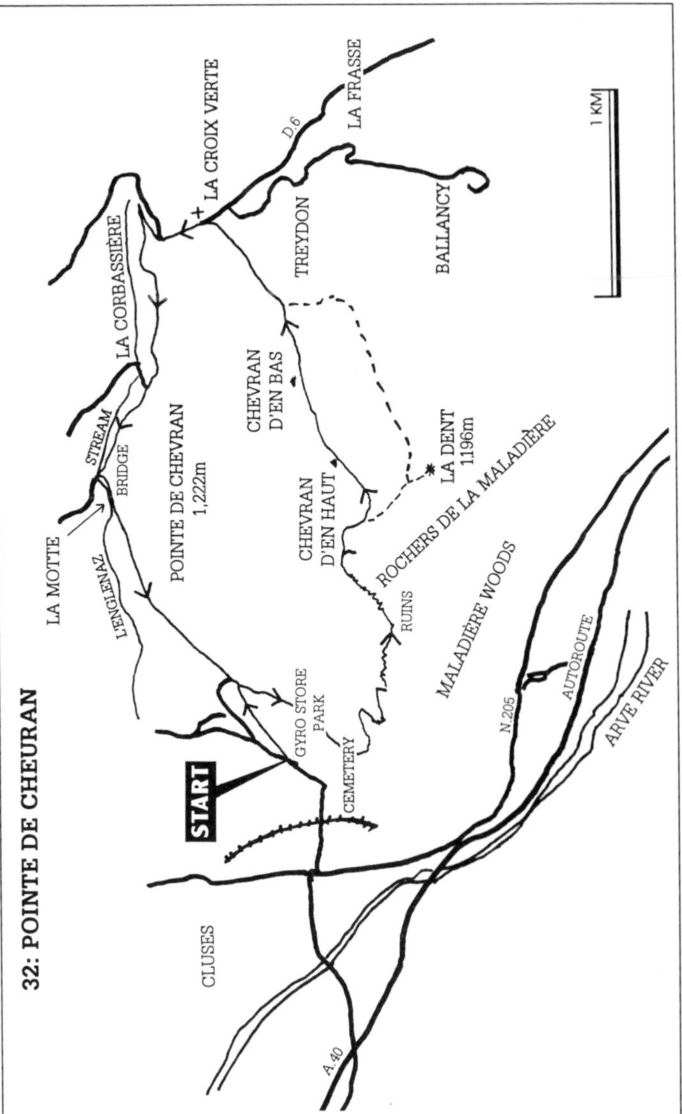
32: POINTE DE CHEURAN
START
CLUSES
LA MOTTE
L'ENGLENAZ
STREAM
BRIDGE
LA CORBASSIÈRE
LA CROIX VERTE
D.6
LA FRASSE
TREYDON
BALLANCY
1 KM
POINTE DE CHEVRAN
1,222m
CHEVRAN
D'EN BAS
CHEVRAN
D'EN HAUT
LA DENT
1196m
ROCHERS DE LA MALADIÈRE
RUINS
GYRO STORE
PARK
CEMETERY
MALADIÈRE WOODS
N.205
AUTOROUTE
ARVE RIVER
A.40

down on the left (green/red splashes on a rock). As you walk down through the woods the road runs parallel up on the right for a short while. Continue following the red/green splashes and the yellow mountain cycle signs and ignore any paths branching off. Go down steeply through coniferous and beech woods, crossing a dry stream bed, to the hamlet of La Corbassière, alt. 797m, which is at the end of an asphalt road (2hrs 50mins).

Walk down the road for a short while and then turn off left on the corner (green/red flashes and bike markings). You are now on an attractive path through woodland and meadows with a stream called the Ruisseau de l'Englenaz flowing down on the right and beyond the stream there is an upward sweep of meadowland with the occasional old chalet and fruit trees. Before reaching the hamlet of La Motte you cross a bridge made of flat slabs of stone and then a few metres later turn left over a second concrete, moss-covered bridge. *An idyllic spot, the sort of place where one has to dawdle and gaze down at the water as it gurgles around the weedy rocks and if tired and hot you can dip your feet into the shallow, icy water.* Continue on the path round the side of the hill with a ravine on the right and in places quite a drop! Suddenly you are in the open and there is another spectacular view of the town of Cluses.

The path reaches the cross-roads at the start of the walk. Turn left *(if your car is at the alternative start keep straight on the main path)* and follow the smaller track for about 5mins till you reach your car (3hrs 35mins).

Remarks: A really attractive walk at all times of the year, especially on a hot day in summer as much of the walk is in shade. Note: this walk is called Pointe de Chevran (pointe meaning point or summit). On the board at the alternative start it looks as if there is a path to it. However, after two futile attempts to reach the pointe and abortive telephone calls to the tourist office in Cluses, who did not seem to know much about it, I was put in touch with someone from the Forestry Commission. He assured me that there is no path to the pointe, just a circular walk round the mountain. So that solved the mystery, and the walk is lovely anyway!

33: LAC DE VOGEALLE - Alt. 2,001 metres

(Faucigny/Haut Giffre region)

Difficulty: Difficult. The way up is very steep and not for anyone suffering from vertigo. However, one can always go up and down by the return route which is longer but easier.

Time:	6hrs 45mins.
Height gain:	1,053 metres.
Maps:	Editions Didier & Richard IGN No.3 Massifs du Chablais Faucigny & Genevois 1:50,000. Cartes IGN 3530 ET Top 25 Samoëns/Haut Giffre 1:25,000.
Depart from:	Plan du Lac, near Sixt - 955 metres.
Signposting:	Good.

How to get there (from Geneva)

Take the motorway direction Chamonix and exit at No.15, Boëge/St. Jeoire. Then turn left briefly on the D.903 and watch for the D.9 right signposted Fillinges, Samoëns and Vallée Verte. Follow this road to the Pont des Fillinges and then turn right on the D.907 direction Taninges/Samoëns. (ALTERNATIVELY go through Annemasse and take the D.907 direction Taninges/Samoëns.) At Samoëns follow signs to Sixt. Go straight through the village of Sixt (do not turn at the bridge) and you will come to an impressive roundabout called Plan des Lacs at the Fer à Cheval (horseshoe) which is the terminus of the road; here there is plenty of parking space.

Directions

From the Plan des Lacs parking area at the end of the horseshoe, with the Chalet de Cirque de Cheval in front, go up to the right where there is a wide jeep track and a horse riding area. The chalet of the bureau d'accueil/réserve naturelle/bureau de tourisme is on your left. Go down the wide jeep track to a large board showing all the different walks in the area and signposts saying La Fond de la Combe 1hr (a walk to the end of the valley) and Lac de Vogealle 3hrs, where you are heading. Look up behind here for a dramatic view of the peaks of the Cornes du Chamois, alt. 2,562m. You are now entering the Sixt Nature Reserve.

Go straight through deciduous woodland, past two attractive ponds and into a gravelly open area. Cross over a dry river bed by a green, wooden bridge and then, when the track forks, go left following signs to Buvette de Prazon. A few minutes later take another left fork over the Giffre river by a second wooden bridge (20mins).There is a sign here saying Pas de Boret/ Vogealle. Keep on the main cindery track with the river on your right and you arrive at the little Buvette (café) de Prazon (30mins).*When we were there early in the morning it was unfortunately shut though attractively surrounded by a flock of sheep. On our return in the afternoon it was crowded with hordes of Sunday afternoon strollers - I preferred the morning scenario.*

Take the little path which goes to the left of the buvette (there is no sign but a wooden cross dated 1968 and a red flash on a rock). This is a narrow stony path which goes gently upwards towards the end of the open valley through a gate marked Réserve Naturelle and across a dry river bed, following red splashes. You start to climb up the side of the valley passing a small commemoration stone to Hubert Ducroz, with an inscription "et sa vie dans ces montagnes" (and his life in these mountains). After scrambling across several rushing streams the path becomes steeper and rockier. Be careful to follow the red arrows and splashes. *On this walk the red splashes seem to turn orange and then finally to pink - did the painter run out of paint?*

This is a very impressive path called the Pas de Boret. It winds up the left-hand side of the incredible horseshoe of towering cliffs with countless streams coursing downwards, often ending in dramatic waterfalls in the valley below. The path gets steeper and is very exposed. In the more vertiginous places there are lengths of wire hawser to hang on to (these were in bad condition when we did the walk). A stone dated 1826 (1hr) is evidence that this is an ancient pathway.

After the stone the path becomes less exposed and there is no longer a huge drop on the right. The grassy, rocky path seems to go into the mountain, undulating through woodland and bearing round to the right before arriving at the Chalet de Boret on a grassy shelf at alt. 1,380m (1hr 30mins). There is a notice on the side that this is a communal refuge, open to everyone at all times, but should only be used in case of necessity (bad weather) - in the summer priority is given to the shepherds. The inside is very rudimentary with a wood stove and a small sleeping area.

Go up to the left of the hut following the signpost to the Refuge de Vogealle; straight on indicates Fond de la Combe (this is the high path to the end of the valley by which you will return). There is a shrine, dated 1848, with an empty stone niche which obviously once held a statue. The path goes through meadowland and stunted vegetation and then becomes more exposed again with some patches of flat rock and scree and a number of dry stream beds to cross. It becomes steeper and rockier as it zigzags up and you have to watch where you are heading. Keep checking for the red/orange flashes on the rocks.

You pass under a high rock face and across river beds before coming to a new cross dated 1991, with a sign saying Refuge de Vogealle 45mins. The path becomes less steep, though still rocky and strewn with big boulders, as it clings round the mountain underneath an impressive cliff face called Le Dardet (2hrs 30mins).This is followed by another fairly steep climb negotiating rocks and boulders; you do not see the Swiss Alpine Club refuge of La Vogealle, alt. 1,901m, until you are almost there, as it is tucked back in a grassy area (3hrs 10mins).

It is better not to stop at the hut (which is off the path to the right) until

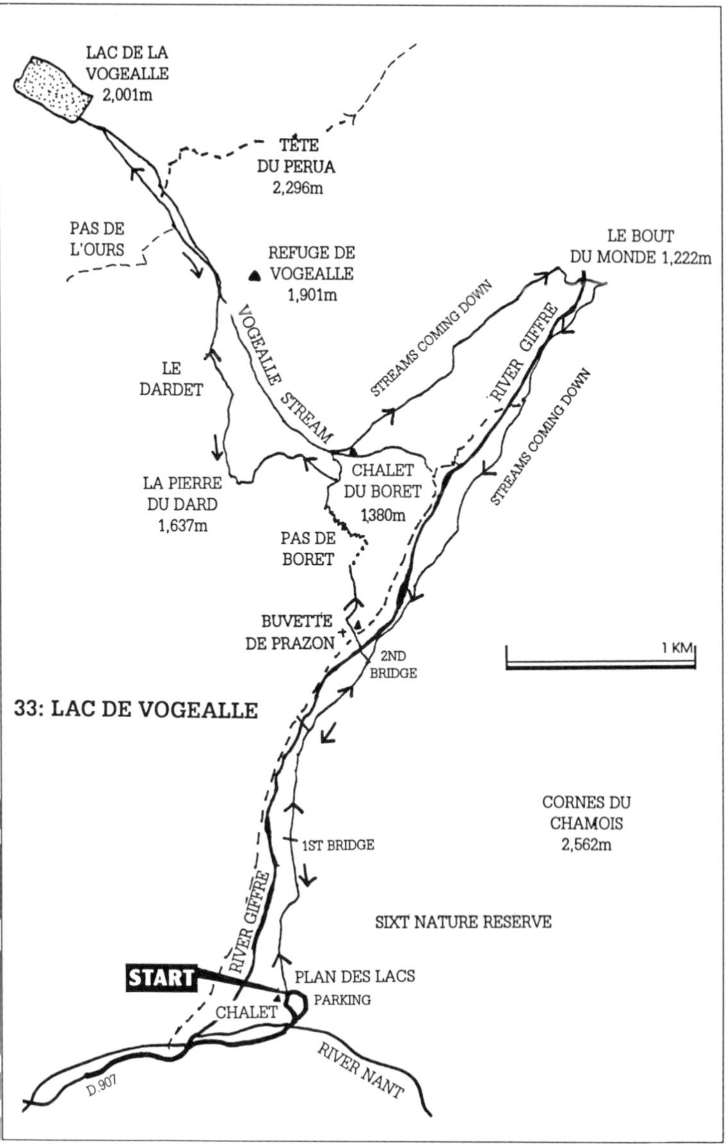
LAC DE LA VOGEALLE 2,001m
TÊTE DU PERUA 2,296m
PAS DE L'OURS
REFUGE DE VOGEALLE 1,901m
LE BOUT DU MONDE 1,222m
VOGEALLE STREAM
STREAMS COMING DOWN
RIVER GIFFRE
LE DARDET
LA PIERRE DU DARD 1,637m
CHALET DU BORET 1380m
STREAMS COMING DOWN
PAS DE BORET
BUVETTE DE PRAZON
2ND BRIDGE
1 KM
33: LAC DE VOGEALLE
CORNES DU CHAMOIS 2,562m
1ST BRIDGE
RIVER GIFFRE
SIXT NATURE RESERVE
START
PLAN DES LACS
PARKING
CHALET
RIVER NANT
D.907

you have visited the lake which is another 25mins on the same path climbing upwards for 100m with a stream down on the right. The path is not so rocky which is rather a relief, and climbs medium steep into a magnificent hanging valley (a hanging valley is a valley you have to climb up into). Walk straight down the valley past a signpost half way and a path off to the right to the Mont Ruan, till you reach the lake. *When we were there in late August it was practically dry and rather a disappointment - it would be better visited in early June (snow permitting) when all the streams are cascading down the mountains.* Retrace your steps to the refuge (4hrs) where you can stay the night and also get food (see further details below).

Take the same path back to the Chalets du Boret (5hrs). Then, leaving the way you came, go round the hut to the left and follow the signpost to Bout du Monde.This is an easier path which undulates through alpine pastures, intermittent woodland and rocky places into the head of the valley. If you look back you get an impressive view of the path you came down from the refuge. A few minutes from the Chalets de Boret you cross a stream with lots of boulders by a rickety wooden bridge, and follow the signpost which says La Fonde de la Combe. The path marked with occasional pink splashes is well defined but may be muddy and slippery after rainfall. It crosses a number of streams and dry river beds and goes through some lovely stunted beech woods to a big sign saying La Combe in pink plus an arrow on the side of a rock (5hrs 30mins). As the path wends round to the head of the valley you can hear the constant sound of gurgling water from the numerous streams that are rushing down to the valley floor; the view of them tumbling down off the sheer rock faces is really magnificent.

After crossing two tricky streams you arrive at the head of the valley (5hrs 45mins). You are now at the Bout du Monde (end of the world!) but there is no sign except a red arrow on a large rock. The path starts to wind down towards the end of the valley with some flashes which now seem to have turned pink but the path is self evident as you can see it from above. The gradient is fairly steep and you pass a large rock with a house painted on it and Boret written underneath (referring to the hut above) on the way to the Giffre river on the valley floor (6hrs). *The Giffre is quite a torrent in all seasons and in spring the banks are a profusion of flowers, including the white alpine anemones (pasque flowers), lily of the valley, globe flowers and butterwort.* Keep to the left on a wide path crossing several bridges, some made of wooden slats.The path goes along the dry edge of the river bed which is very wide but I would imagine there are times of the year when it is full of water. The streams are rushing down off the cliffs and there are some fantastic waterfalls. After more scree and river bed you cross the river at an easy point and take the wide path down towards the end of the valley - bear right where it says Buvette de Prazon/Pas de Boret if you want to have a drink or continue straight back to the car (6hrs 45mins).

Remarks: This is a superb walk best done in late spring when the waterfalls and lake are more impressive but beware of snow; the flowers are also varied and abundant at this time. The Fer à Cheval is a horseshoe of high dramatic mountains ringing a flat valley and because of its beauty and easy accessibility it is very popular with families, so if possible avoid weekends in the high season.There are a lot of picnic areas, kiosks, cafés and also a riding school. When we arrived early on a Sunday in August there was not a soul about,. but when we got back the place was crowded. However, fewer leave the valley floor and once you start climbing you are relatively on your own. I have also rewalked this route in late autumn and seen nobody all day, except a lone chamois.

34: LAC DE GERS (Sixt) - Alt. 1,533 metres

(Faucigny/Haut Giffre region)

Difficulty:	Medium steep walk up to the lake.
Time:	4hrs 30mins.
Height gain:	765 metres.
Maps:	Editions Didier & Richard IGN No.3 Massifs du Chablais & Faucigny/Genevois 1:50,000. Cartes IGN 3530 ET Top 25 Samoëns/Haut Giffre 1:25,000.
Depart from:	Le Fay near Sixt - 768 metres.
Signposting:	Adequate though could be better - difficult to find the alternative path down from the Lake though the choice is signposted on the way up.

How to get there (from Geneva)

Take the motorway direction Chamonix and exit at No.15, Boëge/St. Jeoire. Then turn left briefly on the D.903 and watch for the D.9 right signposted Fillinges, Samoëns and Vallée Verte. Follow this road to the Pont de Fillinges and then turn right on the D.907 direction Taninges/Samoëns. (ALTERNATIVELY go through Annemasse and take the D.907 direction Taninges/Samoëns.) At Samoëns follow signs to Sixt. At Sixt turn right across the bridge and then right again at the bureau de tourisme which is the old railway station. Turn left at the next intersection (a sort of cross-roads) and you will arrive at the hamlet of Le Fay. Leave your car just before the bridge.

Directions

There are signposts before the bridge indicating straight on to Lac de Gers 2hrs 30mins on the GR.96 and left the Tour du Giffre Haut on the GR.5. Walk across the bridge over the River Giffre, which is a rushing torrent, and up the asphalt road. On the left you can see the village of Salvagny and behind you are the dramatic mountains of the Fer à Cheval (horseshoe) beyond Sixt with the tops of the pylons which disfigure the Lac d'Anterne area.

After 15mins you arrive at Englène which is a cluster of attractive chalets with a big old stone cross. Continue straight on a wide stony track (there is a GR.96 sign on a fountain to the right) past a notice that you are entering a nature reserve *(yet each time I have done this walk I have met Landrovers coming down with hunters and dogs!).* The path winds up fairly steeply through pretty, mossy woodland, consisting mainly of birch, and you can hear the sound of rushing water all the way which is the Gers stream coming down from the lake. Keep to the main path passing a shrine set in the side of the rock and then an attractive watery grotto. *At the shrine and grotto are some intriguing white crosses with two parallel white lines across instead of the usual one. I was told that this is the cross of the French Resistance but the tourist office assures me that nobody was killed in the Sixt area during the war and that this is the Cross of Lorraine, although why they are there is a mystery.* The path crosses the stream by a bridge (40mins) at a lovely place where the water tumbles over huge boulders. Then the stream disappears for a while. 15mins later follow a sign straight ahead to Lac de Gers (there is an unsigned path to the left).

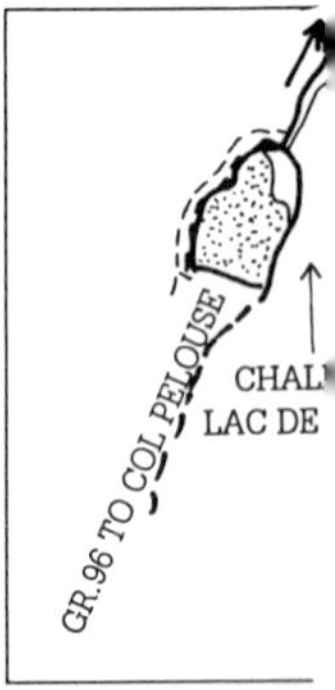

You are now curling round the mountain with the stream down on your right. You come to a second bridge (1hr 10mins) which leads only to a building called Les Challenies hidden in the trees, so do not cross over but continue on the path straight up. 5mins later you cross the river on a third bridge, made of iron, and after a few metres there is a tall rock face on the left with water trickling down and a huge GR.96 sign on the stone. *If you happen to do the walk after a frost the icicles on this rock face are very impressive.* Eventually the path comes out of the forest and you can see a lovely chain of mountains on the right and a little hut on the left with slopes of coniferous trees behind.

When you reach a T-junction go right, following the sign to Lac de Gers par Porte (1hr 30mins). It also indicates Lac de Gers to the left and this is where you will come out on your return. This path curls round the side of the mountain and you can see where you have walked up if you look back; there

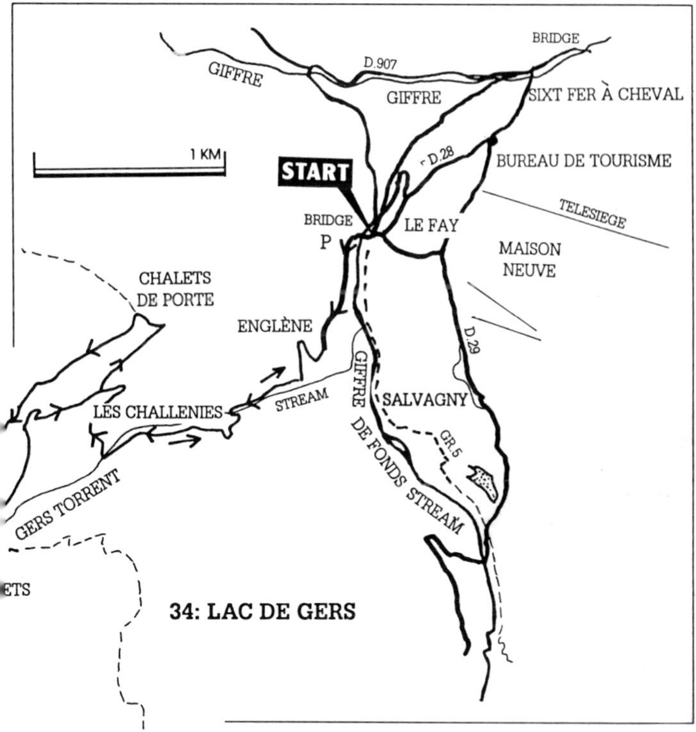

are steep slopes with dense coniferous woods to the left and dramatic views down into the valley to the right. When you arrive at the four scattered huts of the Chalets de Porte (1hr 45mins) follow the sign left towards Lac de Gers (the path to the right is signposted Samoëns and eventually joins the GR.5 at the Giffre river in the valley). You go through lovely woodland on an easy, undulating path which doubles back round the mountain.

The path comes out into a beautiful wide valley (2hrs 5mins) apparently unspoilt until you see the top of a ski-lift on the skyline to the right. This is one of the lifts coming up from the well-known ski resort of Flaine which is just over the brow - in fact higher up the valley is another ski-tow coming down but it is not visible. The path turns into a wide track as you walk down the valley to the lake (2hrs 30mins), where there are some small huts and a café (buvette) which also sells goat's cheese. This is a very attractive lake with mountains all around and little habitation to spoil the natural beauty of the area. It is worthwhile strolling round the lake to select a picnic spot away from the chalets where there are lots of goats and goat droppings! *Later in the season the café is shut but the advantage is a stillness and silence, only interrupted by the barking of deer, the cries of birds and the odd rock fall.* You can see the path at the end of the lake which continues up to the Col de Pelouse.

Go back down the valley for approximately 10mins and turn right on a grassy path (no sign) towards some scattered chalets, heading for the last two which are spaced about 50m apart. Bear left in front of the left-hand chalet (do not cross the stream) and you will see a red arrow on the side of the building saying Sixt. You are joining the path which comes down from the Chalets de Foges (see explanation below). This is a narrow, grassy path which becomes rockier and steeper as it meanders through woods, bracken and raspberry bushes, with the river down on the right; follow the yellow arrows and splashes. The path flattens out before it goes down to a small hut with a sign on it saying Sixt (3hrs 10mins). A few minutes later you come out onto your original path. Retrace your steps back to the bridge (4hrs 15mins).

At Le Fay there is a gîte d'étape (Sixt/Salvagny area).

Remarks: This is a delightful walk at any time of the year but especially dramatic after lots of rain when the Gers stream rushes impressively down the wooded mountainside, over rocky boulders and narrow gorges, on its way to join the Giffre river. There is plenty of shade on a hot summer's day, but I prefer late autumn just before the first snow, when the mountains seem to rise out of the mist like illustrations in Chinese paintings and the precipitous waters are muted by glistening icicles. Note: it is possible to make this walk much longer by continuing from the lake through the Combe de Gers to the Col Pelouse, alt. 2,227m, then circling back under the Téléski de Gers past the minuscule Lac Parchet and the Chalet de Foges on your right.

35: LA CROIX DE COMMUNE - Alt. 1,969 metres
(area Faucigny/Haut Giffre)

Difficulty:	Medium - a steep climb at the end towards the cross!
Time:	5hrs (or 4hrs 15mins if you drive to Passy).
Height gain:	1,000 metres.
Maps:	Editions Didier & Richard IGN No.3 Massifs du Chablais Faucigny & Genevois 1:50,000.

	Cartes IGN 3530 ET Top 25 Samoëns/Haut Giffre 1:25,000.
Depart from:	Maison Neuve Alt. 814m or Passy Alt. 1,112m.
Signposting:	Adequate.

How to get there (from Geneva)

Take the motorway direction Chamonix and exit at No.15, Boëge/St. Jeoire. Then turn left briefly on the D.903 and watch for the D.9 signposted Fillinges, Samoëns and Vallée Verte. Follow this road to the Pont de Fillinges and then turn right on the D.907 direction Taninges/Samoëns. (ALTERNATIVELY go through Annemasse and take the D.907 direction Taninges/Samoëns.) At Samoëns follow signs to Sixt. At Sixt turn right across the bridge on the D.29 and park in the village of Maison Neuve (between Sixt and Salvagny) at the Auberge de Salvagny which is opposite a road up left which goes to the hamlet of Passy.

Alternatively drive up to the hamlet of Passy - there is not much parking space but it does save you some 45mins in total walking time, OR in July and August take the chair-lift up to Les Vagnys (the starting point is between the villages of Sixt and Maison Neuve) thus saving even more time.

Directions

From the Auberge de Salvagny take the tarmac road to the left signposted Lavoisière/Le Planay and Passy. This winds up through meadows and occasional chalets crossing under the Les Vagnys chair-lift which goes from Maison Neuve up to a ski area where there are quite a number of lifts.

At the tiny hamlet of Passy (30mins) there is a small car park (as mentioned above), a few chalets including a big farm which is inhabited all the year round and a dear little chapel. The chapel has an old tiled roof and a lovely onion-shaped steeple with a weather-vane in the shape of a cockerel, which looks much too big for the small building underneath. You walk under the chair-lift coming up from the valley and the road deteriorates into a jeep track going upwards medium steep to Les Vagnys. After 5mins follow the signpost round to the right to Commune and do not go straight.

The track flattens out as it winds along the right-hand side of the mountain with views of the valley to the left through light coniferous and deciduous woodland; it then steepens again before coming out into the open. You walk between some old huts called Les Coppons on the way and pass under the chair-lift at least three times as you follow the path up. Eventually you can see over on the right the start of the valley to the Chalets de Sales and the Pointe de Dérochoir, and also the dramatic rock face of the Rochers des Fiz.

You arrive at an open, grassy area called Les Vagnys (35mins) with a bar/

restaurant and the arrival point of the chair-lift over on the right. There are also several other lifts starting up in various directions, to take the skiers even higher. The wide path continues upward past a wooden cross (erected 1955) on the right. Continue round to the left signposted Commune; straight on is signposted Le Grenairon, where there is the Chalet-Hôtel Buet, a good spot to pass the night if you are planning a longer walk.

Cross the Torrent du Vivier which is often dried up in summer and pass by two wooden shacks, marked as Verduize on the map, before going through light woodland again on an undulating wide track running along the side of the mountain with the valley far below on the left. There is a new wooden cross on the side of the track, dated 1991; *in fact there are three in total dated the same year on this walk. The tourist bureau assures me that this has no special significance, but that the people in the region are very religious and, when a cross falls down, it is immediately replaced by a new one, either by the farmer who owns the land or, in this case, by the commune.* Cross the Saugy stream where a dramatic, sheer sheet of rock traverses the path and continues steeply downwards; the stream itself is usually a mere trickle, except after a storm.

There is a sign on a tree saying Réserve

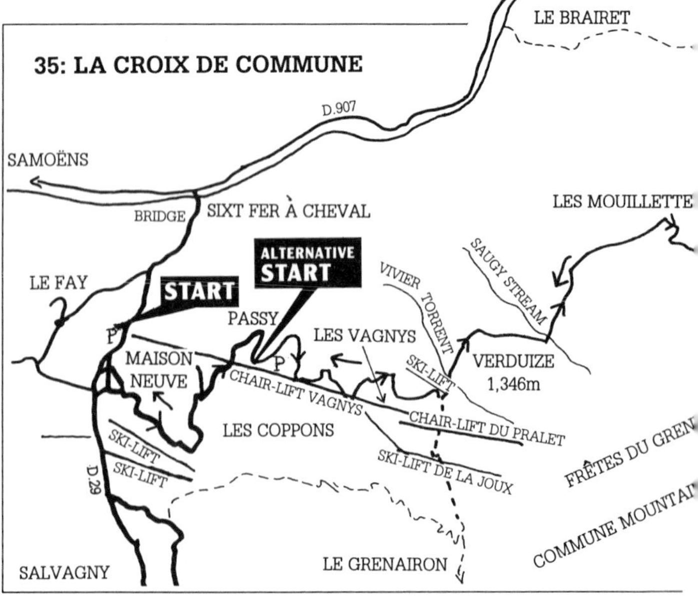

Naturelle - faune, flore protégée (see section on Reserves) before you come to another huddle of huts called Les Mouillettes, alt. 1,434m (1hr), with another cross. After this you start to climb a bit, still through scattered woods, and then come out onto the open mountainside (1hr 20mins). There is the rocky Frêtes du Grenier to the right and in front the dramatic rock faces of the Fer à Cheval (horseshoe) mountains. On the horizon you can now see the cross of the Croix de Commune which is your destination - it looks frighteningly high up but at least relatively easy to get to.

The path goes through a small area of flat serrated rock with big boulders dotted around. There is a large rock on the side of the path with a deep indentation (you feel there should be a statue inside) and behind is a hut (1hr 45mins). In fact there are a number of small huts here (some brand new) with mounds of rock and earth behind them as protection against avalanches which sweep down the precipitous mountain slope. The path undulates over the bare mountain crossing four streams. Immediately after the fourth rivulet, which is on a slight corner, take the little path up to the right going right beside the stream, through initial scree and then over alpine pasture. As it is a short cut, this path is rather undefined, but basically keep going up the steep slope towards the ridge till you meet the official path coming up from les Praz de Commune. ALTERNATIVELY go on to the huts which are visible ahead (Les Praz de Commune) where you will see a signpost to the right saying Croix de la Frête.

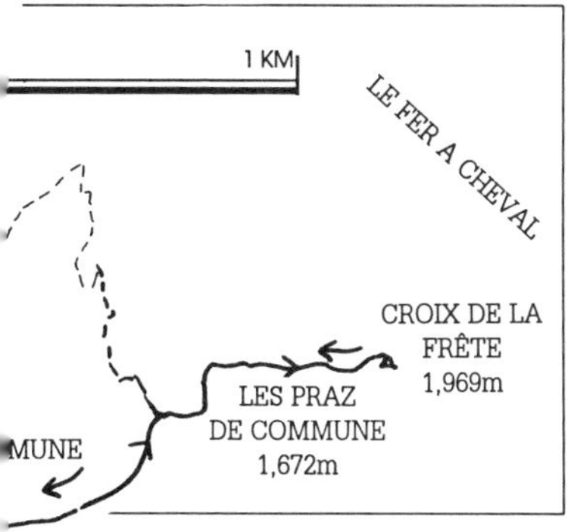

Alternative return route: You can continue through Les Praz de Commune on a track which leads down to the hamlet of Le Blairet in the valley towards the Fer à Cheval from Sixt. However, in order to do this you really need two cars (see map).

The path up to the Croix de Frête, alt. 1,969m, is steep, exposed and boggy over alpine pasture with occasional bushes. The height gain from the turn-off is 300m and for much of the way you cannot see the wooden cross, dated 1988, on the summit of the ridge. However, it is a welcome relief when it appears after half an hour of climbing! (2hrs 30mins).

The effort is worth it as there is a breathtaking view of the entire Fer à Cheval which really is a horseshoe of dramatic, rocky mountains plunging to the valley floor beneath with numerous streams cascading over the precipitous surfaces and glinting in the sunshine. On the horizon are the equally magnificent mountains of the Swiss Valais dominated by the Grand Mont Ruan and its glaciers at alt. 3,040m.

Retrace your steps the way you have come up (4hrs 15mins from Passy).

Remarks: I have yet to discover why this walk is called the Croix de Commune in all French guidebooks when the cross on the summit is called the Croix de la Frête! This is a glorious walk and a chance to see the magnificent Fer à Cheval mountains without joining the hordes of people who flock to the area below to picnic and stroll; I would not do it on a very hot day as much of it is steep and exposed. Look out for ibex and chamois, as this walk is in a National Reserve and the animals are protected (see chapter on Reserves).

36: LAC D'ANTERNE/REFUGE DE SALES - TWO DAY HIKE

Alt. 2,104 metres (day 1) - Alt. 2,220 metres (day 2)
(Faucigny/Haut Giffre region)

Difficulty:	Medium - A rather long haul up from the Chalets des Fonds the first day and short steep climb to the Pointe du Dérochoir the second day.
Time:	Day 1 = 5hrs. Day 2 = 6hrs 20mins.
Height gain:	1,093 metres (day 1). 411 metres down - 823 metres up (day 2).
Maps:	Editions Didier & Richard IGN No.3 Massifs du Chablais Faucigny & Genevois 1:50,000. Cartes IGN 3530 ET Top 25 Samoëns/Haut Giffre 1:25,000.
Depart from:	Les Fardelay - 1,054 metres.
Signposting:	Excellent - this is a popular walking area.

How to get there (from Geneva)

Take the motorway direction Chamonix and exit at No.15, Boëge/St. Jeoire. Then turn left briefly on the D.903 and watch for the D.9 right signposted Fillinges, Samoëns and Vallée Verte. Follow this road to the Pont de Fillinges and then turn right on the D.907 direction Taninges/Samoëns. (ALTERNATIVELY go through Annemasse and take the D.907 direction Taninges/Samoëns.) From Samoëns follow all signs to Sixt. At Sixt turn right across the bridge, go through the village of Salvagny and on past the Cascade de Rouget waterfall (worth stopping to look at) and park at the Chalets de Fardalay, a small group of old chalets above the road. There is a small open space for parking on the right just before the chalets.

Refuge de Larrieux with Chaine des Aravis in background
View of the Sous-Dine when walking towards Roche Parnal

Lake Annecy seen from the summit of La Tournette
Walking towards La Tournette

Lac d'Anterne

Directions

Day 1: Chalets de Fardalay to Refuge Alfred Wills, Lac d'Anterne

Walk up the road from the car park and just beyond the chalets you will see a wide clearing on the left where there is a sign (hidden by branches) saying Chalets des Fonds. 50m further on there are additional signs on a rock and a tree to Les Fonds 1hr 30mins. The path is wide and stony through woods with the rushing Le Giffre stream, which starts in the nearby Le Buet mountain, down on the left and high rocky cliffs beyond. Cross the river on a bridge at a pretty ravine called Creux de Oua (15mins).

Continue straight up the path which starts to climb, but not steeply at first, following blue markings on the trees. The rushing stream falls away on the left. This is the start of a 330m climb up to the Chalets des Fonds and the path initially goes through coniferous forest with some open areas and little huts. It meets a jeep track coming from Salvagny at La Celière and more signposts (30mins). Follow the sign Les Fonts (they have mis-spelt Les Fonds!) to the right, on a wide track following the stream. The towering crags to the left are marred by huge electricity pylons and wires which march across this region.

You negotiate several rivulets trickling off the rock on your left and spilling across the path to cascade into the river far below on the right. Further on cross another bridge above a ravine where the river crashes impressively over big boulders (1hr 15mins). Continue up to some small

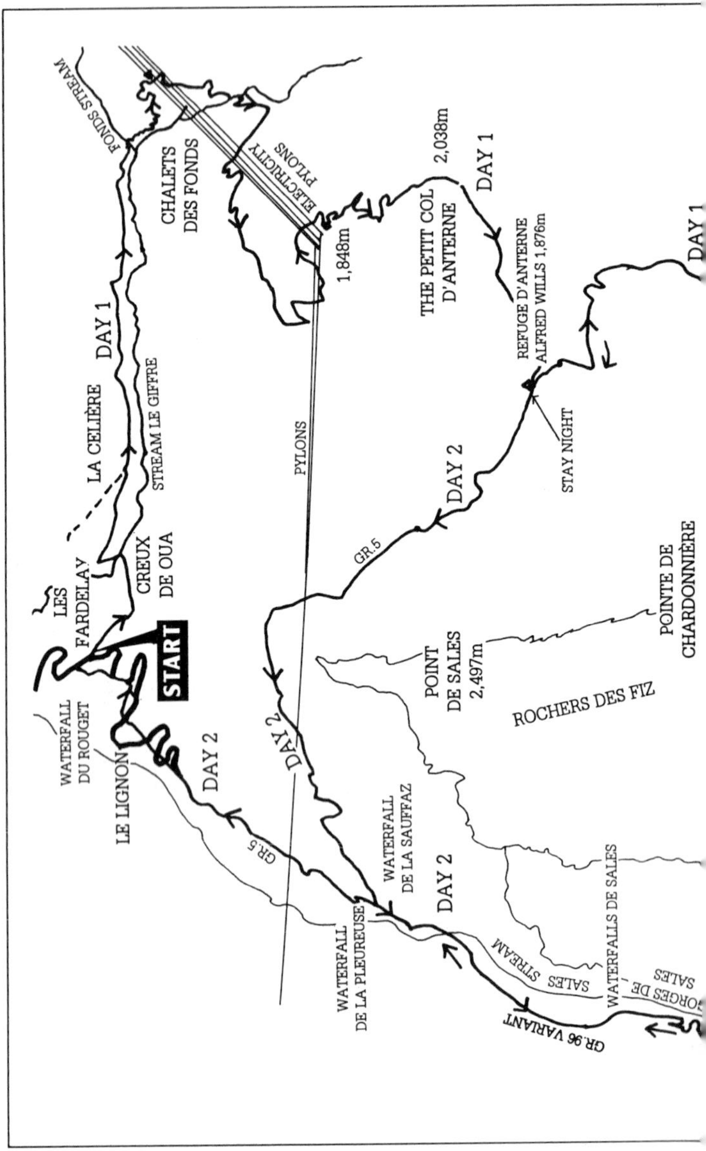
FONDS STREAM
CHALETS DES FONDS
ELECTRICITY PYLONS
2,038m
DAY 1
THE PETIT COL D'ANTERNE
1,848m
REFUGE D'ANTERNE ALFRED WILLS 1,876m
DAY 1
LA CELIÈRE
STREAM LE GIFFRE
PYLONS
DAY 2
STAY NIGHT
GR.5
CREUX DE OUA
LES FARDELAY
START
POINT DE SALES 2,497m
POINTE DE CHARDONNIÈRE
ROCHERS DES FIZ
WATERFALL DU ROUGET
LE LIGNON
DAY 2
DAY 2
GR.5
WATERFALL DE LA SAUFFAZ
DAY 2
WATERFALL DE LA PLEUREUSE
WATERFALLS DE SALES
SALES STREAM
SALES
GR.96 VARIANT
DAY 1

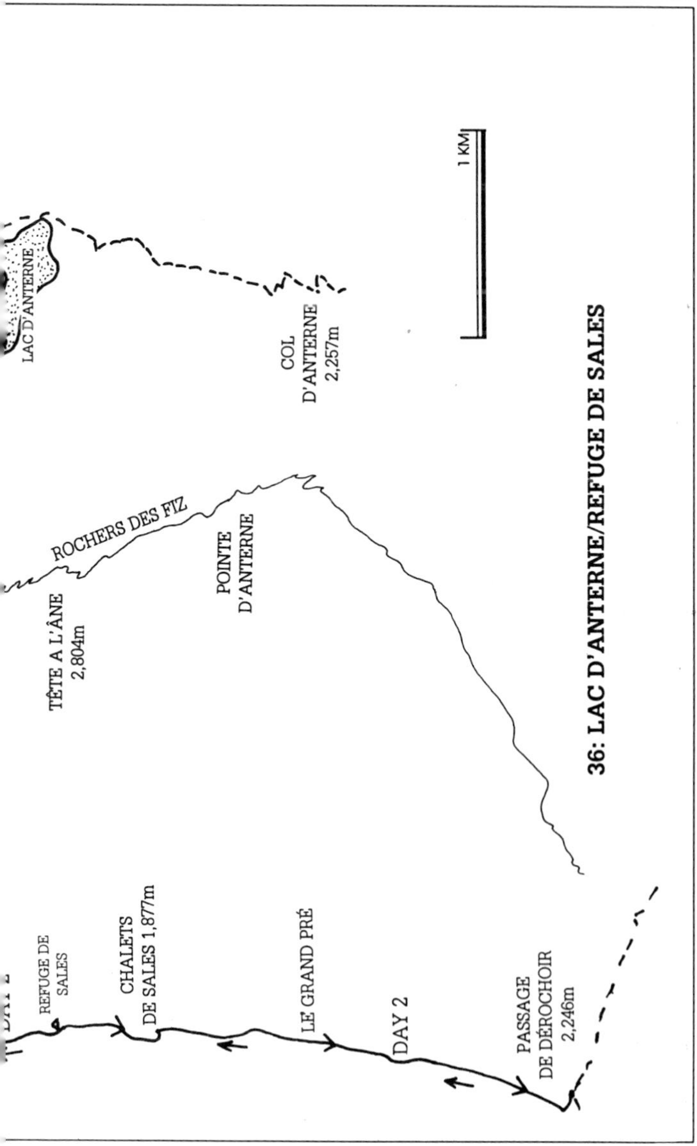

36: LAC D'ANTERNE/REFUGE DE SALES

chalets which are set in a circle of imposing peaks (1hr 30mins). This is the Cirque (circle) des Fonds. The large old chalet on the left is called the Nid d'Aigle (eagle's nest) and was built in 1858 by an Englishman called Alfred Wills (more information below). Just after is the Refuge des Fonds, alt. 1,380m (see below for details).*This is a good spot to stop for refreshment and to sample their delicious bilberry tart if you are walking in early autumn.*

Refuge des Fonds (privately owned), 74740 Sixt Fer à Cheval, tel. 50.34.44.05. Accommodation for 40 people (dormitories) - food available.

From the refuge bear round to the right on a wide stony path through coniferous trees until you come to more signposts. There is another path off to the right, but continue straight on as indicated Anterne/Buet/Chamonix. *In August or early September you will see big bunches of blue willow gentians which, unlike their spring flowering dwarf counterparts, are tall with lots of blooms on one stalk.* The path comes out of the forest and into another cirque (circle), only narrower, with the Giffre stream still flowing nearby.

At another sign follow right in the direction of Anterne (1hr 45mins) curling up round the hillside. You can see the Chalets des Fonds below on your right - it is about 400m up to the Chalets d'Anterne and another 200m to the lake. The path is mossy and wet with lots of tall gentians and ferns growing on the banks, depending on the time of year, and there are lovely views down into the Samoëns valley. Leaving the trees behind, the path winds round through open pasture with glorious views to left and right; *one feels diminished by the sheer immensity and height of the mountains in this area which contrast with the more graceful, friendly Chablais peaks to the north.*

The path continues across the top of the mountain through dwarf alder bushes and right under the wires of five enormous electricity pylons. It passes a big fir tree on the left where someone has painted all the ends of the sawn branches bright orange! Looking back you can see the entrance of the valley to the Chalets des Sales and Pointe de Dérochoir where you will be walking the following day. Still with an impressive view down to the Chalets des Fonds huts, which seem an incredible distance below, you pass a tiny pond and come to a rock indicating you are at 2,076m, with signs Pas d'Anterne/Lac d'Anterne - Réserve naturelle, chiens interdits (3 hrs).

You are now right on top of the mountain where the terrain is open, undulating and boggy with lots of heather, bilberry bushes and white bog cotton flowers. When you come to another signpost at the Petit Col d'Anterne, alt. 2,038m, which says Refuge 30mins follow the sign left to Lac d'Anterne 1hr (Col 1hr 45mins). *In foggy weather it is wise to go directly to the refuge as it is easy to get lost here.*

Follow the obvious path which goes through some black shale and over rocks, pools and river beds which may be empty in dry weather. The towering long rock wall of the Rochers des Fiz, 800m high, is over on the left. When the lake finally appears below (4hrs) one is agreeably surprised at how big it is, shaped rather like a whale. Ahead you can see the path winding up and over the Col d'Anterne, alt. 2,257m. If you do not wish to go down to the lake cut across the hill to the right and join the path going back to the refuge (you can see the path from above). There are lots of marmot holes so look out for these furry creatures which you can often see bounding over the countryside. There is always a marmot on sentry duty and he will give a piercing whistle to warn the others of danger.

Otherwise when you reach the lake take a U-turn round to the right and follow the red signs to the refuge - a defined path, through shale, rocks and grassland (you are now on the GR.5). After you pass a cairn you can see down to the refuge which nestles in a grassy alpine plain with the huge Rochers des Fiz behind. The path snakes down for about half an hour towards the refuge (5hrs), which is quite small, surrounded by six other mountain huts. You can see that this used to be a small alpine hamlet as there are traces of broken down walls where crops were grown. Just before arriving, cross over the Ruisseau (stream) d'Anterne, which runs right through the valley, with signposts to Chamonix back towards the lake and Chalets des Fonds to the right.

Refuge d'Anterne Alfred Wills, Plaine d'Anterne, 74740 Sixt Fer à Cheval, tel. 50.34.49.36. (Privately owned).

Open June to October. Situated on the GR.5 between Sixt and Chamonix, this is a small refuge, clean but fairly rudimentary with one cramped dortoir (dormitory) housing 50 people. There are no showers and only one small basin with cold water in the toilet. However, there is a pipe outside with running water. The food is basic but adequate.

This refuge is dedicated to Alfred Wills, an Englishman who lived from 1828 to 1912 and was a founder of the London Alpine Club. He came to the valley of the Giffre (Sixt area), fell in love with it and constructed a large chalet Nid d'Aigle, in 1858 in the Cirque des Fonds. There is a picture in the refuge of Alfred standing in front of his chalet in 1877.

The present guardians of the refuge (which is private) got very excited when they heard my name (Norton). The daughter of Alfred Wills married a Norton and lived in the Nid d'Aigle for many years. The family, according to hearsay, lost their fortune in India and so sold the chalet to the Lucas family who still own it.

Day 2: Refuge Alfred Wills, Lac d'Anterne to Chalets de Sales and Pointe de Dérochoir

Walk down the valley with the high flat wall of the Rochers des Fiz on your left. The valley floor is boggy with flattish rocks on the left from ancient glacier formation. You are now on the GR.5 which goes all the way from Sixt to Chamonix. Cross a small river by a wooden bridge; the path goes by large rocks and is well-defined, winding up round the mountain to the base of the electricity pylons. You quickly lose sight of the refuge round the corner, but there is a good view back down the valley with the snowy Mont Blanc range rearing up behind the Col d'Anterne. You can see the path you went up the day before over on the right. The Fiz escarpment ends dramatically at the Collet d'Anterne, alt. 1,796m, where there are signposts and a first view down to the Samoëns valley beyond (45mins). Here there is a narrow path heading up to the right to the refuge Le Grenairon which can be seen half way up the side of the mountain. Ignore this path and continue straight on down.

There are wonderful views down to the valley and village of Salvagny as you wind round the mountain, going gently downwards at first and then much steeper, crossing dry river beds and in and out of woodland, on a path which is sometimes quite rocky and, in wet weather, slippery and muddy. Follow the GR red/white signs carefully all the way until you finally reach a T-junction (1hr 35mins) with the spectacular waterfalls of the Cascades de la Sauffrez and Pleureuses in front. *Here you can go right and walk back to the car (30mins) - route details below.*

Turn left and follow sign to the Refuge de Sales 1hr - you are now on the GR.96 which is a variant of the GR.5. Follow the stony path which goes quite steeply up the side of a ravine with the stream rushing below on the left. This is a watery, boulder area with two rock faces each side, making the ravine narrow before it opens out. On the left is the other side of the sinister Rochers des Fiz. After 20mins you reach a plateau and cross the stream before starting to climb up along the other side of the ravine. This walk is characterised by its flattish stretches and then steepish climbs with three dramatic waterfalls. The interesting thing about these waterfalls is that the river bed may be empty in dry weather and the water tumbling down the boulders seems to come from an underground source. At the first waterfall the path becomes a ledge going under a cliff; however there is a solid protection rail so it is no problem. At the third waterfall the path deviates to the right following a dry tributary of the main river. You reach the final plateau at a cross with a small 17th-century chapel on the left. Continue to the Refuge de Sales. alt. 1,886m (2hrs 35mins) - details below. This is an ideal place to stop for a refreshing drink before starting to climb up to the Pointe de Dérochoir.

Refuge de Sales, 74740 Sixt Fer à Cheval (privately owned), tel. 50.34.47.01. A more sophisticated refuge than Alfred Wills - can house 80 people in various dormitories.

The path is fairly flat for a while and goes between a small group of renovated huts which must have originally housed the shepherds guarding the huge flocks which were kept up here during the summer months. After 10mins you go past an old stone water trough and up over rocks onto a slightly higher plateau in a wide grassy valley called Le Grand Préau (my Oxford dictionary translates this as "the big courtyard"). This valley is very attractive with two small ponds and there are cows and horses grazing in summer. You come to a junction where there is a sign on a rock. Keep left towards the Pointe de Dérochoir. The right fork goes to the Col de la Portette and eventually to the Chalets de Platé, another refuge in an area called the Désert de Platé, a desolate region of flat creviced rock. You can see up on your right the top of the cable-car coming up from the ski resort of Flaine.

After 30mins from the Chalet de Sales you start the serious climb to the col which is fairly steep but on a defined path. The top is a narrow ledge with a steep drop over cliffs on the other side and magnificent views; you can see right down the Chamonix valley with the Lac Vert far below and the glistening snowy peaks of the Mont Blanc range (4hrs). *This is a walk which is really worth the effort as the view is one of the most dramatic in the region. What a spot for a picnic! - the only snag is that in summer the col is often crowded.*

Retrace your steps to the Chalets des Sales and then the Cascade de Sauffraz at the junction where you arrived from the Col d'Anterne. Continue straight down until you reach the Chalets de Lignon, alt 1,180m. The path is wide and easy, though somewhat stony, through spaced coniferous woods with four waterfalls on the way. Keep right when you get to the Chalets de Lignon where there is a car park, café and lots of signposts, one stating that you are entering the Sixt National Reserve. Continue down the tarmac road, making use of the obvious short cuts to avoid the bends until you reach the car parking at the Chalets de Fardelay (6hrs 20mins).

Remarks: A wonderful and varied two-day walk in a beautiful alpine area which is very popular so you will meet a fair number of people. It is possible to split the walk into two separate one-day hikes. Another alternative is to make a complete circle by continuing past the Lac d'Anterne and over the Col to the Refuge d'Anterne where you can spend the first night. You then continue on a variant of the Mont Blanc path before turning up right to the Passage de Dérochoir. This option is only for people who do not mind heights and in good weather as there is a tricky passage involving chains and ladders.

37: CHALETS DE CRIOU - Alt. 1,664 metres
(Faucigny/Haut Giffre region)

Difficulty:	Medium walk with no steep gradients until the chalets. Steeper if you go on to the Aouille.
Time:	4hrs 15mins.
Height gain:	954 metres.
Maps:	Editions Didier & Richard IGN No.3 Massifs du Chablais Faucigny & Genevois 1:50,000. Cartes IGN 3530 ET Top 25 Samoëns/Haut Giffre 1:25,000.
Depart from:	Vallon d'en Bas - 710 metres.
Signposting:	Adequate on the upward path, not so good on the return - signposts but no splashes!

How to get there (from Geneva)
Take the motorway direction Chamonix and exit at No.15, Boëge/St. Jeoire. Then turn left briefly on the D.903 and watch for the D.9 right signposted Fillinges, Samoëns and Vallée Verte. Follow this road to the Pont de Fillinges and then turn right on the D.907 direction Taninges/Samoëns. (ALTERNATIVELY go through Annemasse and take the D907 direction Taninges/Samoëns.) Drive through Samoëns towards Sixt and take the first turning to the left marked Les Vallons. Go directly to the little chapel in Vallon d'en Bas and park nearby.

OR if there is not enough parking space near the chapel, continue towards Vallon d'en Haut 5mins up the road - turn left at the fountain and park further on where there is plenty of room. It is also possible to start the walk from here by taking the jeep track straight ahead.

Directions (from Vallon d'en Bas)
Take the stony path which goes up to the right of the little chapel, initially between mossy stone walls. After a few minutes turn sharp right to Criou. Keep to the main track which goes through woods with the Samoëns valley down on the right. At a T-junction (15mins) turn up left at a sign to Alpage du Trot 1hr 20mins (if you come from Vallon d'en Haut you will continue straight at this sign). 5mins later you pass an attractive wooden trough fountain called Fontaine du vin blanc.

This is a wide defined jeep track through deciduous and coniferous forest. When you come to a fork, bear right to Criou (to the left is where you come out on your return). Keep on the main path (ignoring all paths going

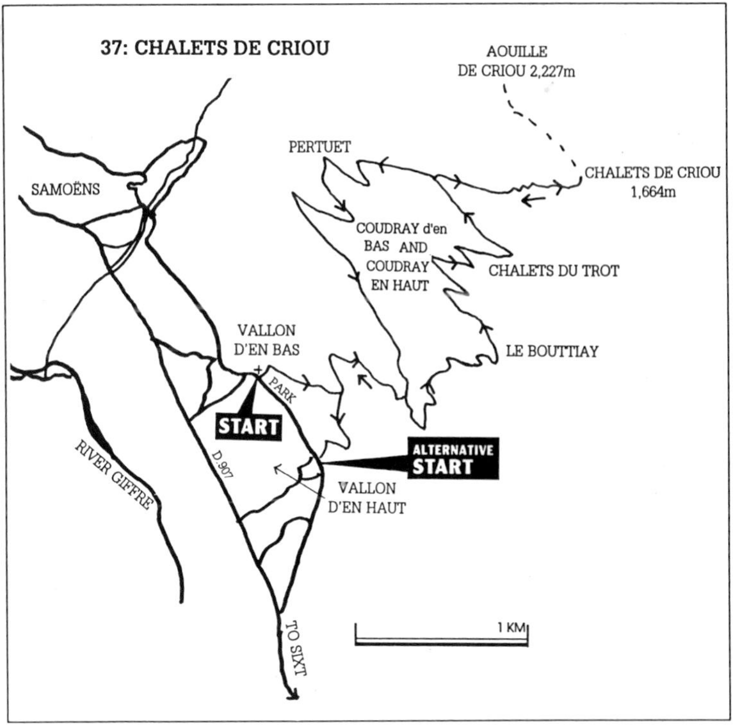

off) following signs to Criou. You reach Le Bouttiay (50mins) consisting of two little huts, and 30mins later others at Coudray d'en Bas and Coudray en Haut. The woods give way to attractive open alpine pasture, covered in bright blue forget-me-nots and early purple orchids in springtime, just before you reach a collection of wooden huts called Le Trot, alt.1,400m (1hr 30mins). There is a sign saying Boissons/Buvette. If you have time take a drink at the attractive wooden chalet and buy some of their delicious goat cheese - the goats are all around you!

Take the steep path straight up between the chalets following the sign to Criou and turn left at a T-junction. The path winds round the mountain with the odd hut dotted here and there. This is probably an old mule track as much of the path appears man-made, hewn out of the mountain, with intermittent low stone walls. The slopes are partially covered with a flat fissured rock formation, this ancient glacier type terrain being fairly common in the Samoëns area. *In summertime there are lots of butterflies, particularly the tiny blue ones which cluster round the dried goat dung. I have also seen swallow-tail butterflies, mottled whites and a camberwell beauty, the latter being among the rarer species.*

At the Chalets de Criou (2hrs 30mins) there is a sign and a big arrow on a rock. Walk through the chalets skirting a big round modern water tank, until you come is an attractive old stone trough higher up, which must have been the original source of water for the cattle and goats. The chalets look old and unspoilt, apart of course from the inevitable corrugated iron roofs. Above the water trough is a large rock with Criou painted in red. This rock is the highest point of the walk - there is a splendid view of the Giffre valley below and beyond the rearing peak of the Roc d'Anterne which is the end of the impressive Rochers des Fiz ridge and to the left the Mont Blanc range. Straight ahead on the horizon are the tops of the ski-lifts coming up from the well-known ski resort of Flaine. From the rock there is a path going steeply upwards to the Aguille de Criou, alt. 2,227m, which takes about 1hr 30mins. However, the path peters out and you have to find your own way to the top. (I have not done this walk.)

Retrace your steps until you come to the first major turn where there is a board on a tree (2hrs 45mins) but no indications. You get more extensive views of the Giffre valley as you continue straight, even though there is no path but lots of muddy cattle tracks. Skirt south of the fir trees and you will come to a defined path leading to the old chalets you can see below you called Pertuet, where you can refresh yourself at an old wooden water trough. Here there are one or two chalets with the original tavaillon roofs which you see so rarely in the Alps nowadays. In summer many of these rustic chalets are used as holiday homes and have been tastefully restored.

After Pertuet you are on a jeep track (if the leaves are off the trees you can already see the village below with its little chapel standing as a landmark) going down through woodland with a steep drop one side and passing a cascade of slate rock to the left before reaching the original path (3hrs 45mins). From here you can retrace your steps to the chapel. Alternatively, if you go straight (where you should turn right to Vallon d'en Bas) you reach the next little village of Vallon d'en Haut where there is a charming fountain at the finish of the walk. It has water coming out of duck heads and a notice saying Fontaine de Chernieux, Oeuvre (designed by) François Mugnier 1820 to 1900. *It is worth taking a look at the beautiful wild garden of the old farm opposite. When we did the walk in July the garden was ablaze with purple and pink and the rare yellow Mongolian variety of clematis, plus clusters of highly scented white stocks. The old farmer's wife was delighted to show us around!*

Turn right and walk along the road for about 10mins, flanked by some dilapidated Savoyard farms, till you get to Vallon d'en Bas (4hrs 15mins).

Remarks: Considering these little villages are very near the bustling ski and summer resort of Samoëns they are curiously unspoilt, maybe because they are off the main road. It is obviously an area which has a lot of history as the chalets are old, some as yet untouched by renovation. Vallon d'en Bas is a charming hamlet of weathered Savoyard farms with not many modern chalets - what a find!

We did this walk in high summer and saw very few people. It is also a good choice on a hot day as much of it is in shady woodland and the way up is not too steep. The views down the Giffre valley and off the surrounding mountains are superb, even more so in early winter when there are no leaves on the trees. I thought that the French word Aouille (de Criou) might have a specific meaning but the tourist bureau at Samoëns assures me it does not!

38: TÊTE DE BOSTAN (Samoëns) - Alt. 2,406 metres
(Faucigny/Haut Giffre area)

Difficulty:	Medium - the walk to the Col de Bostan is long and steep but there are no airy places.
Time:	6hrs.
Height gain:	1,261 metres.
Maps:	Editions Didier & Richard IGN No.3 Massifs du Chablais Faucigny & Genevois 1:50,000. Cartes IGN 3530 ET Top 25 Samoëns/Haut Giffre1:25,000.
Depart from:	Les Allamands - 1,030 metres.
Signposting:	Good in parts.

How to get there (from Geneva)

Take the motorway direction Chamonix and exit at No.15, Boëge/St. Jeoire. Then turn left briefly on the D.903 and watch for the D.9 right signposted Fillinges, Samoëns and Vallée Verte. Follow this road to the Pont de Fillinges and then turn right on the D.907 direction Taninges/Samoëns. (ALTERNATIVELY go through Annemasse and take the D.907 direction Taninges/Samoëns.) The main street of Samoëns is a pedestrian precinct so follow signs to Sixt which will take you round the village. Then turn left where it is signposted Centre ville (town centre) and Morzine. Take the first turning right (D.354) to Les Moulins/Morzine on a narrow uphill road and then at a left-hand bend take the still narrower road straight ahead, signposted Les Allamands/Les Chavonnes/Refuge de Tornay (this is easy to miss so be careful). Continue up this road by two car parks and through the hamlet of

Les Allamands (just over 4km) till you get to a third car park where you leave your car.

Directions

At the entrance to the car park there is a sign which says Refuge Tornay/Bostan, alt. 1,763m, 2hrs. The way up is at the end of the car park to the left where there is no sign but there are red/white GR marks on a rock. The wide, stony path goes up through woodland and, after 5mins, you get your first view of the imposing rock face of the Dents d'Oddaz to the right. This magnificent wall of rock accompanies you all the way to the Col de Bostan. Ignore the sign to the right which says Boston Palatieu (according to the map this could be a shorter way but I have not tried it). Go straight on and through an iron gate (45mins) and a few minutes later you are out in the open in a sort of narrow valley, which never really opens up fully. Here the towering rock face of the Dents d'Oddaz is really impressive; if you look behind you can see the tops of the ski-lifts which come up from the ski resort of Flaine.

38: TETE DE BOSTAN

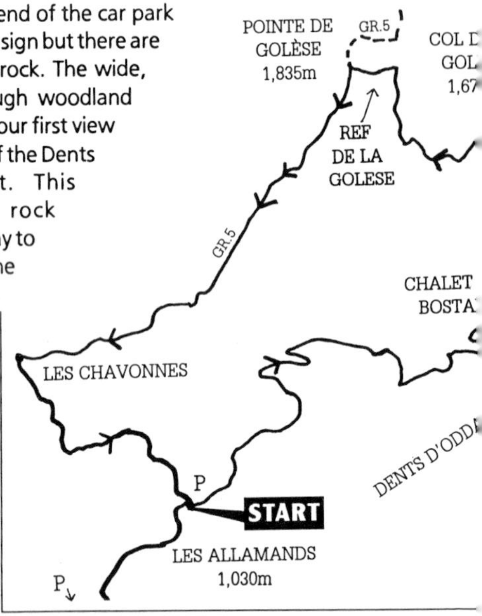

Continue upwards through alpine pastures passing the old cattle hut of Chalet de Bostan, alt. 1,602m, on your right (1hr 5mins) and, shortly after, an old stone water trough which is in a very strategic spot for a drink on hot day. Keep going past a more modern chalet with the Refuge de Tornay visible ahead. There is a sign to the left to the Col de la Golèse (this is where you will return if you cut through before and go via the col). The Refuge de Tornay, alt. 1,763m (1hr 45mins), is a fairly recent building and a popular overnight stop for people doing the Dents Blanches circular walk which takes about six days. *They serve delicious fruit tarts here and it is a delightful place to stop for a drink and a snack.*

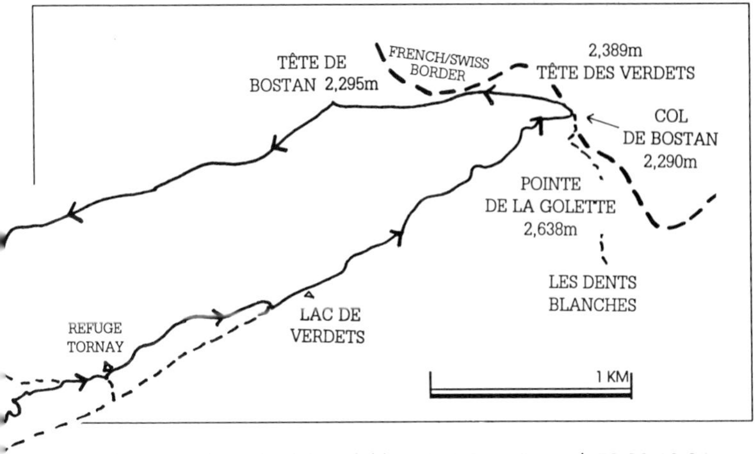

Refuge de Tornay (French Alpine Club), 74340 Samoëns, tel. 50.90.10.94. Open summer and winter seasons plus weekends and holidays.

From the refuge you take a grassy, undulating path following the red/ white splashes on the left-hand side of the valley. Here you get the flat, glacial rock terrain which indicates that hundreds of years ago the valley was covered by a glacier. 15mins from the refuge you get your first view of the Col de Bostan on the horizon. When you come to the Lac de Verdets down on your right (it shrinks to a small pond in summer) the path crosses over and joins another path coming up from the right. You are now climbing more steeply through a jumble of big boulders. *In July and August you will see lots of tall purple monkshood, the lilac coloured hairy adenostyles with their big leaves and clusters of deep forget-me-nots, amongst a profusion of other flowers.* Take time to turn round and appreciate the magnificent view down the valley.

You need a lot of puff for the last part of the climb which is steep but not too difficult and the path is easy to follow. When you reach the Col de Bostan, alt. 2,290m (3hrs 30mins), you are rewarded by sweeping views on all sides; in front is Planachaux, the top of the ski resort of Champèry in Switzerland, with the Rhône valley beyond. On the skyline are the Vaudois alps with the ski resort of Leysin nestling halfway up. To the right are the daunting peaks of Les Dents Blanches (meaning white teeth), from the Pointe de la Golette, alt. 2,638m, to the Dent de Barme, alt. 2,756m, and to the left is the green mound of the Tête de Bostan. There is a signpost pointing right to the Refuge de Vogealle and Refuge de Folly. *This is the path you would take on the difficult way round the Dents Blanches - it is often covered in snow even in summer and should only be attempted by experienced walkers.* The col is on the French/Swiss border and there is a yellow signpost with the timings to the Swiss destinations of Pas de Bide and Chalets de Barmaz. *It is the obvious place for a picnic before tackling the rather airy way round to the left.*

The path goes round the back of the Tête des Verdets ridge and is quite exposed with a steep slope down on the left as you approach the Tête de Bostan. After 15mins you come to a fork (3hrs 45mins). The left fork takes you round the bottom of the Tête de Bostan and the right one up to the summit, so take your choice! It is worth going up to the top, alt. 2,406m, as you get a good view of the peaks around Morzine and Les Hauts Forts ridge (the highest point in the Chablais region). You can now see the top of the Mont Blanc range behind the Dents d'Oddaz, which is a magnificent sight, the glistening snow covered peaks contrasting with the sombre d'Oddaz ridge, which from here really does look like a row of teeth. The path continues along the top of the wide, exposed ridge gradually losing height and then going down steeper. Down on the right are interesting rock formations and the valley of the Dranse river down to Morzine. Towards the end of the valley is an attractive, small lake where there is the Hôtel/Refuge Mine d'Or, a popular stopping off place for tourists.

After approximately 40mins (4hrs 10mins) you come off the Bostan hump and meet the lower alternative path. Continue straight on through a wooden gate (there is an electric fence here) until you meet a signpost, about 1hr from the col (4hrs 30mins). If you go left you get back to the Refuge de Tornay and can then take the original route back to the car. It is a narrow, rocky path but quite easy.

Otherwise, continue straight following the Col de Golèse signpost on a path which is open and easy. Ahead is the Pointe de Golèse which looks most inviting with a clump of trees on the summit, but it is a 200m climb from the col and you would have to return by the same path or make a long detour. As your path curls round the hillside you can see down to the refuge at the col and the long jeep track going up to it. Pick your way down to the refuge as there are a number of paths (5hrs 10mins). The building is not very attractive as it has a rusty corrugated iron roof with a modern extension stuck on the end. However, when it is open, it has tables and chairs outside and is a welcome stop for refreshment.

Refuge de la Golèse, Col de la Golèse, 74340 Samoëns, tel. 50.34.43.80.
Accommodation for 60 people in three dormitories.

You have now joined the the GR.5 on a jeep track going down through open pastures for quite a long way with a shallow valley to the left. There is the odd alpine hut and occasional chalets lower down with more woodland as you lose altitude. The track becomes a tarmac road about 10mins from the car park. It is easy walking all the way and, if less interesting than the way up, at least a relief from having to negotiate down a tricky path. It takes 45mins from the refuge to the car park (6hrs).

Remarks: The Dents Blanches is the first high mountain range rising from the lower slopes of the pre-alpine region - it is separated from the main Mont Blanc peaks by the Chamonix valley. This is a challenging walk at a fairly high altitude but with no technical difficulty and, therefore, within the possibilities of most fit people. It is very popular so you risk meeting a number of people in the summer season. There are magnificent views into the Rhône valley and over the Vaud and Valais peaks in Switzerland. It is interesting to note that the Col de Golèse is one of the two main migrating routes for birds flying north/south over the Alps and every year thousands of birds are ringed and checked by ornithologists here. It is also traditionally a great smuggling area and the legend goes that one Christmas Eve a Swiss customs man met a heavily laden Frenchman coming from the direction of Samoëns. When challenged as to what he carried, the Frenchman replied that he was the Angel Gabriel!

39: POINTE DE MARCELLY - Alt. 1,999 metres

(Faucigny/Haut Giffre region)

Difficulty:	Medium except for the last climb to the Pointe where there are chains although you can avoid these by going round - this is a ridge walk so not for anyone suffering from vertigo.
Time:	4hrs.
Height gain:	470 metres and 69 metres.
Maps:	Editions Didier & Richard IGN No.3 Massifs du Chablais Faucigny & Genevois 1:50,000. Cartes IGN 3429 ET Top 25 Bonneville/Cluses 1:25,000.
Depart from:	Praz de Lys - 1,510 metres.
Signposting:	Adequate as the path is obvious except at the end of the walk - orange & turquoise splashes along the ridge and small signposts.

How to get there (from Geneva)

Take the motorway direction Chamonix and exit at No.15, Boëge/St. Jeoire. Then turn left briefly on the D.903 and watch for the D.9 right signposted Fillinges, Samoëns and Vallée Verte. Follow this road to the Pont de Fillinges and then turn right on the D.907 direction Taninges/Samoëns. (ALTERNATIVELY go through Annemasse and take the D.907 direction Taninges/Samoëns.) From Taninges take the D.902 signposted Les Gets and at Le Pont des Gets (7km out of Taninges) turn left on the D.328 and then left again on the D.308 signposted Praz de Lys. Go right through the ski station in the direction of the Col de Ramaz following signposts to the Restaurant Jean de la Pipe at a place called Les Molliettes. Park your car opposite the restaurant.

Directions

Walk up the road from the restaurant and on the first corner there is a signpost to the left saying Lac du Roy. Take this narrow defined path which climbs fairly steeply over bare hillside up to a crest where you can see the lake. Here there is a signpost (20mins) indicating right to Chalet de Roy/Pointe de la Couennasse/Pointe de Marcelly which is a shorter way to the ridge you are heading for. However, for what I consider a more interesting route, cross a stream and take the path round the side of the lake. Do not continue right round the lake but go straight on the path at the end until you see large chalets over the crest. Then bear right on a grassy track which goes round the lake higher up and reaches the path coming up from the signpost to the Pointe de la Couenmasse; (as it is open hillside you can see all these connecting paths from far away including the one you want on the side of the hill, so you can't get lost!).

Turn left when you get to the path (50mins) and climb fairly steeply for 10mins till you reach the ridge at 1,862m. Bear left towards the Pointe de Marcelly (the right one goes to the Pointe de Perret, alt. 1,941m and Pointe de Haute Fleury, 1981m). You are now walking along a wide ridge with impressive views of the surrounding peaks on either side; down on the right you can see the road you came up and the valley of the Giffre with Taninges and below on the left the Lac de Roy and Praz de Lys. About 10mins along the ridge there is a danger sign which means there is a rather difficult short scramble down some rocks, with a steep drop on the right and a wire rope for support. If you do not like this, take an earlier detour down to the right, dropping steeply for a short distance, and then turn left at a T-junction back up to the original path. Continue along this glorious, wide ridge following the orange and later turquoise markings.

You reach the Frête de Penaille, alt. 1,892m (1hr 15mins) which is the first peak along the ridge and 15mins later on you come to the second peak

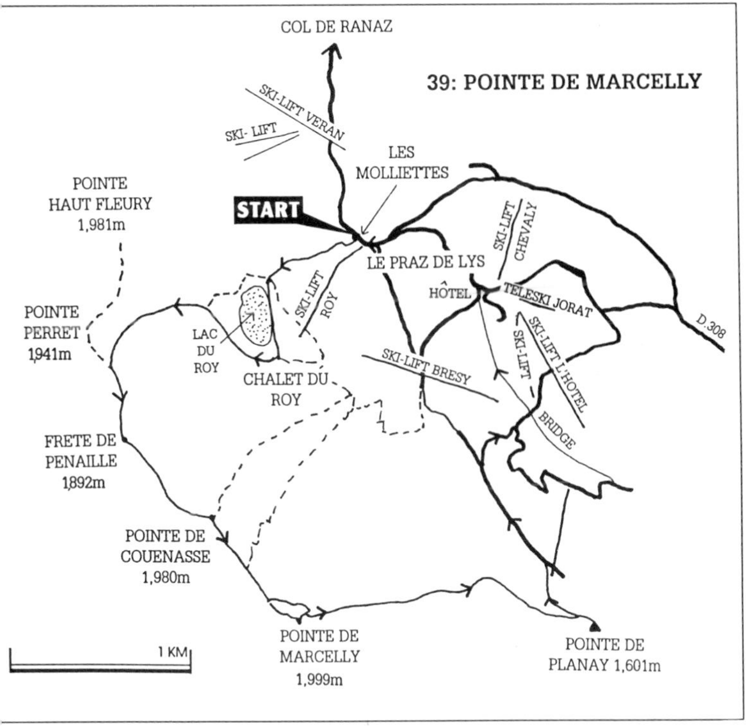

called the Pointe de Couennasse, 1,980m (1hr 30mins); the name is marked on a rock so you know you are there! You can now see the Pointe de Marcelly in front - a towering rock with a large cross on top and a magnificent view of Mont Blanc beyond. Watch for a path off to the left just before you reach the airy scramble to the top. This path goes round and up behind the pointe which is much easier. Otherwise the path becomes quite precipitous and at the end you are scrambling over rocks hanging on steel cables for about 40m! The climb is not difficult for those who like doing this sort of thing (I find it exhilarating), but do not attempt it if you suffer from vertigo.

From the top of the cables there is a short walk to the summit marked by an ugly, tall, iron cross painted yellow and held down by long wires (2hrs). There is an incredible view from the pointe, alt. 1,999m. The peak juts out over and dominates the town of Taninges; beyond you have a magnificent, uninterrupted view of the entire Mont Blanc range. *This is a good place to have your picnic if it is not too windy and you are there on an uncrowded week day - otherwise you could find that there are lots of people up here and it is not exactly peaceful.*

Do not go down via the cables but take the rocky path which comes up from the back. This will lead you to the path that goes round the Pointe from the bottom and continues along the ridge, gradually losing height; you have to pick your way along the ridge carefully as there are lots of boulders but it is not dangerous. The surroundings are open with glorious views on either side, but later on there are continuous patches of low woodland. You come to a large wooden cross (3hrs) on the left which is a memorial to Marc Claude who died here on Christmas Day 1974 (one wonders how as it is not a dangerous place). Walk along till you come to the top of the Téléski de Planay. Ignoring any paths branching off, continue straight until you reach the Pointe de Planay, alt. 1,601m, which is a hump at the very end of the ridge and a popular jumping off spot for parapenting (3hrs 15mins).

Here there are even better views of the surrounding peaks and countryside and you can see right up the Arve and Giffre valleys, from Cluses almost to Chamonix and from Taninges to Samoëns. Retrace your steps for about 100m and then take the grassy jeep track down right over an open slope with some woodland - another path coming down from the ridge joins from the left. The path goes under the Planay ski-tow and about 10mins later joins a narrow road going to a chalet with a small parking area opposite (it is possible to start the walk from here). Turn left down the road and you come to the first chalets of the Praz de Lys area. Continue for another 10mins and just before a bridge which you can see from the hill, take the path left indicated Praz de Lys (3hrs 35mins). This track crosses the plateau area with ski-tows and various chalets. It deteriorates just before the end but continue straight and you will reach the road again by an ugly block of flats with a tiny chapel beyond (3hrs 50mins).

Turn right in front of the flats and then almost immediately left at a T-junction with a sign to the Jean de la Pipe restaurant. Follow the road for about 10mins till you reach your car (4hrs).

Remarks: The Pointe de Marcelly is a dramatic walk as the long ridge with its enormous cross at the summit dominates the town of Taninges and is a landmark for the entire region. It is very popular as the views from the ridge are magnificent, especially of the Mont Blanc range. Although an airy ridge walk, it is within the capabilities of most walkers with a head for heights, but it should not be attempted in wet weather when the rocks are slippery. As this is a classic walk of the region it is best to avoid the inevitable crowds on Sundays in July and August.

40: POINTE D'UBLE - Alt. 1,963 metres

(Faucigny/Haut Giffre region)

Difficulty:	Medium though steep in places; don't walk along the ridge if you suffer from vertigo.
Time:	4hrs 45mins.
Height gain:	798 metres.
Maps:	Editions Didier & Richard IGN No.3 Massifs du Chablais Faucigny & Genevois 1:50,000. Cartes IGN 3528 ET Top 25 Morzine Massif du Chablais 1:25,000 or Cartes IGN 3429 ET Top 25 Bonneville/Cluses 1:25,000.
Depart from:	Les Côtes - 1,165 metres.
Signposting:	Good some of the way.

How to get there (from Geneva)

Take the motorway direction Chamonix and exit at No.15, Boëge/St. Jeoire. Then turn left briefly on the D.903 and watch for the D.9 right signposted Fillinges, Samoëns and Vallée Verte. Follow this road to the Pont de Fillinges and then turn right on the D.907 direction Taninges/Samoëns. (ALTERNATIVELY go through Annemasse and take the D.907 direction Taninges/Samoëns.) At Taninges take the D.902 signposted Les Gets and at Le Pont des Gets turn left on the D.328 towards Praz de Lys. Continue for about 2km to a place called Les Côtes. Park your car below a hairpin bend just after the D.328 goes off to the right, where the D.308 comes in from Praz de Lys.

Directions

Walk up the road and take the narrower tarmac road which goes straight on at the hairpin and is signposted to La Crotte and Les Munes. You are walking along an attractive, narrow wooded valley with the Boutigny river rushing down on the right in a ravine and a wooded hill up on the left. After 10mins the path becomes level with the stream and you cross over a bridge into coniferous trees, where you will find a variety of mushrooms growing in the autumn. The road is flat and easy.

You reach a large wooden barn on the right called La Crotte (25mins). The road degenerates into a jeep track here and continues on. However, take the wide path up to the right which says Pointe d'Uble/Les Munes. You go through an iron barrier (presumably to keep out vehicles) and up the mountain through scattered firs; over on the left you can see a chair-lift.

15mins later you reach the Chalets de Rosset (40mins). Go straight through the huts and continue on the path which then bears to the right curling steadily upwards round the hill. 5mins later go straight on at another signpost towards the Pointe d'Uble (left is indicated Les Munes/Pointe de Ramaz). You pass the ruins of Les Perrières and cross some tiny streams to the Chalets d'Uble ruins, where there is a wooden sign with a green spot on it pointing upwards! Follow the green spot ignoring a path off to the left; the track goes up medium steep and is poorly defined in places especially when it is wet and muddy.

You reach a humpy ridge (1hr 30mins) where there are masses of large purple violets in springtime. From here you can see Mont Chéry, the top of the ski conglomeration above Les Gets, and the jagged peaks of the Roc d'Enfer on the left. Do not make for the large wooden cross on the right but turn left at a muddy T-junction and then continue up the saddle of the Pointe d'Uble. There is a signpost but it has fallen down (it could be removed or replaced in the future), indicating left Pointe d'Uble and right to Bonnavaz/Parteset. The path is not always clear but you can see the summit above as you climb over open alpine pasture. The 1hr climb up the grassy mountain is steep and tiring. The path winds over to the left and become slightly rocky and fragmented, so it is really easier to pick your own way to the top!

The terrain suggests that the Pointe will be another grassy hump but in fact you come on to a ridge, the ground dropping away in front very abruptly, which is most unexpected. This is the Pointe d'Uble, alt. 1,963m (2hrs 30mins). The views all round are impressive, especially the Roc d'Enfer straight ahead with the Pointe de Chalune to the left and the Haute Pointe behind; below to your left is the Lac de Roy and the jagged crest of the Pic de Marcelly above Praz de Lys. If you walk to the end of the ridge, which takes 5mins, you can appreciate the sudden dramatic drop!

Retrace your steps to the fallen down signpost (3hrs 30mins) and make for a small chalet down the hill in front of you which you reach in about 10mins. Then go straight down the hill (there are two paths but take the right-hand one) for about 10mins to a jeep track (3hrs 50mins). Turn down into the woods - there is a sign which says Bonnavaz (this is a hamlet on the D.338. You will have to walk down the road to the hairpin bend).

After 30mins of winding down the forest jeep track you hit the road at a sign pointing back saying Chalet d'Uble/Pointe d'Uble/La Crotte (4hrs 20mins).

Turn right and walk down the road with the River Foron on the left. Pass the hamlet of Bonnavaz on the right with its little chapel and then cross the Boutigny stream which rushes attractively over boulders before joining the River Foron. After 25mins you arrive at the hairpin bend and the point of departure (4hrs 45mins).

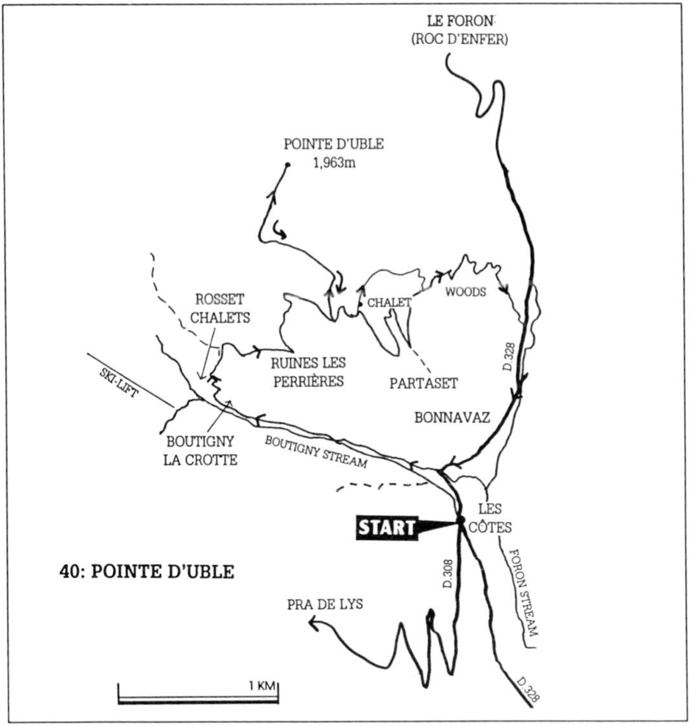

Remarks: The walk is quite a surprise because the way up to the Pointe is not so interesting but when you reach the ridge summit there is an unforgettable panorama, especially of the Roc d'Enfer ridge, one of the most impressive mountains in this area. The flowers in springtime are lovely and in the autumn the woods are full of interesting mushrooms, including the large red ones with white spots.

41: ROC D'ENFER - Alt. 2,243 metres
(Faucigny/Haut Giffre region)

Difficulty: Tough - only for competent walkers not afraid of some scrambling over rocks and ridge walking with steep drops each side.

Time:	6hrs.
Height gain:	888 metres.
Maps:	Editions Didier & Richard IGN No.3 Massifs du Chablais Faucigny & Genevois 1:50,000. Cartes IGN Top 25 3528 ET Top 25 Morzine Massif du Chablais 1:25,000.
Depart from:	Le Foron - 1,355 metres.
Signposting:	Some red splashes but few signposts. However, when you are on the ridge the way is obvious!

How to get there (from Geneva)

Take the motorway direction Chamonix and exit at No.15, Boëge/St. Jeoire. Then turn left briefly on the D.903 and watch for the D.9 right signposted Fillinges, Samoëns and Vallée Verte. Follow this road to the Pont de Fillinges and then turn right on the D.907 direction Taninges/Samoëns. (ALTERNATIVELY go through Annemasse and take the D.907 direction Taninges/Samoëns.) At Taninges take the D.902 direction Les Gets and at Pont des Gets turn off left on the D.328 towards Praz de Lys. After about 2km turn right on a small road which says Col de l'Encrenaz (actually you are still on the D.328). Before you get to the col there is a T-junction with the farm of Le Foron off to the left. Leave your car in the grassy space on the right before the farm.

Directions

Turn left up the tarmac road and through the farm, crossing a stream, after which the road becomes a wide level jeep track before narrowing through intermittent trees and on to open hillside going gently upwards. You reach a fountain, dated 1933 and the big cowshed of the Chalets de Foron du Milieu (20mins). With the farm behind you and facing the fountain, bear up to the right. There is no sign but you will come to a defined track which you follow upwards. If the day is clear, and you should not attempt this walk in poor weather conditions, you can see the Col de Foron between two humps to the left of the rocky crest of the Roc d'Enfer (which is on your right) so basically make for the col. You come to two more barns, invisible from the slope lower down, called Foron d'en Haut. The path continues straight on after the barns and climbs quite steeply over open mountainside covered with alpine roses and bilberry bushes. The Col de Foron is among a few stumpy fir trees slightly to the right of the rocky Pointe de Chalune which you can see ahead. There are signposts just below the col (1hr 10mins), indicating right to the Roc d'Enfer, left to the Pointe de Chalune 1hr, and straight on to Petit Souvroz and La Chèvrerie. It also says Crêtes de Bellevaux, which is a three-day circular walk.

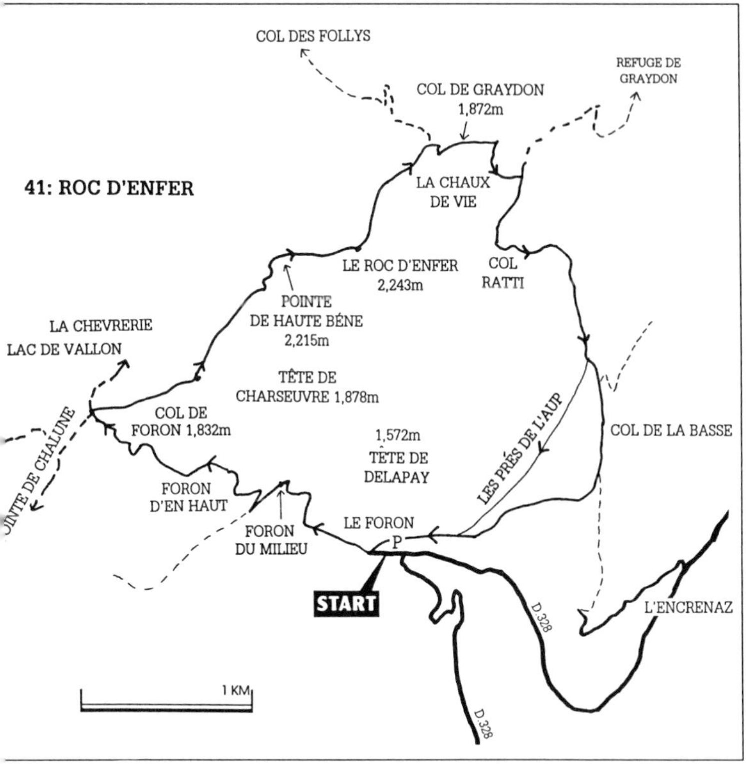

The next part of the walk is on a ridge with blue/red flashes on the rocks and sheer drops on each side. You can see right down into the valley, the path you came on past the two farms and the Mont Blanc range on the horizon. The track goes over the first hump and then along another ridge with a good view down to the left of the hamlet of La Chèvrerie and the Lac de Vallon and behind the village of Praz de Lys with the Pointe de Chalune and the Pic de Marcelly. The path leaves the ridge and goes round the Tête de Charseuvre, alt. 1,878m. You then come to a steep rocky gully where you need both hands to help you scramble up (do not look behind!). This goes up to a narrow saddle between two rocks where you turn right along the ridge (2hrs 20mins). Basically, the Roc d'Enfer has two summits, the Point de Haute Bene 2,215m and the Roc d'Enfer itself at alt. 2,243m. On some of the difficult stretches there are cables to help you.

The north side of the Roc d'Enfer ridge

Following the odd red splashes you climb up to the Pointe de Haute Bene, alt. 2,215m (2hrs 40mins), a grassy knoll where there is an iron cross. This is followed by a delicate scramble down and along the ridge to another small iron cross (3hrs) put up to commemorate the death of Joseph Rey from Bellevaux who died here aged 58 in 1918.

About 20mins later the path joins the ridge again, having passed mainly below the summit on the north side. Turn sharp right to reach the summit about 20m further up. You are now on the Roc d'Enfer, alt. 2,243m, where there is a small concrete IGN triangulation point. Stop here for your picnic if the weather is fine, to contemplate the fantastic panorama of mountain peaks in all directions: the Chablais summits of the Dents d'Oche, the Cornettes de Bise and Mont de Grange, the Chaine des Aravis with the Pointe Percée and on the horizon the Mont Blanc peaks with the Dents du Midi and the Vaudois mountains. To the north is Lake Léman (Lake Geneva) with the Jura a smudge on the skyline.

Retrace your steps for 20m, then carry straight on along the ridge to another minor summit where there is a white cross (3hrs 45mins). Look back here and contemplate the way you have come along the difficult ridge; it is quite impressive! Careful now as the ridge starts to go down fairly rapidly for about 300m and you have to watch that you do not slip. The one thing that saves this path from being really scary is that the grassy hump on the left or right most of the way along hides the fact that the other side is a precipitous drop! However, there are a number of rocky descents and tricky passages so go slowly! You can see the path leading down to a narrow pass in the mountain and then continuing along the side of the mountain towards the hamlet of Graydon where there is a SAC (Swiss Alpine Club) refuge.

After an hour from the summit you reach the Col de Graydon, alt. l,892m (4hrs 30mins). There is no sign except one saying that where you have come from is dangerous with "accidents mortel" (fatal accidents), which gives one a thrill as it is better to see that sort of notice after you have done it rather than before!! Take the path to the right which winds back down the side of the high ridge with some red marks on the rock.The path initially crosses some scree and then becomes easier as you go lower.

At this juncture we saw a huge marmot sitting up on a rock, silhouetted against the sky with the Mont Blanc range in the background - an impressive picture which was unfortunately too far away for a photo even with a telescopic lens.

The path is well defined, with red splashes, and continues to circle back underneath the Roc d'Enfer, along the side of a combe (valley) called la Chaux de Vie (quicklime). You can see a low ridge ahead called the Col de Ratti, alt. 1,900m, which you climb gently towards; a mere nothing compared to what you have already done so you hardly notice it! (4hrs 55mins). When you reach the col you can see the Mont Chéry above Les Gets with all its disfiguring ski installations on the horizon ahead; you are now round the front of the mountain again. Turn left at the top of the col on a defined path which goes down to the Col de la Basse. You are gradually dropping into a wide grassy valley with a stream in a shallow gully. About 15mins along this path you will see an isolated pile of rock to the right. Turn right here (if the visibility is good and with the rocks behind you aim for a path immediately below the cross on the Pointe de Marcelly on the horizon).

Careful here as there is no defined path but lots of cattle tracks which is rather confusing. It is important to stay low as you want to skirt the Tête de Delapay which just out above Le Foron - ahead of you is the grassy summit of the Point d'Uble with the Pic de Marcelly beyond. Remember to keep right of the little stream and aim for one of the cattle tracks curling round the middle of the shoulder. This is rather a tedious part of the walk (just when you want a rest) through what is called Les Prés (meadows) de L'Aulp. You will eventually see the road to Le Foron below and the hamlet of La Villiaz de Combafou. Eventually you will stumble on a defined path which takes you down to where you park your car. If you miss it keep going and you will find a path running parallel to the road and in 15mins you reach the car park (6hrs).

Remarks: This walk is not called the Roc d'Enfer (Hell's rock) for nothing and is one of the classics of the Haute Savoie region. Although hundreds of people climb it every year it should not be attempted by the faint-hearted or anyone suffering from vertigo. There is a fair amount of rock scrambling, often with chains to give support, but the drops behind you are quite considerable so a head for heights is essential! It is one of the most dramatic walks I have ever done as the views, in all directions, are breathtaking.

42: LA HAUTE POINTE - 1,958 metres
(Faucigny/Haut Giffre region)

Difficulty:	Medium, though steep in places.
Time:	3hrs 30mins plus 1hr if you climb to the Pointe.
Height gain:	550 metres.
Maps:	Edition Didier & Richard IGN No.3 Massifs du Chablais Faucigny & Genevois 1:50,000. Cartes IGN 3429 ET Top 25 Bonneville/Cluses.
Depart from:	Sommant - 1,413 metres.
Signposting:	Sporadic but difficult to get lost.

How to get there (from Geneva)
Take the motorway direction Chamonix and exit at No.15, Boëge/St. Jeoire. Then turn left briefly on the D.903 and watch for the D.9 right signposted Fillinges, Samoëns and Vallée Verte. Follow this road to the Pont de Fillinges and then turn right in the D.907 direction Taninges/Samoëns. (ALTERNATIVELY go through Annemasse and take the D.907, direction Taninges/Samoëns.) Follow this road to Mieussy and then take the D.308 direction Messy/Sommant/Col de Ramaz. Continue uphill for about 11km to Sommant, a downhill and cross-country ski station situated in an attractive wide bowl in the mountains. Turn left in front of the café/buvette (towards Col de Ramaz) and leave your car in a small parking lot on the left-hand side, just after a new self-service bar.

Directions
Take the first left turning after the new self-service bar on a jeep track which goes behind scattered chalets. It soon becomes grassed over with a low crumbling wall to the right; there is a blue arrow on a rock to the left. Follow a wooden signpost to Col de Cordon (10mins) and then a second one left to Col de Cordon/Charmettes (15mins). You are in open country with a stone wall and fence on the right of the path which narrows and becomes less defined. Stick to the fence until you reach the end of the fir trees and see a rock over on the left with another blue wooden sign to Col de Cordon/Charmette. (The last time I did this walk there was a new sign, still to be put

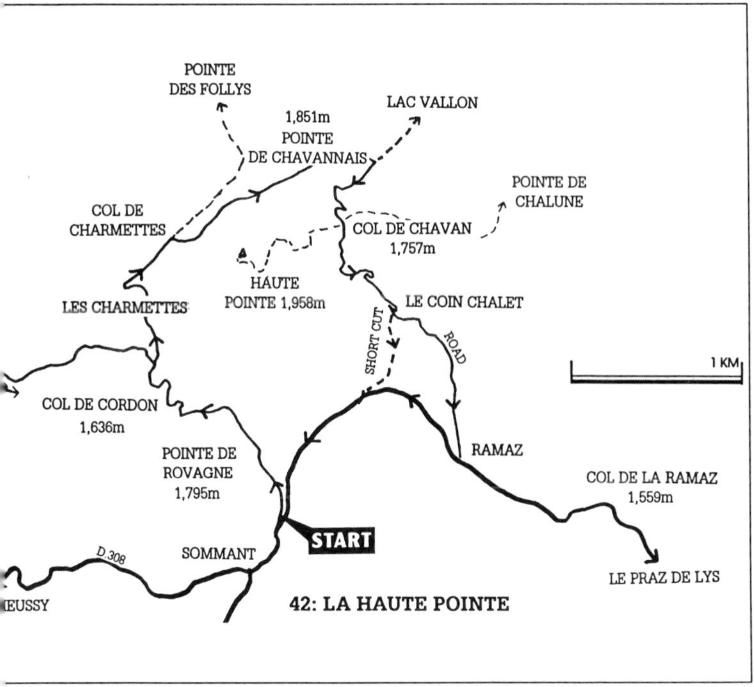

up, before you came to the rock. It really doesn't matter which sign you follow as both paths meet up a short while later!)

Follow the track, marked with intermittent blue and white splashes on the rocks and a red/white GR sign, through an attractive dell where there are lots of interesting orchids in springtime. Up ahead on the left is the rocky pinnacle of the Pointe de Rovagne, alt. 1,795m. When you reach the Col de Cordon ridge at alt. 1,636m (45mins) you can see both ways - back to the Mt. Blanc range and Col de Ramaz and ahead to the mountains of the Vallée Verte, Les Voirons and the Jura on the horizon.

From the Col de Cordon there is a path straight down into the valley but continue instead on the well defined path which goes right signposted La Charmette; there are blue marks on rocks. The path undulates round the mountain towards the Chalets de Charmettes with fairly steep slopes descending on the left into a wide, attractive, unspoilt valley. This is followed by a rocky, scree type terrain which is natural marmot country. *If you keep quiet you may well see one of these huge furry creatures running across the rocks. Listen for the piercing whistle which is uttered by the marmot who is acting as sentry to warn the others that danger is approaching.* Watch out for a white arrow on a rock saying Sommant where the path descends to meet the jeep track going to the Chalets de Charmettes, alt. 1,620m; turn right and walk up towards the chalets.

Go past the chalets and at the next corner take the narrow, grassy path which goes straight on (there are no markings here). You can already see a signpost at the col on the skyline, so make for this landmark. Turn right when you meet another path going across the side of the hill, still making for the signpost about 100m ahead. *Alternatively, keep on the jeep track which goes to the top of the col but further left; then turn right and walk along the ridge to the gate.*

There is a fence and a gate at the Col des Charmettes (1hr 10mins) and also a signpost left to Tigny/Les Charmettes. BE CAREFUL AT THE GATE: do not go through it, which seems the most obvious way to go, but turn right on a narrow grassy track which curls back the way you came but higher. You eventually see an isolated yellow/red splash on a rock to the left. Keep a look out as this area is riddled with marmots. *Every time I have done this walk I have seen a marmot at this spot. It is amusing to take time to watch the antics of these big furry creatures, as they amble around sniffing at rocks and rooting for food (see section on alpine fauna for more details).* Follow the poorly defined path which goes straight and very steeply up the side of the mountain. About three-quarters of the way up, just before some scree, take a grassy track to the left. This is easy to miss, but not the end of the world if you do, as you can still go up to the top and meet the path there. However this way is much steeper. If you look back you have a good view of the impressive Môle mountain which stands out in splendid isolation.

Walk along the top of the ridge to the Col de Chavannais (2hrs). There is a steep drop on the left over the edge of a huge cliff (Roc de la Tournette) and a good view down to the Bellevaux valley. The path goes slightly upwards to a grassy spot which is a convenient picnic spot though it might be too exposed for some people. You can walk on further to the Pointe de Chavannaise, alt. 1,851m, but the path peters out and it is somewhat vertiginous.

DO NOT take the obvious path which goes straight down from the col as it has been partially washed away by a landslide where it comes to a tricky expanse of steep scree (you cannot see this from above). INSTEAD take the path to the right which you can see going right along the mountainside - when it forks take the lower path (the higher fork peters out). It is not as difficult as it looks but you should go back if there is too much snow. This is the north side of the mountain so the snow can stay in patches till quite late in the season.

The path goes over some scree and in places you have to pick your way; at one point it climbs up over some rocky steps. There are no splashes anywhere and in places the path is difficult to see, but just keep going round and it becomes better defined as you reach the Col de Chavan, alt. 1,757m (2hrs 30mins).

From the col it is possible to follow the sign up to the Haute Pointe; the path is marked with intermittent blue splashes and is fairly clear except when going up the grassy slope to just below the summit where it seems to be "pick your own way" - the path along the top is well trodden and the view on all sides is spectacular - starting from the west in a semi-circle: the Pointe des Brasses, the Pointe de Miribel, the Hirmentaz ridge and Les Voirons in the Vallée Verte, the Grand Rocher de Nifflon and Pointe de la Gay near the village of Bellevaux with the La Dent d'Oche in the background; the Pointe de Chalune with the Roc d'Enfer behind, the Pointe de Folly and the Pointe d'Uble near Praz de Lyz, the cross of the Pointe de Marcelly ridge dominating Taninges with the nearby Pointe Fleurie and finally the lone Môle peak - on the skyline; south are the higher alpine ranges, including Mt. Blanc.

From the Col de Chavan follow the blue marking down the grassy hillside to a new looking chalet at the start of a jeep track where you turn left down towards the road you can see below going towards the Col de Ramaz. Just beyond the next chalet (called Le Coin on the map but marked L'Escape on the chalet) watch for a narrow path going down to the right which is a short cut down across the meadows, crossing a stream and then keeping the woods to the right and the stream to the left. However, if it has been raining, this way is very boggy and it is easier to stick to the jeep track. When you reach the tarmac road (3hrs 10mins via the jeep track) turn right and walk down to the parking spot (3hrs 30mins).

Remarks: Once you get round the other side of the mountain away from Sommant where there are a number of ski-lifts, you come into unspoilt and peaceful mountain scenery. Do this walk in springtime as the flowers are particularly abundant here, especially the big trumpet gentians, various orchids and also king cups and marsh marigolds in the valley. However, make sure that the snow has left the north side as too much makes walking round impossible. It is worth the extra effort to go to the Haute Pointe summit if you want a panoramic view of the entire region - don't forget to look out for marmots!

43: POINTE DES BRASSES - 1,503 metres
(Faucigny/Haut Giffre region)

Difficulty:	Medium - uphill for quite a long way but nothing difficult.
Time:	5hrs.
Height gain:	823 metres.
Maps:	Editions Didier & Richard IGN No.3 Massifs du Chablais Faucigny & Genevois 1:50,000. Cartes IGN 3429 ET Top 25 Bonneville/Cluses 1:25,000.
Depart from:	Entreverges - 680 metres.
Signposting:	Good in parts - yellow splashes then blue splashes.

How to get there (from Geneva)

Take the motorway direction Chamonix and exit at No.15, Boëge/St. Jeoire. Then turn left briefly on the D.903 and watch for the D.9 right signposted Fillinges, Samoëns and Vallée Verte. Follow this road to the Pont de Fillinges and then turn right on the D.907 direction Taninges/Samoëns. (ALTERNATIVELY go through Annemasse and take the D.907, direction Taninges/Samoëns.) Continue straight through the traffic lights at Le Brochet (Viuz-en-Sallaz to the left), and about 2.5km later look for a small sign off to the left saying Entreverges (just before the D.26 to St. Jeoire). Go up this narrow road and take the first turning to the left signposted Les Brons. The road becomes stony and at the first fork go left (there is a tarmac road right to new flats and straight goes on to a disused quarry). There are parking places along here, or if you continue (the road becomes stonier however), you will reach a larger parking area where there is a big board with information about the walk.

Directions

It takes about 5mins from the fork to the notice board which is headed Pointe des Brasses No.6 (see below). You start walking up a wide wooded gorge with the Entreverges stream initially on your right and then crossing under the path to the left after about 10mins. The jeep track goes up medium steep through beech and coniferous woodland. When you come to an intersection (25mins) go straight on, there is a yellow splash further up on a tree (do not go down to the left). Ignore other paths branching off (one is where you come out on your return) and keep going up right leaving the river down on your left; there are no signs.

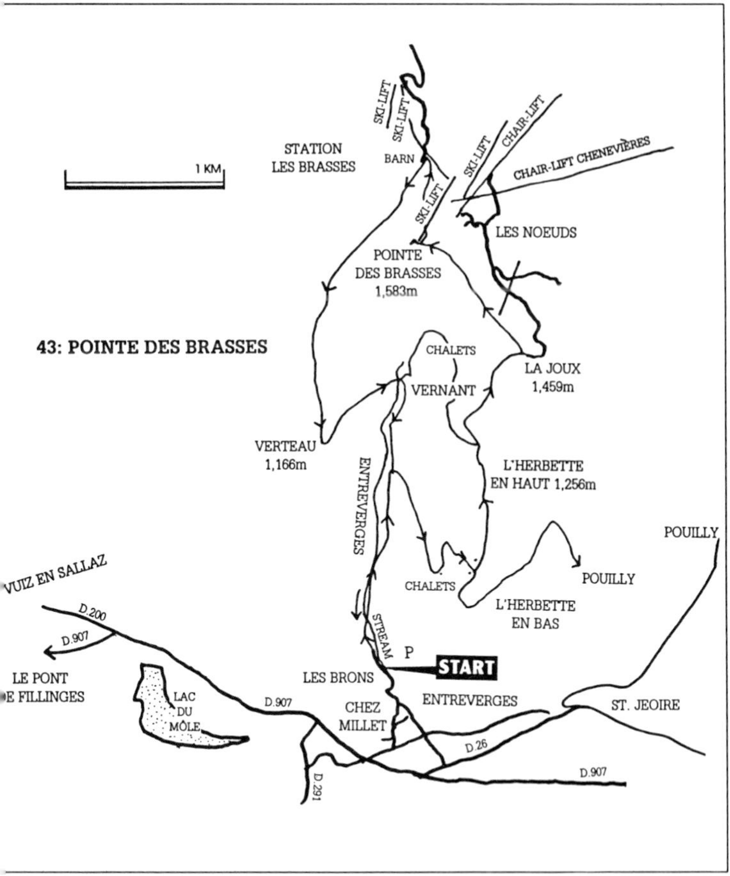

You initially climb up fairly steeply and then the path levels out somewhat as it starts curling round the mountain; through the trees (if there are no leaves) there are tantalising glimpses of the Arve valley below and the village of Viuz-en-Sallaz. At a fork, go left following a yellow splash; the right path goes down to a large chalet which you can see. Here there is a sign saying Réserve de Lièvres (hare reserve) - *I have never seen such a notice before and we looked for hares madly but not a sign of life!* Shortly afterwards you come out of the woods proper and into an attractive glade where there is another large chalet. The path is still defined and goes round the building and then winds up through meadowland with occasional trees to a newish chalet which you pass behind; (when this chalet is in sight do not take the path down to the left). Soon after another path merges from the right (this is the way up from Pouilly). Here you come to your first blue signpost, to L'Herbette, and from now on you follow blue splashes as well as the odd yellow one. Turn left towards L'Herbette which takes you up onto the wide shoulder of the mountain (1hr 15mins).

Go past the few chalets of L'Herbette en Bas on your right (no signs) and then continue upwards towards the chalets of L'Herbette en Haut which are visible ahead. From this wide shoulder you get your first views of the magnificent peaks on your right; from left to right the Haute Pointe, Pointe de Chalune, Roc d'Enfer and the Pic de Marcelly above Taninges, with the Mont Blanc range on the horizon. Behind is the distinctive peak of the Môle. You come to another sign saying L'Herbette, wedged in a tree on your right. Continue following the ridge past L'Herbette en Haut, alt. 1,256m, which consists of three houses and two outside toilets, one shabby looking and the other distinctly upmarket with a little path to it. Near the large farmhouse down on your right there is a smart bath on a platform surrounded by tiles! On the top of the main door of the large farm it says Domaine des Balisiers, Peney, Genève - Caves des Palais de Justice SA. *The mind boggles; is this where the law courts hide their reserves of wine so that they can come up to this relatively hidden spot and drink it? Does the Lord Chief Justice sit in the bath with his wig on and have a nip or two? One really does discover some intriguing places on these mountain walks!* Note that since the author first did this walk an impenetrable fence has been put round these chalets.

After the farm look up on the right and you will see a small grotto in the rocks with a cross (rather spoilt by a sheet of galvanised iron over it). It is worth going to have a look inside as there is a charming natural stone statue of the Virgin Mary with a lovely maternal expression on her face; normally the statues in these alpine grottoes are painted, cheap looking and expressionless.

Following the blue splashes, keep to the path which curls up behind the hill in front. You pass a sign which says Pointe des Brasses and then negotiate a stile before coming to more signs, ahead to La Joux and left to Pointe des Brasses (2hrs). Go straight to La Joux. You can see the top of the chair-lift at Les Brasses up on your left. The path follows the contour of the mountain through occasional coniferous trees; keep a look out for the cross of La Joux, alt. 1,425m up on your right and either cut up across to it (no defined path to start with) or stick to the path which goes to the first chalet of La Joux itself. Then turn up right to the cross (2hrs 25mins) from where you get another magnificent view of the surrounding mountain peaks. Below are the half a dozen chalets of La Joux with a jeep track going up to them and a small pond.

Pointe des Brasses. View up the Giffre valley with Mont Blanc behind

Make your way along the defined path on the grassy ridge, which goes behind a ski-tow. You can see the path you will take back round the mountain and also the arrival point of the chair-lift from Les Chenevières, as well as other chair-lifts and ski-tows coming up from all directions.

You come to a large new chalet (2hrs 40mins) which you go in front of to reach a jeep track path, where you can see a blue sign left to the summit of Les Brasses. This is a 15mins steep walk to the summit of Les Brasses, alt. 1,583m which is rather ugly, being the end of a ski-tow and the site of a walkie-talkie transmitting station. However, the view is extensive as you can not only see all the surrounding peaks but also into the Vallée Verte down on one side and on the other Lac Léman (Lake Geneva) with the Salève ridge and the Jura on the skyline (3hrs).

Follow the ski-tow down and bear left where there is a defined jeep track (you can see the chair-lift below). There are blue flashes here and you are obviously going down on a ski slope. At the bottom of the wide grassy track there is a big barn and signposts at a T-junction. Bear left towards Verteau (3hrs 15mins) past the barn on a grassy jeep track, beside an old stone wall where there are a row of stately fir trees. After lovely meadowland the path drops down through intermittent woodland and then levels out somewhat as it starts to curl round the mountain. You will come to another T-junction where you follow the sign left to Verteau/Vernant (do not go down right where there is a blue cross on a stone).

Keep on past a small new chalet on your right. Shortly after there is another big chalet and a little shrine. Continue straight past the shrine ignoring any tracks branching off, on an undulating path which continues round the mountain, through woodland. You arrive at two large chalets, a rusty old plough and another shrine below (3hrs 55mins). Keep up left here, (further on there is a sign saying Verteau, alt. 1,166m and Venant ahead. The path goes gently at first and then down again, still curling round the mountain. There is a little spring along this jeep track with a padlock on it and one wonders why on earth someone wants to lock up a water supply! You come to Vernant, alt. 1,225m, which is a pretty group of chalets, and an intersection (4hrs 10mins) where there are signposts. Go down right (straight on would take you back to L'Herbette/La Joux). You now follow the Entreverges stream again, below on the right, as you go down medium steep through woodland on a defined jeep track. 20mins from Vernant you get back to the branch where you went up right to L'Herbette. From here you retrace the path to the car (5hrs).

Remarks: A really lovely walk with magnificent views - it is just a pity that the landscape is marred by so many ski-lifts. This is Walk No. 6 from a map sold by the local tourist bureau, Promenades et Randonnées Pedestres, Massif des Brasses, *with short explanations in French only.*

44: LE MÔLE - Alt. 1,863 metres
(Faucigny/Haut Giffre region)

Difficulty:	Medium though very steep at the end and somewhat airy coming down off the top. The traditional way is easier.
Time:	3hrs 45mins.
Height gain:	703 metres.
Maps:	Editions Didier & Richard IGN No.3 Massifs du Chablais Faucigny & Genevois 1:50,000. Cartes IGN 3429 ET Top 25 Bonneville/Cluses 1:25,000.
Depart from:	Chez Béroud - 1,160 metres.
Signposting:	Erratic - more needed in strategic places.

How to get there (from Geneva)

Take the motorway direction Chamonix and exit No.15, Boëge/St. Jeoire. Then turn left briefly on the D.903 and watch for the D.9 right signposted

Fillinges, Samoëns and Vallée Verte. Follow this road to the Pont de Fillinges and then turn right on the D.907 direction Taninges/Samoëns. (ALTERNATIVELY go through Annemasse and take the D.907 direction Taninges/Samoëns.) Continue on the D.907 until you reach the cross-roads and lights in Les Brochets (Viuz-en-Sallaz to the left). Turn right on the D.12 following signs to Perillonnex/Bonneville. At the first roundabout turn left and follow all signs to St. Jean-de-Tholome, briefly on the D.9 and then right on the D.200. At the church in St. Jean turn up left (there is a signpost saying Le Môle). Continue upwards for 5.5km through the village of Bovère to Chez Béroud at the end of the tarmac road. There is a small restaurant, Le Relais de Môle, on the left-hand side.

Directions

At the start of a defined wide jeep track to the right (no cars allowed sign) there is a yellow signpost to Le Môle. The going is medium steep uphill through shrub and woodland. There is a short cut up to the left which meets the jeep track. Follow all signs saying Le Môle/Petit Môle (there are steep short cuts which are evident). BE CAREFUL; after about 15mins do not go straight but steeply up to the left on an initially wide forest track (there is no sign here).

ALTERNATIVE WAY: The path straight on is the main route to the summit and the easiest way up. It goes past the chalet/buvette of the Petit Môle.

Continue on the forest path which goes in and out of woodland as it

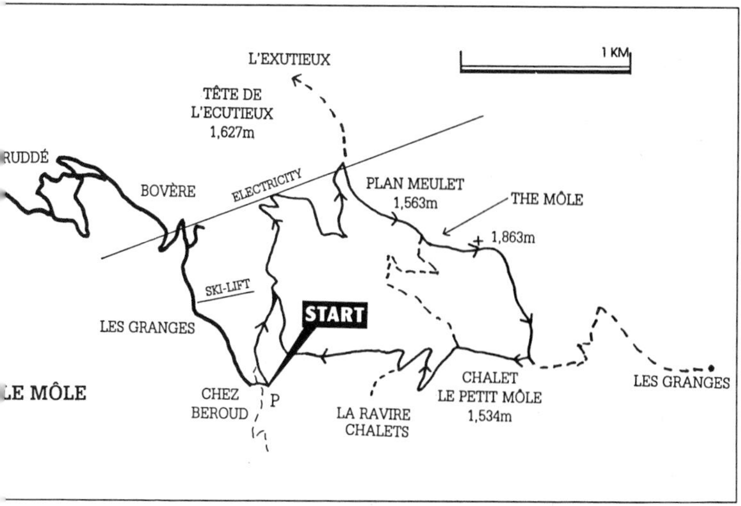

snakes up round the mountain; ignore tracks branching off to the right. Watch out for a sign up on a tree to the right indicating Ecutieux (35mins) which is where you are going! The path seems to go back slightly downwards the way you have walked up, only higher. At the next T-junction bear up to the right (45mins); there is no sign. Keep a look out for overhead electricity wires ahead as you will go under these later. The path is still wide and winds fairly steeply through scattered woodland and firs. 10mins later, at another T-junction (55mins), keep on the main path bearing left. After going through a cattle fence you come out on to alpine pasture underneath the pylon wires at Plan Meulet, alt. 1,563m (1hr 5mins). To the left is the hump of the Tête de l'Ecutieux at 1,627m (there is a track leading to the top). Straight on is a path down to the hamlet of l'Ecutieux and a glorious view into the Giffre valley and the town of St. Jeoire.

You can see the Môle summit up on your right. Go to the right of the pylon and keep to the side of the ridge with the firs on your left; there is a sort of grassy path but very undefined which goes over a small hump and alongside a fence before going through it by a sign (1hr 15mins). You then start to climb up another steep hump. Keep the fence on your left and the track becomes defined as it winds up very steeply through scrubs and raspberry bushes; keep climbing and higher up ignore small paths off to the right. It takes about half an hour to reach a parapenting jump off spot (two small flag sticks) and it is quite a tough climb (1hr 45mins). The path curls round the edge and then you can see it clearly ahead, going up steeply over open pasture to the summit of the Môle which is another steep path over open pasture. Look right for a splendid view over Bonneville in the Arve valley and to the left the Giffre and town of St. Jeoire. You have done the worst part of the climb as the path levels out along the ridge and you come to the first cross (this is new and was not there when I did the walk for the first time). Continue for a few minutes and you come to another cross which marks the top. The drop on the other side is very abrupt so be careful (2hrs).

It is worth the rather tough haul up for the magnificent open views on all sides of the surrounding Haute Savoie countryside which includes Lac Léman (Lake Geneva) with the Jura behind and the entire Mont Blanc range.*This is a favourite picnic stop so there may be lots of people at the weekend.*

If you have a good head for heights continue along the ridge (otherwise go back by the one of the various paths you can see snaking down the bare mountainside to the chalets below). This ridge path is rather airy and rocky, so watch your feet; it descends steeply for about 20mins to a large concrete block dated 1909, where there are cows grazing in summer (2hrs 20mins). Walk along the continuation of the ridge for approximately 10mins to a parapenting flag and take a few minutes to appreciate the strategic site of this magnificent mountain which stands alone at the confluence of the Giffre and Arve valleys. You can see the Giffre river flowing into the mightier Arve waters and in front is the town of Cluses with Mont Chevron (Walk No. 32) behind. Return along the ridge and with your back to the concrete block go straight on a narrow path, back round the side of the mountain through scattered fir trees and shrubs. Follow the easy undulating path till you come out at the Petit Môle chalets where there is an incredible assortment of animals such as goats, cows, geese and turkeys. There is also a little buvette (café) where you can buy drinks in summer (2hrs 45mins).

Skirt the chalet onto a wide jeep track at the side which goes across the open mountain to two other little chalets and then follow the wide defined path downwards in and out of woodlands with lovely views into the valley below (this is the classic way up and down). You join the path you came up (3hrs 20mins) which you should follow back to the starting point (3hrs 45mins).

Remarks: From Geneva the lone peak of the Môle stands out clearly in front of the Alps - in fact some tourists mistake it for Mt. Blanc itself! Dominating the confluence of the Giffre and Arve valleys with the splendid panorama of the Haute Savoie Alps all round, this walk is a classic and if any walk in the region should be done this is the one! As it is not far from Geneva it is a very popular outing, so avoid sunny weekends in summer if you want to escape the "madding crowd". On a golden week day in September I was alone and "master of the world" at the top - this is how it should be walked!

45: BOUCLE DES CONFINS (La Clusaz) - Alt. 1,395 metres
(Aravis/Bornes region)

Difficulty:	Easy - ideal with visitors.
Time:	3hrs 30mins plus time visiting lake.
Height gain:	About 300m - undulating.
Maps:	Editions Didier & Richard IGN No.2 Massifs des Bornes-Bauges 1:50,000. Cartes IGN 3430 ET Top 25 La Clusaz/Grand-Bornand 1:25,000.
Depart from:	La Clusaz - 1,095 metres.
Signposting:	Good - lots of signposts and also yellow and blue markings.

How to get there (from Geneva)

Take the motorway direction Chamonix and exit at No.16, Bonneville/La Clusaz. Follow the N.203 signposted St. Pierre-en-Faucigny/La Clusaz and shortly after turn left on the D6 direction St. Pierre-en-Faucigny. At the roundabout in the village continue on the D.6A over the railway line and then turn right on the D.12 signposted La Clusaz. This road takes you up the Borne river valley, a narrow, twisting road through the villages of Petit-Bornand and Entremont. Continue on the D.12 to St. Jean-de-Sixt and then take the D.909 to La Clusaz. At the start of the village go straight (do not bear down right, signposted Centre) and you come to a roundabout. Park near here or in the underground parking.

Directions

Walk to the roundabout and then up the road up signposted Piscine (swimming pool). Turn left at the antique shop (an old chalet) and continue till you see a wooden signpost on the right to La Perrière/Tour de Village/ Circuit des Houches/Col des Mouilles. Take the grassy path up between new chalets, marked with yellow flashes, which is medium steep and goes behind apartment blocks. You come to an impressive jumble of huge grey rocks left behind by a massive landslide in the 19th century. Stop here and enjoy a

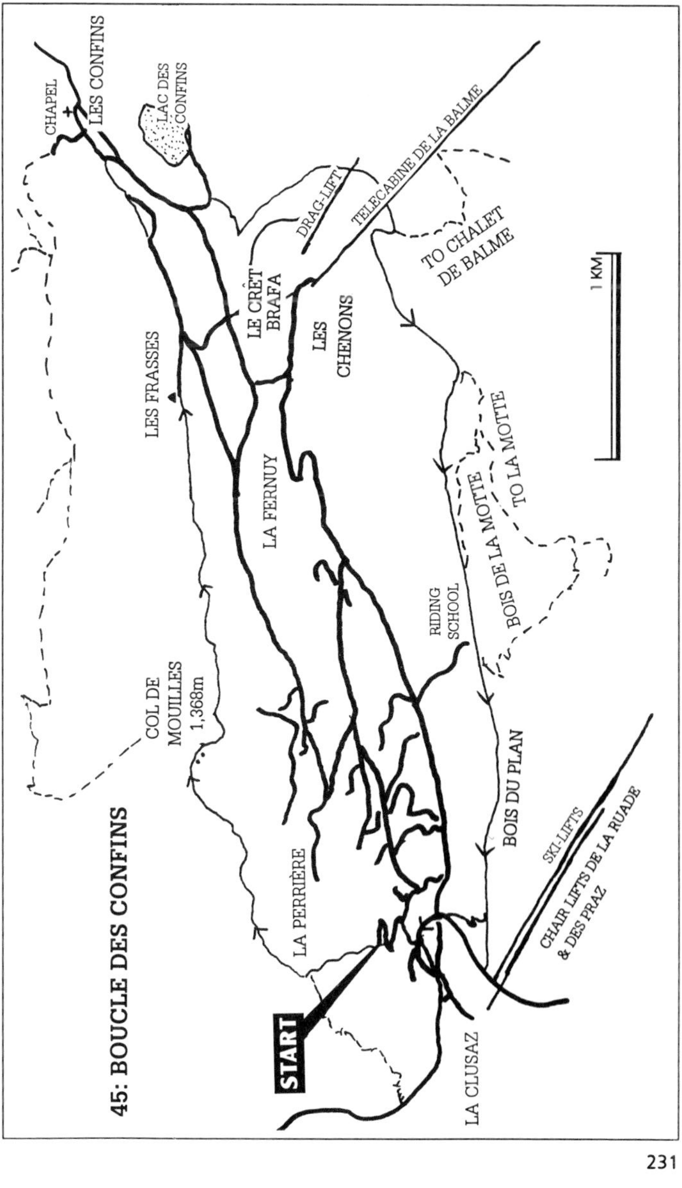
45: BOUCLE DES CONFINS
START
LA CLUSAZ
LA PERRIÈRE
COL DE MOUILLES 1,368m
LES FRASSES
LA FERNUY
LE CRÊT BRAFA
LES CHENONS
CHAPEL
LES CONFINS
LAC DES CONFINS
DRAG-LIFT
TELECABINE DE LA BALME
TO CHALET DE BALME
1 KM
TO LA MOTTE
BOIS DE LA MOTTE
RIDING SCHOOL
BOIS DU PLAN
SKI-LIFTS
CHAIR LIFTS DE LA RUADE & DES PRAZ

panoramic view over the valley and village of La Clusaz. The path becomes rocky; at a wooden cross follow a yellow splash and sign to Circuit des Houches/Toutes Directions. Take a right turn at a T-junction called La Perrière at the top of the rock-fall (10mins) - left is to Les Houches. Keep going upwards and ignore a turning shortly after to the right signposted Clusaz/Nant/Le Bossonnet. If you are walking in summertime the plants along this path are usually labelled.

Climb some wooden steps and go left at another T-junction with no signpost (the right turning peters out into nothing) through scrubs and trees before coming to yet another signpost. Turn left to Les Confins following the yellow splashes and arrows on a path climbing gently through dense vegetation and deciduous woodland. You arrive at Sur La Perrière, alt. 1,395m, and another host of signposts (20mins). Turn right to Col des Mouilles (amongst other destinations). You have stopped climbing and are now on a wide undulating path through woods and open spaces. Continue straight ignoring VTT mountain bike signs and a path left to Boucle du Danay. You come out into lovely open meadowland at the Col des Mouilles, alt. 1,368m, where there is an old barn (1hr 10mins). On your right there are lovely views of the outskirts of La Clusaz with ski-lifts on the horizon beyond. At another bevy of signs continue straight to Les Confins. You can now see the path going back to La Clusaz along the other side of the valley below the splendid peaks of the various summits of the Aravis mountain chain. The path becomes a jeep track along the open side of the hill with lovely old chalets dotted around.

Just past an old chalet on the left cross over a narrow stream to some more signposts. Take the path up to the left indicated Les Confins following the yellow flashes. Pass two old chalets, one displaying the name Plattuz en Haut. From here you start to descend gradually following yellow splashes towards the head of the valley. You arrive at a lovely old Savoyard farm with chickens, a cat, geraniums hanging from the windows and the wood stacked up at the side ready for the winter - of course there is a big TV aerial and an electricity pole to spoil the illusion but never mind! Just past the farm there are other chalets and a sign announcing you are at Les Frasses, alt. 1,372m. Keep straight and you come immediately to a tarmac road and then later on to a wider road.

Turn left (signposted Confins) and further on there is a sign to the right indicating Boucle des Confins/La Clusaz par La Motte which is where you want to go (2hrs). However, it is worth a detour along the road for about 5mins to the hamlet of La Claiseraz and the pretty little lake of Les Confins - in springtime invaded by frogs and tadpoles. *There are many little cafés and restaurants and it is a good spot for lunch. Walk a few minutes further up the road to the little chapel dedicated to the 40 martyrs, St. John the Baptist and St. John the Evangelist. It was constructed a year after the big freeze in 1833 which, during the night of 2/3 September, destroyed the wheat and potato harvest causing local hardship. The people of the valley made a petition to God, promising that if he gave them a good harvest the following year they would build a special chapel in thanksgiving - their wish was granted! Near the door there is a plaque in memory of a young couple, members of the French Resistance in the World War II, who were killed by Italian Fascists in August 1943.*

Go back to the signpost to Boucle des Confins/La Clusaz par la Motte and take the track which curls round the head of the valley. On the right you look down into the valley where there are roads, car parks and some ski-lifts. You go over the Crête de Brafa at 1,338m (though it is not marked) and come to a ski-lift. There are a number of signs which makes it rather confusing, but follow all indications to La Clusaz par La Motte. The wide unpaved path goes under the Télécabine de la Balme and shortly after there is a turning to the left which goes to the Chalet de Balme and later on another left turning which says GR Tour d'Aravis, but ignore these and keep straight following yellow flashes.

You arrive at the Combe du Fernuy (3hrs) which is a wide jeep track going through deciduous and coniferous woods on the edge of the Bois de la Motte. Keep to the track, crossing several rivulets. This takes you to Le Recorbaz which is a big riding centre and shortly after you can see the outskirts of La Clusaz down on the right. The jeep track narrows to a path and continues on over open meadows past the top of a drag lift; the ski beginner slopes of La Clusaz are down to the right and you are quite high above the village. Follow the path round and down to a T-junction where you turn right to Bossonnet (do not go to Clusaz centre). When you meet the road below turn right past a grotto with a statue of Our Lady, there are lots of signs and you could equally well do this walk the other way round (3hrs 30mins). Walk back to where you parked the car.

Remarks: A truly delightful walk as the path goes round a beautiful valley with glorious mountain scenery. There is no climbing or scrambling over rocks and the way is well signposted - a real must and within the capabilities of even the most hesitant walker. Not long after the snow melts the slopes are bright with a myriad of alpine flowers which continue until late summer.

46: LE TROU DE LA MOUCHE (the fly hole!) -
Alt. 2,450 metres (Aravis/Bornes region)

Difficulty: A tough walk and not for anyone suffering from vertigo.
Time: 5hrs 30mins.
Height gain: 981 metres.
Maps: Editions Didier Richard Cartes IGN No.8 Massifs du Mont Blanc/Beaufortain 1:50,000.
Cartes IGN 3430 ET Top 25 La Clusaz/Grand-Bornand 1:25,000.
Depart from: L'Arpette, Les Confins (La Clusaz) - Alt. 1,419m.
Signposting: Signs at the beginning and end - some red arrows.

How to get there (from Geneva)
Take the Chamonix motorway and exit at No.16, Bonneville/La Clusaz. Then follow the N.203 signposted St. Pierre-en-Faucigny/La Clusaz and shortly after turn left on the D.6A direction St. Pierre-en-Faucigny. At the roundabout in the village continue on the D.6 over the railway line and then turn right on the D.12 signposted La Clusaz. This road takes you up the Borne river valley, a narrow twisting road, through the villages of Petit-Bornand and Entremont. At St. Jean-de-Sixt take the D.909 to La Clusaz. In La Clusaz follow a sign Lac des Confins onto a narrow road. After about 10mins (4.5km) you pass through Les Confins where there is a little lake and continue to the end of the road where there is a large car park called L'Arpette.

Directions
Take the narrow tarmac road out of the car park which becomes a jeep track after a large farm on a bend to the right (La Lanchette) selling the delicious Reblochon cheese. After about 5mins there is a sign on the right to Combe de Grand Crêt. This is the real start of the walk, on a defined path over open grassy hillside, climbing steadily and often steeply, becoming rocky in places. Over on the right are dramatic slabs of fissured rock which look like a series of waterfalls. Follow the infrequent red arrows on the rocks marking the path.

When you arrive at a large rock (1hr) you have to be careful. Take the path to the right which is marked Chemin des Paturages - this is a gentler path winding round the mountain. (Straight up will also take you to the Trou but you must turn right at some ruins which are not easy to see and you could make the same mistake as we did the first time and find yourself on a steep slope of scree!) To the left is the Pare de Joux mountain, a towering rock

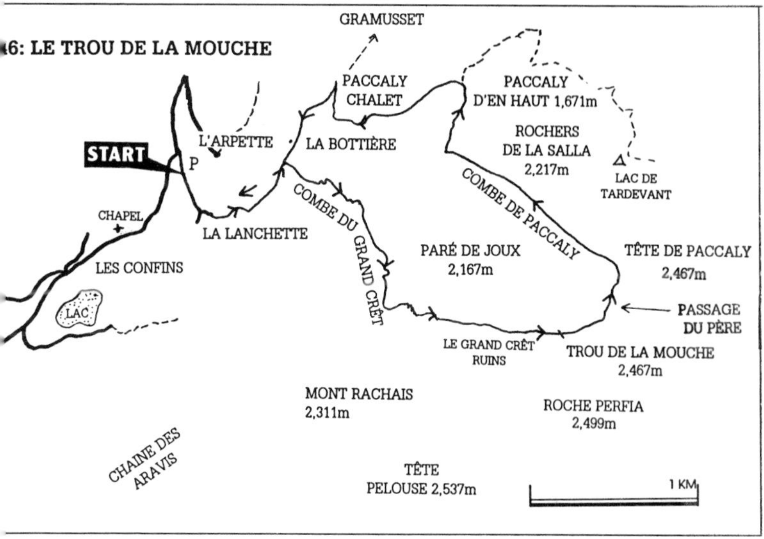

2,167m high. At the foot of the rock face there is a large cave, in front of which there is a sort of open stone coffin (sarcophagus) which looks as if it should house an Egyptian mummy, but I am sure has been converted as a watering trough for cows instead! (It is worth taking about 5mins to walk over and see this.)

The path makes a wide detour towards the Mont Rachais mountain, alt. 2,311m, on the other side of the combe. It then winds back over steep pasture and zigzags upwards till it goes by some ruins (1hr 20mins). Note: it is easy to walk by these ruins; all that remains is the stone outline at grass level which is only clearly visible from above. However, it does not really matter as you just continue up the path all the way.

You will eventually see the Trou de la Mouche ahead which tunnels through the gigantic Roche Perfia. It looks as if there are two holes from below but in fact there is only one. The last part up to the hole is across a sort of wide stony saddle where there is some grass. CAREFUL HERE - try and keep to the path which is not always easy to follow and is quite steep. It is also muddy and slippery in wet weather. Down on the right is an imposing valley of scree which should be avoided. Just before you get to the top keep to the left where it is less steep.

On our way up we met two dear old men who later informed us proudly that they were in their seventies and had been walking all their lives - one of them had climbed Mt. Blanc in 1936. They knew every peak on the horizon and their estimate of how long it would take to the Trou and their advice to keep to the left at the top were spot on! Although starting after us they nipped down the steep centre of the combe on the way back and were well ahead. One cannot but admire these incredible "men of the mountains".

The long steep haul to the top is worth it when you pass through the dramatic arched hole of solid rock (3hrs). The view is magnificent; straight ahead is the continuation of the Aravis range terminating in the regal peak of the Pointe Percée at 2,750m. To the right is the nearby snow covered Mont Blanc range in all its glory and further right in the background are the Grande Casse and other mountains of the Vanoise; below is the Val d'Arly with the road going through Mégève to join the Arve valley - this is one of the most extensive and breathtaking views in the whole region!

The path down from the Trou is marked on the map with little blue dots and not without reason as it is indeed steep and very exposed. This is not a path for anyone suffering from vertigo and should not be done in wet weather. Pick your way down carefully (on the map it is called the Passage du Père). Sheep tend to congregate here in the summer. If they are blocking the path, gently insist on your right of way rather than go round them as they are certainly more sure-footed than you.

It takes about 20mins to get down this steep slope following the infrequent red markings. There is an incredible wall of rock to the right which culminates in the Tête de Paccaly, alt. 2,467m. The rock face is fissured with narrow black lines and looks completely unscalable. As you make your way gingerly down this slope, it echoes back your voices along with the sinister cry of the alpine choughs that circle around the rocky summit. It is a relief to arrive at a ridge, alt. 2,420m (3hrs 20mins). If you are lucky you may also spot a large bird of prey with white markings on its wings - this is the gypaète (bearded vulture - see Flora and Fauna) reintroduced into the area a few years ago.

The path goes down on the left but for a really good airy view keep to the top of the ridge. Look back and you will get an impressive view of the Trou which already seems a long way above you. After the ridge follow the path ahead down the Combe de Paccaly, crossing stones, rocks and shale; be particularly careful on the shale as these small stones move easily. The path becomes steep and alternates between rock, scree and grass so you have to pick your way down and concentrate!

After about 1hr it gets easier. There are red splashes from time to time on the rocks. The view of the valley is impressive with La Clusaz at the end and straight ahead mountain peaks, including the Pic de Jallouvre and the Aiguille Verte which dominates the Lac de Lessy.

The path is clearly defined with red markings on the rocks, going steadily down the combe (narrow valley) dominated by the precipitous slopes of the Rochers de la Salla. alt. 2,217m, on the right and the Paré de Joux, alt. 2,167m to the left. After about 30mins you come to the first stunted fir trees and some bushy vegetation and, not long after, a small wooden hut with a number of signposts, alt. 1,674m. Straight on is the Combe and Lac de Tardevant. Follow the signpost sharp left marked La Clusaz. One is rather puzzled at first about the little hut until you realise it used to be the outhouse of the Paccaly-d'en-Haut chalet which is round the corner and marked on the map! The path is still well defined and less steep, the vegetation getting more varied with stunted birch amongst the firs and pines.

You arrive at the Chalet de Paccaly (5hrs) which is a mountain café/restaurant. Take the jeep track left in front of the chalet (the right fork is signposted Gramusset which is the refuge at the foot of the Pointe Percée). This track meets the narrow road which you walk along for 15mins, past La Bottière chalet on the right, till you reach the car park (5hrs 30mins).

Remarks: This is a really dramatic walk - one that gets the adrenaline flowing and you feel scared (at least I did). The views of Mt. Blanc and surrounding peaks are unforgettable. WARNING: DO NOT DO THIS WALK UNLESS THE WEATHER IS GOOD, YOU ARE FIT AND ABOVE ALL DO NOT SUFFER FROM VERTIGO. However, a friend over from England strolled up it in his sneakers and declared it was nothing!

This walk can also be done the other way round (often shown in guidebooks). The advantage is that you can see the Trou from the very bottom and you avoid going the wrong way as we did the first time. However, you don't get the dramatic view of Mt. Blanc as you go through the Trou and you go up the very steep slope instead of down it - a question of choice!

The hidden mine: It is said that there is gold to be found in the Aravis, although the gold seekers who came in 1914 left again shortly after having looked in vain. The legend of the Saint-Jean-de-la Mine is interesting. In the evenings a stranger would often pass the chalet of Paccaly-d'en-Haut from the direction of the Combe de Tardevant. Heavily laden it seemed he had struck gold but no one knew where his mine was to be found as he put his shoes on back to front to confuse pursuers. Years later, having made his fortune, he returned to La Clusaz from Paris and confided the whereabouts of the mine to two of his friends. Armed with a plan they set off for the Combe de Tardevant. Unfortunately on the way they drank too much "eau de vie" and lost the directions - the site was never discovered!

47: LE CIRCUIT DES ANNES - Alt. 2,162 metres
(Aravis/Bornes region)

Difficulty:	Medium - quite a climb but nothing difficult.
Time:	5hrs.
Height gain:	912 metres.
Maps:	Editions Didier & Richard IGN No.8 Massifs du Mont Blanc/Beaufortain 1:50,000. Cartes IGN 3430 ET Top 25 La Clusaz/Grand-Bornand 1:25,000.
Depart from:	Les Troncs (Grand-Bornand) - 1,250 metres.
Signposting:	Excellent.

How to get there (from Geneva)
Take the motorway direction Chamonix and exit at No.16, Bonneville. From the exit take the N.203 signposted St. Pierre-en-Faucigny/La Clusaz and shortly after turn left on the D.6A direction St. Pierre-en-Faucigny. At the roundabout in the village continue on the D.6 over the railway line and then turn right on the D.12 signposted La Clusaz. This takes you up the Borne river valley, a narrow twisting road, through the villages of Petit-Bornand and Entremont. At the end of the valley bear left on the D.224 which leads onto the D.4 where you turn left again towards Grand-Bornand. In the village of Grand-Bornand follow a sign down to the right to the Vallée de Bouchet/Les Plans. Bear right at the little chapel in the hamlet of Les Plans, go past Le Centre Nordique on the left and continue through the hamlet of Les Troncs to the end of the road where there is a large car park (the last 100 yards is a rough jeep track).

Directions
Go to the end of the car park and take the path up through the woods where there is a sign to Les Troncs/Col de Borne Ronde/La Pointe Percée/La Balme/Refuge de Gramusset/Col des Annes. Shortly after go straight on at a second sign to the Refuge de Gramusset (left to La Balme). The path is well defined and rocky, winding up quite steeply through open beech and tall firs at the side of a gully with a stream running through it. After 5mins bear left (straight on is a dead end) and then a few minutes later go left again where the sign indicates Toutes Directions; there are also red splashes on rocks. Follow the next signposts (10mins) to the Refuge de Gramusset/Pointe Percée. Cross a stream on a rather primitive wooden bridge and then turn right at a T-junction further on towards the Refuge de Gramusset sign. At the top of the

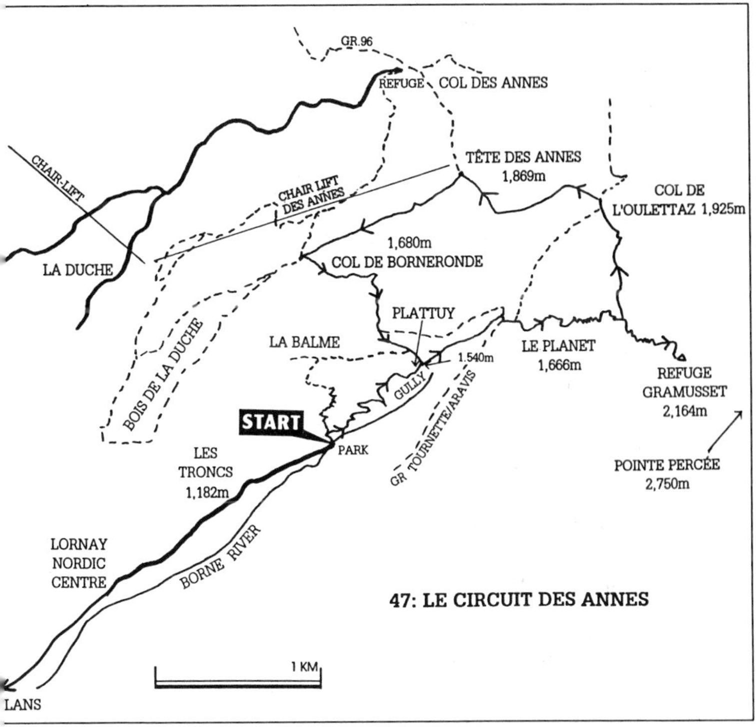

gully in an open area (45mins) go straight on ignoring signs left to Borne Ronde/Bois de la Duche (this is where you will come back). Continue over a low rocky rise and past the chalet of Le Plattuy, alt. 1,540m, down on your right (45mins) and follow all directions to Le Gramusset.

The path goes up through an attractive open valley to the big old farm of Le Planet, built 1813, alt. 1,666m (1hr), which is decorated with colourful geraniums in summer. Bear right behind the chalet (more signs) and then steeply up through a small chimney where a bit of scrambling is involved. At the top of the chimney bear left at another signpost to Le Gramusset. This is the start of a long, tough haul up but it is compensated by a lovely view back down the valley to the hamlet of Les Troncs and in front are the towering slopes of the Pointe Percée. Look out for a blue arrow on the right pointing to a primitive little shrine hewn out of the rock with a bright blue grill in front; you can also see a cable which is used to haul up supplies to the refuge. There are red/yellow splashes all the way up. You start to climb in earnest after the shrine on a well defined path but take time to look back at the impressive Tournette mountain which dominates Lake Annecy.

You come to a junction with signs indicating straight on to Col des Annes and to the right Refuge Gramusset which you can now see above you (2hrs). There is still a steep 25mins climb so the faint-hearted can go straight to the Col des Annes if they wish. The Refuge de Gramusset (2 hrs 25mins), alt. 2,162m, belongs to the French Alpine Club (details below). Although the surroundings of the hut are bleak and rocky this is a popular refuge as it is the start for all climbs to the Pointe Percée. Although it is possible to walk to the summit it is a steep and difficult climb, and much nicer to sit on the terrace and watch the people toiling up - you can see the successful climbers silhouetted on the summit!

Refuge de Gramusset, 74450 le Grand-Bornand, tel. 50.0240.90.

Open May to end October (depending on climatic conditions). Refreshments and meals available. Accommodation in dormitories for 60 people.

Retrace your steps to the signpost and head for the Col des Annes (2hrs 40mins). The track goes around the mountain at the end of the valley with some splendid views. It is fairly steep and some of the rocks you clamber over may be slippery; follow the red/yellow splashes carefully. At one spot there is a large deep hole in the rocks with snow at the bottom at all times of the year. The path drops down until about 200m before the Col de l'Oulettaz, alt. 1,965m, and then goes steeply up again. Look back from the col (3hrs 15mins) and you will see the path you came up from Le Planet and an impressive view into the Arve valley with the Roc d'Enfer on the skyline. Turn left and follow a path along the ridge (there is a short stretch of chain here but it is not difficult). There is a fork where you can either bear down to the right and follow the path beneath the ridge (less airy!) or stay on top which is more dramatic. From the next fork keep up on the ridge and follow red/ yellow splashes, making for the chair-lift you can see at the Tête des Annes. The path undulates along the ridge up to a pile of rocks, alt. 1,950m, and then goes down fairly steeply for 100m to the ski-lift at the Tête des Annes (3hrs 50mins); there are lots of alpine rose bushes along the path.

ALTERNATIVELY you can take the bottom path which you can see going down to the Col des Annes, alt. 1,722m, a group of large barns where the cattle are housed - there are usually big herds around and the noise of the bells is quite deafening! Here you can buy the famous Reblochon cheese which they make on the premises (see notes about the different Savoy cheeses) and there is a bar/restaurant (Frederic) which is open only in season. There may be lots of people and cars as the col can be reached by road. To get back on the main walk follow the sign to the Tête des Annes.

It was at this spot that we saw two magnificent gypaète barbu (bearded vultures) gliding majestically and slowly towards the Pointe Percée (see Flora and Fauna). From the Tête des Annes follow the signpost straight ahead to the Borne Ronde.

You are now walking along a bushy wide ridge, initially with the chair-lift on your right going all the way down into the valley. The path can be quite slippery and muddy if there has been wet weather. At the Col de Borne Ronde, alt. 1,680m (4hrs 15mins), take the left fork to Le Plattuy/Les Troncs. The path is fairly flat for a while through as it winds back round the mountain. After 10mins go straight down at a junction (the path to the left says Gramusset) on a wide path through coniferous woods. You lose height fairly rapidly until you arrive at the signposts you went by on the way up, just before the chalet of Le Plattuy. Retrace your steps following the signs to Les Troncs (watch for the small path signposted Les Troncs which is easy to miss). You can see the car park far below quite a while before you get there (5hrs).

Remarks: This is a delightful day's hike though you have to be reasonably fit. It is best to avoid busy summer weekends. The Pointe Percée is a very popular mountain, one of the highest in the area and a real challenge for serious walkers. In autumn there are lots of interesting mushrooms in the woods including the traditional big red ones with white spots.

48: BOUCLE DU LAC DE LESSY - Alt. 2,045 metres
(Aravis/Bornes region)

Difficulty:	Medium - a switch back walk, going up and down three times!
Time:	4hrs 35mins.
Height gain:	244m, 729m and 214m.
Maps:	Editions Didier & Richard IGN No.3 Massifs du Chablais Faucigny & Genevois 1:50.000. Cartes IGN 3430 ET Top 25 La Clusaz/Grand-Bornand 1:25,000.
Depart from:	Vieux Chinaillon - 1,308 metres.
Signposting:	Very good as it has been recently redone. Large boards at various locations.

How to get there (from Geneva)

Take the motorway direction Chamonix and exit at No.16, Bonneville/La

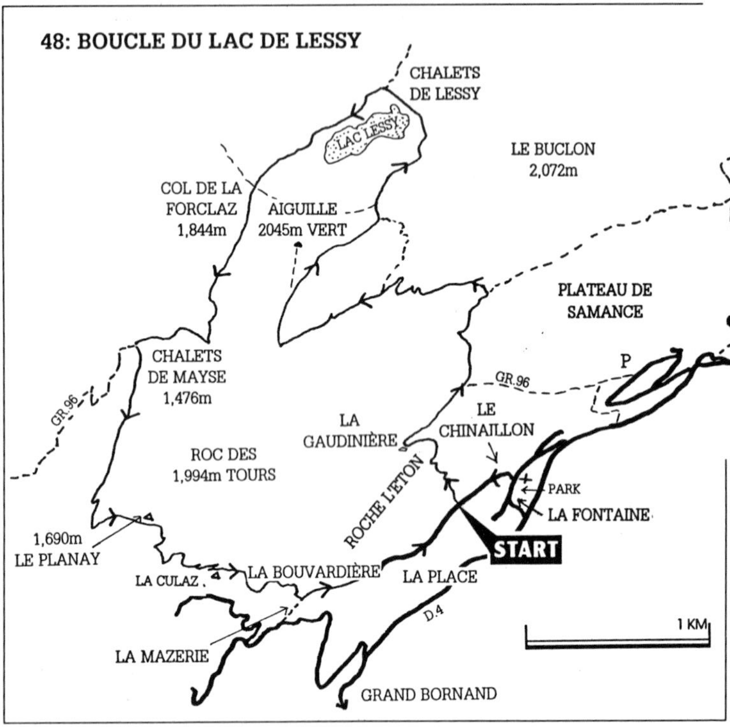

Clusaz. Follow the N.203 signposted St. Pierre-en-Faucigny/La Clusaz and then turn left on the D.6A direction St. Pierre-en-Faucigny. At the roundabout in the village continue on the D.6 over the railway line and then turn right on the D.12 signposted La Clusaz. This road takes you up the Borne river valley, a narrow, twisting road through the villages of Petit-Bornand and Entremont. At the end of the valley bear left on the D.224 which leads onto the D.4 where you turn left again towards Grand-Bornand/Col de la Colombière. Go through Grand-Bornand towards Chinaillon. At the entrance to the village take the road going back left signposted to Lac de Lessy. At the hamlet of Vieux Chinaillon park your car on the right beyond the little church and opposite the café/restaurant La Fontaine.

Directions

Walk back up the road for a few metres and then turn left at the signpost to La Bouvardière/Lac de Lessy. Go up for 300m past some newly constructed

chalets and, just where there is a sign indicating straight on Lac de Lessy, take the narrow path right (no sign) which starts off quite steeply over open hillside and then into scattered woodland. The well-trodden path skirts the rocky wall of the Roche de L'Eton with obvious steeper short cuts if you want to take them. Take a look back over Vieux Chinaillon where many of the old chalets grouped round the church still have roofs of wooden tiles called tavaillons.

You reach the top of this first climb of 244m at a smart sign which says Borne No.10 La Foret/Sentier de Decouverte followed by some quaint old chalets called La Gaudinière, alt. 1,562m. Here you find Borne No.9 Flore Specifiques des Chalets (40mins). *These numbered reference points (bornes) are part of a discovery walk round Chinaillon (see below).* The path continues through the chalets, with a smart sign just after the second chalet to the Lac de Lessy. You are now on a wide track which narrows as you approach Borne No. 8 Chalets de la Gaudinière by a big old chalet (50mins). It then goes down for a while and levels out as it curls round the front of the mountain. There are beautiful views of the other side of the valley with its many ski-lifts going up to the Mont Lachat. Behind is the Chaine des Aravis dominated by the majestic Point Percée. When you come to signpost, Borne No.7 Faunes des Montagnes (55mins) go straight on towards the Plateau de Samance/Lac de Lessy. This is where the GR.96 comes in on the right from Chinaillon. *(Alternative route - you could get to this point by taking the GR from Chinaillon itself.)*

The path undulates through open meadow called the Samance Plateau to a further sign left to the Aiguilles Vertes/Lac de Lessy and straight on to the Chalets de Cuillery/Col de la Colombière. Turn left; this is where you start to climb for the second time on a medium steep, but well-trodden path over alpine pasture which is populated by the Abondance breed of brown and white cows in summertime. As you go higher there are even better views of the Aravis range, especially as the snow-covered peak of Mt. Blanc becomes visible in the background. You can also see Chinaillon in the valley below and the road going up to Col de la Colombière. The path becomes easier as it bears right below the grassy mountain ridge of the Aiguille Verte.

Turn right at the next signposts to the Aiguille Verte/Lac de Lessy (1hr 50mins) - straight ahead goes to Col de la Colombière/Chalets de Cuillery and left to the Roc des Tours. You can see the grassy hump of the Aiguille Verte above as you skirt round the mountain. 10mins later there is a further sign left to Aiguille Verte for those with the energy to climb to the top and back (about 30mins).

Follow another signpost to Lac de Lessy with a good view in front of Le Buclon mountain, alt. 2,072m. You are now on a ridge and you get your first view down the other side to the green waters of the Lac de Lessy which is an attractive kidney-shaped lake of glacial origin, nestling in a bowl in the mountains, with the dominating Buclon to the right and the white flat mass of the Rochers de Leschaux behind. To the left is the Col de la Forclaz and between the mountains you can see rolling countryside as far as Lake Geneva with the Jura range smudging the horizon. Just above the lake is a cluster of huts, including the Refuge de Lessy which is a good place to stop for refreshment and to eat thick slices of Reblochon cheese on fresh bread. Alternatively, stop for a picnic just beneath the ridge so that you can enjoy the beautiful views.

Refuge de Lessy, tel. 50.25.98.32.
Dormitory accommodation.
Open from May to 15 October depending on climatic conditions.

Follow the signed path which you can see going down towards the lake. About halfway down there is a possible short cut on a path to the left which cuts across above the lake and meets up again at the Col de la Forclaz - this saves about 10mins. Otherwise continue to the chalets, which are rather forlorn looking with galvanised roofs, and then turn left to Chalets de Mayse/ Col de la Forclaz (right goes to Col de Sosay/Dent de Jallouvre). The wide path goes round above the lake to the col, alt.1,844m, where you have a beautiful view down into the Nant valley and the Chalets de Mayse where you are heading. Go straight over the col (the sign right indicates Linvouet Paradis). This is a rather tiring descent of 368m down a winding wide path which is eroded in places and can be muddy and slippery if it has been raining.

The Chalets de Mayse (3hrs 30mins) consist of about 12 buildings in a fold at the end of the valley, one of which is a refuge. They have a big herd of goats here and you can buy fresh goat's cheese - be careful of the geese guarding the refuge as they are quite fierce! From the chalets you can see the path going up the mountain on the left back to Chinaillon. In fact there is a large notice above the chalets telling you to go left so it is difficult to go wrong here. From the chalets you have a lovely view of the valley of the Overan up from Entremont up to the Col de la Buffaz, flanked by the rugged Rochers de Traversiers on the left and the Montagne des Auges on the right.

Refuge de Mayse - Proprietor Philippe Bibollet - tel. 50.22.47.15.
Dormitory for 30 people.
Open from May to 15 October depending on climatic conditions.

Follow the signpost left to Le Chinaillon par La Cula, walk down a jeep track for a few minutes and then go up left by another signpost. This is where you leave the GR.96 which continues down the valley. It is also the start of the third climb which is 214m up a steep slope. At first the path is open and then you reach three big fir trees where you can have a rest before tackling the next section which is through alder bushes and woodland. The path becomes rocky and tricky but only for a short distance up to Le Planay, alt. 1,690m. The climb takes approximately 35mins (4hrs). You are now on the other side of the mountain; above you on the left rears the impressive square rock face of the Roc des Tours, alt.1,994m.

It is now a great relief to go gently downwards on a delightful path past some chalets with the Roc des Tours on the left and the Chaine des Aravis in front. After a signpost you start dropping down the mountainside in earnest on a stony path through lovely light, mixed woodland. At the bottom of the slope (4hrs 20mins) there is a signpost right to the Parking de la Cula and left to Chinaillon. Go left along an easy path which meanders around the bottom of the mountain, initially with an old stone wall on one side, past the chalets of La Cula down below and La Mazerie. Take a pause to appreciate the lovely rolling alpine country on your right and the rocky mass of the Roc des Tours on your left. Bear right where it is signposted Chinaillon on a narrow path through intermittent tall fir trees to a T-junction. Then turn left towards Chinaillon (4hrs 30mins) on a narrow unsurfaced road which goes underneath electricity wires.

From here you can clearly see the ugly ski slopes on the other side of the valley; what a shame the slopes are defaced in this way; it always looks worse in summer to see the green hillsides criss-crossed with chair lifts and wires. Nevertheless the path is still very attractive as it meanders through woods and then open meadowland, past a little shrine with a cross, before reaching the chalets of La Bouvardière. Walk down the road, past the turning you took on your outward journey, to the village where your car is parked (4hrs 45mins).

The tourist bureau in the centre of Grand-Bornand sells a very good map showing the various walks in the region, including the Sentier Découverte mentioned above. There are also helpful notes in English.

Remarks: This is probably the best signposted walk in this region and it would be difficult to take the wrong way. I would call it a good family hike, provided all members are fit, as there is lots of variety. There are usually crowds of people on sunny weekends in July and August.

49: BOUCLE DE SAINT JEAN-DE-SIXT - 960 metres
(Aravis/Bornes region)

Difficulty:	Very easy.
Time:	3 hrs.
Height gain:	Practically none - 50m.

Maps:	Edition Didier & Richard IGN No.2 Massifs des Bornes-Bauges 1:50,000. Cartes IGN 3430 ET Top 25 La Clusaz/Grand-Bornand 1:25,000.
Depart from:	St. Jean-de-Sixt - 960 metres.
Signposting:	Good in parts.

How to get there (from Geneva)

Take the motorway direction Chamonix and exit at No.16, Bonneville/La Clusaz. Follow the N.203 signposted St. Pierre-en Faucigny/La Clusaz and shortly after turn left on the D.6A direction St. Pierre-en-Faucigny. At the roundabout in the village continue following the D.6 over the railway line and then turn right on the D.12 signposted La Clusaz. This takes you up the Borne river valley, a narrow, twisting road, through the villages of Petit-Bornand and Entremont. Continue on the D.12 to St. Jean-de-Sixt and park your car in the centre of the village in front of the syndicat d'initiative.

Directions

Walk back down the road you drove in by and turn left after 50m where there are a number of signs including Camping/Caravaning Municipale and a beautiful old chalet set back on the left. The road goes gently up, then levels off at Crêt St. Jean, alt. 1,000m, and goes down. There are beautiful views down the Thônes valley with Mt. Lachat on your right, the Aravis range on your left and La Tournette mountain ahead. At a road junction (over on the right is a telephone box) bear left and you will see a sign saying Le Suet/Mt. Lachat par Les Plans. Follow the sign till you come to the hamlet of Forgeassoud. All along this road there are some very attractive chalets, some old, some new. At Forgeassoud there is a pretty little chapel, built in 1631 but recently renovated. Continue till the road peters out at a typical old Savoyard farm called Les Plans, where Reblochon and goat's cheese are offered for sale (30mins).

Take the track which goes in front of the farm (signs) and across a meadow (you may have to negotiate some electric fences as there are lots of cattle here). After 100m there is a sign straight Mt. Lachat/right Le Suet. Continue straight, climbing round the side of the field with woods on the left. When the path meets a wide stony track at a T-junction, go down left signposted Les Villards, Bourgeal (the path up to the right goes to Mt. Lachat). This is a wide balcony path along the side of the hill, through some deciduous woodland but with more lovely open views down to the Thônes valley on your left backed by the rearing peak of La Tournette. The track becomes a tarmac road and then gets wider as it winds all the way down to the valley floor. You are on the route de Perrière where there are a number

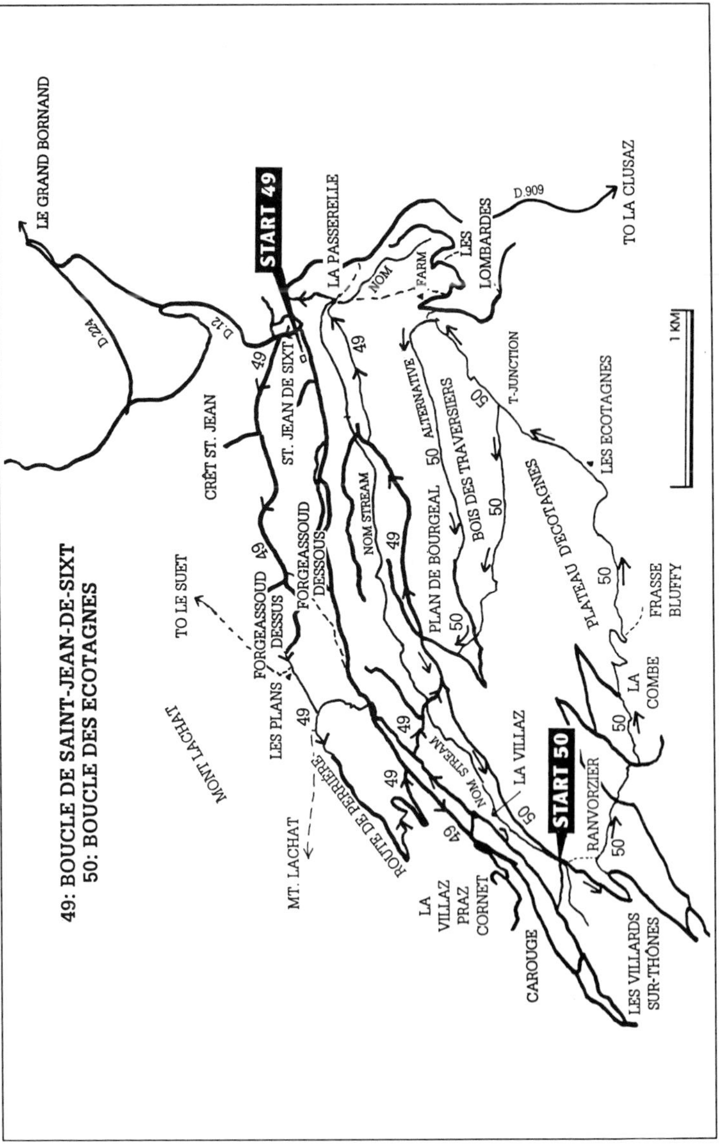
49: BOUCLE DE SAINT-JEAN-DE-SIXT
50: BOUCLE DES ECOTAGNES
LE GRAND BORNAND
D.224
D.12
START 49
LA PASSERELLE
NOM
FARM
LES LOMBARDES
D.909
TO LA CLUSAZ
CRÊT ST. JEAN
ST. JEAN DE SIXT
49
ALTERNATIVE
50
T-JUNCTION
1 KM
LES ECOTAGNES
PLAN DE BOURGEAL
BOIS DES TRAVERSIERS
NOM STREAM
FORGEASSOUD DESSOUS
FORGEASSOUD DESSUS
TO LE SUET
PLATEAU D'ECOTAGNES
FRASSE
BLUFFY
LA COMBE
LES PLANS
MONT LACHAT
ROUTE DE PERRIÈRE
MT. LACHAT
LA VILLAZ
START 50
RANVORZIER
LA VILLAZ PRAZ CORNET
CAROUGE
LES VILLARDS SUR-THÔNES

of authentic old Savoyard chalets and farms.

This road joins the D.909 from St. Jean-de-Sixt to Thônes. Turn right (1hr 15mins) and walk along the main road for about 10mins to the hamlet of La Villaz - *there used to be a short cut across the main road down into the lower valley by a small shrine, but work on the widening of the road has destroyed the turning. It could be that they replace it when all the work has finished.* Just outside La Villaz there is a sort of cross-roads where you turn down left (no sign).There is a telephone box over on the right and a sign to Praz Cornet. A few minutes later bear right at a T-junction and continue on a narrow road through some prosperous new houses till you come to the hamlet of Carouge and a shrine to the Virgin Mary on the left (1hr 30mins). *This is a very Catholic part of France and there are numerous shrines in the region - if you recite three Hail Marys in front of this statue you get 100 days' indulgence in Purgatory.*

Turn left here, signposted St. Jean par l'Envers/Les Plans 1.5km, and cross the bridge over the Nom river. Turn left again and walk along a pleasant road with the river on your left. This takes you to the hamlet of Plan de Bourgeal (2hrs) where there is another chapel (built 1839). Further on there are numerous signs by a wooden bench concerning cross-country ski trails. Continue on the road towards St. Jean-de-Sixt and when you reach a junction with more signs, follow the direction St. Jean/Circuit de l'Envers.

This narrow road goes through picturesque meadows with ancient fruit trees and some really lovely old Savoyard farmhouses, complete with balconies bright with flowering geraniums, and flourishing vegetable gardens. Follow the sign L'Envers de Forgeassoud which enters lovely beech and fir woods (called the Bois de l'Envers), with the river Nom flowing down on the left in a narrow gorge. Cross the river by a green iron bridge called La Passerelle, where the stream has turned into a rushing torrent. Turn up left out of the river valley to the main road and turn right into St. Jean-de-Sixt. When you get to the roundabout in the centre of the village, with the church straight ahead, turn left towards the syndicat d'initiative.

Remarks: A delightfully easy stroll within the capabilities of anyone. Much of the walk is on tarmac road but there is little traffic (except for the 10mins on the main road). The countryside is beautiful, quiet and pastoral. This is the place to come if you want to see old authentic Savoyard farms and a way of life which is fast disappearing.

50: BOUCLE DES ECOTAGNES - (See map p247)
Alt. 1,280 metres (Aravis/Bornes region)

Difficulty:	Easy through steep woods.
Time:	3hrs 45mins or 4hrs 15mins.
Height gain:	528 metres.
Maps:	Edition Didier & Richard IGN No.2 Massifs des Bornes-Bauges 1:50,000. Cartes IGN 3430 ET Top 25 La Clusaz/Grand-Bornand 1:25,000.
Depart from:	Pont de Carouge, Les Villards-sur-Thônes 752 metres.
Signposting:	Good - follow yellow splashes.

How to get there (from Geneva)
Take the motorway direction Chamonix and exit at No.16, Bonneville/La Clusaz. Follow the N.203 signposted St. Pierre-en-Faucigny/La Clusaz and shortly after turn left on the D.6A direction St. Pierre-en-Faucigny. At the roundabout in the village continue on the D.6 over the railway line and then turn right on the D.12 signposted La Clusaz. This road takes you up the Borne river valley, a narrow twisting road through the villages of Petit-Bornand and Entremont. Continue on the D.12 road to St. Jean-de-Sixt and then take the D.909 towards Thônes. At the village of Les Villards-sur-Thônes, turn left down a hill where it says Chef-Lieu. At a T-junction bear left following sign to Ranvorzier and shortly after go right at a shrine over a narrow bridge called the Pont de Carouge and park on the other side.

Directions
There is a board here which shows you the different walking possibilities, including raquette (snow-shoe) walks. This is the first time I have seen a map for this activity, which consists of walking across the snow on things that look like tennis rackets.

Walk up the road following the sign to Ranvorzier. Look down into the valley and you have a good view of the Pont de Carouge and an old mill over the River Nom with a waterfall down the side where you feel the water-wheel should be (on closer inspection it turned out to be a dilapidated sawmill); underneath the bridge you can see another man-made waterfall. Follow the yellow splashes to a hairpin bend and then go off the road (still following the yellow splashes) on a path which goes up through the woods with a stream down on the left. There are widely spaced wooden steps and a large old chalet to the right.

Close-up of carved balconies, Lombardes Farm, Boucle des Ecotagnes

You come to a small wooden sign saying Chemin de Ranvorzier (20mins) which confirms you are going in the right direction (the second time I did this walk the sign had disappeared). Cross the stream and into open meadowland; at this stage you are going through the garden in front of an attractive chalet called Pranpraz but this is an official walk and the owners don't mind! The path becomes undefined, especially in springtime when the grass is tall, but continue medium steep straight up the hill towards another big old chalet following the yellow splashes. There is a beautiful view of the valley behind with the village of Les Villards-sur-Thônes. Shortly after the upper chalet you meet the narrow road.

Cross the road at a point where you can see that you have cut off a huge bend (30mins). You can see the hamlet of Ranvozier to the right but you don't actually go through it. Climb up the hill by a bench quite steeply through open meadowland; the path is not defined so keep a look out for the yellow splashes on trees. The path becomes clearer as you go into light woodland past a sign saying Beauregard and also some red splashes.

You meet a jeep track (1hr) - a continuation of the same road you crossed previously. Go left and almost immediately steeply up to the right where there is a sign saying St. Jean-de-Sixt. This path is steep and there is a lot of tree felling which sometimes makes the path tricky to find - the red marks also get mixed up with the yellow ones! It comes out at a jeep track where you bear up to the right. Continue along the track for 20mins, and 5mins after a sign pointing straight to Les Lombardes you come out on to the Plateau Les Ecotagnes by a newly built hut (1hr 30mins); this is an attractive sweep of open fields with views across the valley to the dramatic rocky ridge of the Mont Lachat - there is a lovely clump of trees in the middle of this meadow which is a pleasant spot to stop and have lunch.

Continue across the pasture where there is no clear path and it is rather boggy. Follow the fence which goes all the way along the top on the right; beyond is an old chalet (called La Combe). At the end of the meadow continue straight through the fence, still carefully following the yellow flashes and you find yourself on a defined path which goes to another old chalet with no name and a sign saying Beauregard (1hr 45mins). From here you can in fact walk up to the Pointe de Beauregard (blue flashes), which is the arrival point of a number of ski-lifts coming up from La Clusaz. Keep straight on, following the sign to St. Jean-de-Sixt and the yellow flashes. The path plunges into dense fir forest and goes down around the mountain towards St. Jean-de-Sixt. Ignore any paths off to left or right. At a point where the path comes into the open there is a superb view of the Chaine des Aravis mountain range with the Pointe Percée at one end.

When you come to a T-junction (2hrs 15mins) turn left towards Villards-sur-Thônes (right goes to Les Lombardes - see alternative way below).* The path plunges down through bush rather than woodland and at times is not well defined, so keep checking for the yellow splashes; this region is called the Bois de Traversiers (meaning "going across"). Later on the path becomes clearer, rather like a ditch which increasingly resembles an old mule track. You pass by a ruin; typical of many in the Alps where one can envisage the peasants scratching a living from their small patch of cultivable land, with few cows and hens. *Now many of these places are jumbles of rock and fragments of creeper-covered wall, with nothing left to say who lived and died there, except perhaps an ancient apple tree - sort of sad and yet triumphant. Probably the terrain was open when this particular place was inhabited and* *the coniferous forest has been planted since.* Continue on the mule track which goes down through ancient beeches till it meets a road.

Cross the road (2hrs 45mins), still following yellow splashes, and take the short cut down; there are now old and new chalets on either side. You come to another road with a convenient bench and signposts pointing back the way you have come. Turn left and walk through the hamlet of Plan de Bourgeal, past the Roman styled Chapelle de Plan du Bourgeal dated 1839 with a rather quaint tower, marred somewhat by the galvanised iron roof. Walk down the narrow road with the River Le Nom on the right, still following the yellow flashes, till you come to the bridge at Pont de Carouge (3hrs 45mins).

*Alternative way back: Follow the sign right to Les Lombardes. Continue down through the forest (rather muddy if it has rained) till the path meets a tarmac road. There is a sign left to Les Villards par Les Traversiers which is a lower path back. However, walk down the tarmac road, past new chalets, till you see on the left one of the unusual farms built by Jean Marie Favre Lorraine at the beginning of the century. Unfortunately, it is uninhabited and has fallen into disrepair but you can still appreciate the intricately carved balconies and huge glass veranda. Hopefully it will soon be tastefully restored.

Go back to the signpost and take a wide path through tall birch woods, still following the yellow splashes carefully (some of the way there is quite a drop on the right), till you come to a defined jeep track where you turn left following the sign Les Villards. This turns into a tarmac road with woods on the left and lovely meadows on the right. Follow this road down through the hamlet of Plan de Bourgeal (see explanations for higher path) till you get to the bridge.

Remarks: A very attractive low altitude walk within the capabilities of even the most hesitant walker, despite the occasional steep stretch. It is nice to do on a hot day in summer as there is lots of shade.

51: LA POINTE D'ORSIÈRE - Alt. 1,750 metres
(Aravis/Bornes region)

Difficulty:	Medium - goes steeply up to start with but there are no difficult places.
Time:	*4hrs.*
Height gain:	790 metres.
Maps:	Editions Didier & Richard No.8 Massifs du Mont

	Blanc/Beaufortain 1:50,000.
	Cartes IGN 3531 OT Top 25 Megève Col des Aravis 1:25,000.
Depart from:	La Gutary (Manigod) 960 metres.
Signposting:	Good in parts, look for yellow triangles. Do not follow Circuit d'Orsière signs from the summit (see remarks below).

How to get there (from Geneva)
Take the motorway direction Chamonix and exit at No.16, Bonneville/La Clusaz. Follow the N.203 signposted St. Pierre-en-Faucigny/La Clusaz and shortly after turn left on the D.6A direction St. Pierre-en-Faucigny. At the roundabout in the village continue on the D.6 and then turn right on the D.12 signposted La Clusaz. This road takes you up the Borne river valley, a narrow, twisting road, through the villages of Petit-Bornand and Entremont. Continue on the D.12 to St. Jean-de-Sixt and then take the D.909 to Thônes. From Thônes take the D.12 direction Serreval. After 1km bear left on the D.16 to Manigod. In front of the church at Manigod take the turning down to the right, signposted Tournance/La Charmette, which goes into the narrow Fier valley. Follow all signs to La Charmette, through the hamlets of Choseaux, Joux and Tournance; just before the hamlet of La Gutary you come to a bridge over the river signposted Bionière (although on the map this is the Nant Gothier stream!). and beyond on the left is a shrine in a rock. At the bridge are various signposts, including one saying Circuit d'Orsière No. 38.

Directions
Take the narrow path to the right of the bridge which goes down into the woods and is signposted La Balme/Le Macheux/Sur Le Freu/Circuit d'Orsière. At first the path follows the river on the right and then goes over a bridge to a cross-roads (5mins). Bear up to the right (signs Val Sulens/Circuit de Banc) on a steep uphill path through beech and coniferous woods. There are yellow diamonds and orange splashes on rocks and trees. After 20mins you come to a stone commemorating the accidental death of Francis Avettand on 31 January 1944 at the age of 36. *Whether he fell or was shot by the Germans is anyone's guess.*

240m higher up the path comes out into beautiful open meadowland and a few minutes later you reach the Chalet de la Balme, alt. 1,200m, which has been recently renovated. There are signposts here, one saying Circuit d'Orsière and you get a marvellous view of the surrounding peaks including the nearby Montagne de Sulens (Walk No. 53). Continue on the jeep track to a T-junction; turn left and then after the first corner go up right for about 50m (careful, this is not obvious). There is another bevy of signs up on a tree including one for the Circuit d'Orsière. Turn left on a narrow track which goes up steeply through woods and round the mountain for about 30mins, with occasional steep drops down one side - there are yellow diamonds and orange splashes.

When the path meets a jeep track (1hr 10mins) turn up left and then out into open meadowland again with the Crozet chalet, alt. 1,406m, on your left. Here there is a good view of the narrow valley below, and the Parmelan mountain behind which dominates the northern end of Lake Annecy. *In early spring the surrounding slopes are covered with narcissi, alpine daffodils and trumpet gentians.* Continue on the jeep track curving gently uphill round the mountain to the chalets of Le Macheux, alt. 1,598m (1hr 30mins). Turn up right, signposted Circuit d'Orsière, and you can see the signposts at the top of the Pointe d'Orsière 150m higher up. Keep left on the ill-defined track which is quite eroded in places (there are yellow and orange splashes) or make your own way up the open hillside.

You arrive at the Pointe, alt. 1,750m (1hr 50mins), which has a signpost at the top saying Circuit d'Orsière. There are glorious views all round and particularly of the Chaine des Aravis mountains, from the L'Etale to Mont Charvin peaks (one does not often see them from this angle). In front is the impressive L'Aiguille de Manigod (Manigod needle) which seems part of the mountain chain itself, but looks more needle-like from a lower level.

Although the official Circuit d'Orsière path continues across the ridge (see remarks below) retrace your steps back to Le Macheux chalets (2hrs 5mins); on the way down there is a good view of the ski installations at the Col de Merdassier, part of the La Clusaz complex. Turn left at the chalets down the same jeep track and continue past the path in the woods you came up (2hrs 20mins). The track goes down through open alpine pastures and occasional coniferous trees, past a big tumble-down barn on the right, before reaching the chalet of L'Arbarête, alt. 1,404m (2hrs 35mins). *For this part of the walk you are on the Circuit de Banc No. 27.*

10mins later bear down to the right at a T-junction which takes you to another big old chalet (Les Charmettes*) (3hrs), where there is a signpost saying Circuit de Freu No. 30 which you will now follow. (*There is a certain confusion as to the names of the chalets as maps differ. However, according to the Didier & Richard map the first chalet is not named and the second chalet is La Combe.)

Here you can either take a short cut over the hill (it is marked La Tête on the side of the chalet) or take the jeep track left. NOTE - If you go right you will eventually arrive back at the Chalet la Balme where you can retrace your steps down through the woods. Otherwise take the jeep track left past the chalet of La Combe* where you bear down right towards La Tête (3hrs 15mins), a working farm with lots of brown and white cows around.

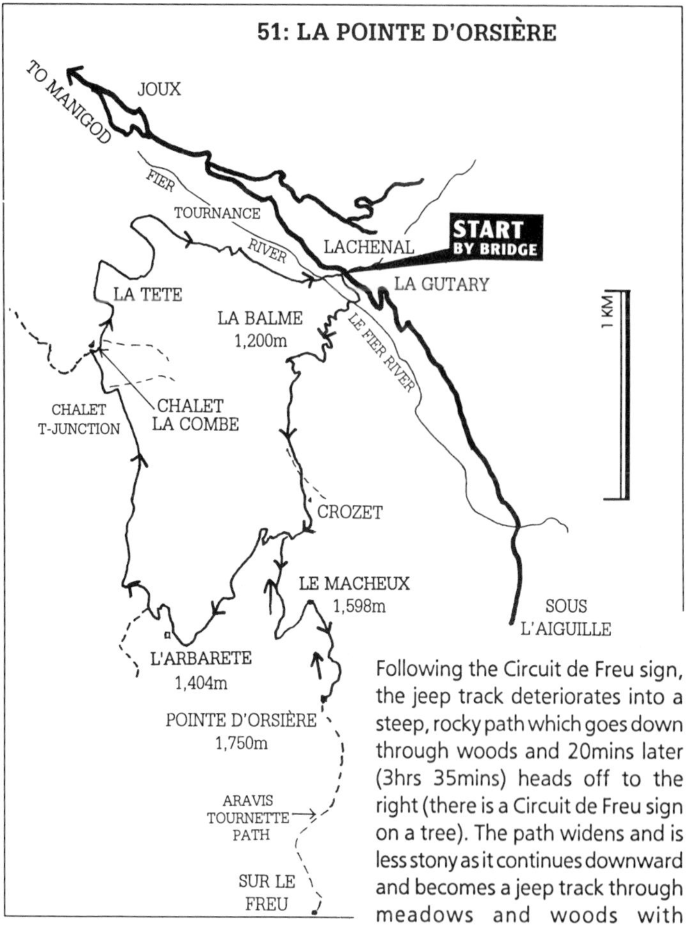

Following the Circuit de Freu sign, the jeep track deteriorates into a steep, rocky path which goes down through woods and 20mins later (3hrs 35mins) heads off to the right (there is a Circuit de Freu sign on a tree). The path widens and is less stony as it continues downward and becomes a jeep track through meadows and woods with occasional chalets.

Cross the Fier river where the water looks very welcoming on a hot day as it tumbles over big boulders. You are now on a wide jeep track which goes beside the river and finally to the bridge where you have left your car (4hrs).

Remarks: A beautiful walk in an unspoiled region. There are wonderful views of the Chaine des Aravis, Mont Charvin and the nearby Sulens mountain. Since this walk was originally done the Manigod tourist office have re-

signposted the entire region and changed the original circular walks. I have not followed their Circuit d'Orsière as there is a long difficult descent into another valley, plus a lengthy stretch down a road which makes it rather tedious; it also impinges on the Tour de la Tulle itinerary (Walk No. 52). My personal feeling is that they have overdone the signs and made directions more confusing. A map is available at the Manigod tourist bureau, price FF.30 (explanations in French only).

52: TOUR DE LA TULLE - Alt. 2,072 metres
(Aravis/Bornes region)

Difficulty:	Strenuous rather than difficult. There is one steep descent near the end of the walk.
Time:	5hrs.
Height gain:	872 metres.
Maps:	Editions Didier & Richard No.8 Massifs du Mont Blanc/Beaufortain 1:50,000. Cartes IGN 3531 OT Top 25 Megève Col des Aravis 1:25,000.
Depart from:	Sous l'Aiguille (Manigod) - 1,200m.
Signposting:	Follow all signs Tour de la Tulle until you get to Les Fontanettes; then follow signs Tour de Sulens (yellow diamonds).

How to get there (from Geneva)

Take the motorway direction Chamonix and exit at No.16, Bonneville. Follow the N.203 signposted St. Pierre-en-Faucigny/La Clusaz and shortly after turn left on the D.6A direction St. Pierre-en-Faucigny. At the roundabout in the village continue on the D.6 over the railway line and then turn right on the D.12 signposted La Clusaz. This road takes you up the Borne valley, a narrow, twisting road through the villages of Petit-Bornand and Entremont. Continue on the D.12 to St. Jean-de-Sixt and then take the D.909 to Thônes. Soon after entering Thônes turn left on the D.12 direction Serreval. After 1km bear left on the D.16 to Manigod. In front of the church at Manigod take the turning down to the right, signposted Tournance/La Charmette, which goes into the narrow Fier valley. Follow all signs to La Charmette and continue through the hamlets of Choseaux, Joux, Tournance, Gutary and La Charmette to Sous l'Aiguille, which is right at the end of the valley. Park your car in the parking space where the tarmac road gives way to a jeep track. There are lots of signs at the entrance including one saying Tour de la Tulle.

Directions

There is a sign indicating Lac Charvin at the start of a wide jeep track which ascends medium steep through light coniferous wood, with the precipitous rock faces of the Orsière, La Riondaz and La Tulle ahead. You can either keep to the jeep track all the way up or take a short cut at the first corner (marked with a yellow splash on a rock), which is a narrow path along the River Fier which takes about 10mins before joining the jeep track again. You cross the river by a bridge (15mins) and then, a few minutes later, a dry river bed before passing a Tour de Sulens signpost on a small hut (30mins).

Shortly after you come out of the woods onto open alpine pasture. You can see the path in front, curling round the Tulle mountain, and the chalets of L'Aulp de Fier d'en Bas. Ignore the steep path on the right, signposted Circuit d'Orsière, which goes up to the Sur le Freu chalet (this is the way you will return). Continue on the wide jeep track and turn up right following signs Tour de la Tulle/Lac de Charvin (50mins) and ignore another turning to the left which goes to the chalets of L'Aulp de Fier en Bas and the Lac du Champ Tardif. The wide path climbs upwards as though you are winding round a large bowl, crossing a number of streams, through a rocky austere landscape where you can see the cavernous openings of caves above you (there are obvious short cuts if you want to take them). You arrive at the cow barns of L'Aulp de Fier en Haut, alt. 1,756m (1hr 25mins). *In summer there are lots of cows and we saw an enormous bull who luckily didn't take any notice of us. In the barn itself there were at least 20 pigs.* Here there are further signs indicating Tour de la Tulle/Lac de Charvin.

Continue past the barns on the defined, narrow path; you can see it curling up higher round the bowl of mountains to the Col des Portets, with the peaks of La Rouelle, La Goenne and Mont Charvin, alt. 2,409m, dominating the skyline. There are occasional yellow splashes to follow and a steep short cut if you want to take it.

The path winds up medium steep round the wide bowl and if you look back you can see the two groups of chalets clearly; there is a bit of a scramble over a rocky gully but the path is not difficult. You reach a signpost (fallen down when I did the walk) which says left to Lac de Charvin and straight on Col de Portets (2hrs). It is worthwhile to make the 10min detour to see this lovely mountain lake, even though there is quite a steep path up to the crest of the hill from where you look down onto the lake (it takes about another 10mins to get to the lakeside itself). It is said to be one of the prettiest of the region's alpine lakes and nestles in a ring of grassy mountain slopes, dominated by the Goenne peak one side and Mt. Charvin the other.

From the crest of the hill overlooking the lake you can see a path crossing over to rejoin the one you were on to the Col des Portets (2hrs 20mins) actually there are three paths crossing over so take your choice! You then traverse a scree slope for about 15mins, not technically difficult but care should be taken nevertheless. After the scree there is a short steep climb up to the Col de Portets (2hrs 50mins) where there is a gate in a fence. Look back and appreciate the path you have taken which you can see all the way to the chalets. At the Col des Portets, alt. 2,072m, you are on the other side of the ridge with the rocky Tulle mountain jutting out to your right and the Mont Charvin now on your left. Below, the path winds down to a grassy plateau and you can see the villages in the valley far below. *This is the time to take a well earned break and picnic, as most of the rest of the walk is downhill.*

There is no signpost at the col but you don't really need one; just take the path to the right which curls round the mountain and then goes down quite steeply into the grassy plateau at the foot of the Tulle ridge; way over on the left you can see woods and chalets (there is also a higher path which goes along the ridge and down but I have not taken it. Ignore a path off to the left, which is the way to the summit of Mt. Charvin and is quite difficult. Instead continue down following the sign Tour de La Tulle (2hrs 55mins). From here

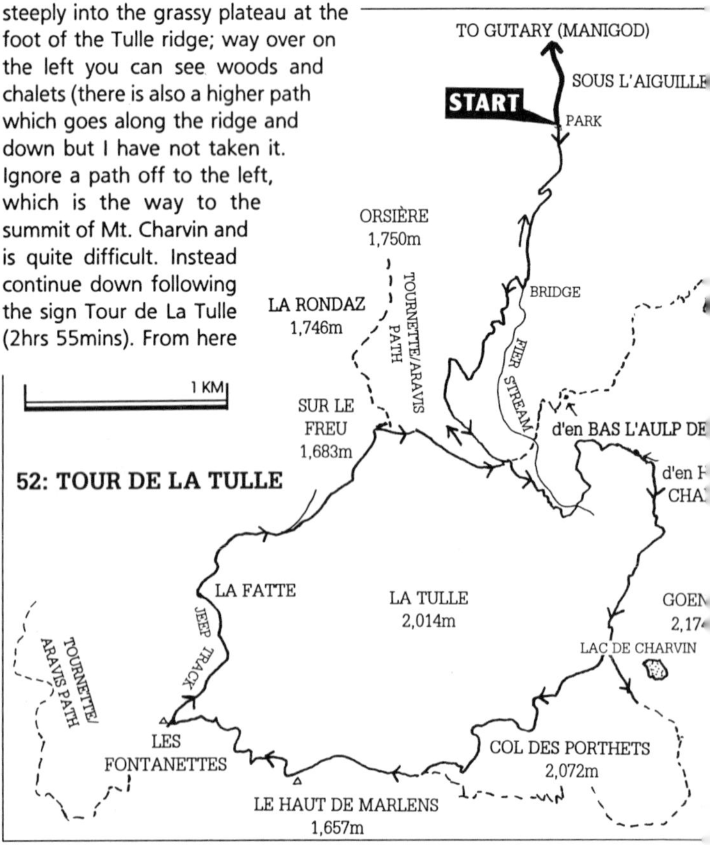

the path gets easier and less steep as you cross pleasant alpine pastures to the Chalets Le Haut de Marlens, alt.1,657m (3hrs 10mins). In season this is a café/restaurant and there is accommodation.

Refuge Haut de Marlens (privately owned), 74230 Bouchet Mt. Charvin, tel 50.44.40.89. Open in summer only, according to climatic conditions.

From these chalets continue on a wide jeep track which curls down (obvious short cuts) to the Chalets Les Fontanettes (3hrs 25mins). This is another café/restaurant, on a lovely open site, a popular stop in summer; there is a jeep track off to the left but you turn right signposted Tour de Sulens. Note: Here the Tour de la Tulle signs disappear and you continue on the Tour de Sulens circuit (indicated by a yellow diamond).

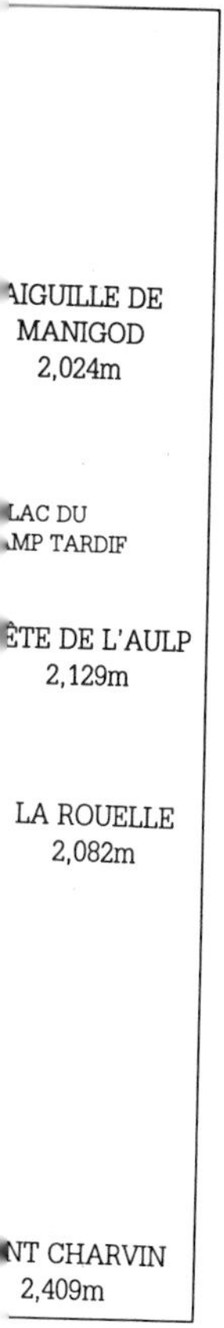

This pleasant, wide, easy path goes past the odd barn and chalet, round the front of the mountain with the rocky mass of the Tulle up on the right. After 15mins turn right off the jeep track at a Tour de Sulens sign (3hrs 40mins) and a yellow marker, climbing again up the side of the mountain but not steeply (there is a little over 200m height gain between Les Fontanettes and the Chalets de Freu). There is a good view of the Orsière summit on your left with the Sulens mountain behind. The large cow shed of Sur Le Freu, alt. 1,683m, sits exposed on an open ridge (4hrs 5mins). Ignoring signs on the left to Tour de Val Sulens par Le Freu and Orsière/Tour de la Tulle, go straight from the front of the barn to the edge of the ridge where you can see a signpost. There is no defined path for the 5mins stretch to the signpost, which says Circuit d'Orsière, but you can see a clear path down into the valley you came up originally. Be careful as this is a vertiginous path and can be slippery after rainfall. You cross some dry water courses with scree and further down the path becomes rocky with long grass; follow the yellow splashes all the way. When you get to the bottom you are on your original path (4hrs 35mins). Retrace your steps back to the car (5hrs).

Remarks: This is a strenuous walk in unforgettable scenery. If you prefer to avoid the steep descent from the Sur Le Freu chalet you can always do the walk in the other direction. This description follows the Tour de Tulle circuit as it used to be and the signs are still there for most of the way. However, the local tourist office have recently re-routed many of the walks, numbered them and put signs in all directions. There is a map available at the Manigod tourist bureau, price FF.30 (explanations in French only and rather confusing).

53: TOUR DE SULENS (Thônes) - Alt. 1,615m
(Aravis/Bornes region)

Difficulty: Easy jeep track most of the way - one medium steep ascent.

Time: 3hrs 45mins.

Height gain: 316 metres.

Maps: Editions Didier & Richard IGN No.2 Massifs des Bornes-Bauges 1:50,000.
Cartes IGN 3531 OT Top 25 Megève Col des Aravis 1:25,000.

Depart from: Col de Plan Bois - Alt. 1,299 metres.

Signposting: Excellent - follow all signs Tour de Sulens - lots of signposts and yellow splashes.

How to get there (from Geneva)
Take the motorway direction Chamonix and exit No.16, Bonnneville/La Clusaz. Follow the N.203 signposted St. Pierre-en-Faucigny/La Clusaz and shortly after turn left on the D.6A direction St. Pierre-en-Faucigny. At the roundabout in the village continue on the D.6 over the railway line and then turn right on the D.12 signposted La Clusaz. This road takes you up the Borne river valley, a narrow, twisting road through the villages of Petit-Bornand and Entremont. Continue on the D.12 to St. Jean-de-Sixt and then take the D.909 direction Thônes. Soon after entering Thônes turn left on the D.12 direction Serraval, and then be careful to take a small road to the left, about 2km later, signposted Les Clefs. At the entrance to the village bear back sharp right on a narrow road and follow all signs to Col de Plan Bois; this is a winding road uphill for about 6km. The Col de Plan Bois consists of a café/restaurant with a grassy parking area in front just before the road starts to wind down again to Manigod.

Directions
Start walking in the direction you came up by car. Do not take the first sign left which says Le Mont Sulens 1hr 45mins but continue down the paved road for about 500m. As you walk down you have an uninterrupted view of the vertical cliffs of the Parmelan mountain behind Annecy and to the left the majestic Tournette peak at 2,351m. You pass La Frasse which consists of farm buildings and an attractive little chapel (10mins). Shortly after take the wide track to the left signposted Tour de Sulens/La Frasse which undulates gently through forest, open fields and the barns of Les Rottes and Les Gay.

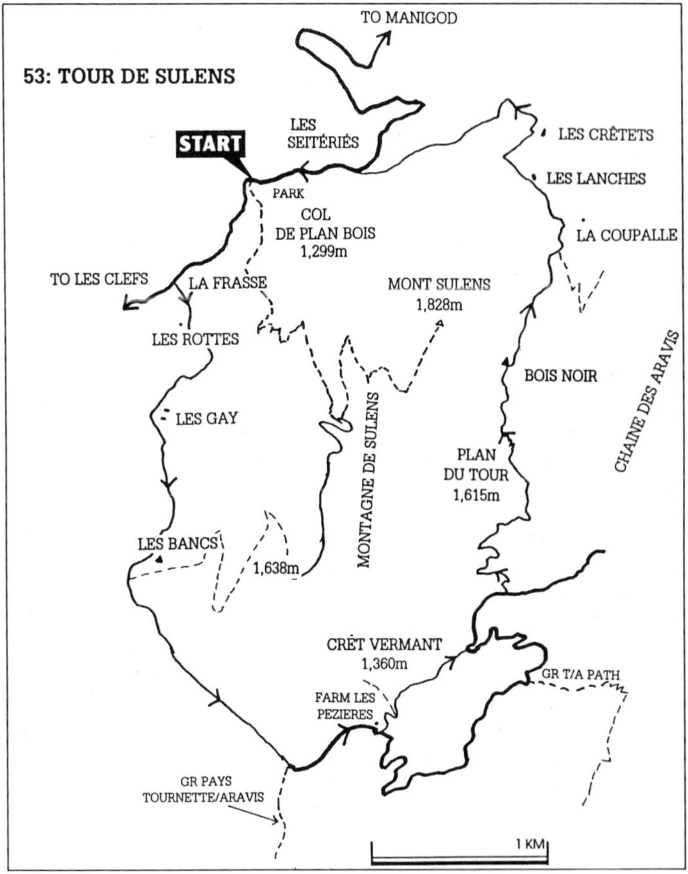

At a sign indicating Les Bancs left (35mins) keep to the main track. Shortly after go left following sign Tour de Sulens/Le Mont/Col de la Bottaz. Ignore a further sign to the left saying Sulens 2hrs and keep on main Tour de Sulens path which 10mins later goes past a new barn on the right (55mins). 5mins after the barn ignore stony jeep track to the left and when you come to a fork follow the Tour de Sulens sign to the left (you are now on the Tournette/ Aravis GR. red/yellow Route de Pays path till the next farm). There are lovely open views as you walk down; over on the right are farms and hamlets nestling in an unspoilt valley with mountains behind and straight ahead is an impressive view of Mont Charvin, alt 2,409m and the Aravis chain of peaks including La Tulle (Walk No. 52). On the left are the grass covered slopes of Mt. Sulens. This path meets a paved road which continues to a typical large Savoyard farm called Les Pezières. *At this farm you can not only buy the local Reblochon cheese, you can also watch the farmer making it!*

Go through the farm and round the back on a stony jeep track. Bear right on a wide grassy path signposted Tour de Sulens (1hr 15mins) which goes alongside a fence on the right for a short while with yellow splashes and further signposts, so you can't go wrong. You can see a large barn ahead at the Crêt Vermant, alt. 1,360m. Go up right behind the barn on a jeep track (signs here again) and then left at the next fork following the signpost indicating Tour de Mont Sulens (don't go down right which says Mt. Charvin). 5mins later turn left following the sign Plan de Tour up a wide stony path which winds up the mountain medium steep for about 40mins. There is an ugly cow shed at the top which is the highest point of the walk at alt. 1,615m. There are sweeping views all round, especially of the Chaines des Aravis mountain range with the nearby fearsome mass of Mt. Charvin. The path winds round before you reach the cowshed (follow yellow splashes) into a dip in the mountain at the Col du Plan du Tour, and on your left is the long grassy Sulens ridge with its rather curious indentations and on the other side is a low hill with some trees (2hrs 15mins).

The path starts to go down (left is up to the cowshed) and after 15mins you come to a big barn left, marked on the map as Bois Noir, alt. 1,1550m. Far above on a ridge is a cross - the highest point of the Sulens mountain, alt. 1,818m, which is really a long shoulder culminating at this point. Continue following yellow splashes and signs past the barns of La Coupalle, Les Lanches and Les Crêtets with magnificent views over the lush farm-dotted countryside. You can see down to the valley and the village of Manigod, dominated by its church with a high steeple; you are now walking round the front of the mountain and the rocky cliff of the Parmelan swings into view again. You can also see across to the Col de Plan Bois where you have left your car.

The path becomes more wooded as you get lower and then hits a tarmac road (3hrs 30mins). Turn left and walk back up the road past some old working farms to the col (3hrs 45mins).

Remarks: There is something very satisfying about walking round a mountain instead of having to go up and down it! However, you do have an option to go to the top if you feel more energetic. This is an easy, well signposted circuit all the way with no worries about getting lost. The views of the surrounding countryside and mountains (Parmelan, La Tournette, Chaine des Aravis, Mt. Charvin amongst the many peaks), are really outstanding. This is real farming country (no nasty ski-lifts to be seen) and there are lots of brown and white Abondance cows feeding in the lush meadows, plus herds of goats, not to mention the chickens, ducks and geese scratching round the farms. This walk is best done in spring or early autumn as there is little shade on a hot day - due to the rich soil the flowers are particularly abundant and the rare lady's slipper orchid can be found here.

54: TOUR DE L'AIGUILLE DE LA TOURNETTE - Alt. 1,739 metres (Aravis/Bornes region)

Difficulty:	Medium but some difficult patches; going down from the Col de Vorets is steep and over scree.
Time:	4hrs 30mins.
Height gain:	689 metres.
Maps:	Editions Didier & Richard IGN No.2 Massifs des Bornes-Bauges 1:50,000. Cartes IGN 3431 OT Top 25 Lac d'Annecy 1:25,000.
Depart from:	La Molloire (Serraval) - 1,050 metres.
Signposting:	Excellent all the way round - look for yellow splashes and triangles.

How to get there (from Geneva)

Take the motorway direction Chamonix and exit at No.16, Bonneville/La Clusaz. Follow the N.23 signposted St. Pierre-en-Faucigny/La Clusaz and shortly after turn left on the D.6A to St. Pierre-en-Faucigny. At the roundabout in the village continue on the D.6 over the railway line and then turn right on the D.12 signposted La Clusaz. This road takes you up the Borne river valley, a narrow, twisting road through the villages of Petit-Bornand and Entremont. Continue on the D.12 to St. Jean-de-Sixt and then take the D.909 direction Thônes. Soon after entering Thônes turn left on the D.12 direction Serraval. Approximately 1km after the Col de Marais take a right turn to L'Ermite/Montaubert. Follow this road which climbs for 600m to L'Ermite. At L'Ermite keep right direction Montaubert and then, just after a bend where Montaubert comes into view, take a narrow stony track signposted Gîte de Cernay (careful, it is easy to miss!). Drive to the end of the stony track which stops at a farm called La Molloire. Park your car away from the farm or better still at the bend below where there are signposts indicating Tour de Val de Sulens and Tour de l'Aiguille.

Directions

La Molloire is a delightfully dilapidated Savoyard farm complete with yapping dogs and a majestic billy goat. The only discordant note is a ski-lift which ends just above the farm where there is a sign on a tree indicating Tour de l'Aiguille. From the ski-lift take the jeep track which climbs up fairly steeply heading south-west. In front there is a good view of the dramatically austere L'Aiguille mountain with a cross on the summit. For the first 100m you walk through open country and then the path turns northwards into woods; there are yellow splashes and diamonds on trees. Continue round the flank of the mountain, climbing most of the time quite steeply (ignore the grassy path going off to the right).

The path gets narrower and steeper as it curls round to the right. After 2km of climbing you come out through open alpine pasture to the Trois Vargnes hut, alt 1,400m, which is new and rather ugly (Trois Vargnes means three fir trees). The path bears left and there are wooden signs on a tree saying Tour de Val de Sulens and Tour de l'Aiguille. Look for the yellow diamond signs as the track goes over a fence and undulates down through woods for about 10mins. The path becomes rocky as it starts to wind round the mountain again and there is some scrambling over rocks and scree and at one stage you negotiate a sheet of rock. BE CAREFUL here as there is a yellow right-angled sign which means you go right - you could easily miss it.

The rocky path continues down to the Clairière de l'Arpettaz, alt. 1,250m (clairière means a clearing) (1hr). This is a delightful spot in springtime as it is full of marsh marigolds, orchids and lilies of the valley. There is also meant to be a "source" (spring) but we couldn't find it. Ignore the path to the right leading to the hamlet of Les Pruniers and continue through the clearing to a wooden signpost indicating Tour de l'Aiguille. The narrow path goes through beech and coniferous woods undulating round the flank of the L'Aiguille mountain and then steepening as the vegetation changes to stunted bushes sprinkled with an abundance of flowers in season. Follow a mark on a rock to Chalet des Vorets and the yellow signs; there is a good view of the Aiguille up over on the left. After 250m the path flattens out somewhat and then steepens round the flank of the mountain away from the Aiguille heading north-east.

At the ruins of the Chalet des Vorets, alt. 1,538m (1hr 30mins), there is a good view of Thônes down on the right in the valley. You have climbed 300m since leaving L'Arpettaz and there is another 200m up to the Col des Vorets which is the highest part of the walk. Turn left at the chalets by a yellow mark on the wall; at first the path is level and seems to be going in the wrong direction, but it then turns sharply left as it steepens again. At this stage watch carefully for the yellow markings till you come to further signposts. Bear left to Val de Sulens/Praz Dzeures (also written in yellow on

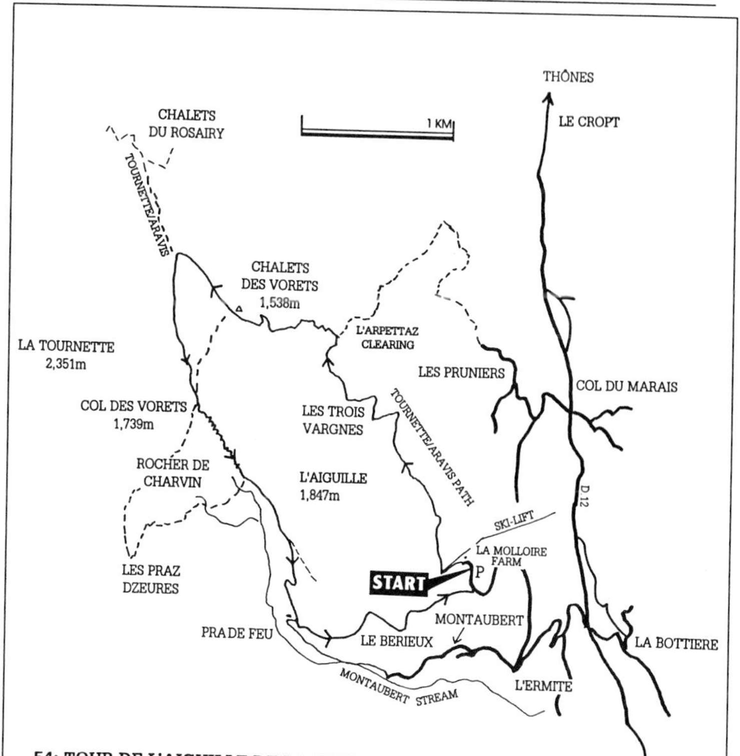

54: TOUR DE L'AIGUILLE DE LA TOURNETTE

a rock is Tour de l'Aiguille) - the path on the right to the Refuge de Rosairy and the summit of La Tournette. You still have 100m to gain and the track climbs up past a refreshing spring through patches of scree. There is a shallow depression on the top just before the pass which is bare and rocky. BE CAREFUL here, it is easy to lose the yellow signs as the path is undefined - keep to the left of the combe (depression) going upwards.

At the top of the pass (2hrs 15mins) there is a signpost saying Col de Vorets, alt. 1,739m/Tour de Val Sulens, and if you continue straight you can see over the side where it says Sentier escarpé Prudence. In other words the slope goes steeply down, so be careful! Take the path down which you can see from the top curling round the mountain. This is not too bad at first and there is an impressive view of the other side of the Col d'Aiguille, with precipitous rock slopes terminating in what looks like a row of caves, then scree and finally woods, to the rocky bed of the mountain stream. Follow the yellow signs carefully as you go down steeply, crossing a dried up river bed. After a while you will see a sign on the left-hand side of the rock face saying Tour de Sulens. Take the path down left marked Tour de l'Aiguille or, for a less precipitous descent, go up right signposted Tour de Sulens par Praz Dzeures which leads to a new refuge. This is a longer way round, beginning with a 60m climb up to the hut.

The direct route goes down over river beds and flat rocks and is quite tricky in places. At times the path is undefined so watch out for the yellow signs as they are easy to miss. Stay together when it becomes difficult and precipitous over scree and boulders and be careful not to dislodge stones in case they gather momentum and hit someone further down the slope. There is approximately 20mins of this terrain before entering woodland which is a welcome respite - there is more scree but this time you are going across and not down. The wood path is narrow and also steep and comes into the open on a high bank parallel to the river. It eventually meets a stream bed and a wide jeep track before winding back over the river and up to Les Praz Dzeures where there is a sign (3hrs).

Turn left along the jeep track which is wide but less steep than earlier. The stream is down on your right and you lose height rapidly through woods and open country with yellow diamond signs on the trees.To the right there is a dramatic view upwards to the Rocher de Charvin and you pass a pulley which takes supplies to the refuge which you can just see high above.

When the path forks go right through open meadowland till you reach the two barns of Pra du Feu. ALTERNATIVE: you can take the left fork signposted La Tournette/Les Praz Dzeures, which has red diamond markings. This takes you via an old hermit's refuge to La Molloire and you approach the farm from above which means you don't have to walk up the jeep track at the end (I have not personally been this way but friends have).

From the top of col to the barns is a descent of 600m. On the corner between the two buildings there is a wooden sign ahead to Montaubert and left to Tour de Sulens and La Molloire; there is another wooden sign on a tree saying Tour de l'Aiguille. Turn left to La Molloire through an electric fence and across a field of cows. Keep on a low path where there are yellow splashes on a rock.There is another sign on a tree at the end of the field.

This is an easy undulating path curling gently down towards La Molloire through fir and beech woods across a number of streams. After passing the ruins of a house on the right buried in undergrowth, the path continues down until it reaches an open field (sign on tree). Bear left in the field alongside the fence and you reach the rough track you drove up to the farm. Here there is another wooden sign saying Tour de Sulens. Walk up the road for 5mins to La Molloire (4hrs 30mins).

Remarks: This is a fairly tough but rewarding walk, though personally I find The Aiguille (needle) a rather daunting looking mountain. Although it is right next door to the magnificent La Tournette peak which is so popular with walkers, it has the advantage of being less known and is therefore uncrowded during the summer months. You must be fit and prepared for precipitous downward slopes as well as climbing. However, the walk is not dangerous and has lots of variety i.e. woodlands, flowers, rock, scree and open meadows. It is well signposted all the way round but keep your eyes peeled for the yellow diamond flashes!

55: BOUCLE DES TERVELLES - Alt.1,850 metres
(Aravis/Bornes region)

Difficulty:	Hard slog up through woods for 752m to start and then a further height gain of around 200 metres from the refuge - worth it!
Time:	5hrs 15mins.
Height gain:	1,070 metres.
Maps:	Editions Didier & Richard No. 8 Massifs du Mont Blanc/Beaufortain 1:50,000. Cartes IGN 3431 OT Top 25 Lac d'Annecy 1:25,000.
Depart from:	Montremont, near Thônes - 780 metres.
Signposting:	Good - follow Boucle des Tervelles signs.

How to get there (from Geneva)

Take the motorway direction Chamonix and exit at No.16, Bonneville/La Clusaz. Follow the N.203 signposted St. Pierre-en-Faucigny/La Clusaz and shortly after turn left on the D.6A direction St. Pierre-en-Faucigny. At the roundabout in the village continue following the D.6 over the railway line and then turn right on the D.12 signposted La Clusaz. This takes you up the Borne river valley, a narrow, twisting road, through the villages of Petit-Bornand and Entremont. Continue on the D.12 to St. Jean-de-Sixt and then take the D.909 to Thônes. In Thônes watch for the tourist office and then go left, signposted Montremont 6km. At Tronchine (just outside Thônes) bear left again and park just before the hamlet of Montrement, opposite wooden signposts and a wide new jeep track going up on your right.

Directions

The signs say Boucle des Tervelles/Refuge du Larrieux and other directions, with numbers which correspond to a map sold at the tourist office. The jeep track goes up fairly steeply through light beech and coniferous wood with some nice views of the narrow valley below and the end of Mt. Lachat behind Thônes. Follow a sign to the right saying Boucle des Tervelles/Larrieux (30mins). The path is marked by red and yellow splashes and gets narrower and steeper as it winds up through beech woods for about 750m. It is quite a long, painful climb but the shade of the trees is very welcome on a hot summer's day; the path is well defined all the way so you can't go wrong. After 1hr 15mins you come out of the woods and are rewarded with a magnificent view of the Chaine des Aravis on the right with the Pointe Percée rearing above at the end. The path continues through intermittent woodland and crosses a stream (1hr 25mins). *The water from this stream tastes delicious, but that may be the result of climbing up steeply for over 700m!* After the stream the path goes across alpine pasture to a signpost (1hr 35mins).

Go left towards Larrieux, cross a dry stream bed and follow the yellow/red splashes over a low rise to the Refuge de Larrieux, alt. 1,532m (1hr 50mins). Just before the refuge there is a small memorial stone dedicated to Alpagiste Frank Hofer, 1876 - 1989, with the inscription "he has made Larrieux a meeting place, of which he was the warm and kind guardian". The building looks smart (restored in 1976) with a green galvanised roof and little wooden troughs and tables for picnickers, all rather twee; there are also glorious views of the surrounding mountains.

Refuge Larrieux (privately owned), tel. 50.02.19.52.
35 places in two dormitories (telephone ahead if you require a meal).
Open in season (mid-June to mid-September).

If you face the refuge as you arrive, you can see red/yellow splashes on the wall and a signpost which you should follow up on the right to the Col de Nantes (do not take the Circuit de Larrieux No. 21). Further up there is another sign indicating GR.96 Nord Vallée de Cruet/Sud Col de Nantets/Boucle de Lindion No. 19. You are climbing round a delightful green alpine bowl in the mountains (you can see that the Circuit de Larrieux is a path round this) and straight ahead of you is a beautiful view of La Tournette, one of the highest peaks in the region at alt. 2,351m.

Keep to the left at a T-junction 5mins after the refuge and follow the red/yellow signs carefully. The climb is medium steep with lovely views back down into the grassy, green bowl with the refuge and the Chaine des Aravis behind. You come to a ridge at the top (2hrs 20mins) and find there is quite

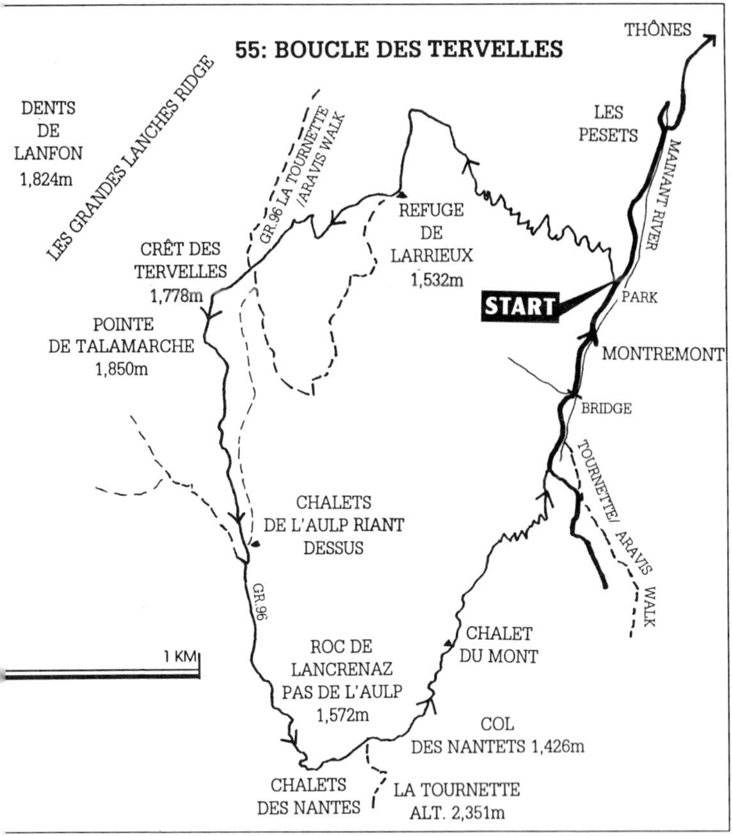

a drop the other side down to an ugly square man-made watering place for cattle, lined with blue plastic. The path goes left behind the hump of the Crêt des Tervelles, alt. 1,778m, and then down and up again marked with splashes, to a col where there are more signposts. Go straight on up the slope, indicated Boucle des Tervelles/Chalets de l'Aulp Riant Dessus (2hrs 30mins); the path to the right goes down into a shallow valley, where you can see three ugly blue plastic ponds, to Lindion/ Gîte d'Alpage; the path on the left goes to the Chalets de Talamarche. This is quite an important cross-roads where the GR.96 and the Tour du Massif Tournette Aravis path comes up from Le Lindion and stays with you to the Col des Nantets.

There is now a climb of about 150m to the Pointe de Talamarche, which is part of Les Grandes Lanches ridge. Follow the white/red GR signs which are not always easy to see. Go left at a T-junction (2hrs 45mins) - there is a white/red cross to the right which means do not go that way. You are now on the bumpy, wide, rocky ridge of Pointe de Talamarche, alt. 1,850m. Go straight on at a cairn down into a short shallow depression and then up again; through the trees to the right you catch your first glimpse of Lake Annecy and the jagged peaks of the Dents de Lanfon (they do look like teeth!) before arriving at the top of the Talamarche where there are more extensive views including the Tournette, the Chaine des Aravis and Mont Blanc to the east (3hrs). As you leave the top and go round the corner of the Pointe you look down the other side into an attractive, long wide alpine valley with the Chalets de l'Aulp Riant Dessus in the middle; beyond is the Pas de l'Aulp which you have to cross on the way down to the Col des Nantets.

Walk down into the valley, following the white/red GR splashes towards the signposts you can see opposite the chalets where another path goes off to the right (3hrs 20mins). Follow the signpost which says Boucle des Tervelles/Pas de l'Aulp/Col des Nantets/Montremont. You are now on a jeep track to the Chalets de l'Aulp Riant Dessus where in summer there is a big herd of cows. 5mins later, just before a corner which leads down to the barns, go straight on a narrow grassy path. There is no sign here but further on there is a GR mark on a rock; look back for an impressive view of the Talamarche Pointe and the path you have taken through the valley. You are on an open, grassy path which goes gently up, through a fence, over the Roc de Lancrenaz, to the Pas de l'Aulp, alt. 1,580m (3hrs 45mins). From this col there is an impressive view of the southern end of Lake Annecy and the surrounding mountains, especially of the nearby Tournette. A rocky, airy path then winds down to the Chalets des Nantets far below and you have to watch your feet as you do some clambering over rocks. However, it is not technically difficult and the views on the way are spectacular. Still following the GR red/white splashes, the path drops 150m to the first chalet, alt. 1,440m, and then 5mins later goes above the Chalets des Nantets towards a low hump with an iron cross on top and a signpost beyond; this is the Col des Nantets, alt. 1,426m (4hrs), where there are signposts.

Go straight on down indicated Boucle des Tervelles and Montremont. You are now leaving the GR.96 which continues right to the Chalets de l'Aulp (one of the starting points for climbing La Tournette) and on to the Col de la Forclaz. Up ahead on the left you can see the Refuge de Larrieux which shows you have done a long semi-circle. Now follow blue signs and Walk No. 22 down through high scrub and then light beech and coniferous wood until you arrive at the Chalets du Mont which are set in an attractive open meadow (4hrs 25mins). Cross a stile and go down a narrow path with high banks, like an old water course. You get occasional glimpses of a stream at the bottom

La Tournette seen from Pointe de Talamache, Boucle de Tervelles

of a steep ravine on your right. The path becomes a wide spur covered with woodland and there are ravines each side. As the woodland thickens, the path gets narrower and steeper, winding down seemingly forever to a dry river bed (4hrs 55mins). At a big barn there is a road going off up to the right signposted Tour de La Tournette 6hrs 30mins. (This is the Tour du Massif Tournette Aravis circle walk.) Turn down left at the next T-junction (more signs here) and you come to the tarmac road, where you cross the river and walk through the hamlet of Montremont till you arrive at your car (5hrs 15mins).

Remarks: One feels that having made the long slog up through the woods it is a pity to have to go back down again a few hours later! - of course it is possible to stay overnight in the Refuge Larrieux (telephone first to make a reservation). This is a wonderfully satisfying walk in a beautifully unspoilt area where you do not see a single ski-lift all day; the views over Lake Annecy and La Tournette mountain are spectacular.

56: LA ROCHE PARNAL - Alt. 1,896 metres
(Aravis/Bornes region)

Difficulty:	Difficult - there is one spot where you have to climb round a rock face hanging on to a chain, putting your feet on iron spikes - not for anyone suffering from vertigo.
Time:	4hrs (+ 45mins if you go to the summit).
Height gain:	522m (724m if you go to the summit).
Maps:	Editions Didier & Richard IGN No.3 Massifs du Chablais Faucigny & Genevois 1:50,000. Cartes IGN 3430 ET Top 25 La Clusaz/Grand-Bornand 1:25,000.
Depart from:	Le Chesnet (Orange) - 1,172m.
Signposting:	Adequate - yellow splashes plus some red/white GR markings.

How to get there (from Geneva)

Take the motorway direction Chamonix and then the A.41 direction Annecy, exiting La Roche-sur-Foron (first exit). (ALTERNATIVELY go through Annemasse and take the D.907 direction Taninges/Samoëns. At the village of Bonne, about 8km from Annemasse, turn right on the N.503 to La Roche-sur-Foron.) At La Roche-sur-Foron look for the D.2 direction Orange. Do not turn left into the village of Orange but continue straight on the V.6 Chemin de Chesnet (also signposted Chalets de Balme) and continue on till the road ends at a car park. There is a sign saying Chalets de Balme 1hr.

Directions

Take the wide stony jeep track going steeply up through fir and deciduous wood, following yellow splashes and ignoring any paths branching off. Where there has been a lot of tree-felling, there is a beautiful view on the right of the impressive rock wall of the Montagne de Sous-Dine. After about 20mins go up left at a fork (the path to the right is where you will return) following the yellow flashes on rocks and tree trunks.The path narrows and goes in and out of the woods on the side of a ravine with the Flan river rushing below. To the right is the Sous-Dine, to the left the rocky edifice of the Sur Cou, alt. 1,809m, and ahead is the Roche Parnal, alt. 1,896m, looking rather formidable! *These rocky, limestone mountains, the first range of the Alps rising abruptly from the fertile Geneva plain, are particularly impressive - the pitted, light grey rocks make a sharp contrast to the intense green of the woods and fields.* You come out onto the open hillside and continue on the path till you go through a fence and arrive at the Chalets de Balme (1hr) with tables outside and refreshments available in summer.

At the chalet go left following the sign on the wall indicating Circuit de Balme/Col de Cou (red/white GR markings on a stone on this path). 5mins later go straight up the steep grassy hill in front signposted Col de Freu 45mins, still following yellow markings (the main path to the left is marked Circuit de Balme). At the top you go through a stile and are at the Col de Sur Cou; take time to admire the numerous peaks you can see from this viewpoint: (from left to right) the solitary Môle, the Pic de Marcelly above Taninges and, on the horizon between the Pointe d'Andey and the nearby towering cliffs of the Rochers de Leschaux, the serrated teeth-like peaks of the Dents du Midi - an unforgettable panorama! There is also a sweeping view down into a valley, sprinkled in springtime with thousands of buttercups and marsh marigolds where melting snow at altitude causes streamlets to flow through the rich green grass.

Bear up to the right still following yellow splashes, towards the sheer, smooth rock face of the Roche Parnal. At first the path goes through fir trees and is somewhat boggy if it has been raining, but it later becomes defined and rocky as it curls round the base of the mountain. There is an iron cross nailed to the rock (1hr 30mins) which commemorates a young lad who fell here on 8 January 1938. *It makes one reflect on the risks people take - at that time of the year the path was probably covered in snow and it would certainly have been a dangerous walk to have undertaken.* There are red/white GR signs on the rock face which is sheer with black granite veins scaling the surface. As you start to climb to the Col de Freu the path becomes steep and rocky; at times you have to watch your footholds and you need both hands to grip the rocks but it is not technically difficult though it can be quite slippery after rainfall.

When you go through a stile at the Col de Freu, 1,694m (1hr 45mins), there is a glorious view down into the unspoilt Champ Laitier valley with the long tree-covered hump of the Montagne des Frêtes, part of the famous Plateau des Glières. Beyond are the jagged peaks of the Chaine des Aravis culminating in the Pointe Percée and the Mont Blanc range on the horizon.

DETOUR (add around 45mins): Although not marked on the map there is a path to the right of the col which goes up to the top and a borne (reference marker), alt. 1,896m. It is quite steep and airy but worth the effort as the panoramic view from the summit is supreme - to the south the entire Alps, and to the north the Geneva plain, the lake and Jura range on the horizon. Return the same way and then cut across when you see the path going round the base of the hill to the Col de Sable.

OTHERWISE: Take the defined narrow path which curls round the south

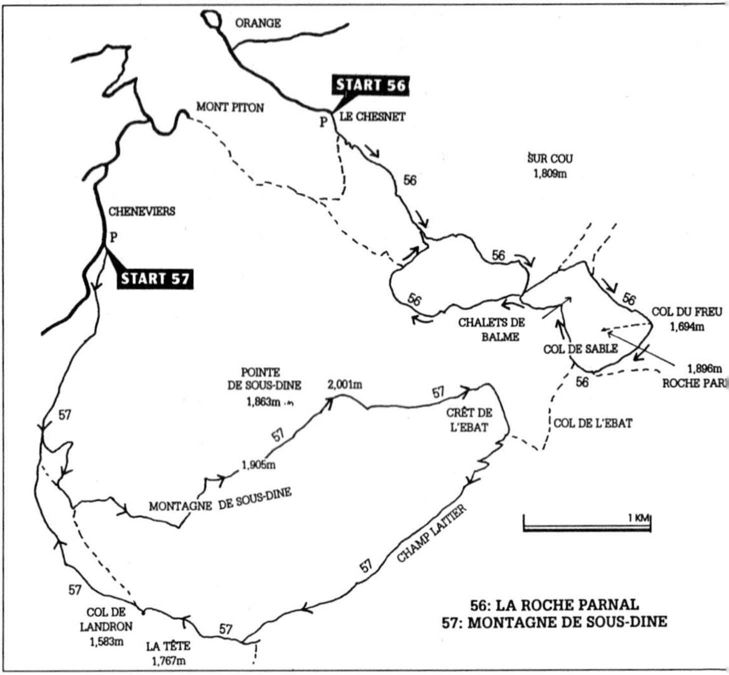

side of the mountain to the Col de Sable (do not take the one you can see going straight on round the base of the Sous-Dine). Just before you reach the col there is a path going up the mountain to the right - this is another way to the summit, but the path peters out after about 10mins. *In springtime the flowers are particularly striking and include the yellow vanilla and early purple orchids, alpine daffodils, trumpet gentians, clumps of pansies, harebells, forget-me-nots and creamy pasque anemones.*

At the Col de Sable (2hrs 30mins) you go through a fence and are now back round to the north face of the Roc Parnal. You are rewarded with a beautiful view right over the end of the lake with the Salève in the foreground and the Jura beyond. 5mins from the col you come to a chain which goes round a large rock with iron bars to put your feet on - there is quite a precipitous drop. This is only for people who do not suffer from vertigo but it is not difficult. The only scary thing is that you cannot see in advance where to put your feet and at one spot there is rather a long gap between the iron bars - long legs help! If you do not like it retrace your steps back round the mountain. You can see the path going down to the Chalets de Balme, past

View of the Sous-Dine from the Roche Parnal

a small hut which used to be a refuge but has now fallen into disrepair.

Pass in front of the Chalets de Balme (3hrs 10mins) and take the jeep track down (GR red/white signs and yellow splashes). This is easy walking down through intermittent woodland to start, passing a memorial stone on the right, dedicated to a François Chappot who died 11 June 1989 (one wonders how as this is not at a dangerous spot). Further down, the woods become denser and you cross some streams till you join the original path back to the car park (4hrs).

Remarks: In summer this is a popular spot though most people go no further than the meadows around the Chalets de Balme. The sweeping views of the Alps, the lake and surrounding countryside are unsurpassed. Because this area is of rocky limestone formation it has not been disfigured by ugly ski-lifts! The Roche Parnal is quite exposed with little shade so a very hot day is not recommended - however, watch out for patches of snow which linger on the north side. The spring flowers, especially on the south side, are abundant. Note: this walk can be done in either direction - some people prefer to go up the rock on the iron bars rather than down, the advantage being better visibility.

57: MONTAGNE DE SOUS-DINE - (See map P274)
Alt. 2,001 metres (Aravis/Bornes region)

Difficulty:	Medium/difficult but should not be done by anyone suffering from vertigo - there is a chain at one spot for scrambling round a rock face.
Time:	6hrs 15mins.
Height gain:	1,000 metres.
Depart from:	Cheneviers (La Roche-sur-Foron) - 1,090 metres.
Maps:	Editions Didier & Richard IGN No.3 Massifs du Chablais Faucigny & Genevois 1:50,000. Cartes IGN 3430 ET Top 25 La Clusaz/Grand-Bornand 1:25,000.
Depart from:	Chenviers
Signposting:	Adequate - follow yellow and red splashes.

How to get there (from Geneva)

Take the motorway direction Chamonix and then the A.41 direction Annecy, exiting La Roche-sur-Foron (first exit). (ALTERNATIVELY go through Annemasse and take the D.907 direction Taninges/Samoëns. At the village of Bonne, about 8km from Annemasse, turn right on the N.503 to La Roche-sur-Foron.) At La Roche follow the D.2 signposted to Orange. Do not turn left towards the village of Orange but continue on the road and then take the C.16 left to Mont Piton/Cheneviers. Drive through the hamlet of Cheneviers (there is a nice café/restaurant here called the Mont Piton) and continue on until the end of the road where there is a large parking area.

Directions

At the car park there is a signpost indicating Circuit de Sous-Dine/Col de l'Enclave/Champ Laitier where a wide jeep track starts gently upwards under shady deciduous and coniferous trees. After about 5mins follow a sign right to Circuit de Sous-Dine with a yellow splash on a tree. 10mins later turn right at a T-junction (red splash on a tree) and continue on a wider jeep track with yellow splashes (do not follow the red ones). Cross a forestry road (30mins) and continue straight. *Note: the white blobs with a red line through them are the signs for the wood-cutters only - they are not directional signs. There is a lot of forestry and construction of new roads in this area so some yellow splashes may disappear in the future.* Where there is a sign 18 on a tree (40mins) take the left fork following the yellow splashes. As you continue upwards there are tantalising glimpses through the trees of the littoral plain

A bouquetin (ibex) on the Sous-Dine

with Lac Léman (Lake Geneva) beyond.

10mins later you come to signposts - Sous-Dine par le Monthieu up to the left and Sous-Dine par l'Enclave up to the right. Take the left-hand fork towards Sous-Dine par le Monthieu. Here is an example where logging has modified the path as, after a few minutes, you come out onto a new stretch of wide stony road where you turn left. Ignore any paths branching off and follow the yellow splashes on the main track which curls around the mountain fairly flat through tall fir trees. When you eventually come out into the open (1hr) you have a magnificent view of the plain below, the Salève (the mountain just behind Geneva), the town of La Roche-sur- Foron and part of Lac Léman with the Jura mountains on the horizon.

The path becomes pleasantly flat as it circles round the mountain through trees and open spaces, and you can see the precipitous rocky mass of the Sous-Dine rearing up in front of you. 15mins later take the sign to the right to Sous-Dine/Monthieu (yellow arrow on rock) when you come to a clearing. The path starts to climb up. Be careful - after another 15mins (1hr 30mins), where the woods start to thicken again, do not follow the main jeep track round to the left but take a narrow track straight ahead. There is a cairn of stones and a yellow arrow but no sign. The path is dark through tall, dark, coniferous forest (it seems as if one is walking back the way one came only much higher up). *We came across a very high ant-hill by the side of the path crawling with ants going about their business. Ant-hills are fairly unusual in the Alps but are frequent in the nearby Jura mountains.* The path bears round over scree for about 5mins and you have open views again with the rocky crests of Sous-Dine up on the right.

Suddenly you come to an exposed corner where if you went straight on you would go over the edge! (1hr 50mins). Take time here to admire the plain below and the splendid view of the adjacent Roche Parnal mountain with the Chalets de Balme refuge nestling in the valley. Beyond are the peaks of the Chablais region. The path bears round to the right and becomes narrow and rocky as it starts to climb quite steeply up the open mountainside - this is not for anyone suffering from vertigo as sometimes you need both hands to clamber over the rocks. Over on the left you have a spectacular view of the Môle with the jagged peaks of the Dent d'Oche in the background. The path goes through a narrow rocky gully to the Col de Montieu and then slackens off as you walk through knee-high vegetation and lovely mountain flowers in a fold in the hillside before going up the shoulder and along a crest with a dramatic drop on one side (happily not always visible from where you are walking). The path undulates over grassy terrain with occasional stunted firs and flat limestone rocks.

The Sous-Dine is a flattish, rock-pitted, limestone mountain so there is no dramatic summit. You reach a wide, grassy area (2hrs 55mins) where there is a yellow arrow on a flat grey rock pointing back the way you have come and a red arrow pointing down the other side saying Landron (this is an alternative shorter path off the mountain down to the Col de Landron). Continue upwards for 5mins to a small stone cairn which is on the edge of the mountain and is a good place for a picnic (3hrs). From here you get one of the best views in the Chablais region - it is fascinating to pick out and name the dozens of surrounding peaks; in the Jura to the north, the Alps to the south and the Thorens-Glières plateau on the immediate left.

Continue along the ridge crest on the path which is sometimes indistinct with occasional red markings. The crest is rocky and indented and it looks like there are obvious short cuts but it is safer to keep to the path as there are unexpected narrow crevices in the rocks. As you progress the path becomes more difficult as you start picking your way down over small crevices and large rocks into a narrow rocky defile. At one stage there is a drop down a rock face with a sort of stirrup to put your foot into. If you do not care for this you can descend more easily by climbing down a rocky ledge on the left. *When we did this walk in high summer we came face to face with an inquisitive bouquetin (ibex) who did not seem the least bit timid. He seemed to regard our scrambling efforts with amusement and kept us company for quite some time.*

Continue following the red splashes downwards. The path is not technically difficult but you are climbing around boulders so care is needed.

Finally you have to lower yourself across a sheer rock face by a chain. The best way to do it is to grab hold of the chain, face into the rock and move your feet along the cracks, like rappelling. These chains are only about 3m long and there is no steep drop below. After this the worst is over and you can see the path below which goes round the other side of the mountain from the Col de l'Ebat. Make for this path by going down the slope as you please because there is no defined track; this area is called the Crêt de l'Ebat.

Turn right at the bottom and you walk into a gloriously unspoilt valley called the Champ Laitier. The coniferous trees on the hillside to the left seem to sweep right down to the valley floor, the dark forest green giving way to the emerald green of the alpine pastures; a stream meanders through and there are no ugly buildings to mar the tranquil scene. On the right are the dramatic rocky slopes of the Sous-Dine. *But this lovely valley has known death and destruction. The reason there are so few farms is because they were burnt down during the war by the Germans. This is one of the famous Thoren-Glières valleys where the last of the gallant French Resistance bands held out against the enemy. On the forest covered hillside are hidden bunkers and caves where the soldiers were relentlessly hunted out over many months and at great cost of life.*

1hr 20mins from the top you arrive at a rough jeep track which goes down along the right-hand side the valley (4hrs 20mins). Walking along this delightful path, which is flattish and skirts the valley side, you get a good view of the Parmelan mountain which dominates Annecy; on the horizon to the left is the dramatic summit of the Tournette, the highest peak in the area.*There is an isolated farm/chalet along the path. When open, kindly shepherds will let you renew your water supplies as there is little shade on this hike and being a limestone mountain all the streams run underground.* If you walk down this valley in mid August you will notice that the slopes are covered with glorious purple thistles. The path leaves the valley and skirts up right past a solitary barn.

After roughly 15mins keep straight on the path going uphill towards the pass (left bears down into the valley) passing a barn set back on the right. It is then a short grind till you reach the Col de Landron, alt. 1,583m, though there is no signpost saying you have reached the top! (4hrs 40mins). To the left is an interesting peak called La Tête, alt. 1,767m, and you get your first views of the coastal plain again as you have walked right round the mountain. The path continues through open spaces and woodland - there is a big sign announcing that you are in the protected area of the Fôret Dom de la Haute Filière and just after the sign a path up to your right which says Sous-Dine; this is the shorter way down from the red arrow at the top. Way over down on the left you can see the road up to the Plateau de Glières.

The path passes a high rock face and gets stonier and wider as it goes down fairly steeply through cool forest. Keep to the main path till you get back to the signs Sous-Dine par l'Enclave/Sous-Dine par Le Monthieu. Continue down the same way as you came up (6hrs 15mins).

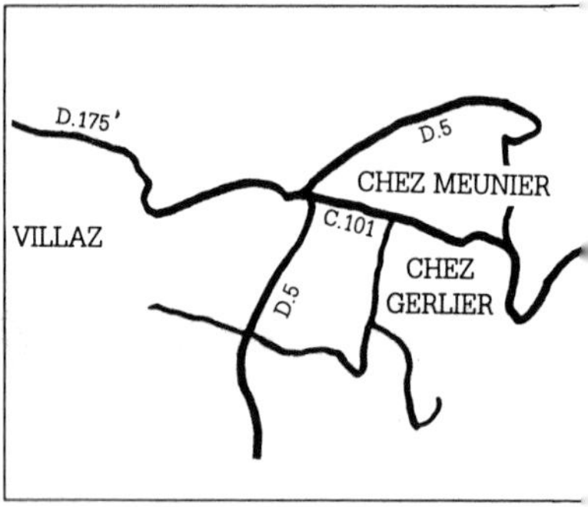

Remarks: This is one of my favourite walks as the views are so extensive. The first range of Chablais mountains rising out of the Lac Léman plain give contrasting views of undulating green fields and the lake, stretching from Geneva to the start of the Rhône valley, with the long line of Jura mountains on one side and the varied jagged peaks of the Alps on the other. Although I have only done this walk in high summer I would suggest that a better time is in spring or autumn, as there is little shade and no streams where you can quench your thirst. This is a good area for seeing bouquetins (ibex), the agile alpine sheep with their long serrated horns. The Sous-Dine is a limestone mountain, pitted with rocks and crevices, not unlike the Parmelan near Annecy. The difference is that it is not so well known and even at the height of the summer season you will see few people.

58: LE PARMELAN (ANNECY) - Alt. 1,835 metres
(Aravis/Bornes region)

Difficulty:	Medium, but do not go up the Grand Montoir if you suffer from vertigo; there is a way round.
Time:	4hrs.
Height gain:	635 metres.
Maps:	Edition Didier & Richard IGN No.2 Massifs des Bornes-Bauges 1:50,000. Cartes IGN 3431 OT Top 25 Lac d'Annecy 1:25,000 (only shows part of walk).and/or Cartes IGN 3430 serie bleu Annecy (nord-est). Thorens-Glières 1:25,000 (the serie bleu series are being phased out so difficult to find).
Depart from:	Above the village of Villaz - 1,200m.
Signposting:	Excellent all the way round; follow yellow splashes.

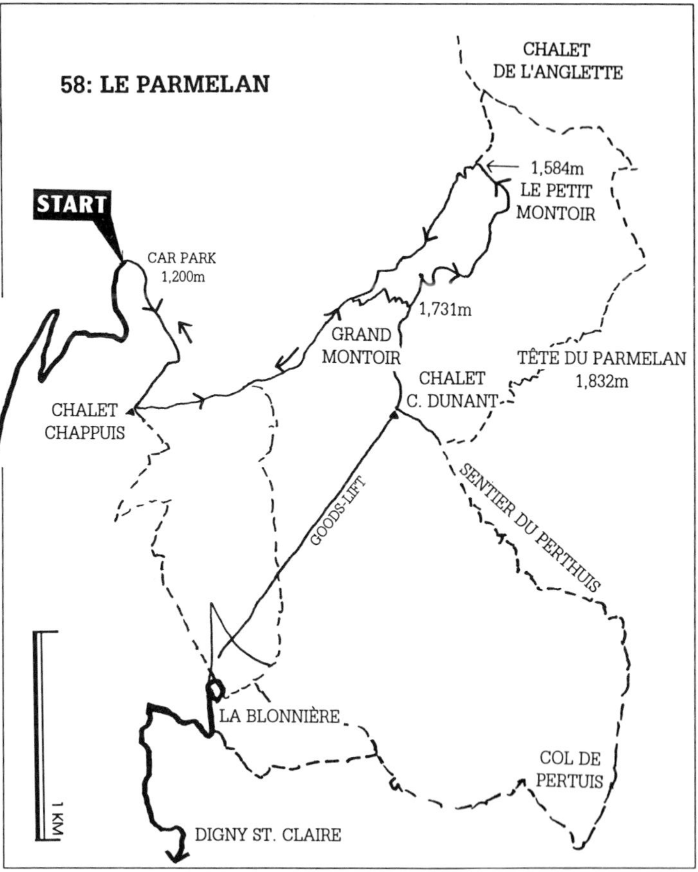

How to get there (from Geneva)

Take the motorway direction Chamonix and then the A.41 signposted Annecy/Grenoble/Lyon. Exit Annecy Nord and follow all signs to Annecy-Le-Vieux and then Thônes on the D.16. Look for the D.5 to Thorens/Villaz and then a sign saying Villaz which takes you to the centre of the village. Follow the Parmelan sign up to the D.5 where you turn left and then shortly after right up a small road, C.101 signposted Parmelan. The road goes on for 5km before ending in a parking area. ALTERNATIVELY take the N.201 direction Annecy which goes into France through the new Bardonnex customs (by-passing St. Julien-en-Genevois). Follow all signs to Annecy and then Annecy-Le-Vieux from where you continue as above.

Directions

At the end of the parking area there is a notice board with a map showing the different walks on the Parmelan. Take the wide stony track beside it bearing upwards through tall firs. After 5mins turn right at a sign on a tree to Chalet Chappuis and continue on a wide, fairly flattish path, winding round the base of the mountain. The Chalet Chappuis (15mins) serves drinks and snacks and is splendidly situated in an open area which juts out of the mountain. You get a magnificent view straight down the Thônes valley framed by the mountains around Lake Annecy. It is a delightful place, a popular spot to linger and enjoy the surroundings before continuing.

Follow the sign Boucle de Parmelan on a narrow path still going upwards through woods. Turn up left to Refuge de Parmelan at a signpost (30mins) which indicates straight on to Parking La Blonnière - *this is an alternative way up (see below).* The path curls round the mountain becoming wider and then narrower again. There is a sign on a tree saying Club Alpin Français Refuge de Parmelan Pointe de Vue remarquable 1hr. A few minutes later you have your first close view of the high cliff face of the Parmelan and you wonder how you are ever going to get up it!

Still in shady woodland, you arrive at a choice of direction (50mins). Straight ahead is the Petit Montoir, an easy path following the contour of the mountain, or you can go right up the Grand Montoir. The path to the right goes steeply up the face of the mountain. It is not technically difficult and there are chains or an iron rail to hang on to, but it is not for anyone who suffers from vertigo (there is a sign here saying it is not dangerous but vertiginous). If you are not afraid of heights take this path as it is an exciting climb up the rock face. The going is rocky but well trodden and there is a steep, treeless drop on one side.

After 25mins of climbing (1hr 15mins) you reach the shoulder at a signpost indicating that you have rejoined the path via the Petit Montoir. Turn right and continue up the shoulder. You now appreciate that the top of this mountain is an incredible limestone plateau of long corrugated rock fissures, dotted with stunted firs and criss-crossed by narrow, deep crevices and cavernous holes; this is a weird lunar landscape, which was a glacier thousands of years ago. It is dangerous to walk over if you do not stick to the paths or the fog comes down. On the horizon rises the glistening Mt. Blanc range with the renowned Plateau de Glières in the foreground (where the last of the French Resistance fighters held out in World War II). Behind is the Annecy valley, with the Pont de Caille bridge clearly visible, and beyond Lac Léman (Lake Geneva) and the Jura mountains.

Continue on the well-trodden rocky path and suddenly, over a slight rise, you come to the Refuge Camille Dunant, alt. 1,825m, belonging to the French Alpine Club (2hrs15mins). Built in 1883 it is large and rather ugly with a corrugated iron roof. There are actually two buildings, the newer one being an annexe with additional dormitory accommodation.

Refuge du Parmelan (Club Alpin Français), Digny St. Claire, 74230 Thônes, tel. 50.27.29.45. Open from 26 June to 12 September (weekends until 10 October). The refuge serves a variety of food and drink and can accommodate 50 people in three dormitories.

This is the summit of the rocky Parmelan and a favourite spot for picnickers.

There is a breathtaking panoramic view over the town of Annecy and the mountains surrounding the lake, with a glimpse of the end of the lake through the Col de Bluffy. Straight ahead are the serrated teeth-like cliffs of the Dents de Lanfon with the high peak of the Tournette rearing up beyond. Over on the left are the snow covered peaks of the Mont Blanc range and below is the winding green Thônes valley; no wonder it is crowded with people on summer weekends!

Further on from the refuge there is a sign to La Blonnière par le Col de Pertuis 3hrs/Grotte de l'Enfer 1hr/Chalet de l'Anglette 1hr 30mins/Villaz 2hrs 45mins. *La Blonnière par le Col de Pertuis is a longer way round to the alternative start of this walk. I have not done it but am told that it is quite difficult. If you have time take this path and then branch off after about 10mins towards the Grotte de l'Enfer (clearly marked). The Grotte de l'Enfer is difficult to find and the path, though clear at first, gets tricky further on. However, if you persevere along the path for about 15mins you get a good idea of the glacial type terrain and you can peer into the awesome limestone holes and crevices. In spring and summer there is an abundance of wild flowers in the patches of fertile soil between the rocks. It is then wiser to retrace your steps to the refuge.*

Retrace your steps to the signpost Grand Montoir/Petit Montoir facile (meaning easy) and go straight on towards Petit Montoir on a stony path round the back of the mountain. It is attractive and well defined, snaking through the serrated rocks and fissures of this limestone region, dotted with shrubs and small fir trees, but watch your feet in places! This path is longer than the Grand Montoir as it goes right round the Parmelan cliffs. At a sign to Chalet de l'Anglette right and Villaz straight, go straight on over the col (crest) when you will see the Annecy valley again and the path ahead going right along the hill.

Continue along the front of the mountain with the daunting, rocky face of the Parmelan on your left and the valley down on your right. It is a delightful, undulating path and a welcome change from the steep haul up the rock face, though there are occasional steep drops where the mountain falls away on your right. There are numerous hidden caves in the rock face and at one spot you notice a complete change of temperature (more noticeable on a hot day), presumably due to cold air emanating from the deep rock fissures. The path goes into cool fir woods back to the signpost indicating left up to the Grand Montoir (3hrs). You are now on the path you came up. Be careful to take the right fork to Chalet Chappuis (not left to La Blonnière) and continue back to the car park (4hrs).

Remarks: There are two ways up this mountain, one from the forestry road beyond the village of Villaz and the other from above the village of La Blonnière. I have chosen the way up from Villaz as it is easier to find, there is more parking space and the path is less steep. This walk is a classic and a must if you are staying in the Annecy region as the panoramic views are breathtaking. It is extremely popular as the local population love to traipse up on weekends and picnic at the top by the refuge. So beware weekends in high summer as you will find the mountain swarming with people! If you have the time, stay at the refuge and watch the sun rise at dawn, but remember you will not be alone!

59: CASCADE D'ANGON (Talloires) - Alt. 781 metres
(Aravis/Bornes region)

Difficulty:	Easy though there is a short steep path to start.
Time:	2hrs 45mins.
Height gain:	300 metres.
Maps:	Editions Didier & Richard IGN No.2 Massifs des Bornes-Bauges 1:50,000. Cartes IGN 3431 OT Top 25 Lac d'Annecy 1:25,000.
Depart from:	Talloires on Lake Annecy.
Signposting:	Excellent - you can't go wrong!

How to get there (from Geneva)

Take the motorway direction Chamonix and then the A41 signposted Annecy/Grenoble/Lyon. Exit Annecy centre and follow all signs to the D.909 Veyrier Le Lac/Talloires which will lead you to the road along the eastern shore of the lake. ALTERNATIVELY take the N.201 direction Annecy which goes through the new Bardonnex customs (by-passing St. Julien-en-Genevois). Follow all signs to Annecy and the D.909 as above. Continue on the lake road,

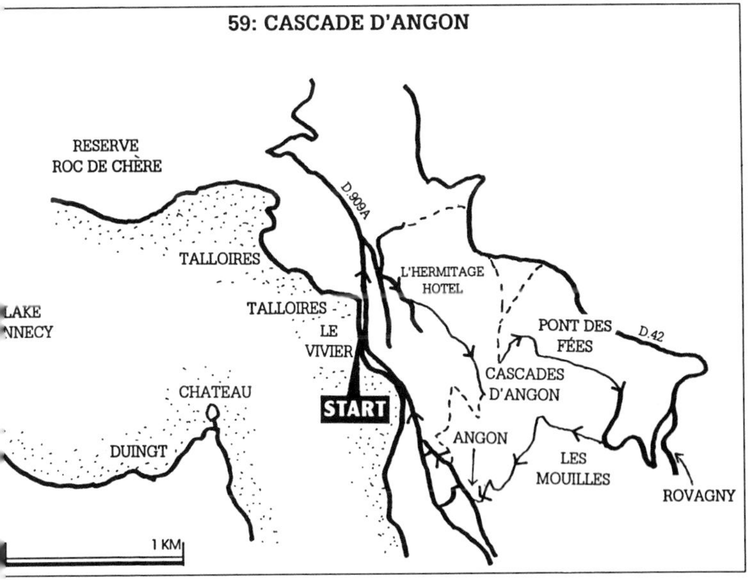

direction Talloires, and just after a sign right to the village you will see two signs left Cascade d'Angon and Hôtel l'Hermitage - there are tennis courts further on the right. Park near here or, if there is no room, continue to the lakeside where there is more parking space.

Directions

Go back to the signs and turn right on the Chemin Vivier. Walk up the road passing the Hôtel l'Hermitage and take a wide stony track to the left, signposted Pont des Fées and Rovagny. The track goes up steeply at first through delightful deciduous woods and then levels off as it bears round the contour of the hill; ignore the path going down right signposted Angon. You come to a sign to Cascade d'Angon (45mins) and an iron barrier. Go through the barrier on a defined path which goes along the edge of a deep wooded gully; there is an iron railing on one side for protection as you often have to bend under the overhanging rock of the cliff face on the other. There are two beautiful waterfalls; the first one is smaller and the path goes underneath it, which can be a rather watery experience if there has been lots of rain. It continues to the second waterfall which is very dramatic as it falls straight off the cliff into the narrow, rocky gully far below. The last few metres to the waterfall is tricky as the path goes up over slippery rocks, although there is a chain and a barrier. As you walk around the gully there are lovely views back over the end of the lake.

Retrace your steps to the gate and the wide track, where you turn right and continue upwards; there is a lovely view here of the château on the promontory jutting out from the village of Duingt across the lake. Take a turning to the right (1hr 15mins) signposted Pont des Fées and Rovagny. You cross over the two streams above the waterfalls, the first one on a wooden slatted bridge where the water flows enticingly over small rocks and the second, the Pont des Fées (fairy bridge), on a more substantial edifice, with the river flowing fiercely below through a deep gully.

After the bridges turn up left (right goes to the edge of the gorge) where the path comes out into beautiful meadowland which in springtime is a carpet of flowers amid long waving grass - purple wild geraniums, bright blue cornflowers, yellow vetch, golden buttercups, tall white daisies and fluffy cow parsley creating a kaleidoscope of colour - a natural place to stop and take refreshment (1hr 30mins) while you admire the colour and scenery; you can see Lake Annecy through the trees and the Taillefer ridge with the Roc des Boeufs behind (Walk No. 61).

A few minutes later you come to the road to Les Mouilles and Rovagny. Turn right, continue till you come to a corner at Les Mouilles and turn sharp right (1hr 40mins), signposted Angon. Follow the defined path which has a tiny stream flowing on the right before it goes through delightful meadowland (the track becomes somewhat undefined amid the waving grass and flowers) and then into woodland where the track is again clear with red splashes. The path is rocky, going down fairly steeply on the other side of the waterfall gorge; be careful if it has been raining as the rocks are slippery.

The track comes out at the village of Argon (there is a big building in front which looks like a school). Turn right and cross the "waterfall" river (proper name Grenant but it doesn't sound so nice!) - look at the huge stone mill wheel to the left which looks as if it is still in use. The road hits the D.909 where you turn right and walk back to your car along the lakeside - this is very pretty much of the way back on a little path right beside the water (2hrs 45mins).

Remarks: Although this walk is short it is well worth doing and perfect for taking visitors and children, who will enjoy the dramatic waterfalls. The contrast between woodland and meadows is delightful and makes this a very satisfying expedition - the views of Lake Annecy and surrounding peaks are spectacular! It is worth going into the charming village of Talloires afterwards and sitting at one of the lakeside restaurants - some of them very upmarket (see Talloires). Note: the road through the village is one way.

60: LA TOURNETTE (Annecy) - Alt. 2,35l metres
(Aravis/Bornes region)

Difficulty:	This is a difficult walk as there is a vertiginous scree slope to cross and then a chain plus two ladders to negotiate to reach the final summit. Nevertheless, hundreds of walkers do it every year.
Time:	6hrs 30mins.
Height gain:	1,024 metres.
Maps:	Editions Didier & Richard IGN No. 2 Massifs des Bornes-Bauges 1:50,000. Cartes IGN 3431 OT Top 25 Lac d'Annecy 1:25,000.
Depart from:	Montmin - 1,094 metres.
Signposting:	Excellent - follow green splashes. The path is defined all the way and you can't go wrong.

How to get there (from Geneva)
Take the motorway direction Chamonix and then the A.41 signposted Annecy/Grenoble/Lyon. Exit Annecy centre and follow all signs to the D.909 Veyrier Le Lac/Talloires which will lead you to the lake road. Just before Talloires look for the D.42 to the left, which is a narrow rather windy road going over the Col de la Forclaz (a popular spot for tourists in summer as the view down the Annecy lake is magical) and on to the village of Montmin. At Montmin park your car beside the church.

ALTERNATIVELY take the N.201 direction Annecy which goes through the new Bardonnex customs (by-passing St. Julien-en-Genevois). Follow all signs to Annecy and the D.909 Veyrier Le Lac/Talloires and proceed as above.

Directions
Near the church there is a board which says La Tournette Circuit No.14 - 4 hrs. Cross the village street and go up the tarmac road as indicated between two old houses. It degenerates into a jeep track, rather like an English country lane, with steep banks of vegetation and occasional chalets. As you walk up you can see down left into the valley and over to the Col de la Forclaz. Take the signpost to the right saying Tournette, following the green splashes which accompany you to the summit. You pass through a gate on to a pleasant stony path going up medium steep through intermittent woodland, getting rockier as you climb higher, with steepish wooded slopes of beech and fir on either side. In front there are daunting views of the massive La Tournette mountain in front.

The path comes out of the woodland and bears left across a dry river bed (30mins) levelling out for a short while before going back into stunted beech woods and climbing again medium steep. As you come of out the woods for the last time (50mins) you can see way over on the right the huge cliffs of the Pointe de La Beccaz, and on the left the Pointe de la Bajulaz with La Tournette behind. The path becomes stonier and then rockier as you pass a small cave (55mins). *When we walked here in October we saw a group of three female bouquetins (ibex) on the mountainside opposite underneath some rocks - they did not seem the slightest bit concerned to see four humans crashing up the path.*

After meandering through a wide rocky gully and over a stile (presumably to keep the sheep in and not the bouquetins) the path starts to steepen again. You come to the Rochers de Charvet, alt. 1,645m, a grassy hump and lookout point with a good view back the way you have come and down to the village and church of Montmin where you left the car (1hr 30mins). From here you can see the path going right up to the col; it almost doubles back along the gully higher up the mountain, steepening as you climb to the ridge, crossing a dry river bed (1hr 50mins) and passing through stunted alder bushes. Down on the right are the ruins of the Chalet du Lars which look as if they are now being used as sheep pens. Here you get your first view of Lake Annecy in the distance and you feel you have come a long way!

On the grassy ridge, alt. 1,899m (2hrs), there is a good view of the other side of the mountain with the valley going towards the town of Thônes. The Pointe de la Beccaz towers to the right but turn left along the ridge towards the Pointe de la Bajulaz. Walk along this ridge, which is airy but not difficult or steep, culminating in the Pointe des Frêtes at 2,019m. You come to a sign which says Gîte pointing down to the right (2hrs 30mins).

There is an imposing wall of rock straight ahead but you can see the path bearing round to the left and going up over the ridge. Care should be taken here because although the path is defined it goes across a rather precipitous scree slope for about 15mins and you have to pick your way along fairly meticulously so that you do not slip.

You reach a col (pass) between the Pointe de la Bajulaz and La Tournette (3hrs). Now the green splashes you have been following diligently are joined by brown markings. The col is rather desolate and rocky and there are still another 160m to climb to the top. Take time to appreciate the view of Lake Annecy with, on the other side of the water, the smudged outlines of the Taillefer ridge, Roc des Boeufs and the Semnoz ridge beyond, the latter extending all the way along the lake to the town of Annecy. You can also see down to the Chalets d'Aulp and the path winding up the mountain - *this is one of the alternative ways to the summit and halfway up is the French Alpine Club Refuge de la Tournette.* Continue, following the green splashes,

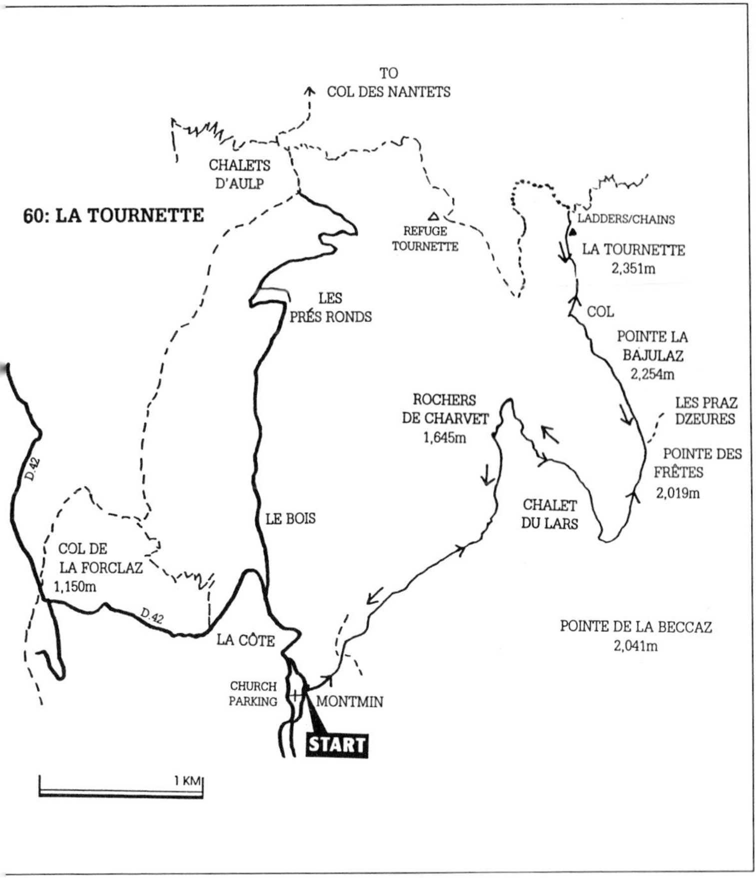

along a defined path which curls upwards round the mountain which is a jumble of magnificent rocks with numerous small crevices, caves and holes. In some places there are precipitous drops on the left but thankfully not too near the path! *In the autumn we saw mottled brown and white ptarmigan picking industriously at something tasty on the rocks but, like the bouquetins, they did not seem concerned by our approach.*

Turn right at a T-junction where there are arrows in all directions (3hrs 15mins) - the left path goes down to the Refuge de la Tournette and then to the Chalets d'Aulp. There is also a sign saying Fauteuil (armchair), referring

Pointe de la Bajulaz, La Tournette

to the rock perched on the summit of the mountain which from afar does look rather like an armchair. The path winds round the rock which has a cross inscribed on the face. It is dedicated to Jean-Pierre Dufour who died here on 16 August 1962 at the age of 22 years. *You come across such monuments to walkers who have tragically fallen on just about every altitude walk in the Haute Savoie. It is a tragic reminder that walking in the mountains can be a dangerous activity should the weather turn bad or there is a moment of inattention.* A few metres on there is a chain across a rock face, about 50m in length but not tricky to negotiate as there are plenty of footholds. It leads into a narrow chimney where there are two ladders (17 rungs on the last ladder), up to a flattish rocky area with a cross at the end - you have reached the summit! This is the obvious place to stop and have a picnic while admiring the fantastic mountain ranges in all directions plus the whole of Lake Annecy (4hrs).

There is no other way off this summit but to return down the ladders which I read with interest were installed in 1968. Retrace your steps the same way back to the car (6hrs 30mins).

Refuges:

Refuge de la Tournette (French Alpine Club), tel. 50/68 52 30
Refuge/Hôtel La Rosairy (privately owned), tel. 50/02 0026
Refuge Le Casset (privately owned), tel. 50/68 54 11

Remarks: La Tournette is the highest peak in the Annecy region and very popular with more experienced walkers. If you look at the map you can see that the summit can be reached from various starting points and it is possible to do a two-day circle staying in one of the refuges (see above for list). This is a tough walk but within the capabilities of any fit person not suffering from vertigo; it is worth the effort as the view from the summit is unforgettable. There is something very satisfying about achieving a challenging walk, especially as many people are hesitant to hang on to chains and clamber up ladders but are thrilled when they have done so! The fact that in summer there are often queues to get to the "fauteuil" shows that this is one of the popular "Alpine classics". If you want to do this walk and be relatively alone it is better to go during the week outside the busy months of July and August.

61: LE ROC DES BOEUFS - Alt. 1,335 metres

(Aravis/Bornes region)

Difficulty:	Medium as far as Entrevernes and then a steep climb to the Col de la Cochette.
Time:	6hrs 15mins.
Height gain:	885 metres.
Maps:	Editions Didier & Richard IGN No.2 Massifs des Bornes-Bauges 1:50,000. Cartes IGN 3431 OT Top 25 Lac d'Annecy 1:25,000.
Depart from:	Duingt (on Lake Annecy) - 450 metres.
Signposting:	Good - though not always obvious.

How to get there (from Geneva)

Take the motorway direction Chamonix and then the A41 motorway signposted Annecy/Grenoble/Lyon. Exit Annecy sud and follow all signs to Albertville. Take the N.508 which goes along the western shore of the lake till you get to the village of Duingt which is three-quarters of the way down where it narrows, with Talloires on the opposite shore. There is an attractive small château jutting out into the water. In the village take the first turning to the right after the church (there is a sign saying Grotte du Notre Dame du Lac/Taillefer). Follow this narrow road for above 200m till you come to a car park on the right and a sign to Notre Dame du Gorge. Park your car here.

Directions

Walk up the road from the car park and shortly you will see a number of wooden signs up on the right to Taillefer Panorama 45mins/Circuit Entrevernes 2hrs/Grotte du Notre Dame du Lac/Belvedere Saint Michel. This is the start of a pilgrimage to the grotto and on the left is the first of the stone shrines depicting the five Joyful, Sorrowful and Glorious Mysteries of the life of Christ. It is interesting to look at these shrines, and at the same time to admire the glorious view down to Duingt and over Lake Annecy, as you follow the stony path, obviously well used by pilgrims over the years. After the shrines, the path goes up left but continue straight on for a few metres to the huge grotto hewn out of the rock, called Notre Dame du Lac. Standing lonely amongst the boulders is a rather sad statue of the Virgin Mary with lots of plaques dotted about the rocks, thanking Our Lady for favours granted. There is also an inscription asking for protection against the enemy, dated 24 June 1940. *The building of grottoes to the Virgin Mary was very popular at the turn of the century and you will find them scattered about the Savoie area which has always been a bastion of Catholicism, in contrast to the Calvinism of its northern neighbour Geneva.*

Go back down and take the path (which is now on your right), where there are signs to Crêt du Taillefer/Crêt du Bourg 765m 1hr. This is an easy, well defined, medium steep climb through a reserve of Corsican pines and larches. After about 5mins of twisting path you come to a small circular glade with an imposing statue of the Archangel Michael crushing the devil with his foot. From here there is an impressive view down the lake all the way to the town of Annecy. *I think the devil looks more interesting than St. Michael whose face seems rather smug, with eyes hooded and peering over the lake, rather than at the devil whom he is meant to be killing!* This is where the pilgrims and Sunday strollers give up and walk back; there is a path on the left which goes down near to the lake at La Maladière where there is a way back to the start.

Keep to the main track going upwards through stunted woodland. Soon after you reach another viewpoint with a magnificent panorama to the left of the Dents de Lanfon with the Col des Frêtes on the other side of the lake. You are now walking along the wide Taillefer ridge which juts out into the lake so there are impressive watery views on both sides.

Ignore the path going down on the left (20mins) but continue up towards a clearing and a squat concrete borne (marker) at 638m. After 15mins there is a signpost right to Duingt (this is an alternative way back for those preferring a shorter walk). The path becomes rockier with stunted vegetation, mainly juniper and oak - there are sporadic orange splashes but they look rather old. There are still magnificent lake views and you are exactly opposite the imposing La Tournette mountain, alt. 2,351m, which dominates the southern end of the lake (see Walk No. 60). The Col des Frêtes and the Dents de Lanfon are visible again and also the Parmelan overlooking Annecy

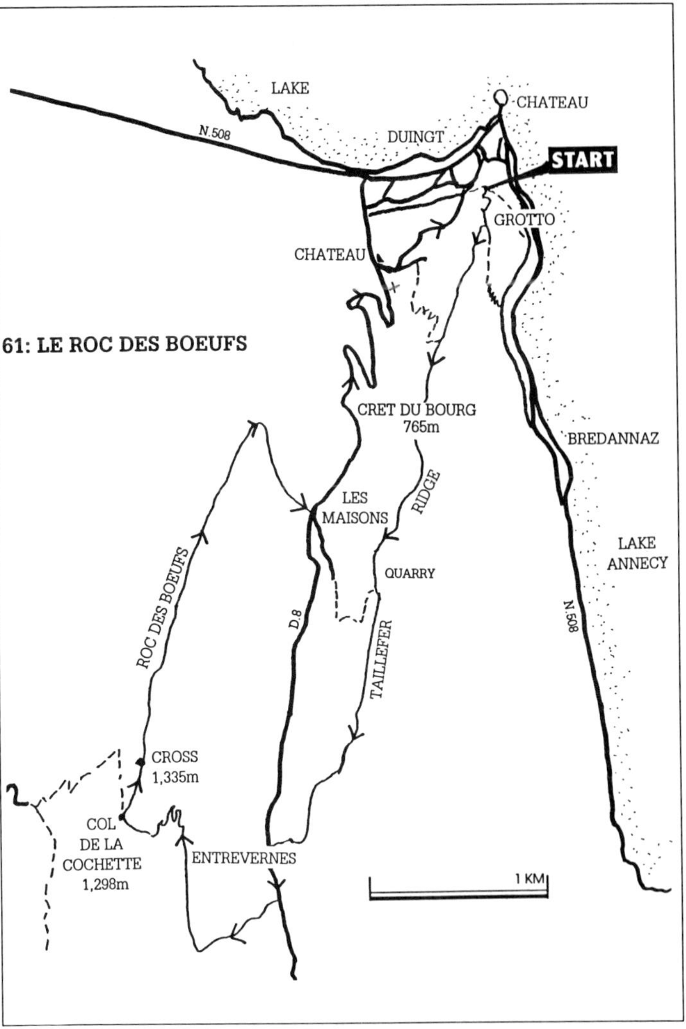

with the Jura mountains in the background. In the foreground below is the little château on its promontory, like an island in the sparkling water. As views go this one is breathtaking!!

You arrive at the Crêt du Bourg, alt. 765m, though there is no sign to say you are there! (45mins). The path gets rockier and you start clambering upwards over boulders - you are still going along the ridge with the end of Lake Annecy in view but to the right is now a narrow green valley which looks gloriously unspoiled apart from a road through it to the villages of Les Maisons and Entrevernes. Down on the left is a huge limestone quarry (this is a real eyesore and the enormous white gash it makes in the green hillside can be seen more clearly when walking along the other side of the lake). You come to two short stretches of iron railing as you skirt the quarry and you can see down to where a railway of metal carts transports the chalk down the hillside. We expected to hear explosions any minute but there was an eerie silence - nothing seemed to be functioning.

At a T-junction (1hr) take the left-hand fork (right is just a picnic area). The lake is now behind you as you skirt round the back of the quarry. You come to a fence with a sign on it saying Carrière de Lathuile et Duingt - Danger, Explosion de Mine, so keep to the path bearing downwards which then bears up to the ridge again. You can see the village of Les Maisons over in the valley to the right.

You come to a signpost and a yellow arrow (1hr 30mins) - be careful as it is easy to miss. Follow straight to Entrevernes - down to the right is Les Maisons (no sign). However, about 5mins further on, after a bit of a rock scramble, there is another group of signposts at a jeep track. Go straight again (right is Les Maisons); if you are tired at this stage take the right path down to Les Maisons and at the village take the road back to Duingt. The path becomes easier with thicker woods on each side.

If you do this walk in autumn you will see a variety of mushrooms along this path. Some are quaintly conical, others with a sinister watery blue tinge, and of course the colourful "picture book" variety, the bright red ones with white spots. It is an art to know your mushrooms as some are deadly poisonous and you should never pick them unless you know they are edible. To make sure take them to any pharmacie (chemist) who will examine them for you. A friend told me an interesting anecdote: the woodland bolets (species of mushroom) only grow with the rising of the moon!

After 20mins you come to a sign down right to the village of Entrevernes (1hr 50mins). At this point the path seems to disintegrate but it is not difficult to cut across the field and then find the defined path again which goes along the side of a hill with a stream down on the right. You come into a lane where you follow the little river down. Leaving the stream on the right the path then goes up into the village by a restored farm and the old village bakery.

A quaint little Savoyard village, renovated tastefully so that it looks spruce but retaining an old world charm. When looking down on it from the other side we noticed that most of the roofing was new and there was not a single dilapidated building. On the day we walked a deadly calm hung over

View of the Taillefer ridge with the Roc des Boeufs behind

the village - I suppose the inhabitants were enjoying their sacred midday meal. We saw a Gîte de France, and a little café which was sadly shut.

When you reach the main street after the bakery, turn left and walk along for a few minutes till you see a sign on the right on an old stone wall (2hrs), to La Cochette. From the village to the col is a 450m steepish climb. The path takes you along the hillside parallel to the village with the church down on the right, through an ancient orchard, the stunted gnarled trees covered in lichen.

After the orchard the path goes upward through meadows with stately chestnut and walnut trees and then starts to snake towards the Col de la Cochette. After passing two small huts you enter woodland again; there are red marks on a stone here (2hrs 30mins). The gradient is steep but technically easy and as you get higher the vegetation is replaced by beech and oak. The path becomes a defined, stony mule track winding round the mountain; look back and you have a good view of the ridge you walked along, with the lake beyond. The going becomes rockier as you reach the top, winding all the way. Just before the summit there is a fairly steep scramble towards the cliff face of the col but the path is easy to follow; you cross under the high-tension wires of a long line of electricity pylons which march across these ridges to goodness knows where, but, as always, ruining the landscape.

When you arrive at the wide woody ridge of the Col de la Cochette, alt. 1,298m (3hrs 30mins), take the signpost up to the right saying Duingt. (If you go straight you will go down the other side of the ridge and eventually reach

St. Eustache in the next valley.) Over to the left is a high-tension pylon. Go up the ridge for about 10mins following blue flashes until you see a blue splash on a large rock to your left. If you can manage it, clamber up this rock and you are on a small rocky summit where there is a cross (3hrs 40mins). It is a dramatic spot for a picnic as you have an uninterrupted view of all the surrounding mountains including the Bauges and Beaufortain ranges.

The path becomes rocky with lovely open areas and you can see all the way to Annecy. Follow along the ridge which now starts to go down gently. You arrive at a clearing with a medley of signs and a bench! (4hrs 30mins). To the left says St. Jorioz, which is a village north of Duingt which you can see further down in the valley. Take the sign straight saying Les Maisons/ Duingt. The path gets wider and the trees taller as you start winding down, at first gently and then later on medium steep. 15mins later, if you watch out on your left, you will see a large flat, grey rock. This is a jump-off point for parapenters but it is also a good spot to stop and rest, with a chance to admire the view down Lake Annecy with its surrounding peaks.

The path gets wider and arrives at a T-junction where you turn right. After coming to a field and a fence meet the road at the hamlet of Les Maisons (5hrs 30mins). Here you have a choice - you can either go through the hamlet and follow the signs to Taillefer which takes you back up on to the ridge and you retrace your steps. OTHERWISE turn left and walk down the valley. The road is very easy with few cars and you can take the obvious short cuts.

You come to a cross, from which you can see down to the church and the car park at Duingt. A few minutes later you come to some old farms and an ancient château on your right with an original slate-tiled roof topped with a weather-vane (6hrs). Turn right here in front of the château and continue down, crossing a bridge over a stream with a small waterfall falling over mossy hummocks. Walk along this charming road which follows a stream. The road passes another shrine with a large cross and then goes under the old railway bridge to the car park (6hrs 15mins).

Above the bank in front of the small car park you can see the start of a tunnel. It is fairly long and was originally a railway tunnel which has recently been restored and converted into a bicycle track!

Remarks: There is a Mediterranean aspect about this walk, mainly due to the stunted oak and juniper bushes on the Taillefer ridge. It is lovely on a hot summer's day as there is plenty of shade but you get better views of the surrounding peaks if you walk when the leaves are off the trees. However, you will not be disappointed at any time of the year as it is one of the most charming and beautiful walks in the Annecy region. The second part of the walk, namely up to the Roc des Boeufs, is steep though not difficult, but less enthusiastic walkers can go as far as Entrevernes and either return by road or back along the Taillefer ridge.

GLOSSARY OF USEFUL FRENCH WORDS

(in alphabetical order)

Au bout de	=	At the end of (something)
L'aigle	=	Eagle
L'aiguille	=	Needle (summit of a mountain)
L'arbre	=	Tree
L'arête	=	Ridge
L'auberge de jeunesse	=	Youth hostel
Bas	=	Low
La borne	=	Boundary marker (usually concrete)
La boucle	=	Circle or loop (used to describe a round trip)
Le buisson	=	Bush
Le boulet	=	Type of mushroom
Le bourg	=	Market town (borough)
Le bouquetin	=	Ibex
Le brouillard	=	Fog
La buvette	=	Café
Les cailloux	=	Stones, rocks
La canne	=	Walking stick
Le carrefour	=	Cross-roads
La carte	=	Map
La cascade	=	Waterfall
La chambre d'hôte	=	Bed and breakfast
La chapelle	=	Chapel
Le champignon	=	Mushroom
Le chemin	=	Path
Le cheval	=	Horse
La chèvre	=	Goat
La chute de pierre	=	Rock fall
Le ciel	=	Sky
La clairière	=	Clearing, glade
Le col	=	Pass
La combe	=	Shallow valley
La commune	=	District (small)
La corniche	=	Overhanging mass of hardened snow at the end of a precipice
Le couloir	=	Corridor (in mountain terms, a narrow passway through rocks)
Le coup de soleil	=	Sunstroke
La crête	=	Top or ridge
La croix	=	Cross
Le danger (dangereux)	=	danger (dangerous)

Descendre	=	To go down
L'église	=	Church
Entrée interdite	=	No entry
L'est	=	East
L'étang	=	Pond
La falaise	=	Cliff
La ferme	=	Farm
La foudre	=	Lightning
La fleur	=	Flower
Le gîte	=	Refuge - (see chapter accommodation)
Le gouffre	=	Large hole, chasm
La grotte	=	Grotto
Haut/e	=	High
Le hameau	=	Hamlet
Là-bas	=	Down there
Là-haut	=	Up there
Le lac	=	Lake
Le lièvre	=	Hare
Marcher (se promener)	=	To walk
La mairie	=	Village hall (literally means mayor's house)
La montagne	=	Mountain
Monter	=	to go up
La moraine	=	Debris (rocks) carried down by a glacier
Le moulin	=	Mill
Le mouton	=	Sheep
La neige	=	Snow
Le nord	=	North
Les névés	=	Glacier-snow - treacherous snow patches
Le nuage (nuageux)	=	Cloud (cloudy)
L'oiseau	=	Bird
L'orage	=	Thunderstorm
L'oratoire	=	Wayside shrine
L'ouest	=	West
Le papillon	=	Butterfly
Le parcours vita	=	Exercise route (usually in woods)
Le pèlerin	=	Pilgrim
La pente	=	Slope, gradient
Le pic	=	Peak or summit (e.g. Pic des Mémises), also means woodpecker
La pierre	=	Stone
La piste	=	Track (usually meaning a man-made path for skiers)
Plagne, plan	=	Mountain term for small plain or plateau
Le plateau	=	Plain, plateau, upland
La pluie	=	Rain

La pointe	=	Point or head (e.g. Pointe de la Gay)
Le pont	=	Bridge
Le poteau (indicateur)	=	Signpost
Le pré/praz	=	Field, meadow
La randonnée	=	Long walk (ride)
Le ravin	=	Ravine, gully
Le réfuge	=	Mountain refuge (hut)
Le renard	=	Fox
La rivière	=	River
Le rocher	=	Rock
La route	=	Road
Le ruisseau	=	Stream or rivulet
Le sac de couchage	=	Sleeping bag
Le sac à dos	=	Rucksack
Le sanctuaire	=	Sanctuary
Le sapin	=	Fir tree
L'herbe	=	grass
Le sentier	=	Marked path
Le serpent	=	Snake
Le soleil	=	Sun
Le sommet	=	Summit
La source	=	Spring (water)
Le sud	=	South
Le taureau	=	Bull
Le télécabine	=	Cable-car
Le télésiège	=	Chair-lift
Le téléski	=	Drag, tow or pommel lift
Le temps	=	Weather
La tempête	=	Thunderstorm
Le terrain privé (propriété privée)	=	Private property
Le trou	=	Hole
Le tonnerre	=	Thunder
La vache	=	Cow
La vallée	=	Valley
Le versant	=	Side (of a mountain)

NOTES

Printed by CARNMOR PRINT & DESIGN
95-97 LONDON ROAD, PRESTON, LANCASHIRE, UK.